101

Proofs

For

GOD

EYE-OPENING NEW INFORMATION SHOWING THERE HAS TO BE GOD

By JIM STEPHENS

ISBN 978-1-48357-991-7

Table of Contents

Table of Contents

Table of Contents

Preface

Whether you are deeply religious or only casually interested in God, this book has something for you. It compiles a massive amount of scientific knowledge into a readable and digestible form.

Look through the Table of Contents until something catches your eye. Read a little. See if it isn't "eye-opening" as mentioned in the sub-title.

The average person doesn't have the time or inclination to dive into scientific research.

For many years science and technology seemed to be turning us away from God. But that has all changed now.

Unfortunately, the news is slow getting out and entrenched interests are fighting against new discoveries that lead to strong evidence for God's existence.

Jim Stephens has done all the work for you. This book shows the total failings of Darwinism to scientifically explain life and the fossil record and it will teach you critical thinking skills to use when you hear arguments against God.

Chapter after chapter will give you "eye-opening" new information. Learn again and again that scientists cannot explain what they see right in front of their eyes. That's not to mention that they are totally unable to create anything remotely similar.

Parents and grandparents will be able to fascinate children with facts about animals from this book. Homeschoolers will find this an indispensable resource. Church small groups will love it. Pastors will want it on their bookshelf. Anyone with a friend who might be questioning the existence of God will find this a perfect gift.

Last but not least, because it is written from faith and inspiration, it will touch your heart.

Introduction

Buy this book. In the future you are going to want to have it handy for the information it contains.

The time has come to have a discussion about God because the world is in such sad shape.

The time has come to talk about God from the point of view of technology and science.

Believers don't need to have any fear of a scientific discussion about God anymore. The eye opening information of modern scientific discoveries leads straight to the existence of God as the only possible explanation.

This book puts its contents into plain language which can be understood by middle schoolers to technologically-challenged seniors. New scientific truths have been discovered which will force school textbooks advocating evolution to be thrown out.

Actually Darwinism as a theory was all but abandoned many years ago in 1972 (see Chapter #73), but the believers in godlessness never abandoned their faith in no God. Learn the truth in this book in understandable language about how mutation and natural selection totally fail to produce a single new species even when intelligent scientists try to make it work. Applying intelligence invalidates the theory, but they soldier on.

This book lays out one by one over one hundred explanations of why there has to be God. Take your pick. There's surely one to appeal to everyone. Thousands more could be added.

Each chapter can be read in a few short minutes. Read one for morning meditation and inspiration. Talk about one over dinner with your children or grandchildren. Start up a conversation with your friends. Share a page from the website: www.101ProofsForGod.com. Sharing God will always make you feel good. Try it.

I wrote this book because God wanted me to. Five years ago I had a very deep prayer one night sitting on my bed. I was sixty-two years old and thought I would ask God what He wanted me to do with the rest of my life. I wanted to dedicate it to helping Him.

I will never forget that prayer. After I spoke that question I was overwhelmed with a feeling of loneliness from God, universe-wide loneliness. He is an incredibly loving parent but so few of His children make any effort to have anything to do with Him. So few know anything about His Heart. So many lead lives fruitlessly seeking after money, fame, or power. Some even actively campaign against His existence. How would you feel?

This book is to get the truth out. There has to be God. There is no other possible explanation, rational, logical, scientific, social, historical, technological, biological, chemical, or based on the laws of physics. You'll see if you read this book.

Join me in the new revolution…the true path to happiness. Let's learn science from a God-centered faith perspective. God's plan is the best plan for the world and for each individual in it. Let's go back home to our Father and let's become one family under the real source of joy.

Let's share this journey together and may you feel God and His blessings through these pages.

From my heart to yours,

Jim Stephens

Dedication

This book is dedicated to God, with deepest gratitude for inspiring this 5-year project and continually pushing me along the way.

I also dedicate it to all those living their lives to bring God's literal Kingdom on the Earth and thus give comfort to His lonely heart.

Chapter #1 Male and Female

When people see in their minds a chart of the evolution of mankind, typically it looks like this:

Image 1. Artist's Concept of Human Evolution, but incomplete.
©2016 Nari Hanna

This illustration shows a human evolving through many intermediate stages from an ape to a man. However, one extremely important and totally essential half is left out of this picture. The result is that it gives you the wrong image of reality.

At every single step of the evolutionary process, there must have been a female evolving exactly simultaneously with the male. All of the same genetic and physiological changes of the male would necessarily have to be duplicated in females. Changes in hands, feet, skeleton, organs, hair, everything must be mirrored in both males and females.

Image 2. Artist's Concept of Male and Female Evolution.
©2016 Nari Hanna

However, science tells us that men's and women's bodies are also very different. Our brains are different. Our muscles are different. Our reproductive organs are totally different. Amazingly, male and female bodies are complimentary as well.

If there were to be an "evolution" in the male body of an ape to become more like a human, but no simultaneous and corresponding evolution in the female mate's body, then the trait would not likely be inherited to the next generation. Take opposable thumbs for example. If the male evolved them but the female didn't, what would happen? Likely only some children would have opposable thumbs.

Since all of the people in the world have opposable thumbs, then we have to assume that we all descended from one man and one woman who had such thumbs.

This would also be true for human feet, pelvic bones, on and on.

Also, if we truly evolved opposable thumbs, genetics would have to predict that occasionally there would be people born today without opposable thumbs? If some of my ancestors were without opposable thumbs and some of my wife's ancestors had no opposable thumbs, there is some chance my children would inherit that feature.

(Note: This scenario would also have to hold true for all animals and fish, even plants, or any species with males and females.)

As an even more complicated example, where male and female are complimentary rather than similar, how could the male evolve a penis unless the female must necessarily evolve a vagina simultaneously? Otherwise, what advantage is the penis for natural selection?

If you study the female human reproductive cycle, there are many changes taking place throughout the month. For example, her vagina is normally toxic for sperm. Only during a few days each month does that change and her vagina actually becomes very hospitable to sperm and a mucous is created with fibers that help the sperm along their way to fertilize the egg. This is a phenomenal development that must have occurred at the time that a man got a penis.

And that's not all. Even if a male body evolves some change and a female body develops a corresponding change, they still have to meet each other and mate successfully. In other words, they have to live in close proximity to each other. They both have to be of child-bearing age at the same time. They have to mate. That mating has to produce a male child or a female child that inherits the new advanced trait. Then when that child grows up, he or she must also find a mate with the same advanced trait to mate with successfully. If this doesn't happen, the trait would pass out of the race.

Are you thinking about the odds of all this happening?

I suppose you could assume that the new advanced trait is dominant. Then if any one individual has the mutation, then all of his/her offspring would have it. But isn't that a faith based assertion?

Evolutionists may hold onto faith in randomness and believe in very tiny changes taking place over millions of years. But it still has to pass the test of practical reality of how our species procreates. Evolution is really based on faith and not scientific proof. I think faith in God is a far more elegant explanation. Somehow I'm not able to imagine that evolution produces a viable penis and vagina through tiny incremental changes.

Evolution theory has to postulate that any advancement somehow spreads throughout the entire human population of all males and females. In other words, every one of us had an ancestor that had the trait. Either we all descended from parents that both had the trait or else all those born without the new trait totally died out and never reproduced.

To believe that the above process happened at random without an intelligent creator invisibly guiding the process requires a huge amount of faith, faith in randomness and chaos to produce order and beauty. That's more faith than most of us religious people have.

There must be God.

Chapter #2 Ugly Flowers

You have probably heard the expression "beauty is in the eye of the beholder". That's generally true, but when it comes to flowers, it's different.

Let's think about ugly flowers. Stop a minute and imagine some of all the different kinds of flowers you have seen. How many would you say are ugly? Out of say 100 different flowers, how many would you say are ugly? 1, maybe 2, maybe even 0.

I tried to find out how many different kinds of flowers there are. But nobody really knows. Www.ChaCha.com says this:

"The total number of described flower species exceeds 230,000, and many tropical species are as yet unnamed."

Www.Flowers-cs.com says this:

> "According to the scientists opinion there are more than 270,000 types of flowers. And each flower in his own way is beautiful and unusual and brings a part of pleasure into your life in order to make it happier."

You don't have enough time in a day to look at all the pictures of different flowers you can find on the Internet.

Of all the flowers you have ever seen in your life, do you remember ANY as being ugly? Probably you might rate some of them as just plain and ordinary, but ugly would be extremely rare. Even the lowly dandelion, hated by many, was beautiful to you when you were a child.

And even those flowers that seem so plain to you, I bet you could find some person that says that exact one is their favorite.

If evolution were true, what are the odds by random chance that out of 270,000 different types of flowers, there are no ugly flowers? The odds must be staggeringly astronomical.

Now there are certainly many ugly bugs. There are some pretty ugly animals and fish too. But there are no ugly flowers.

When someone gives you flowers, what is the first emotion that comes to you? The flowers symbolize that they are giving you affection...they like you. Children will do it without being taught.

Imagine that there is a person that makes up 270,000 bouquets of flowers, one for each type, and gives them all to you. What would that feel like? What do you imagine that person would be trying to express to you?

Duh. He or she would be expressing the most amazing, enormous, overwhelming love for you.

For those of us who know God, behind every single one of those flowers is the love God has for me and for you. His love for us motivated the creation of those flowers.

That's why there are no ugly flowers. They are gifts from a loving God.

There must be God.

Chapter #3 Three Sticks

Let's imagine that you are walking through the woods in a very secluded area. As you are walking, you see something on the path in front of you. When you get up close, it turns out to be three sticks arranged like an arrow.

What goes through your mind? How did those sticks appear like that?

Please give me a number on a scale from 0 to 100. Closer to zero means that the sticks happened to become like that totally at random with no interference from any intelligent force. You think there is zero significance or meaning to the pattern.

A number closer to 100 would mean that you are more certain that some intelligent being arranged the sticks in exactly that pattern with some specific purpose in mind. The intention of the intelligent being is to send a message which has meaning and possibly value to an observer.

There is no right or wrong answer. This is just a line of reasoning.

My guess is that most people would give a number in the high 90's, although I haven't yet done the experiment.

OK, next step. Let's go a little further down the path. This time you encounter four sticks instead of three sticks. Look at the two pictures of 4 sticks that follow and think again of a number between 0 and 100.

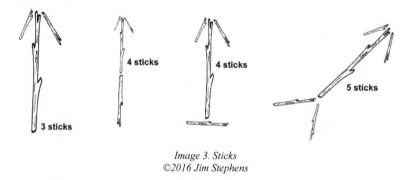

Image 3. Sticks
©2016 Jim Stephens

Did your number go higher or lower? I'm pretty confident when I say that I think your number would go higher. It's getting less and less likely that this was an accident and more and more likely that the arrangement was done by some intelligent being.

6

One more picture and then my conclusion. Imagine again you continue walking in the woods and encounter 5 sticks that look like the above image on the right.

What number between 0 and 100 would describe whether this is random or put there by an intelligent being.

I don't know what number you are at right now, but if your number keeps going up, there will be some point at which it will gets to 99 or 100 as I keep adding more and more sticks.

If it were 1,000 sticks in an arrangement that looks ordered, wouldn't you be certain it originated from an intelligent being?

1,000 is not even getting started when compared to DNA. The human genome has 3 billion "sticks" (recognizable elements).

The human genome is all contained on 23 chromosome pairs. One of the pairs is for sex determination. The number of chromosomes in a sperm or ova is one half of each pair from the parent DNA. Each sperm or egg contains just over three billion DNA base pairs. When combined, the full complement of DNA for a human is over six billion base pairs.

The sperm and egg in humans each contains about 23,000 protein-coding genes.

Now imagine that you are walking with a friend in the woods. Same scenario, you come upon three sticks, then a little while later four, then a little further on five sticks, on and on, ... finally 100 sticks arranged as I have described. Every time you come to a new set of sticks, your friend denies that any intelligent being could possibly have left this trail. Neither of you can see any intelligent being anywhere around, can you?

What do you do? Are you dumbfounded by the foolishness of your friend? Or do you cry for him because he is so lost from his common sense for some reason.

Three billion "sticks" all lined up and organized ... there must be God.

Chapter #4 Order of Assembly

Have you noticed that most things in life that you buy will come with an instruction manual?

All around you there are signs and directions telling you how to do things in the right order or the right way.

Obviously, to be successful at many, many things, you will have to do them in a particular sequence or you get poor results or nothing at all.

Simple machines don't require a lot of instructions. However, as the machines get more and more complicated, the instructions become more and more complicated as well. At a certain point machines require sophisticated training, you are not allowed to perform certain actions unless you are trained and certified. Take for example brain surgery or piloting an airplane.

In order to assemble something correctly, it takes intelligence. You can give a monkey all the pieces to build a Lego submarine, but he's not going to accidentally build it in your lifetime and I'll take odds on eternity. And monkeys are among the smartest of animals.

To correctly assemble something, you have to not only put the pieces in the right PLACE, but you also have to place them in the right ORDER. If you don't get the position and the sequence correct, then the construction will fail.

Imagine the blueprints for building the Empire State Building. First you have to dig a huge hole in the ground and then each step of the way up you would need directions how to lay in all the water pipes, the electricity wires, the plumbing, the air ducts, the heating ducts, on and on.

A human being is sort of similar to a building. We have nerves (like electrical wires), lungs and blood for moving air, water, food, and waste; heating and air conditioning systems. If you were to try to create the "blueprints" for a human body, do you think it would be more or less complicated than the blueprints for the Empire State Building? Absolutely, the human body is 100's if not 1000's of times more complicated than a building. The human body changes and grows. It replaces itself cell by cell. It moves around.

The human body is actually "assembled". I'm sure you have seen books or videos of fertilization and growth of an embryo. That's a clear pattern of assembly going on cell by cell, in a clearly, certain, and planned sequence.

Was there an intelligence that put that all together? It's incomprehensible how it could have happened without intelligence.

There must be God.

Chapter #5 Babies Are Cute

Think of babies with me for a while. Think of human babies that you have known. Think of animal babies, puppies, kittens, baby birds, farm animal babies, going to the pet store or petting zoo. Think of baby fish of all kinds. Even think of baby plants, shoots coming out of the ground, sprouts emerging.

Let's make two categories: "cute" and "ugly". Or make a long line with "really cute" on the left end and "really ugly" on the right end. Now imagine putting all the babies one by one somewhere on the scale. What would it look like?

I'm going to take an educated guess and say that a very huge percentage of the babies are on the left end over by "really cute" or "mostly cute".

Most puppies and kittens have got to be on the "cute" end. Don't you have a calendar somewhere in your house with pictures of kittens or puppies? Do you remember the last time you went to the zoo? The biggest attraction was always the baby animals. Even baby hippos are cute. Were there any babies at the zoo for the "ugly" category? I can't remember any.

Go through "Mammals" in the encyclopedia and check out all their babies. Any ugly there? This will be much more powerful if you actually go look at babies.

Human babies certainly are "cute". They stay that way for years, maybe up to 5 or 6. There is a daycare at the building where I work and all the babies are cute. Maybe a couple get sort of close to the mid-point between "cute" and "ugly" on the spectrum, but definitely I'd still put them on the cute side. That's just on physical appearance. If you add in their little personalities…definitely, definitely cute. If you ask their mother's opinion, would you ever get "ugly"? Nope.

Baby birds almost all follow this pattern of cuteness. I say "almost" because a few might be tending over into the ugly area. Definitely the gigantic majority of baby birds are cute, for sure.

My wife loves gardening and yard work. Baby plants, flowers just coming up, even new grass sprouting are reasons for joy and excitement. If pressed to admit it, I'd have to say that those baby plants are actually pretty cute.

I've left insects for last because I'm a little conflicted where to put them on the scale. Probably, I'd have to get very close to, if not touching, "really ugly" when I'm thinking of baby flies (i.e. maggots). Can't think of too many baby insects that I could put on the cute side. What about you? So I don't mind if the ugly bugs get eaten by birds and mammals. (Maybe bugs were created ugly so we'd avoid attachments to them.)

So all in all, what percentage of the above creatures would be on the cute side? I'd go with about 98% myself when I look at the world. What about you?

If humans and animals are all the result of random accident, why are we all so consistently cute? It makes no sense. Natural selection or survival of the fittest has no connection with cuteness. Ugly can survive and prosper. Do animal parents kick out the ugly ones and only keep the cute ones? Do animal parents have any idea that we humans look upon their offspring and say, "Oh, he's so cute"?

Can we all agree that only humans see "cuteness"? It gives us joy. It also motivates us to act to share our feeling of joy with others.

Human parents expend great time and effort to give joy to their children. Isn't that the whole point behind toy stores and going to the zoo, or buying them a pet?

What about grandparents? You don't know "cute" until you are a grandparent.

The cuteness that I see everywhere in the world is not an accident. It's a deliberate effort on the part of my "original" parent, God, to give joy to me, individually, as well as everyone else collectively. We are God's children.

There must be God.

Chapter #6 Bigness

Things that are big do something to us emotionally. There is just an awesomeness to big things that can take your breath away.

Think about some "big" thing that you encountered in your life that deeply moved you and made you just marvel…"Wow". Here are some of mine: the Grand Canyon, Niagara Falls, the Redwood trees in Muir Woods, the giant Sequoia trees in Yosemite, Luray Caverns in Virginia, and the Twin Towers in New York before 2001.

Big dogs, big people, big houses, big storms, even big bugs all make us stop and take a second look. A big anything will give you pause. "The largest … (whatever)… in the world" makes us pause to see what is it. Just for fun, do an Internet search for "the biggest _____ in the world" and fill in the blank with anything you can think of.

You probably keep some record book in your brain somewhere for each one of the "biggest I ever saw" in every category. You could sit around with your family or friends for hours telling stories about the biggest whatevers you have seen.

I saw a TV show not too long ago about a new building going up in the United Arab Emirates that is going to be the tallest building in the world. It was totally fascinating. As you can imagine there are some really difficult challenges, not the least of which was the 125 degree heat and the very high winds.

Here's my point. Something really, really big takes an incredible amount of effort and energy to bring into existence. The biggest building in the world takes phenomenal resources and time and energy and intelligence in its creation.

Let's take a quantum leap and imagine all the resources, time and energy, it took to create every construction project ever made by human beings in all of history: buildings, houses, roads, bridges, dams, everything. Think of the end results that have been created. But note, the end product is what you can see with your eyes. What you can't see is the intelligence and mind power, the creativity and knowledge that it took to build all those things. In fact, all the thinking took place before any of the building itself was done.

A great amount of knowledge about the principles of construction was required even before the image of the end project could be formed. Otherwise the whole thing would come crashing down. A designer was absolutely necessary for every single project that has come into existence. A planner or engineer was absolutely necessary for everything to come into existence. Even though we cannot see the planner today, we know there was one for every single one of those construction projects. None of them happened accidentally.

Now let's talk about BIG again. As awesome as some of the creations of man are, as big as some of them are, how big are they relative to the size of the earth? Or compare them to the Solar System or the Milky Way. Compare the Milky Way galaxy to the universe. NASA claims there are 3,000 already observed galaxies, and an estimated 125 billion or more. [1]

Now we're talking BIG.

The universe is estimated to be 10 to 20 billion years old. The Milky Way alone is 100,000 light years across and contains from 200 to 400 billion stars. The universe is estimated to be over 14 billion light years across but nobody really knows what's beyond that.

That's BIG. Just trying to imagine the size of the universe seems impossible. Sort of like trying to imagine God. The universe is real. Nobody doubts that it exists even though we can't really get our head around it. But we have more trouble trying to imagine something BIGGER than the universe. Could there really be a being that in fact is the creator of the universe? It is very hard to imagine God in this way, as a being bigger than the universe using 3 dimensional thinking about size. Maybe that's one reason many people stop trying.

I would argue that since anything that we can conceive of from our experience that is orderly and BIG has an intelligent creator, therefore the universe must have a creator because of the need for a planner and builder.

Therefore there must be God.

Chapter #7 Car Mechanic

When your car breaks down, do you try to fix it yourself? Do you take it to a mechanic and then watch over his shoulder telling him how to do his job?

You have probably experienced that there are many different mechanics out there, and some are way better than others. However, almost any one of them or even all of them are better car mechanics than you.

Your passion in life is probably not car mechanics and likely you don't know a thing about it. Thankfully, there are people who do have a passion for car mechanics. They are fascinated by it. They devote a lot of time and energy to studying all about it. They devote many hours to working with the tools of the trade and getting hands on experience. After a certain amount of that, we call them an expert. There are even processes developed to obtain an official "certification" at car maintenance.

Without going through all the training to become an expert, imagine that you proclaimed yourself an "expert" in car mechanics. What would be people's reaction? How much credibility would you have?

When it comes to knowing the truth about God's existence, are there parallels to this story? Is your average person an expert based solely on having a personal belief or opinion? What kind of credentials are needed for a person to be an expert on the subject of God? Is every person's point of view supposed to be considered equally?

Another idea is to take a vote of all the people. If the majority decides whether there is a God or not, does that make it the truth?

I don't think so.

The existence of God is not in the realm of opinion. It is in the realm of facts. You don't get to decide.

It is either true or it isn't. He either exists or He doesn't and no amount of debate, argument, wishing, believing, or demanding is going to change the fact.

When you want to know facts about your car, you would probably trust the word of the experienced car mechanic over a non-mechanic or a novice mechanic. Using the same analogy, we might want to trust the word of those who over their lifetimes had a profound passion to study religious truths.

People like Moses, Jesus, Peter and Paul and other figures from the Bible, St. Augustine, St. Francis, Mother Teresa, and on and on were devoted day in and day out to discovering God and bringing knowledge about God to the rest of us.

Do you personally know anyone like those people mentioned? Do you know someone that you might consider a saint? Do you know someone who is an "expert" on God from their own lifestyle? The expertise that they have is what you want to gain first before deciding whether God exists or not.

Don't be too hasty to think you are an expert on the existence of God unless you have gotten your "certification".

There are many world famous people, past and present, who have revealed their experience of the nature of God from personal experience. Although many of them may have a different experience of the nature of God, all of them would absolutely agree that He exists.

If you are in grade school, it doesn't make much sense to challenge someone with a PhD. Next time you encounter someone denying that God exists, ask them what their credentials are that makes them the expert on God.

I've been having experiences with God for over 43 years. You can take my word (for what it is worth) "There is God."

Chapter #8 Love

Almost every song that you hear on the radio is about love. Many movies are about love and many of the others have a love-centered subplot. An Internet search for images depicting love gets 16.8 billion returns.

The goal of life for our culture is true love. Everybody knows about love. Everybody wants love. But is love something that really exists? No one has ever possessed a physical handful of love.

Let's assume you believe in love, a fairly safe assumption.

How did you come to believe in love? Love is invisible so you didn't see it. It has no physical dimensions.

Some people go so far as to call love "all powerful". How could something invisible and weightless be "all powerful?"

There are different kinds of love: love for parents, siblings, children, grandchildren; love for pets; love of possessions and other inanimate objects; love of money, love of power, love of freedom; on and on.

Love grows. Given time your love for one person can grow greater and greater, stronger and stronger. You can love additional people also, but love is not diminished as if there were a limited quantity. There's more of it. Where does it come from?

Love is not limited by time or space. It doesn't get old. It does not decrease if your beloved is far away.

Someone may love you, but it is possible that you don't know that love for you exists. It's also possible that you can even deny that there is love. When you do, you won't notice the love any longer, but it still exists. It's still there, but beyond your perception.

If we outlive our physical death, love could go on beyond the grave. I happen to believe that after death, your personality continues and therefore your experience of love will continue. Furthermore, it keeps growing and expanding.

Do you still believe in love after realizing all of the apparently contradictory aspects listed? Did you answer "yes"? I think most people would still believe.

If you stop to analyze it, how are the characteristics of this thing called love all that different from the reputed characteristics of God?

It's invisible, not affected by time, no mass or weight, no physical dimensions.

The major difference is that God is a source of love, a creator of love, not the love itself. But what's so fantastic or unusual about there being a creator. You are a creator of love as well, so a being that creates love is not unusual.

If you believe in love, you are very close to believing in God already. If you don't believe in love, you are missing out on what everyone else is getting. Poor you.

The attributes of God and the attributes of love are very similar. God however gets a lot of criticism which I think He doesn't deserve and a lot of blame for things He didn't do.

Where did love come from? My observation is that it always comes from a being who creates the love in order to send it to another being. In every case there is a "source" being that creates the love. Therefore, there must be an original source of love.

There must be God.

Chapter #9 Contest With God

A parable from the future.

Humans have become so technically evolved that they can now make a living, breathing person.

A summit of scientists believed that because they now had the power to create life, God was no longer needed. So they all decided that someone should go and tell this to God.

One of the scientists volunteered to go. So one day he climbed a mountain and called upon God. "God! a bunch of us have been thinking, and I've come to tell you that we really don't need you anymore. I mean, we've been coming up with great theories and ideas, we've cloned sheep, and we're on the verge of cloning humans. So as you can see, we really don't need you anymore, so you can leave us alone."

God nods understandingly and says, "I see. Well, no hard feelings. But before you go, let's have a contest. What do you think?"

The scientist says, "Sure. What kind of contest?"

God replies, "A human-making contest where we make a human being. If you can create a better person than me, I'll go."

The scientist quickly agrees, "Sure! No problem."

The scientist bends down and picks up a handful of dirt and says, "Okay, I'm ready!"

God shakes his head, "No, no, no…you go get your own dirt."

This wasn't exactly a proof for God, but I've always remembered it as a story with a great punch line. I can't be serious all the time about this.

As great as the achievements of science, even to the extent of being able to create life if we ever get to that point, still we are completely within the physical, material world with all its laws and principles. We can't ever create something from nothing. That could only have been the source of everything.

There must be God.

18

Chapter #10 Life After Death

Most of us go through our day to day lives without thinking about or experiencing life after death. But there are some people who openly communicate with spirits and see them constantly. Whole books are written about such experiences with "the dead". There are many such books available with all types of themes and one of the main points they always try to make is to provide documented evidence that these experiences could not be faked.

Unless you have read these types of books and the evidence they present, you might tend to think that this is all hallucinating or some type of scam.

Throughout human history, millions of people have claimed to have had experiences with those who have passed away. How does a materialist explain these phenomena throughout all cultures, all civilizations, and all history?

Are we to totally discount the reams of reports of "near death experiences" coming from people who "died" but somehow were revived? Were they all hallucinating? Do you discard all of the evidence without really taking the time to read what has been reported?

Set aside for the moment whatever your beliefs are about life after death just for the sake of argument. If there really is life after death that would almost certainly cinch the case for there being God. Would you accept that?

Evolution is all about the physical world only. Everything has to follow so-called physical laws of nature, i.e. materialist only nature. If there exists a vast realm of life which is invisible to our eyes which is populated by personalities that used to live on the earth, then where did it come? How did it get there?

If all your ancestors and everyone who has ever lived in history is still alive in an invisible world, is that even conceivable by any process detailed anywhere in the theory of evolution?

Any proofs for the theory of evolution would immediately become infinitely more challenged if they have to somehow account for life after death.

You may not be all that familiar with what are called life after death experiences. Most people are not. But there is a huge storehouse of information available to anyone interested. Many famous mediums communicated messages from the spirit world that have been verified by the scientific community of their times. Many of the mediums were Americans in the late 1800's and early 1900's and very high level leaders of science were present, observing and verifying the results.

Is it possible that they were all fooled somehow?

Check out any library, bookstore, or the Internet. Read up on the documentations and proofs that these experiences with personalities "on the other side" were very real. Scientists who have studied the paranormal may not say they have conclusive proof, but the preponderance of evidence can easily lead to the assumption that there exists life after death, a much easier conclusion than anything else.

(Recommendation: do some research on your own on some of the original sources listed in the footnotes section of this book. Even read their critics if you want. Their disbelief is obvious but their arguments are thin.)

If the human personality lives in the spirit world forever and continues to grow toward higher levels as a loving being, this would make sense as the creation of a loving God who has created humans in His image and likeness. Love should last forever. Loved ones should be together in love after this life.

Do the research and this is what it points to. (See Footnotes and Comments for good resources on life after death and near-death experiences.)

There must be God.

Chapter #11 Purpose

Every movement you make has some kind of purpose. Every sound that comes out of your mouth is for a reason. Every item in the room you are sitting in was created for a purpose.

"What is my purpose in life?" is a nagging question from childhood for many of us. A person with no purpose is a sad sight.

Why does everything have purpose? It makes absolutely no sense that a totally random and accidental process resulted in everything that exists having a purpose.

Our minds even go so far as to demand that things have a purpose. What happens to something that you determine has no purpose? That's right, you throw it away.

If something has no purpose, then it has no value. In other words, it is worthless. A person who surrounded himself with worthless objects would be considered crazy.

If you use a certain tool in your profession and a better tool is invented for the same purpose, you switch to using the new tool. We are constantly evaluating everything according to how well it fulfills some desired purpose.

If it exists, it must have a purpose. Our brains cannot think any other way.

How could this be? Something totally invisible, i.e. purpose, is applied to all materials in the world. Could this have originated exclusively from the materials themselves?

Where does an object's purpose come from? Purpose comes from the creator of an object. If you come across some machine and you don't know what it's for, who do you ask? You ask the person who made it, of course?

When you find God, you find your purpose. That's because He is the creator.

There must be God.

Chapter #12 Chimpanzees

Biologists have told us that Chimpanzees are our closest "relatives" and evolutionists believe that we all descended from ape-like creatures.

It has been repeated for years that the DNA between chimpanzees and humans is 98% to 99% the same. (Actually, human and chimp genome sequencing more recently has put that figure at 95% to 96%.)

That seems like a really small difference and so it's plausible to think that the gap is easily overcome by a few simple mutations. Actually not.

Let's take a closer look at the reality.

Human DNA in a sperm or egg has 3 billion "letters" (base pairs). So what is a 2% difference out of 3 billion? It's 60 million differences.

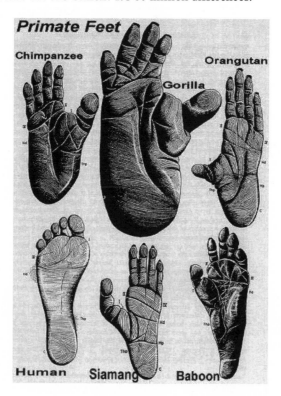

Image 4. Primate feet.

What this means is that an ape-like creature would have to go through 60 million changes to their DNA to get to where it's a human being if there is only a 2% difference. 4% or 5% is going to be way more than 60 million.

60 million characters is something like the equivalent of 20 books of information that are each 500 pages long. (The Encyclopædia Britannica has only about 40 million words on half a million topics.)

The DNA of our ancestral ape would have to "evolve" at least 60 million times to produce a human.

AND we're not just talking about 60 million "mutations". That's because mutations are not necessarily improvements. We're talking about 60 million improvements and advances in the ape's DNA toward a human's.

And if you want to know the truth, scientists have never witnessed any mutation which adds NEW information. Mutations are known to lose or confuse information. The idea that mutation is a method of advanced development is not based on observation, but faith.

The only mutations that scientists can find to study are the ones that cause diseases.

So the number of mutations would have to be many times 60,000,000, because only some tiny fraction of mutations MIGHT actually result in advancements.

But even if we disregard the fact that mutations don't bring advancements and continue this line of thinking, does it work? No, it doesn't.

Remember, for mutation to work its magic, the apes had to reproduce. Reproduction is the only way that mutations can be passed down to descendants. How long does that take? Ape-like creatures will have to grow to be 10 to 20 years old before they mate and produce offspring.

We need to have 60 million mutations to get a human. At that rate, it's going to take a long time. Take a guess.

Imagine the absolute shortest possible route. If there were one successful mutation from an ape toward a human being every single generation (totally against science), it would still take more than 10 years (lifespan) x 60,000,000 changes. It absolutely could not take less than 600,000,000 years.

The typical "evolution clock" showing the history of life on earth indicates that 700,000,000 years ago was when the first multi-celled organisms appeared. It was about 4,000,000 years ago that ape-like mammals appeared. This can't cut it.

As they say, "It doesn't compute." Four million years to go from an ape to a human is what evolutionists need to prove. I just showed why it would take way over 600 million years at the barest minimum.

There must be God.

Chapter #13 The Infinite Monkey Theorem

Since my last post talked about man descending from apes, I'd like to now take a diversion to put to rest The Infinite Monkey Theorem once and for all. You may have heard about this one. It sort of plays tricks on your mind using the concept of infinity. Infinity doesn't really exist in any practical, scientific sense, but if you accept infinity in an argument, then you can end up also accepting that "given infinity, anything can happen," an absurd idea.

Most anyone could immediately think of tens or hundreds of things that could never happen even with an infinite amount of time. The moon will never turn to green cheese for example.

But if you foolishly take the leap of faith from "given infinity, anything can happen" over to the even more absurd premise that "it did happen," you may just be making a leap of faith so great that you are downright foolish.

Here is the description of The Infinite Monkey Theorem from Wikipedia.

"The infinite monkey theorem states that a monkey hitting keys at random on a typewriter keyboard for an infinite amount of time will almost surely type a given text, such as the complete works of William Shakespeare.

In this context, "almost surely" is a mathematical term with a precise meaning, and the "monkey" is not an actual monkey, but a metaphor for an abstract device that produces a random sequence of letters and symbols ad infinitum. The relevance of the theory is questionable -- the probability of a monkey exactly typing a complete work such as Shakespeare's Hamlet is so tiny that the chance of it occurring during a period of time even a hundred thousand orders of magnitude longer than the age of the universe is extremely low (but not zero)." [1]

Note it says "(but not zero)". That is of course a mathematical concept unrelated to any reality we could ever experience. Their emphasis should be placed more on EXTREMELY low probability EVEN given 100's of thousands of times the AGE of the UNIVERSE.

Here is another mathematical calculation that scientists have created which has no real-world application.

Taking one monkey for every particle in the universe and each one typing from the Big Bang (beginning of time) until the universe dies out would not be enough time to type out even one book. Not even close. You'd have to allow that amount of time more than $10^{360,000}$ times.

So let's get real. Here we have a mythical example where they plug in some specific numbers that are incredibly gigantic: the number or particles in the whole universe, trillions times trillions times the age of the universe. Even with all of that, the odds are "nearly zero".

Do you still think "anything can happen"?

Also, remember, we are definitely not talking about a short book that needs to be reproduced in order for the Theory of Evolution to be true. We're talking about reproducing DNA. The DNA of a human contains 3 BILLION characters, and they are not random but exactly in the right order. The Theory of Evolution must also explain all the other millions of species that exist which also have orderly DNA. Randomness cannot produce all the correctly ordered DNA sequences of millions of species in this world.

There has to be God.

By the way somebody did test real monkeys.

Just for your curiosity, there were some professors and students who tried an experiment with real monkeys in England. They never got even one single recognizable word after a whole month.

After punching basically one key many times, the monkeys began hitting the keyboard with a rock. Then they urinated and defecated on it. [2]

Even intelligent computer programmers can't get close to creating words randomly. Funny how they don't seem to notice their own intelligence as part of the creation process of their experiments.

Lots of people never give up their faith very easily. So computer programmers devised random programs to try to get a meaningful sequence. Note again the time span their programs require is billions of times the age of the universe just to get a very short sequence located somewhere inside a whole book.

To produce any exact book would be huge orders of magnitude harder because they can barely get a few letters in a row.

Computer programmers are intelligent beings trying on purpose to do it and they can't do it. And they want us to believe "it could happen"?

Dan Oliver of Arizona in 2004 had a random program that took 42,162,500,000 billion, billion monkey-years to get just this phrase, "VALENTINE. Cease toIdor:eFLP0FRjWK78aXzVOwm)-';8.t" [3]

That's only 19 characters in a row correctly.

Again I repeat, there must be God.

Chapter #14 Empty Space

Scientists tell us that we are made up of mostly empty space. In an atom, there is the nucleus. It is surrounded by the electron(s) which have properties similar to both a wave and a particle.

How much space is there? The current estimate is that the atom is 99.9999999999999% empty space. There are 13 decimal places to the right of the decimal point.

All of the matter of all the humans on the earth could fit inside a sugar cube with room to spare. [1] [2]

To get some perspective, take a grain of rice representing an atomic nucleus and place it at the center of a football or baseball field in a large stadium. Then the seats on the outer limits of the stadium would be similar to the area of the electron field of the grain of rice nucleus. However, you need to think about the stadium as being a sphere and not just a horizontal structure, which makes the empty space a whole lot greater.

If you took all of the space out of your body, you'd instantly disappear and it would take a high powered microscope to find you.

Some scientists aren't even sure if there are really protons and electrons any more. Maybe it's all just energy.

Everything that we experience as hard, cold "reality" is not. It's empty space mostly. A tiny, tiny fraction of it may be energy.

Actually we could say that everything is really mostly nothing...empty space.

Everything that we are experiencing as "something" is because of the amount of energy it has which is oriented in a certain way that we can interact with it and experience it.

Without the form that is given to the energy and the invisible laws and principles that operate on the energy, everything would simply collapse into nothing.

Where did the invisible form, laws, and principles come from? And for that matter, where did the energy come from?

If there is an original source before any of this, even time and space, that must be God.

Energy, time, space, laws and principles, all came from that original source at the same instant.

Can any rational mind really believe that all of this minutely and exquisitely ordered, vastly consistent, awesomely beautiful, extraordinarily complex, and ultimately understandable universe is totally the result of "it just happened."

Where did it all come from?

Simple, there must be God.

Chapter #15 Computers

Most of us use computers on a daily basis. If you have been around computers since the 1980's and 1990's like I have, then you have probably marveled continuously at the amazing explosion in computer technology.

What computers can do is astounding! They have developed greater and greater capabilities while the physical sizes have continued to shrink.

Computers are unbelievably fast at doing one particular thing that they have been programmed by a man to do. The Internet is awesome. For example, you can video conference with someone on the other side of the earth for free.

But always remember that with every stage in advancement, there was always an input of creative genius. Men and women, following electrical and chemical laws and principles, used their intelligence and applied it to make computers faster, smaller, etc.

No computer expert has ever yet invented a computer that is creative and could develop itself. Machines only follow the instructions given them. It may happen one day by way of man's applied creativity, but it won't happen without human input (i.e. intelligent designers). No one thinks that given even millions or billions of years that a computer would get more complex by itself. It would never happen. Given all the correct pieces lying side by side, it would still never happen.

Why do people insist on believing that living beings with brains superior to computers somehow magically developed without any intelligent input?

I found estimates from back in 2009 that the human brain is 40,000 times more powerful than the fastest, most powerful computer in the world at that time, a super-computer. That computer is a really unbelievable machine. Check out this quote from an article in Scientific American Magazine:

> "Computers are lauded for their speed and accuracy, but they don't hold a candle to the human brain when it comes to tackling complex mathematical problems, Dharmendra Modha, director of cognitive computing at the IBM Almaden Research Center, said at today's event."

> "We have no computers today that can begin to approach the awesome power of the human mind," Modha said. A computer comparable to the human brain, he added, would need to be able to perform more than 38 thousand trillion operations per second and hold about 3,584 terabytes

of memory. (IBM's BlueGene supercomputer, one of the worlds' most powerful, has a computational capability of 92 trillion operations per second and 8 terabytes of storage.)" [1]

What did it take to develop such an incredible computer? You'd have to be an amazing computer builder and programmer to even begin to understand it. Could it have possibly been developed without directed intelligence? It boggles the mind in its absurdity.

Scientists are now concluding that the brain is not even a computer. It's something else way beyond what a computer is, just a super-fast calculator with lots of storage. It takes in trillions of information bits each second and constantly monitors everything, your heart and circulatory system, lungs and respiratory system, digestive system, excretory system, eyes, ears, nose, mouth, skin, etc. And all of that is being done and you aren't even aware of it consciously.

If computers are nowhere close to being a human brain and they were absolutely designed by intelligent beings, then it is totally incomprehensible that anyone could even think that the human brain did not have a creator of far superior intelligence. The brain had to have been designed and created by a higher intelligence than us.

What would you think of a person who decides that no intelligence at all was behind the appearance of computers and then he/she ridicules you for believing that intelligent beings created computers? Is there a real discussion possible with that person?

There must be God.

Chapter #16 Your Brain

There is way too much information on the brain for me to cover in a short chapter, but I want to give some convincing highlights (probably more that you want to read). Here is a quote that will get us started.

> "Scientists claim that the most complicated and mysterious thing in the universe is the human brain. Scientists know more about stars exploding billions of light years away than they know about the brain." [1]

The brain is a vast mystery and our greatest scientists have not figured it out. That makes a great case for me that it must have been created by a higher intelligence than ours. To think that it happened accidentally when our greatest minds are very far from understanding its complexity is preposterous. Accidents do not create order.

The human brain consists of approximately 100 billion neurons. That, by the way, is about how many stars there are in our Milky Way Galaxy.

Each neuron has somewhere between 1,000 and 10,000 synapses, equaling about 1 quadrillion synapses. Some say there are up to 40,000 synapses per neuron.

There are possibly as many connections in your brain as there are stars in the known universe.

If all the neurons in the human brain were lined up, they would stretch 600 miles.

A piece of brain tissue the size of a grain of sand contains 100,000 neurons and 1 billion synapses, all "talking" to one another.

Human brains are comparable in computing power to the world's greatest computers, but fantastically better at almost every other task while fitting inside your skull and using only the power of a small lightbulb.

> "The world's most powerful supercomputer, the K from Fujitsu, computes four times faster and holds 10 times as much data. And of course, many more bits are coursing through the Internet at any moment. Yet the Internet's servers worldwide would fill a small city, and the K sucks up enough electricity to power 10,000 homes. The incredibly efficient brain consumes less electricity than a dim lightbulb and fits nicely inside our head." [3]

A human brain is 75% water and has the consistency of tofu, custard, or gelatin. You could cut it with a table knife.

Note also that the human brain accomplishes everything at a relatively slow speed, nothing like a computer. Impulses travel at only about 223.56 miles per hour.

"Axons, the long output connection from a cell, come in two types: myelinated and unmyelinated. Myelinated axons have an extra layer of "insulation," a fatty substance, which allows the impulse to travel about 10 to 100 meters per second. Unmyelinated axons only transmit at about 1 meter per second. When the signal reaches the end, it has to cross the synapse to influence the next cell, which adds about 5 ms." [4]

Ten meters per second equals 22.356 miles per hour. 100 meters per second equals 223.561 mph. So your brain impulses are moving really slow compared to the speed of light and the speed of computers. The speed of light in a vacuum is exactly 299,792,458 meters per second, or 186,000 miles per second. Light goes at 670,616,629 miles per hour.

A 20-year-old man has around 109,000 miles of myelinated axons in his brain, which is enough to wrap around the earth's equator four-and-a-half times. [5]

Here is an amazing fact. Three year old babies have twice as many connections in their brains as adults.

"Babies are born with around a 100 billion brain cells, but only a small number of neurons are actually connected. By three years of age a child's brain has formed about 1,000 trillion connections, about twice as many as adults have. At around 11 years, the brain begins to prune unused connections. Connections that are used repeatedly in the early years become permanent; those that are not are eliminated." [6]

There are more than 100,000 chemical reactions happening in the human brain every second.

The human brain has around 100,000 miles of blood vessels. 750 to 1,000ml of blood flows through your brain every minute. That's enough to fill about 3 full soda cans. [7]

"In 2001, researchers from Harvard found that certain parts of the brain were differently sized in males and females, which may help balance out the overall size difference. The study found that parts of the frontal lobe, responsible for problem-solving and decision-making, and the limbic cortex, responsible for regulating emotions, were larger in women. In men, the parietal cortex, which is involved in space perception, and the amygdala, which regulates sexual and social behavior, were larger." [8]

Here is a quote from Jeff Hawkins about computers and brains in his 2004 book "On Intelligence."

"A human can perform significant tasks in much less time than a second. For example, I could show you a photograph and ask you to determine if there is a cat in the image. Your job would be to push a button if there is a cat, but not if you see a bear or a warthog or a turnip. This task is difficult or impossible for a computer to perform today, yet a human can do it reliably in half a second or less. But neurons are slow, so in that half a second, the information entering your brain can only traverse a chain one hundred neurons long. That is, the brain 'computes' solutions to problems like this in one hundred steps or fewer, regardless of how many total neurons might be involved. From the time light enters your eye to the time you press the button, a chain no longer than one hundred neurons could be involved. A digital computer attempting to solve the same problem would take billions of steps. One hundred computer instructions are barely enough to move a single character on the computer's display, let alone do something interesting."[9]

Even if humans compete against single minded computers on a particular task, we have to remember the human brain is doing thousands if not millions of other things at the same time. Millions if not billions of nerves throughout our bodies are sending signals to the brain for processing. Your eyes, your ears, your heart, your lungs and all your other organs, your muscles, well just about everything is sending messages to your brain.

The more we discover about the brain, the more wondrous and awesome it is. If you think that computers are even remotely close to being like a brain, do some research like this article "Brain Versus Computer" on LucidPages.Com.

"So far, no research team has been able to pinpoint where in the brain memory is and how it functions." [10]

Here is a little bit of information on how synapses work in the brain. This should leave you awestruck.

"Neural synapses in the human brain are extraordinarily complex structures. Responsible for relaying information between neurons, chemical synapses govern the release of over 100 different kinds of neurotransmitters, while electrical synapses deliver information via electricity for rapid-fire reflexes." [11]

"When a nerve impulse gets to the end of an axon, its message must cross the synapse if it is to continue. Messages do not "jump" across synapses. Instead, they are carried across by chemical messengers called neurotransmitters. These chemicals are packaged in tiny sacs, or vesicles, at the tip of the axon. When a nerve impulse arrives at the tip, it causes the sacs to release their contents into the synapse. The neurotransmitters diffuse across the synapse and bind to receptors in the membrane of the cell on the other side, passing the signal to that cell by causing special ion channels in the postsynaptic membrane to open. [12]

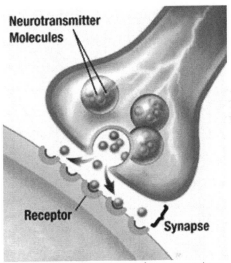

Image 5. Chemical reactions and neurotransmitters.

This setup is awesome. There is a tiny gap between all the connections of nerve cells. Complicated chemical processes have to take place in order for the message to be transferred from one nerve cell to the next.

Not only is it complicated to send a signal, but there are also mechanisms in place to stop the chemical reaction. If it were not stopped, then whatever message was sent would continue to be sent. If you had wanted to raise your arm, it would keep on rising and never stop.

Why the gap between neurons? It absolutely has to be there because if all the neurons were connected without a gap, then when one fired off, they would all fire off. It would be like wiring all your electrical circuits in your house to one circuit, no individual on and off. When you turn on the lights, they would all go on in the whole house. Try to imagine if all the nerves in your body were firing at the same time. Total chaos.

As you can imagine, I'm just getting started. Hundreds of books have been published on the brain and thousands more will be. I have even read where some people now believe that your memories are stored in all the cells of your body, not just inside your skull. People who receive heart transplants are also receiving memories and habits of the former owner of the heart.

Our existence is a total and absolute miracle. Only a supernatural cause could possibly be an explanation for our existence. No materialistic cause, and certainly not a materialistic random accident, makes any rational sense what-so-ever.

There must be God.

Chapter #17 Dr. Antony Flew

This proof is what I'm going to call a "piggyback proof". I propose that you accept the word of a really smart person who searched for the truth about God for his whole life in a very unusual way.

In 2004 after about 50 years as one of the world's leading and best known atheists, Antony Flew, came to the conclusion that there must be God.

> "After a lifetime of probing philosophical inquiry, this towering and courageous intellect has now concluded the evidence leads conclusively to God" [1]

> "Antony Flew has been for most of his life a very well-known philosophical champion of atheism." [2]

Other atheists were quick to call him senile and said that he was manipulated in his old age by certain Christians. He denied it and came out with a book called, **There Is A God, How The World's Most Notorious Atheist Changed His Mind** [3]. It tells his story and the arguments that convinced him. (There are videos on YouTube of his appearances if you search under Antony Flew.) [4]

> "I now believe that the universe was brought into existence by an infinite Intelligence. I believe that this universe's intricate laws manifest what scientists have called the Mind of God. I believe that life and reproduction originate in a divine Source." [5]

> "This is a fascinating and very readable account of how a distinguished philosopher who was a militant atheist for most of his working life came to believe in the intelligent design of the universe..." [6]

> "A stellar philosophical mind ponders the latest scientific results. The conclusion: a God stands behind the rationality of nature." [7]

Flew was not your average atheist. He was considered a brilliant philosopher who at a very young age in 1950 published a paper called Theology and Falsification on atheism that is the most widely reprinted over the last 50 years and has been highly influential in philosophy around the world.

He was always involved in the highest levels of the academic world, even having a professorship at Oxford. He kept up on the latest philosophical arguments for and against God as well as the latest scientific research into the origins of life and the universe.

One of his greatest virtues was his commitment to academic integrity and dedication to the Socratic Method of following the evidence wherever it might lead.

Ultimately, it was the developments in modern science that convinced him that there must be an intelligent source that designed and created the universe. The Big Bang Theory, namely that the universe had a beginning something like 13 billion years ago, does not allow for enough time in order for the complexity of life that we observe to have developed according to evolution. Also, research discoveries in micro-biology and DNA led him to the same conclusion, namely that there must have been an intelligent cause.

This man was one of the greatest and most respected philosophical minds of the 20th century. He debated far and wide those who believed in a God. For him to finally change his mind after 50 years of debating, believing, and researching is a monumental change, certainly not done lightly or easily.

His change completely negates the idea that only common people who are uneducated and haven't done the research can believe in a God.

Secondly, he must have known the incredible hatred that would be unleashed on him from the atheistic community if he betrayed their beliefs. He responded as ever with kindness and gentleness, which is all too evident in the book he wrote, **There Is A God**. In it he patiently spells out the philosophical journey he had taken in life and clearly what lead him to change his mind so all the world could know.

"When Antony Flew, in the spirit of free-thinking, followed the evidence where he thought it led, namely, to theism, he was roundly denounced by supposed free-thinkers in the severest of terms. He had, it seemed, committed the unpardonable sin." [8]

This man understood all the arguments for atheism inside and out. In fact, he created some of those arguments himself. He was the author of 30 books. All his life he wanted to follow the evidence to find the truth and he ended up accepting that there must be God.

"In fact, my two main anti-theological books were both written long before either the development of the big-bang cosmology or the introduction of the fine-tuning argument from physical constants. But since the early 1980's, I had begun to reconsider. I confessed at that point that atheists have to be embarrassed by the contemporary cosmological consensus, for it seemed that the cosmologists were providing a scientific proof of what St. Thomas Aquinas contended could not be proved philosophically; namely, that the universe had a beginning." [9]

In 2007, Flew was interviewed by Benjamin Wiker. He said again that his deism was the result of his "growing empathy with the insight of Einstein and other noted scientists that there had to be an Intelligence behind the integrated complexity of the physical Universe" and "my own insight that the integrated complexity of life itself – which is far more complex than the physical Universe – can only be explained in terms of an Intelligent Source." [10]

You could do all the research yourself and study all the arguments for and against God. Or you could just take a short cut and check out what Antony Flew has to say. I enjoyed reading his book very much although at times the philosophy was over my head. He was clearly a brilliant thinker.

There must be God.

Chapter #18 The Fossil Record

Here's the real bottom line on the fossil record: there has never been any substantiation of the Theory of Evolution by Darwin. [Comment 1]

In fact, as more and more and better and better fossils are discovered, the evidence for evolution is getting worse and worse.

Charles Darwin knew in 1859 when he proposed his theory in **On The Origin Of Species** that there were a lot of gaps and "missing links" in the fossil record. He assumed that over time and with new discoveries that there would be more evidence discovered in favor of evolution, but in fact the opposite has happened.

Darwin said in his **On The Origin of Species:**

> "Lastly, looking not to any one time, but to all time, if my theory be true, numberless intermediate varieties, linking closely together all the species of the same group, must assuredly have existed... "[2]

In order for higher species to have evolved from lower species, there must necessarily be many numerous intermediate stages of transformation. If you think about it, there should be more intermediate entities than just the first species and the last one. Astoundingly (if you believe in evolution) there is not even one of the proposed links in the fossil record. Zip. Zero. Nada.

> "Author Luther Sunderland interviewed five respected museum officials, recognized authorities in their individual fields of study, including representatives from the American Museum, the Field Museum of Natural History in Chicago, and the British Museum of Natural History. None of the five officials were able to offer a single example of a transitional series of fossilized organisms that document the transformation of one Kind of plant or animal into another.

> "The British Museum of Natural History boasts the largest collection of fossils in the world. Among the five respected museum officials, Sunderland interviewed Dr. Colin Patterson, Senior Paleontologist at the British Museum and editor of a prestigious scientific journal. Patterson is a well-known expert having an intimate knowledge of the fossil record. He was unable to give a single example of Macro-Evolutionary transition. In fact, Patterson wrote a book for the British Museum of Natural History entitled, "Evolution". When asked why he had not included a single photograph of a transitional fossil in his book,

Patterson responded: "...I fully agree with your comments on the lack of direct illustration of evolutionary transitions in my book. If I knew of any, fossil or living, I would certainly have included them..." [3]

If evolution were true, there should be millions of fossils of the intermediate links between species along every branch of the tree. But there are none. Science needs to find a lot more than just one "missing link". It needs to find millions. But there aren't any to be had.

We keep finding better and better preserved fossils. The most recent discoveries in Chengjiang, China, are the most outstanding fossils ever found, but still no missing links. Since Darwin was alive, paleontologists have uncovered about 99.9% of our current fossil record, but still no missing links. In Darwin's day they only knew of about 0.1% of the fossil record that we have today. Still after all these new fossils, no Missing Links.

"Despite the tremendous increase in geological activity in every corner of the globe and despite the discovery of many strange and hitherto unknown forms, the infinitude of connecting links has still not been discovered and the fossil record is about as discontinuous as it was when Darwin was writing the Origin. The intermediates have remained as elusive as ever and their absence remains, a century later, one of the most striking characteristics of the fossil record." [4]

The second enormous problem with the fossil record for the Theory of Evolution is that the vast majority of species appear at about the same time in history, called the Cambrian Explosion.

Darwin predicted that slowly and gradually over time the higher forms evolved from the lower forms. But the fossil record indicates that almost all life forms "suddenly" appeared during the Cambrian Age which is about 2% of the time line of the life of the earth.

Here is a chart of the actual fossil record for the appearance of species.

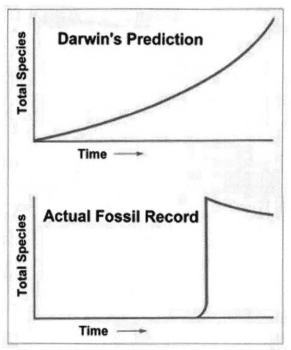

Image 6. Darwin vs. Actual Fossils
©2016 Jim Stephens

Do some research on your own. I suggest you look up "problems with the fossil record" or "Darwin and the fossil record."

Isn't it about time to junk the Theory of Evolution? Darwin said it himself, "If it could be demonstrated that any complex organ existed which could not possibly have been formed by numerous, successive, slight modifications, my theory would absolutely break down." [5] He's correct. It has absolutely broken down.

There must be God.

Chapter #19 Butterflies and Metamorphosis

I think we are all familiar with caterpillars and butterflies. There are over 20,000 known species of butterflies all over the world.

We know that caterpillars go into a cocoon, turn into mush, and then emerge two weeks later as a butterfly. You may have even watched one in school.

This process is called metamorphosis. There is an incredible and fascinating DVD out by the same name, Metamorphosis: The Beauty and Design of Butterflies by Illustra Media.

The DVD shows an animation in great detail of what happens inside the cocoon. Based on MRI research that takes "pictures" of 200 slices of a cocoon, they know which parts of the caterpillar dissolve completely and which parts morph into various parts of a butterfly. Those processes cannot be explained in any way by the Theory of Evolution.

The caterpillar and the butterfly are exactly the same being, just at different stages. BUT we know some parts of the caterpillar dissolved, some parts changed into parts of the butterfly, and in the end the butterfly is capable of reproducing, but the caterpillar could not.

The caterpillar goes into a cocoon and through the process of metamorphosis becomes a butterfly. In this process totally new structures are built from the dissolved cells of the caterpillar. Some of the totally new structures are (a) reproductive organs, (b) a compound eye that can see a larger range of colors than the human eye, (c) a proboscis, a feeding tube which emerges from the cocoon in two halves and is seamed together, (d) six articulated legs that have sensors that can detect a mate or "host" plant over a mile away, (e) two tentacles, (f) wings with veins and scales and all the muscles needed for flight.

One scientist said they don't even know 1/1,000th of what goes on in the tiny butterfly brain.

The Theory of Evolution has no mechanism that can explain metamorphosis.

Those very few who attempt it are making what I call faith statements. Basically they are saying, "We haven't found the evolutionary process yet, but it's out there. Just give us more time." The processes in evolution are random mutation, natural selection, survival of the fittest, and not much else.

There is no known process for this type of sudden and dramatic change in the life of a single individual being.

Here is an interesting analogy which is a very much simplified example. Metamorphosis is much more complicated than this example. Say a Model T Ford is driving along and then it stops. Then part of the engine cover grows to become a garage that completely covers the car. Inside of the garage the car ALL BY ITSELF without any intelligence added takes itself apart, changes the parts into other parts, and reassembles a new vehicle. Two weeks later out comes a helicopter.

If you do a search on the topic "evolution and metamorphosis," there are relatively very few entries and there is no clear scientific research. You'll find words like "cannot explain". You might find some die hard evolutionist believers claiming that scientists just need more time. There are also some proposed changes to standard evolution that are suggested, such as "sudden" evolution. But, with those types of changes you don't have evolution any more. You can't keep changing the definition. A theory has to be a statement that can be proven or disproven. It can't be a moving target.

The Theory of Evolution is just based on faith. It's faith in an unproven and unprovable theory that is changeable all the time. Being changeable makes it untestable. And that makes it a worthless theory.

When a caterpillar goes into a cocoon and starts to turn into mostly mush, there must be some direction ALREADY built into the process or there could never emerge a perfectly formed butterfly out the other side. After that first caterpillar turned to mush, he had to get it exactly perfect coming out as a butterfly THE VERY FIRST TIME or else there would be no more caterpillars reproduced whatsoever.

No caterpillar can reproduce, so it is impossible for evolution to work its "magic". The Theory of Evolution requires myriad changes over long time periods by many, many generations of individuals who reproduced. You CANNOT have evolution in one generation...by definition. The idea that caterpillars could have "evolved" that way is nonsense.

There must be God.

Chapter #20 GPS and Monarchs

Most people are familiar with devices in your car or Smartphone that are called GPS (Global Positioning Satellite) systems and they guide you over short or long distances to exactly your destination.

If you do any research on GPS, you will learn what a modern-day miracle of technology they are.

First you have to have the 31 communication satellites up in orbit circling around the earth. Each one is emitting a signal telling the time and its location. Your GPS device has to be able to pick up at least 4 satellites in order to be able to work for positioning. There is a computer inside the GPS that uses the broadcast information to calculate exactly where you are.

Pretty amazing when you think of all the intelligence and development of science, math, and technology to put those satellites in orbit and in creating the GPS devices themselves.

And the purpose is to create a guidance system in order to give directions to get you where you want to go.

Is it possible for such a sophisticated guidance system to come about randomly without purposeful application of intelligence? Not likely.

Let me tell you about a guidance system even more sophisticated and miraculous. It's the story of the Monarch butterfly.

The normal Monarch butterfly that lives in the spring or summer will only live for two to four weeks. They will mate, lay eggs, and die in that time. However, the generation of Monarchs that are born in late August, unlike their parents and grandparents will live for nine months. Scientists do not know why.

Their desire to mate is turned off and they stock up on nectar and water and begin an incredible flight. They start off in Canada or the northern United States and will fly between 2,500 to 3,500 miles using some type of "GPS" system.

They fly all the way back to the same area and maybe the same tree in Mexico where their ancestors started out. 300 million Monarchs converge from all over North America on the exact same 12 locations in Mexico.

After going into semi-hibernation for the winter, they start the long flight back north. But now their mating instincts are turned back on. They mate, lay eggs, and soon die.

The eggs hatch out caterpillars that eat, make cocoons, emerge as butterflies and continue the flight north, mate, lay eggs, and die. This generation lives only two to four weeks. One, two, maybe three generations are born, reproduce, and die. Then comes late August and the whole thing starts over again with a generation that lives for nine months. This is called the Methuselah generation, and it flies all the way back to Mexico to their ancestral home.

This generation has never been to that spot in Mexico where their "GPS" takes them. Neither were their parents there or their grandparents. How's that for an incredible GPS system!

Each generation included caterpillars that spun cocoons, turned into mush inside, and then reconstituted that mush into a butterfly with that GPS system intact in order to get the Methuselah generation back to "home base".

Scientists don't have any idea yet of how that system works. What does it use for "satellites" for points of reference for guidance? It's obviously more of a miracle of intelligence than the manmade GPS. Only a super intelligence could have designed Monarch butterflies.

Also note how big the GPS in the Monarch is. The brain of a Monarch is about the size of a few grains of sand.

There must be God.

Chapter #21 DNA

Every living thing has DNA in its cells. We can't talk about life without talking about DNA, the "blueprint" of life. Differences in the DNA will determine what type of plant or animal emerges. I'm sure you know a little about it already.

You have about 40 to 100 trillion cells in your body and all of them contain DNA except red blood cells. If you laid the DNA from a single cell end to end, it would stretch about six feet, but would only be about 50 trillionths of an inch wide.

Laying out all your DNA, it would reach to the sun and back about 600 times. (6' x 100 trillion divided by a round trip of 184 million miles). Put another way, it would span the diameter of the Solar System.

If you started typing 60 words per minute for 8 hours a day, it would take you around 50 years to type out the DNA sequence in one of your cells.

DNA is so amazing, there are probably enough facts about DNA alone that I could put together 101 Proofs for God just using DNA.

DNA does almost everything. It sets the patterns for all your proteins. Patterns in your DNA are used for producing the RNA which is then used by ribosomes in your bone marrow to produce hemoglobin. Every second the ribosomes make 100 trillion molecules of hemoglobin. (Can you even believe that?) Hemoglobin carries oxygen to your brain, muscles, and all your cells. Without it, you die.

Humans have 46 chromosomes of genetic material in their cells consisting of 23 pairs. Sections of genetic code on the chromosomes are called genes. We have an estimated 20,000 to 25,000 genes. Each gene is made up of segments of DNA that are about 10,000 to 15,000 base pairs. A "base pair" is like one of the rungs on the "ladder" in the DNA. The genes are the areas of the chromosomes that are passed from parent to child and contain the hereditary information which gives you characteristics like your parents.

The human genome (the exact DNA sequence in a human) consists of about 3 billion base pairs and almost every cell of your body has a complete set. The amount of data in one cell would fill 1,000 volumes of an encyclopedia.

Every time a cell divides the DNA goes through self-replication using cellular protein processes that act like machinery. It makes a complete duplicate of itself, accurately copying the 3 billion base pair genome. Astoundingly impressive! Astronomically impossible to happen accidentally. Your body produces about one billion new cells every hour.

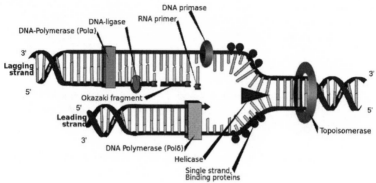

Image 7. DNA Replication Process.

This duplication has just one exception. That is when making a sperm or an egg cell. That process requires ending up with only half the DNA makeup. A man's body makes 1,500 sperm cells per second.

But DNA is not only reproducing itself fantastically fast, it is also helping make every type of protein that is necessary for your life. This is serious multi-tasking.

Watch this 7 minute YouTube video to see an animation of several of the functions of DNA. Astounding mechanical and bio-chemical complexity is taking place. Here is a quote from the video: The DNA is an "assembly line of amazing miniature bio-chemical machines that pull apart the double helix of DNA and crank out a copy of each strand."
http://youtu.be/4PKjF7OumYo

Here is another video (2:36 minutes) that might help in understanding the very complex replicating process: http://youtu.be/wkXgwGn_dGU

Certainly lots more will be discovered about DNA and the human genome, but from what we already know, it is mind boggling in its complexity. There is no entity in the known universe that stores AND processes more information MORE efficiently than the DNA molecule. That some scientists continually exclude any possibility of an invisible hand of God that started the DNA processes is unfathomable. To insist that science must remain godless in the face of all evidence to the contrary is absurd.

Science proves there must be God.

Chapter #22 Life Spans

Living entities that reproduce over longer life cycles, if they had evolved, would have necessarily taken a longer time. May flies that live, reproduce, and die in a day can create descendants way faster than humans.

A rather simple conclusion that must be drawn from the Theory of Evolution is about time. Beings that take years to reproduce must take longer than beings that reproduce in days or weeks. A human being takes about a minimum of 20 years between generations. A fruit fly takes about 8.5 days between fertilization and adulthood.

But the Theory of Evolution has never been demonstrated to be true at all using experiments on species with very short life spans.

Take for example experiments on fruit flies. "It is typically used because it is an animal species that is easy to care for, has four pairs of chromosomes, breeds quickly, and lays many eggs." [1] Eggs can develop into mature adults in roughly 8.5 days. Females will lay about 400 eggs. Research on heredity using fruit flies has been some of the most important research in the history of biology.

If you assume half the eggs are female and each individual of each generation every 8.5 days produces 200 female eggs. They could produce 25 to 40 generations in a year. The number of individuals produced that could possibility have evolved is gigantic. 200 x 200 x 200 ... (25 times) in one year. That's of the order of 3.3×10^{57}.

That's a lot of opportunity to be able to observe some evolution. Compare that to humans which take 20 years to grow to where they can produce a second generation. I'm sure there have been more generations of fruit flies studied by scientists than generations of humans that have ever existed on earth.

Also fruit flies lay 200 eggs every 8.5 days. That's a lot of chance for mutation to work its magic for evolution. Humans take 20 years to grow to maturity and then can only produce a child or two every nine months.

YET (note this is very important!) in all the years of doing scientific research on fruit flies, there has never been any observable evolution. EVEN WHEN THE SCIENTISTS INTERFERE WITH THEIR INTELLIGENCE, they can't get any evolution.

In July, 2012, there was news that scientists had "evolved" fruit flies that could count. [2] Actually, they detected some perceived response to light flashes after 40 generations.

This is not evolution. (A) These are still fruit flies. At most they learned some trick. They did not evolve into some other species, which is what evolution is supposed to be all about. (B) The fruit flies did not change on their own. There was obviously a lot of human intelligence applied. (C) After years of experiments and countless generations, fruit flies are still fruit flies. There is no evidence of evolution. Change yes, but evolution no.

Human beings are millions of times more complicated than fruit flies. Fruit flies mature in 8.5 days compared to humans at about 20 years. That means fruit flies mature 859 times faster.

In the scheme proposed by the Theory of Evolution, the more complicated and highly evolved entities emerged later in time. But this is not feasible because those with longer life spans have to take hundreds of times longer to produce each successive generation.

We can apply this same logic all over creation. Using other insects, fish, or mammals with short life spans that have been studied by scientists, evolution has never been demonstrated. Mice live only for 1 to 3 years. Rabbits live up to 5 years. House flies and bees live about 4 weeks. Pigmy goby fish live only 2 months. Where is there any evolution ever shown in these species? The mayfly that lives less than a day has been around for 300 million years, but it's still a mayfly.

What about all the beings with much longer life cycles? How could they evolve when it takes so long for one generation to reproduce? Elephants take 2 years in the womb. Giraffes and rhinos take more than a year. The lowly velvet worm takes 15 months. Whales and dolphins take over a year and a half. How about the Black Alpine Salamander that takes 2 to 3 years to produce just 2 offspring? Then there is the champion 17 year cicada which takes 17 years between generations.

After you apply years and years of research trying to validate a theory and you still have never been able to find any evidence that it is true, isn't it about time to junk that theory?

There must be God.

Chapter #23 Children and Parents

We are all children of our parents. Inside us are very powerful instincts to have a relationship with our parents. Automatic bonding takes place without a conscious decision.

Even many children who are adopted will go to great lengths to try to learn who their real biological parents are.

We are innately constituted in our very being to having a loving relationship with our parents. This is a win-win relationship for everyone. If our parents are mentally, emotionally, and spiritually healthy and we are in a loving relationship with them, then the odds are huge that we will be healthy also. Even the community around us will benefit.

But this is also a lose-lose proposition. If the parents are immature, then they become an upper limit hampering their children's maturity. If the parents are abusive, then the odds are that the children will also become abusive.

The parent-child relationship is so much of an underlying foundation for our existence that if we are abandoned emotionally and spiritually as children, we will have serious psychological consequences and may even never recover.

The highest revealed understanding of the nature of God is that of a loving Father, i.e. parent. Some religions add a female god or maybe a Holy Spirit/Comforter.

If one does not have God in their life, they are abandoned like a child. He or she is consciously or unconsciously on a search to fill the empty space in that deep inner part of their being.

Many substitutes appear such as money, knowledge, power, sex, or fame which seem for a while to fill the emptiness. But none of them will ever truly satisfy the place reserved for God in our lives. They eventually will be recognized for what they are, false gods.

Sadness, emptiness, bitterness, and resentment, and usually pain are all the results of chasing after these false gods.

It's either a win-win or a lose-lose for each person having a relationship with their parents. Where did this originate? It was not from an accident. We are designed to exist in a loving relationship with God, our eternal parent. Nothing else will ultimately satisfy our hearts.

There must be God.

PS: Allow me to share the final two paragraphs from a recent book I read, **Life In Eternity**, which talks about the cosmic parent-child relationship.

"...as I looked at the sleepy faces of those sitting and standing all around me, I gasped in instantaneous tears. For as I discerned each person's face -- whether that of a child, a young adult, an older man, or a beautiful woman, as well as the faces of many other people from all walks of life -- I became instantly conscious of two extraordinary realities. In the first nanosecond, I saw each human face expressing the sense of being lost and all the myriad pain of disorientation, and the ongoing suffering involved in the lifetime struggle to overcome an unknown amnesia and to live a conscientious life. In the next nanosecond, I saw how much, how desperately, how passionately God loves each person, how tremendously much God longed to be able to assuage each man's and each woman's pain, how much God desired to restore to each person the sense, the living reality of his or her own true identity as an authentic son or daughter of God -- and to reassure each person that they were not only immeasurably loved by God but, as God's child, he or she had a truly cosmic identity as a Being of LOVE, potentially capable of exercising unlimited power to create. I felt so much of God's heart to rescue us, to embrace each of us, so much of God's yearning to reassure us, to heal us -- so that we could finally be immersed in the cosmic joy that is our original birthright.

Slowly, as I stepped back from this realization, I stopped crying. And I simply knew then that, however many dozens, or hundreds, or thousands, or millions of years it might take, God would walk with us every step of the way, that God would recover all of us as His children, who could finally and triumphantly declare: WE HAVE AWAKENED! WE DO KNOW WHO WE ARE! WE ARE THE SONS AND DAUGHTERS OF GOD!" [1]

Chapter #24 Pacific Golden Plover

Take a look at the globe sometime and notice the distance from Alaska to Hawaii. Also note that Hawaii is out in the middle of nowhere and it would be pretty hard to find in the Pacific unless you knew exactly where you were going.

How easy would it be for a bird to hatch from its egg, have its parents leave after just a few days, fend for itself for a couple months, plump up in weight, and then take off flying to Hawaii non-stop for three to four days [1] with no guides, and eventually not miss landing in Hawaii?

The birds that do exactly this are called Pacific Golden Plovers (Pluvialis fulva), known by natives of Hawaii as Kolea. They are small and weigh only about 8 ounces. Every year they migrate between Alaska and Hawaii or other similar routes making nearly a 2,000 mile journey without stopping or resting because they can't swim. It takes them about 70 hours each way and they lose 50% of their body weight. They are known to return to Hawaii to the exact same patch of grass year after year for up to 20 years. Some return to the same backyard and are welcomed by the natives. They like front lawns, parks, ball fields, sometimes even parking lots.

Scientists have been able to track them with small GPS devices and Google Earth images can show their paths across the Pacific. [2]

The parent Plovers live in Alaska from May to August, forage for food, mate, nest, and wait for the young to hatch. In August while the chicks are days old, the parents leave their young behind in Alaska and fly to Hawaii without them. The young have to grow and bulk up on food and water much longer. About October they leave for Hawaii. During the trip they will use up half of their body weight in energy to make the trip.

After winter, by the end of April or early May, all the Plovers will have left Hawaii and journeyed the 2,000 miles back to Alaska. For Hawaiians, the coming and going of the Plovers mark the changing of the seasons.

The Theory of Evolution is based on a process described as slow and incremental changes over long periods of time. There are no partial incremental trips from Alaska to Hawaii for a bird that can't swim. The Plover has to have eaten enough to make the trip and fly exactly to a very small target in the Pacific Ocean the very first time or else die. If it dies along the way, there is no reproduction and hence no evolution.

Darwin himself recognized the limitation of his theory and what scientific facts would invalidate it. He is quoted as saying:

> "If it could be demonstrated that any complex organ existed, which could not possibly have been formed by numerous, successive, slight modifications, my theory would absolutely break down. But I can find out no such case." [3]

It would take a very, very intelligent designer to build a machine capable of flying from Alaska to Hawaii non-stop the very first time. To believe the Pacific Golden Plover happened to learn accidentally over many attempts over longer and longer routes is a fantasy. Darwinism is disproved by his own admission.

There must be God.

Chapter #25 New Zealand Long Finned Eel

The Longfinned Eels of New Zealand grow very slowly but eventually they reach about 6.5 feet long and 40 pounds for females. Males are smaller, only about 2.5 feet. They only mate once in their lives at the very end right before they die and in a place thousands of miles from their home.

To make it even more complicated the males die much younger than the females. Males die at an average age of 23 years old, but females live to an average of 34 (usually ranging from 27 years old to 61), with one recorded as old as 106 years.

Something like this could not happen accidentally, randomly, or by natural selection. There must be a God who created this, probably for the pure fascination of His children. In all the years scientists have studied these eels, they have never located their mating grounds.

Scientists speculate various locations from the deep ocean trenches east of Tonga to the deep trenches near New Caledonia. (Some say the Coral Sea.) They do know the female eels can have millions of eggs in their ovaries, but they don't know what the males do to fertilize them.

Each eel only mates once after having traveled thousands of miles from their home to the mating grounds. Then it dies. The females are usually an average of 12 years older, so there is a huge problem for this species to evolve. How could it possibly have gotten started and continued for so long? Some scientists believe they existed 65 million years ago. Others say 23 million years ago. What if the males and females don't swim to the exact same place over the thousands of miles distance? What if they die en route? What if some males don't show up for a few years and the females die off or vice versa? What if the ocean currents take the eggs out to sea and not back to New Zealand?

When the eels reach the end of their lives, their heads become much more slender and tapered, their skin turns darker, and their eyes double in size. They swim from their fresh water home to the ocean and at that time they stop eating and begin their long journey. They never eat again. They swim over 1,200 miles according to some scientists and over 3,100 miles according to others. Reaching their spawning grounds, the females lay their eggs and die.

In some unknown way the eggs are fertilized. The larvae are called leptocephalus and look nothing like an eel – they are transparent, flat, and leaf-shaped. The larvae reach New Zealand by drifting on ocean currents taking a year to as much as 18 months of floating.

Off the New Zealand coast they change into tiny little eels before going up the fresh water rivers. They are now called "glass" eels because you can see through them. They begin swimming upstream and start to change color to brown as they go along their way. Young eels (called elvers) swim upstream and spend a number of years maturing in freshwater.

They are legendary climbers and have made their way well inland in most river systems, even those with natural barriers. Remarkably they have the ability to get out of the water and travel sort distances on land when they encounter obstacles like waterfalls or dams. Elvers (young eels) swimming up river will climb waterfalls and even dams by leaving the water and wriggling over damp areas. It is not unheard of for an eel to climb a waterfall of up to 20 meters (60 feet). [1]

The theory of natural selection says there is no God and things developed randomly because of some benefit to the organisms or better adaption to the environment. The whole life cycle of the Longfinned Eel at every stage is taking the hard and complicated way, not the easy way. This is a creature that's very existence leaves you feeling a sense of awe.

There are 4 distinct phases in their life cycle. Can a reasonable mind really believe that all these stages could have developed by accident? And even if it happened randomly, why would it possibly be the "fittest to survive?" Only a mind of faith can explain it, so people can choose either faith in a creator God as the source or have faith in some miracle of accidents and coincidences in an extraordinarily long improbable sequence.

It only makes sense that there must be God.

Chapter #26 The Things In Your Room

Look around you in the room that you are sitting in. You could probably identify 1,000 different objects in most rooms.

It's very interesting to go to Google Images and search for "my room". Look at different people's rooms.

Pick just one object and imagine backwards in time as far back as you can regarding that object and the process it went through from the very beginning until it came to exist in your room.

Let's say you bought it at a store. Somehow it got to that store from the manufacturer which could be as far away as the other side of the earth, like China.

There may be hundreds of ingredients that were brought together from various sources by the manufacturer. Is it wood, plastic, metal, or something else? Where did each of the raw materials originate?

How did it get its color? Was it artificially colored? By what? What was that process?

What about the shape of the object? Was it random?

I'm sure you cannot imagine it got that form randomly. Almost absolutely you will know that some intelligent person designed the look and feel and components of that object. He or she designed it over time after much thought and many developmental stages. Blueprints of some kind were made for the construction engineers and the manufacturing process.

Some intelligent person probably laid out an assembly line process and the exact sequence to build the object. Intelligent workers were brought in for each stage of the process. Maybe there were a large number of intricate parts to be assembled, some by machines, some manually by humans. Imagine the sophistication of those machines.

I once watched a documentary on TV about how a simple pencil is mass produced. Once I saw a documentary about potato chips.

Looking again around your room at all of the objects, you know for sure that the most complicated ones were the most difficult to produce. The most complicated objects required the most highly intelligent people to create them.

Ask yourself if there is even one single object in your room that is totally the result of accident and randomness? Is there one single item in your room that exists there which has no purpose? Is there any object that exists which was not caused by intelligent beings?

Nobody in their right mind would argue that any object in your room occurred randomly or by accident with just one exception.

The exception is YOU. Atheists and evolutionists believe that YOU came to exist by accident.

YOU, the most extraordinarily complicated entity in your room (in fact, in the entire universe), somehow got there by accident and a random assembly process.

Preposterous.

Absurd.

There must be God.

Chapter #27 The Truth About Mutation

Those who think there is no intelligent creator of all living beings very often rely on the process of random mutation as the way living species came to exist. They deal with living beings that reproduce and where mutations happen, mostly skipping over how the atoms and other materials got here in the first place.

They believe faithfully that this process could actually produce all the thousands of magnificently functioning attributes of the millions of species that exist.

But does this really make rational sense when you study the truth about mutation, not just assume what is possible "in theory".

When you go to the dentist and have to get X-rays on your teeth, they put a lead vest on you to shield your heart. Why is that? The reason is to prevent mutations of your cells. Another term for it is cancer.

There is a big scare in the media about a hole in the ozone layer around the earth. Why? What's the big deal? It's because if there is less ozone to protect us, there will be more mutations going on, more sickness, more disease.

Most states have a law against getting married to your first cousin. Why? That's because inbreeding of close relatives increases the likelihood of genetic mutations. One famous one is hemophilia.

Every year the "Flu Season" strikes with a new mutated version of last year's flu. Is this a good thing?

If you think about it, you already know that almost all mutation is a bad thing. The odds of bad things happening as a result of a mutation are thousands of times greater than good things happening.

Theodosius Dobzhansky, a prominent evolutionary biologist [1], spent years irradiating fruit flies for thousands of generations to artificially induce mutations. What were the results? When asked, he couldn't think of a single mutant that was more viable out in nature. He could only think of several which might be more viable at unusual conditions like very elevated temperatures.

How about the study of bacteria? Mutation has been studied most extensively in bacteriology because you can experiment with millions of bacteria and thousands of generations in a fairly short period of time. Alan H. Linton, British bacteriologist, wrote in 2001, "Throughout 150 years of the science of bacteriology, there is no evidence that one species of bacteria has changed into another." [2]

We currently have millions of perfectly functioning species on earth all intricately woven together in phenomenal ecosystems connected to the earth. If there was a lot of mutating going on, then where are all the bad results from the mutations? The track record of mutations is mostly diseased and dysfunctional results. Where are they out in nature?

The fossil record does not show any "missing links". This is a well-known fact. But, a missing link is an intermediary step along the "right" path to get to a certain developed species. But think about it. Missing links (if there actually are any) are a tiny, tiny fraction of what would have to be thousands of mutated beings that were the "wrong" path for every "missing link" along the "right" path. No mutants exist in the fossil record either.

All the species on the earth seem to exist in their "final" form, their "perfected" form, and fully functioning. How come scientists don't find any species in nature that are mutating toward something else? There are no records of ever having actually seen instances of evolution for as long as they have been looking. There have of course been changes within a species, but that's not evolution.

Here is an even more fundamental problem for those who have faith in mutation. Mutation requires changes BUT ONLY after there is already a successfully functioning species. Where did that first species come from? You have to have a male and female correctly functioning respectively before they can have a mating relationship which could result in a mutation.

Evolutionists may show us artist's drawings of what types of mutations could possibly occur, but note that before even those changes, they have to assume the original DNA somehow exists. Mutation can only occur after DNA exists. We need to ask Evolutionists to explain the original existence of the DNA.

In the old days people used to think that life could spontaneously "combust" out of nothing. No one believes that anymore. Life only comes from life.

Because there is life, the original source must also have the attribute of life.

There must be God.

Chapter #28 The Lottery

Most of us are familiar with the Lottery, right? Many states have them now and they are being advertised all the time. You know that the odds of winning a lottery are more than a million to one, even hundreds of millions to one in the bigger lotteries. But millions of people buy a ticket anyway and start dreaming of what they will do when they win.

The thing about the lottery that gets people to buy a ticket is that someone is guaranteed to win. Some real person is going to win the jackpot.

Let's apply the concept of the lottery to the existence of life in this universe. Believers in evolution will assert that we "won the lottery" because life exists and evolved into us and the world we live in. It seems to make sense, right? We are here after all.

Ah, but the theory of evolution does not guarantee there will be a winner because it is based on randomness and accident. Would you buy a ticket for the lottery if the likelihood of NO winner was a million to one or even greater?

The mathematical odds of life spontaneously and randomly arising from a "soup" of chemicals has been put by Sir Fred Hoyle at one possibility out of $10^{40,000}$. There are no known chemical reactions or laws of physics that can produce a living cell. [1] The greatest scientists in the world cannot do it.

"He would go on to compare the random emergence of even the simplest cell without panspermia to the likelihood that "a tornado sweeping through a junk-yard might assemble a Boeing 747 from the materials therein" and to compare the chance of obtaining even a single functioning protein by chance combination of amino acids to a solar system full of blind men solving Rubik's Cubes simultaneously." Sir Fred Hoyle (astronomer, cosmologist and mathematician, Cambridge University) [2]

Winning the lottery just once is unbelievable but winning it TWICE IN A ROW is beyond rational comprehension. Can you even conceive of winning the lottery three, four, or five days IN A ROW? The odds of any life happening accidentally are about the odds of you winning the lottery EVERY DAY IN A ROW for over 10 years.

Therefore, the existence of life itself happening accidentally is like winning the lottery every day for over 10 years in a row. Those who believe it might have happened accidentally without a God and that we won this cosmic lottery out of blind luck are lacking some common sense if you ask me. They are trying really hard to believe something against all the odds and the patently obvious and simple conclusion that there must be an intelligent designer.

It is so much easier and more elegant to hypothesize that there is an original source of life outside of the physical universe.

There are only two choices that seem to be available: namely (a) there is God or (b) there is no God. The chances there is no God are less than 1 in $10^{40,000}$ so that leaves us with the chances that there is God. That would be every other chance or $10^{40,000} - 1$.

Note also that the lottery idea above is based on the odds that a single living cell would form by accident. I didn't even touch on the odds of a single cell later developing accidentally into anything more complicated. That would obviously be required before you can have plants and animals. Also the odds just became more complicated.

There must be God.

Chapter #29 Mathematics

Mathematicians have completely refuted the possibility of random action as the source for life or the development of species. The problem is that you have never heard about it and the statements are buried away by deniers of everything but godless evolution.

After the development of superfast computers it became possible for researchers to test out theories by creating computer models. Randomness and survival of the fittest (natural selection) were totally refuted mathematically as the process that could produce advanced species.

I invite you to read up on the Wistar Institute Symposium: Mathematical Challenges to the Neo-Darwinian Theory of Evolution that took place in Philadelphia back in April, 1966 [1]. It was chaired by the Nobel Prize winner, Sir Peter Medawar and only the most distinguished authorities in their fields were invited.

As an example of one of the presentations, Dr. Murray Eden [2] demonstrated that even a single ordered pair of genes could not evolve in the whole life span of the earth. His example started with a preposterous amount of E. Coli bacteria (5 trillion tons covering the planet nearly an inch deep) and showed it was mathematically impossible for a protein to develop. See below for other quotes from the Wistar meeting from Ulam [3] and Schutzenberger [4].

Wistar was followed up by other meetings in Alpbach in 1969 and Chicago in 1980. Each conference became more and more contentious as evolutionists fought against the mathematicians.

As a result, Darwinists had to give up on randomness and gradual change as the process of evolution. So they made up new ideas such as "punctuated equilibrium" which is essentially stating that sudden gigantic changes took place.

Never mind that this is the opposite of Darwin's theory of slow, gradual changes. Also, of course, those unexplained sudden and dramatic changes, which resulted in new species, occurred by an unknown process which they had not discovered yet. By the way it also has to violate known laws of chemistry, physics, and biology.

Many evolutionists hold onto "natural selection" as the magic formula. Somehow it selects out the good developments (mutations) and the bad ones disappear. But we know that a simple bacteria has millions of ingredients that must be correct for it to survive. It's inconceivable that all those ingredients were added one at a time and at each step the resultant being was better adapted to its environment and so became the sole survivor of the species for the next stage to follow.

Even allowing for sudden change and multiple steps at once, we still cannot make enough changes to account for all the necessary developments to get a simple bacteria. What about all the millions of higher order species that are thousands or millions of times more complicated? See Sewell [5].

We know that researchers on mutations have not been able to produce any new species in all their efforts, only change WITHIN a species. In fact, the chances of a "possibly beneficial" mutation are about 1 in more than 1,000. That means 999 mutations out of 1,000 are harmful or neutral.

Let's ignore that fact for a second and use a simple-to-understand example. Let's say we flip a coin. Heads means we have a beneficial mutation. Tales means we have a harmful or neutral mutation. Every time you get a "head," then you move one step forward in evolution. Every time you get a "tail," you move back one step. Just using the laws of probability, how far will you have moved after millions of years???...exactly nowhere. You are in the same place. In this example, you had a 50/50 chance of moving forward in evolution by mutations. But as we know, the odds of a beneficial mutation are not even close to 50/50. They are 1,000 to 1.

The believers in "natural selection" would say that when certain good things happen, then there is no going backwards. That's like saying every time you get 3 "heads" in a row, you make permanent progress toward some unknown destination where you want to end up. So even if you get 3 "tails" in a row, there's no going back. How natural selection really works is a mystery since no one has ever seen it in an experiment. Also, there is no explanation why it goes in a certain direction.

It's like saying "natural selection" got us where we are because we are here. That does not contain proof of anything. It's circular reasoning, right? That's about the essence of the Theory of Evolution. "We know we are here and we must have gotten here by natural selection because there is no God."

I read lots of articles about mathematical calculations for evolution and I invite you to read them and make up your own mind who has a plausible explanation.

Just for fun here is one number that I read which fascinated me. A mathematician [6] calculated the time it would take under very suitable conditions for a usable protein to hook up from available amino acids. That number was 10^{171} years.

When we start getting into really big numbers, they are very hard to comprehend. That doesn't seem like such a big number. (Actually there are only 10^{80} atoms in the universe.) Here is what that number would be in some sense by our reality. If you gave an amoeba 10^{171} years, he could carry every single atom in the universe, one by one, all the way across the universe and back (30 billion light years), more than 600,000 trillion, trillion, trillion, trillion times if he were traveling at the unbelievably slow speed of 1 inch every 15 billion years (the age of the universe). I love it.

There are 3,000 trillion atoms in the period at the end of this sentence.

So if a mathematician calculates the odds of life developing randomly at 1 in $10^{1,000}$, then I would say the argument is over. That's just the kind of impossibly high number we're talking about and thus Evolution is totally impossible mathematically.

There must be God.

Chapter #30 S.E.T.I. and DNA

Another group of scientists are close to recognizing that there must be God. They are astrobiologists.

S.E.T.I. stands for "Search for Extra-Terrestrial Intelligence" and comprises several groups of scientists that were combining their expertise to try to discover if there is intelligent life anywhere out in the universe. [1]

In order to decide how they would recognize intelligent life, they had to determine some basic criteria that they could apply to observed phenomena that would characterize only intelligent origins. For example, if they saw certain patterns like Morse Code in a radio transmission, infra-red radiation, or gamma ray bursts, they would be certain that it had originated only at an intelligent source.

So far they have never detected any intelligent life anywhere else in the universe.

Recently however a couple of these scientists, Vladimir I. shCherbak and Maxim A. Makukovb, had the bright idea to apply the criteria they had created for SETI to the results of the DNA studies that have emerged. The conclusion was exactly one word, "Wow!" [2]

They found that DNA shows patterns that could only have been created by intelligence. The odds of an error were less than 1 in 10^{13}. (1 in 10 trillion)

The obvious conclusion is that DNA is not random, but is the definite result of an intelligent design.

The astrobiologists published their conclusions in a peer-reviewed highly acclaimed journal in their field named Icarus. [3]. Peer-reviewed clearly means that other experts in the same field have poured over their work and their conclusions and have given it their stamp of approval.

Go to my Footnotes and Comments if you want to see some references to the article and the charts of DNA that show the clear proof of intelligent design.

You may not have heard about this if you aren't in the field. But it must be sending shockwaves through a whole lot of research institutes right now and causing panic among evolutionists.

The truth cannot be kept down forever. I applaud the courage it must have taken for those scientists to come forth and go against entrenched dogma of evolutionists and the violent backlash that will surely come. But the truth will win out because it will be undeniable. The odds are 10 trillion to 1 that DNA came from an intelligent source.

There is God.

Chapter #31 The Second Law of Thermodynamics

Most likely you have heard the term, Second Law of Thermodynamics, but may not be able to give a definition. Note that this is a scientific LAW of nature. It's been around and verified again and again for a long, long time and there are no known violations of the Second Law of Thermodynamics, unlike the THEORY of Evolution which is worse than Swiss cheese.

Thermodynamics has to do with the study of energy. The meaning of the Second Law in simple terms is that everything tends toward disorder or lower energy. Energy tends to disperse. Nothing becomes more complex on its own. Everything tends to break down over time as long as nothing new is added to the system from outside.

Hot things cool down as the heat (i.e. energy) disperses. Things tend to go downhill (not uphill) to a lower energy state. Everything wears out and eventually decays. Living things all eventually die. This is the natural order of the universe.

Isaac Asimov (a highly respected evolutionist, and ardent anti-creationist) has said:

> "Another way of stating the second law then is: 'The universe is constantly getting more disorderly!' Viewed that way, we can see the second law all about us. We have to work hard to straighten a room, but left to itself it becomes a mess again very quickly and very easily. Even if we never enter it, it becomes dusty and musty. How difficult to maintain houses, and machinery, and our bodies in perfect working order: how easy to let them deteriorate. In fact, all we have to do is nothing, and everything deteriorates, collapses, breaks down, wears out, all by itself—and that is what the second law is all about." [1]

Since everything in the universe tends toward disorder, it is a violation of the Second Law if they become more orderly and complex all by themselves.

If you leave your room one day and it's a mess, it will stay a mess for all eternity, gradually getting messier and messier until it one day disappears. If you go away for a while and come back and it is cleaner and more orderly, then you know your mother was there. If not your mother, at least some energy force was there with the distinctive, intelligent attribute of order. Energy might have been added but by itself would not be sufficient. There had to be the component of orderliness. Otherwise the random energy would have just added to the mess. Putting a wild bull in there would not have cleaned the room.

This is where evolutionists have a really hard time. They can say all day that there was energy coming down to the earth from the sun, but what about the orderliness that resulted? It requires information and intelligent design.

If there were to exist some primordial soup of chemicals (disregarding where it came from), then for all those chemicals to somehow change into a living cell is a direct violation of the Second Law. They would not order themselves into a living organism that has gigantic numbers of orderly properties like digestion of fuel sources and reproduction.

People who deny the existence of God have a huge problem with the Second Law of Thermodynamics. They usually claim that the energy of the sun qualifies as the outside source that can cause life to form accidentally. That's a huge stretch because there is no order and information in the sun's energy. There are many examples of the sun's energy speeding up the process of disorder, not the other way around. It heats water to cause it to evaporate faster. It wears out the paint on your house.

They also try claim that the earth is an open system and somewhere in the universe changes are going on that balance out the increased order on the earth. That's an extreme level of faith in a mystery greater than the mysteries in the Bible. That's on the order of saying that I'm sitting in my room watching my computer fall apart, so somewhere else on earth a computer is being built all by itself. Except the problem is multiplied millions of times over because living plants and animals are millions of times more complicated than a computer.

Honest evolutionists will admit that they have a problem, but nonetheless go right on having faith. They have faith even though there must have been millions upon millions of violations of the Second Law of Thermodynamics necessary to get to every new stage up the evolutionary ladder from a single living cell, to multi-celled species, to plants, to animals, up to human beings. That would take an unfathomable number of increases in order, each one a violation of the Second Law. The only honest explanation is that an unseen intelligent designer is adding energy and information and order.

> "If Evolution is true, there must be an extremely powerful force or mechanism at work in the cosmos that can steadily defeat the powerful, ultimate tendency toward 'disarrangedness' brought by the Second Law. If such an important force or mechanism is in existence, it would seem it should be quite obvious to all scientists. Yet, the fact is, no such force of nature has been found." [2]

"Using natural processes alone, there's just no explaining how the complex, information-intense organization of even single-celled life and its uniquely inherent and complex processes could have emerged from non-life in the first place, and then could continue to fly in the face of natural law with untold increases in information, complexity and organization to yield all the flora and fauna varieties known to have existed." [3]

"Thus, unless we are willing to argue that the influx of solar energy into the Earth makes the appearance of spaceships, computers, and the Internet not extremely improbable, we have to conclude that the Second Law has in fact been violated here." [4]

There must be God!

Chapter #32 Irreducible Complexity

The concept of "irreducible complexity" was put forth by Dr. Michael Behe, a biochemist, in his book, **Darwin's Black Box:** The Biochemical Challenge to Evolution. [1]

The concept is a strong argument against Darwinian Evolution and in favor of an invisible, intelligent designer. Remember Darwin's evolution was all about lots of small incremental changes over time and many generations. Darwin even said the following:

"If it could be demonstrated that any complex organ existed which could not possibly have been formed by numerous, successive, slight modifications, my theory would absolutely break down. …But I can find out no such case." --Charles Darwin [2]

Years ago before modern equipment like the electron microscope scientists believed that a single cell was basically just a blob of protoplasm, not complicated at all. This is the "black box" that Behe refers to. They did not know what was going on inside. Nowadays, we know for a fact that the tiniest of living bacteria cells is very, very, very complicated.

"Although the tiniest bacterial cells are incredibly small, weighing less than 10^{12} grams, each is in effect a veritable microminiaturized factory containing thousands of exquisitely designed pieces of intricate molecular machinery, made up altogether of one hundred thousand million atoms, far more complicated than any machine built by man and absolutely without parallel in the non-living world." [3]

If a system is "irreducibly complex," this simply means that you cannot take away any single piece at all because if you do, it won't work. Behe uses the example of the mousetrap to try to illustrate his point. It has only five parts, but if you took away any one of them, it would not work.

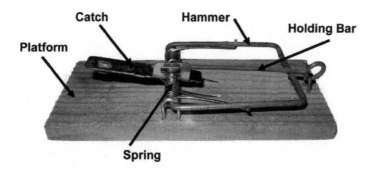

Image 8. Mousetrap.

"If any one of the components of the mousetrap (the base, hammer, spring, catch, or holding bar) is removed, then the trap does not function. In other words, the simple little mousetrap has no ability to trap a mouse until several separate parts are all assembled. Because the mousetrap is necessarily composed of several parts, it is irreducibly complex. Thus, irreducibly complex systems exist." [4]

In his book, Behe gives a few examples, but the one that I like is the flagellum (tail) of a tiny bacteria. Behe has studied those for 20 years. The tail allows it to swim around. The tail works a lot like a machine, an outboard motor on a boat. Behe says there are 40 different proteins that are needed for the flagellum and they have to be assembled in the correct order and sequence. One mistake or one missing piece and it won't work. (Watch an animation of the process on YouTube. [5]) This could never develop slowly piece by piece. All pieces must be present at the beginning and assembled in the correct order.

The big problem for evolution is that it relies on small incremental and accidental steps AND each one has to make the organism better off or it doesn't survive by "natural selection." It has to be BETTER adapted than its ancestor. If a tail begins to develop slowly, the early bacterium is going to have a useless tail. That's not going to be advantageous. It's going to be worse. Evolutionists faithfully believe that this process happens over and over again thousands of times.

Let's take a larger scale example. Evolutionists believe that dinosaurs evolved into birds. How did that supposedly happen? Imagine you are a dinosaur on four legs and you have a baby that has two legs that start to look slightly like wings. Then this baby grows up and has a descendant a few generations later. In this new dinosaur, the same two legs look slightly more like wings. The process repeats itself many, many times. Each time the offspring is somehow more fit to survive. At some point in the middle of the evolution, the dinosaur must have two half-leg/half-wings. How well are they going to work? Obviously, it has to be the two front legs and only the two front legs that change. Back legs changing doesn't work. Two legs changing only on the left side or right side doesn't work. Only one leg changing doesn't work. All this seems preposterous to me, but letting our imaginations go on a little more we eventually get to the midway point. At the halfway point you've got limbs that are almost worthless as legs and totally worthless as wings. You're dead meat.

Naturally the true believers in evolution maintain their faith by using their imaginations to get around the irreducible complexity argument. Check out some of their rebuttals if you want and then follow up with the responses by Behe and others. [6]

Typically the evolutionists have no physical or fossil evidence for their imagined processes so how can you debate their faith. Secondly, their imagined processes always violate one important rule of Darwinism, namely that no directed intelligence is ever allowed at any stage of development because there cannot be God.

In the end, scientific truth will lead to proof that there must be God.

Chapter #33 Caveman Paintings

Have you ever seen pictures of paintings that were done on the walls of ancient caves? There are recognizable pictures of many things, including deer, horses, elephants, humans, and buffalo.

Those markings on the walls have been there for thousands and thousands of years. Who could know how they really got there? People can only take educated guesses, right?

Many people assert with absolute certainty that cavemen painted those formations on the walls. But just maybe the similarity to men or animals is just totally accidental. Maybe we can come up with some explanation about rain water carrying different colored minerals swept into the caves by water so we don't have to assume humans did it. How do we know for sure that intelligent beings created those formations?

Scientists must be using some criteria in order to decide with certainty that those supposedly caveman drawings were made by intelligent beings.

Now I want you to imagine a series of pairs of pictures. First we have a picture of a caveman's painting of a horse and next to it is a picture of a real horse. Next there is a picture of a caveman's painting of some deer and beside that is a picture of some real deer. Third is a picture of caveman's painting of an elephant and next to it is a picture of real elephant. Fourth is a picture of a caveman's painting of a buffalo and next to it is a picture of a real buffalo. Lastly is a picture of a caveman's painting of three other cavemen and next to it is a picture of three men dressed up as cavemen.

Of each pair I want you to choose which one of the two most definitely had an intelligent creator and which picture is of something that came to exist totally by accident WITHOUT any intelligence involved.

If you said that the beings pictured in the second one of each pair had NO intelligent creator, then you would be in agreement with the evolutionists and the atheists, the intelligent ones among us. They believe that horses came to exist accidentally, but that caveman paintings of horses could only originate from an intelligent human being. Etc., etc.

Come on!!! It's patently obvious to me that everything in the pictures described above show signs of an intelligent designer. The actual living beings in the second pictures required a creator with intelligence thousands or millions of times greater than the painters who painted the caveman drawings.

A person can deny the obvious for as long and as loud as they want, but they can't change the truth.

There has to be God.

Chapter #34 The Giraffe

The giraffe is one of the world's most amazing creatures. Children and adults alike will stand mesmerized just looking at it for long periods of time.

The giraffe has many features that could not have evolved following steps in the Theory of Evolution, namely in small incremental steps over many generations. It must have been designed by a supernatural intelligence and come into existence with all of its parts functioning.

Male giraffes can stand up to 19 feet tall and their necks alone can be almost 8 feet long. [1] However, they have the same number of vertebrae in their necks as humans, seven. A large male averages 2,600 pounds but can weigh over 4,200 pounds, almost a small pickup truck. The head and neck on an adult giraffe will weigh over 550 pounds. [2]

Think of the engineering skills it takes to create a crane that can lift over 550 pounds and swing it around. You have to know what you are doing. Evolutionists make up a story, without any evidence to back it up, that somehow the long neck elongated by stretching for higher and higher food. Others think the long neck grew because of natural selection and survival of the fittest. The bones in its neck grew longer by mutations and the giraffes with the longer necks were able to survive better because they could reach more food, a competitive advantage.

They seem to ignore other facts. For instance, it's harder to get a drink and get blood to the brain. It's also harder to breathe and swallow your food. It takes really long nerves to reach from the brain to all parts of the body. As the neck gets longer, all kinds of other mutations would have also had to be necessary simultaneously in order to support the head way up that high.

Evolutionary scientists are always disagreeing with each other. Some research even concluded that longer necks is a disadvantage because they die more in droughts and have a more difficult time getting enough nutrition. [3]

Being tall may help you get more food, especially with a 21 inch tongue, but it also reveals your location to any predators in the area.

One of the problems for the giraffe that must be solved if it could "evolve" is how to get blood up to the brain 18 feet off the ground. It takes a lot of pressure to push a full neck's worth of blood up to the brain. You also have to be sure that it doesn't slide back down in between pumps of the heart. The giraffe's heart is two feet long and weighs 25 pounds. The giraffe has a relatively small heart and its power comes from a very strong beat as a result of the incredibly thick walls of the left ventricle. The left ventricle that pushes out the blood has a relatively small capacity, but it pumps 170 times a minute (humans are 80) and creates a blood pressure twice that of humans. [5] The heart pumps almost 16 gallons per minute. It takes special arteries to take this amount of blood and withstand the pressure, the highest recorded for any animals. [6]

The giraffe also has to have unique veins, as well as arteries, so that load of blood in the brain and neck doesn't gush down the hill and into the body and heart.

Now think about when the giraffe bends down to take a drink of water. And it's a big drink of up to 12 gallons. Its legs are six feet long and the mouth can't reach the water without first spreading his legs. But when his head is down, the giraffe has just the opposite problem with his blood. The blood is now rushing to his head really fast. If the heart keeps pushing with the same pressure, it will blow his brains out. Now his arteries have to slow the blood from going down to his brain too fast. But his veins also have to do the opposite from before and help the blood go uphill. So the blood has to flow downhill 8 to 10 feet and then back uphill another 8 to 10 feet back to his heart. That takes some really specialized systems.

Are you following so far? OK, the giraffe is bent over drinking with his front legs spread apart. Suddenly a lion shows up to eat him. He'll have to raise his head from the ground level up to 18 feet really, really fast and start running. If he's slow, he dies and doesn't reproduce. But what happens to his blood when he suddenly raises his head 18 feet in the air. It stays behind. Mostly likely he passes out and gets eaten by the lion. There is no second chance in nature. You get it right the first time or you don't survive.

Scientists don't really know how all this works. You can read about them putting giraffes to sleep with drugs and trying to simulate these situations and see what's going on. [7]

Here's another issue for the rest of his body since the giraffe has really high blood pressure. All of his arteries and veins need to be adapted for this, especially the arteries and veins in his legs which are 6 feet long. The blood vessels especially in his feet would be under a lot of fluid pressure to burst. Scientists say that the skin on his legs is really tight to prevent pressure building up in his feet.

Baby giraffes take 14 months in the womb so it takes a long time between generations for any supposed mutation and natural selection to work out. Babies weigh up to 150 pounds and are 6 feet tall when they are born. Mothers give birth standing up, which means the baby falls 6 feet when it is born. That's another little ability that baby giraffes are required to have to be born. It had to be there the first time, not evolved. Otherwise they would die and it would take at least 14 months before another baby would be born that might make it.

These are just a few of the special characteristics of the giraffe that all have to come together simultaneously for them to even exist. If only some but not all of the systems are in place, then the giraffe likely dies.

To say every living thing came about via mindless random processes requires a faith that far exceeds belief in a Supreme Creator. As the renown British physicist Lord Kelvin once wrote: "Overwhelming strong proofs of intelligent and benevolent design lie around us." And "The atheistic idea is so nonsensical that I cannot put it into words." [8]

God made the giraffe. He made it for you and me and our children to stare at in wonder and amazement. He made it as a gift for us.

There is God and He shows us His love for us in all the things around us.

Chapter #35 Natural Selection

The concept of "Natural Selection," sometimes used synonymous with "Survival of the Fittest," is often touted as the magic process that when added to mutation will result in advancing steps of higher and higher species and the success of evolution. [1] But I encourage you to read up on what Natural Selection is all about and see that it will NOT lead to evolution. Check out the examples that are given, and see for yourself what a fanciful argument this is for evolution of molecules to man. Actually you can't even start with molecules because Natural Selection ONLY works on a species once it can reproduce.

What they actually mean by "natural selection" is what we believers in God totally accept already. Just we call it adaption to the environment. It's a wonderful God-given quality in Nature that creatures have that allows them to better survive. But it is never a process that will give you a new species.

"Natural Selection" is also sometimes referred to as "Survival of the Fittest". However, as a term used by scientists and evolutionists, it does not refer to what we normally think of as being "fit," which means the healthiest, strongest, smartest, or fastest. For them it actually means the ones who were reproductively fittest and left the most descendants.

To rephrase the term, we could say "Survival of the ones that survived". Pretty unscientific huh? [2] Some of them even understand the problem with their logic, namely saying the same thing twice and calling it a proof. That's tautology and not proof of anything. But then they go right on with the same type of assumptions anyway.

Most of us understand the concept of dog breeding or horse breeding where we selectively try to bring out certain characteristics like speed or size or color. It's mating together certain males with certain females. This is all that Natural Selection claims it is doing EXCEPT it happens "out in the wild" without any interference from humans.

Now, who do you think can do a better job of purposeful breeding and selection, "the wilds of nature" or a human in a controlled environment of matching certain males and females? Need I remind you that humans have never been able to breed a new species with all their efforts (very intelligent efforts, not mindless) over decades of trying? Dogs are always dogs and horses are always horses no matter how much we can change their features.

Let's walk through a simplified example and see if this process makes any sense as a mechanism for evolving any new species. Let's assume there is a wild dog population where the dogs have genes for producing long-haired or short-haired descendants. Suppose also that one gene pair controls the length of hair. If a given dog has both types of genes (L and S for long hair and short hair), then it will have medium length hair.

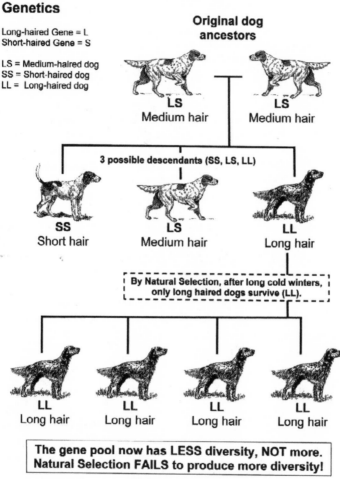

Genetics

Long-haired Gene = L
Short-haired Gene = S

LS = Medium-haired dog
SS = Short-haired dog
LL = Long-haired dog

Original dog ancestors

LS
Medium hair

LS
Medium hair

3 possible descendants (SS, LS, LL)

SS
Short hair

LS
Medium hair

LL
Long hair

By Natural Selection, after long cold winters, only long haired dogs survive (LL).

LL
Long hair

LL
Long hair

LL
Long hair

LL
Long hair

The gene pool now has LESS diversity, NOT more. Natural Selection FAILS to produce more diversity!

Image 9. Dog breeding.
©2016 Jim Stephens

What happens next, the environment changes and gets much colder over time. Natural Selection says the short haired dogs will die out faster, leaving more and more long-haired dogs to reproduce. But looking at the genes, this process is not evolving toward a new or higher species. Actually the dog population is losing genetic diversity and DNA information, not gaining it. The gene for short hair is being lost.

So Natural Selection is not a process that will get you a new species at all because the species is LOSING genetic information. It's going backwards from the way evolution is supposed to go.

This is when evolutionist believers will fall back on mutation as the place where the new genetic information comes from. After there is mutation, then Natural Selection can work its magic. But we already saw in an earlier proof, Chapter 27, that mutation does not work either for creating a new species. [3]

So evolutionist believers count on two processes that demonstrably don't work at all for producing evolution separately, but when combined somehow magically start to work. In mathematics, when two processes are combined, you multiply the odds of success of one process times the odds of success of the other. The odds will be even less likely when the two processes are combined. I remind you that 40 years of intentional and intelligent efforts to develop mutated fruit flies has never gotten anything but fruit flies. None of them that survived was better off (i.e. more "fit") than the fruit flies they started with.

Not even any improvements could be mutated into the fruit flies. But evolutionist believers will still insist that millions of extremely complicated species all happened accidentally. They don't just believe in one very improbable accident, they believe in billions upon billions of progressive accidents one after another building up higher and higher levels of species. There are millions upon millions of species on earth (plants, animals, fish, insects, etc.), each functioning very successfully but with hundreds of different and very distinguishable characteristics.

Another problem at issue for Natural Selection producing evolution is "How do you get the starting point?" Natural Selection only works when there is already a living organism that can reproduce. Natural Selection cannot explain the first original organism. Scientists now know that the simplest of all species capable of reproduction has at least 250,000 ordered genes. Could any accidental process explain ordered genes on that magnitude? Not a chance.

We God-affirming believers do believe in Natural Selection as it is OBSERVED in nature and demonstrated in selective breeding. God designed it and it testifies to God's design skills. The truth about the process of Natural Selection is that it is a conservation mechanism that helps prevent species from going extinct by keeping harmful mutations from proliferating in a population. But as a proof for godless evolution, it fails miserably.

I invite you to do an Internet search for "examples of Natural Selection". All you get are examples of adaptations that creatures have made WITHIN a species, never one species evolving INTO ANOTHER species. Natural Selection fails as a mechanism for evolution. Molecules to man is an extraordinarily long path for evolution to try to walk and it can't.

There used to be an article on the Internet by Discovery.com supposedly on the "10 Examples of Natural Selection." It got taken down. They offer different examples of called "natural selection". There are peppered moths, colored snakes, chemical resistant insects, Galapagos Island finch's beaks, male peacock tail feathers, a certain ability of warrior ants, deer mice changing color, etc., and even humans getting sickle cell anemia. All they talk about is changes WITHIN a species and still they name it evolution. Excuse me. That is NOT the definition of evolving. It's only "selective breeding." Just by waving the magic words, they claim this is the scientific proof of Natural Selection producing evolution. That's fraud. Dirt didn't become dinosaurs. Sorry, natural selection creating new species doesn't exist or they could show it. It's too preposterous.

I must conclude that the evolutionists don't really understand what they themselves are claiming. They don't really have any evidence of a new species. They have already decided the conclusion and are grabbing at straws to justify it. That's very poor science.

Eventually, the honest scientists will conclude along with the rest of us that there must be God.

Chapter #36 The Zoo

When was the last time that you went to the Zoo?

I don't know about you, but I have always been fascinated at the zoo. The educational opportunities are endless and the exhibits are from all over the world, not just our country. It was always really special to go as a kid myself and then later to take my own kids when they were young. Now I'm looking forward to taking my grandchildren as well.

What kinds of animals do they put in a Zoo? Do you see dogs and cats, squirrels, robins and starlings, cows or horses there? No. Zookeepers will always try to put animals there that you will never see in your neighborhood. They go for animals that are somehow amazing, especially for kids.

The largest Zoos in the world are Toronto Zoo and the Omaha Zoo, both with over 17,000 species of animals. Think about that. How long would it take you to study each unique one? Each has a totally different set of DNA and different physical characteristics, lifestyle, digestive system, reproductive systems, locomotion, on and on.

How many animals are there that you have never seen? How about fish or birds? Then there are plants and insects. I saw recently that there are 383 different species of hummingbirds alone.

Nobody knows how many species there are in the world. I searched around for estimates of how many species there are of all the kinds of living beings. A New York Times article reported on an estimate of 8.7 million species. [1] But there are estimates as high as 100 million. Researchers are reporting over 15,000 new species discovered EVERY YEAR. Scientists have named and categorized ONLY 1.3 million so far.

If a zoo has 17,000 species, it only has 1.3% of the already named species, which is a small fraction of the estimated total number of species.

There are 43,271 cataloged species of fungi of an estimated 660,000 to 5.1 million. There are approximately 6,500 species of millipedes. Mollusks, slugs, and snails make up an estimated 100,000 species. Starfish, sea urchins, and their relatives make up 6,500 species.

There are an estimated 5,000 species of mammals, 9,000 to 10,000 species of birds, 23,500 species of fish, 1 million to 30 million species of insects, 298,000 species of plants. The most amazing fact of all is that scientists really have no idea of how many species are yet to be discovered and estimates vary all over the place.

The following is from About.com [2]

Total Animal species: estimated 3-30 million species

    Invertebrates: 97% of all known species
        Sponges: 10,000 species
        Cnidarians: 8,000-9,000 species
        Mollusks: 100,000 species
        Platyhelminths: 13,000 species
        Nematodes: 20,000+ species
        Echinoderms: 6,000 species
        Annelida: 12,000 species
        Arthropods-
            Crustaceans: 40,000 species
            Insects: 1-30 million+ species
            Arachnids: 75,500 species

    Vertebrates: 3% of all known species
        Reptiles: 7,984 species
        Amphibians: 5,400 species
        Birds: 9,000-10,000 species
        Mammals: 4,475-5,000 species
        Ray-Finned Fishes: 23,500 species

"We've only touched the surface of understanding animal life," said entomologist Brian Fisher of the California Academy of Sciences. "We've discovered just 10 percent of all living things on this planet." [3]

I personally guess he might be overestimating what we know.

Go to the websites of various zoos and look at some of the strange and unusual creatures in their zoos. Imagine that there are literally millions of other beings for each one of those you see. This is an extremely small sampling of amazing creatures.

If you want to be even more amazed, just go to the Internet and search for images for moths, butterflies, birds, snakes, dogs, cats, fish, or whatever else you can possibly think of. Then look over those images for a while.

Evolutionists say they believe that every single one of these species exists totally and absolutely by accident, without any intelligence behind it. It was all godless mutations and survival of the fittest. They want me to believe that every color of flower, strange shape, or unique ability came into existence because it was the result of millions of mutations and then natural selection choosing that character trait because it was the most "beneficial" for survival. To me that is so implausible as to be incomprehensible. I am flabbergasted that anyone could believe it.

I hope that they will go spend some time at the Zoo. In fact, let's all go there.

There has to be God.

Chapter #37 Information

"There is enough capacity in a single human cell to store the Encyclopedia , Britannica, all 30 volumes of it, three or four times over." [1] This is a quote from atheist Richard Dawkins. Note, that is just one cell and your body has over 35 trillion and maybe up to 100 trillion.

I don't know about you but if I came across an encyclopedia that was three or four times the size of the Encyclopedia Britannica, you could never get me to believe that it came into existence without any intelligence behind it. But that's what Richard Dawkins, atheist, believes and evangelizes, and probably also makes a lot of money espousing.

> "To illustrate further, the amount of information that could be stored in a pinhead's volume of DNA is staggering. It is the equivalent information content of a pile of paperback books 500 times as tall as the distance from the earth to the moon, each with a different but specific content." [2]

Let me say that in a different way for you. The distance between the earth and the moon varies, but the average is 238,900 miles (384,400 km). Imagine a stack of paperback books, all different, that is 11,945,000 miles high. Now shrink down all that information until you can put it on a pinhead. That is the reality of the world around us. That's how much information exists all around us in every square millimeter of the plants, animals, and people we see. Almost incomprehensible!

Atheists do not believe there was any superior intelligence behind all that information. It all comes from accidental mutations and natural selection (which I have already written about as processes that LOSE information). The more scientists discover about DNA and microbiology, the harder atheists have to work to keep believing in nothing as the source of life.

> "...But in all the reading I've done in the life-sciences literature, I've never found a mutation that added information. ...All point mutations that have been studied on the molecular level turn out to reduce the genetic information and not to increase it." [3]

(NOTE: Let me say that in layman's terms. The very type of mutation that evolutionists depend on happening billions of times to produce all current life forms has NEVER EVER been observed even once in the history of science.)

Life cannot exist without order and information. Every living being starts out with a single cell which contains all the information needed to eventually build the complete organism. When scientists tried to determine the smallest amount of information necessary to still end up with a potentially living organism, they came up with 256 genes. But they profess this theoretical organism might not be able to survive on its own.

> "More recently, Eugene Koonin and others tried to calculate the bare minimum requirement for a living cell, and came up with a result of 256 genes. But they were doubtful whether such a hypothetical bug could survive, because such an organism could barely repair DNA damage, could no longer fine-tune the ability of its remaining genes, would lack the ability to digest complex compounds, and would need a comprehensive supply of organic nutrients in its environment." [4]

> "Is it really credible that random processes could have constructed a reality, the smallest element of which – a functional protein or gene – is complex beyond our own creative capacities, a reality which is the antithesis of chance, which excels in every sense anything produced by the intelligence of man? Alongside the level of ingenuity and complexity exhibited by the molecular machinery of life, even our most advanced artifacts appear clumsy…" [5]

Encyclopedic amounts of information are required for the most basic form of life to exist. It could not be assembled step by step and then suddenly come to life. The information had to already be there at the beginning of life.

Imagine the most complex system you can think of, say a supercomputer, a skyscraper, a spaceship, whatever. The amount of information to build those systems is not enough to build the first living cell. Life is no accident.

There has to be God.

Chapter #38 Practice Makes Perfect

From the time that we were little children, we have heard the axiom that "Practice makes perfect."

We all know the meaning of it, namely that just about anything in life that is worth doing or learning takes practice. You don't get it right the first time. From potty training, to learning to walk, to brushing your teeth, to kindergarten, to playing a sport, playing a musical instrument, getting a job, to cooking your dinner, to about everything else, it takes practice to get it right.

Do you find anyone out there advocating "It takes an accident to make it perfect?" When you get right down to the bottom line, that's what atheists believe. Life itself was an accident. For each higher level of species, there were more accidents (mutations) followed by some process of survival of the fittest.

They must believe the Big Bang was an accident of some kind. The appearance of life from non-living chemicals was an accident.

Most atheists will admit that random mutation cannot generate successful changes for producing evolution so they will add in "natural selection" as the cure all because it magically adds a "positive" directedness. But as I detailed in a previous Chapter, Proof for God #35, natural selection is never the source of new information. It only acts on what exists already which can be inherited. No new information comes from it.

If mutation does not work and natural selection does not work, then adding them together or multiplying them will not work. "Practice makes perfect" obviously means good practice, not bad practice. Bad practice added to bad practice makes a worse result.

You and I might be able to conceive of one or two accidents that happen to go "right" (i.e. toward the direction of evolution), but millions upon billions upon trillions of accidents that go right is NOT conceivable.

Michael Jordan made 49.69% of his shots in his career by practicing a lot, not by accident.

The number one hitter of all time in baseball, Ty Cobb hit successfully 36.6% of the time in his career by practicing a lot, not by accident.

Nobody is any good at anything complicated by accident.

People who decide to be atheists have concluded that all the incredible complexity from the biochemical level up to the intergalactic level including all the flowers, fish, birds, and animals exist by accident followed by reproductive selectivity, followed by another accident, followed by more selectivity on and on to the millionth degree.

Huh?

I believe that atheists start out with a decision that there is no God and then proceed to conjure up a way that this observable world "might" have come about. Then they believe in that. They don't start with the observable data known to science today and propose a theory. They start with the assumption that there is no God and a theory from 154 years ago. Conclusions and theories should come after analysis of data, not the other way around.

Many examples of people falsifying the data (on both sides admittedly) exist in the scientific fields. Also many advances in science have proven previous theories were false. But the "old truths" were slow to die because those who believed in them could not give them up. We have to be careful who we bow down to as our authorities. Darwin thought a cell was mostly an uncomplicated mass of protoplasm. That's far, far distant from what biochemists know today since the electron microscope was invented.

Even Albert Einstein admitted he fudged the data when it led him to the conclusion that the universe was expanding. That would have meant the universe must have had a beginning at a certain point in time which would clearly imply a creator. Later when the research of others like Hubble also concluded the universe was expanding, Einstein admitted his falsification. [1] and [2] He called it his "biggest blunder."

Science is clearly closing in on atheists and making it harder and harder to sustain their beliefs.

Dr. Paul Zulehner, dean of Vienna University's divinity school and one of the world's most distinguished sociologists of religion, has said that atheists in Europe have become "an infinitesimally small group. There are not enough of them to be used for sociological research." [3] Also, "John Updike's observation, 'Among the repulsions of atheism for me has been its drastic uninterestingness as an intellectual position,' appears to have become common currency throughout much of the West." [4]

"And if you think it is challenging to be a Catholic parent, try being an Atheist parent! Some 70% of Americans raised to believe that God does NOT exist end up being a member of a religion as an adult." [5]

That is the worst retention rate of any "faith".

Real scientists go where the evidence leads. They don't cling to unverifiable dogma. The truth about God and evolution will not be suppressed for much longer in science.

There must be God.

Chapter #39 Trees

I'm going to assume that almost every person loves trees. They are everywhere around us with about 100,000 different species, but we often take them for granted.

Without trees we wouldn't exist. They take the carbon dioxide that we exhale out of the air and return to us oxygen that we need for survival. What a phenomenal coincidence if you don't recognize that a master designer created trees. The whole amazingly complicated and delicately balanced ecosystem exists and allows for perfect support for human existence.

Trees have a vascular system that passes water and nutrients throughout all the cells in the tree, somewhat similar to our own circulatory system of blood.

Trees produce for us an amazing variety of fruits that we love. They are almost all tasty in our mouths and at the same time very healthy for our bodies. Yet, there is a tremendous variety: apples, oranges, citrus, peaches, pears, cherries, coconuts, and so many others.

Trees produce in great abundance, far more than is needed for their own survival…almost like they do it for us. Trees are the great "givers" in nature. I will always remember there was a big old cherry tree that my aunt and uncle had in their backyard. That thing produced so many cherries that they could never give enough away to the whole neighborhood. As hard as they tried, the ground would always be covered with a layer of rotting cherries.

Forests of trees support the life and very existence of many other plants as well as myriads of insects, birds, and animals.

Trees give us shade from the hot sun and they shelter us from the rain like a big protective friend.

Trees give us their wood for building our houses and thousands of other creations. For thousands of years we burned the wood of trees to keep warm and to cook meals.

Many a romantic moment has happened in front of a burning fire. One of the greatest joys of going camping is sitting around the fire in the evening.

Trees give us paper. The vast majority of human knowledge that was ever shared in history was made possible by paper from trees.

Chapter #39 Trees

Trees directly or indirectly provide jobs for a large segment of the population.

Another incredible aspect of trees is that they start from a small seed. A seed is truly a miracle in itself, containing nourishment to begin its life and all the DNA information needed to build the tree for its whole lifetime. The first thing to emerge from the seed is the "taproot" which always goes straight down into the ground no matter how the seed is oriented.

Some of the largest seeds we know come from trees, but the largest tree, Sequoiadendron giganteum, produces one of the smallest tree seeds.

Ancient trees that are now under the earth have turned to coal which has also been another huge contributor to human development; heating buildings, driving steam engines for manufacturing and locomotives to move people and business; and making steam power to generate the majority of electricity in the world.

Every little boy who ever walked in the woods has picked up a stick and done wondrous things with it.

Trees can touch the sky like the one Redwood in California named Hyperion that is 379.5 feet high.

Trees remind us of the past like the Great Basin bristlecone pine called Methuselah. It has been dated by drilling a core sample and counting the annual rings at 4,844 years old in 2012.

The largest living thing on earth is the Sequoia named General Sherman at 52,508 cu ft.

Trees can also be miniaturized like the Japanese Bonzai to display elegant beauty. Or what about the awesomeness of the Kapok tree?

Every autumn I try to make a trip to upstate New York when the leaves are changing color. It is spectacular and I never get tired of it. The trees do it for us every year like a living painting.

Trees are not an accident or some plant that happened to have the best materialistic, heartless survival abilities. Trees were designed with us in mind and are a precious life-giving gift to us from someone who loved us before we were born.

We could not exist without them.

There must be God.

Chapter #40 - Chirality: Chemical Handedness

Here's a great proof for God from Chemistry that I recently learned about.

"When two molecules appear identical and their structures differ only by being mirror images of each other, those molecules are said to have chirality. Your left and right hands illustrate chirality and so do your left and right feet. Your hands may appear to be identical, but in reality, they are only mirror images of each other, hence the term handedness." [1]

You probably know that DNA is made up of four simple nucleotides and that DNA is in the shape of a spiral staircase. Well, actually, getting even more specific, DNA is always in the shape of a right-handed spiral staircase.

When amino acids are formed in the laboratory, they can result with either chirality, "left-handed" or "right-handed" in a 50% to 50% ratio.

"In our body, every single amino acid of every protein is found with the same left-handed chirality. ... "

"When a random chemical reaction is used to prepare molecules having chirality, there is an equal opportunity to prepare the left-handed isomer as well as the right-handed isomer.... There are no exceptions." [2]

"The DNA molecule is made up of billions of complicated chemical molecules called nucleotides, and these nucleotide molecules exist as the "R" or right-handed optical isomer. The "L" isomer of nucleotides can be prepared in the lab, but they do not exist in natural DNA. There is no way that a random chance process could have formed these proteins and DNA with their unique chirality." [3]

If the chemicals were produced in a random process there would be a 50-50 mix. Yet the results are all proteins have a left-handedness and all DNA has a right-handedness. The orderliness is astounding, absolutely not random.

To make a strand of DNA step by step as evolutionists claim and still make the correct spiral, all the steps in the strand must bend the same way, i.e. right. In another chapter I talked about how human DNA has over 3 billion "steps on the ladder" or characters in the chain. All those characters have to be in the correct order or you don't get a human being.

Chirality adds an even more impossible level of difficulty for DNA to have formed by accidental mutation as the evolutionist faith believes. In building

93

up the DNA staircase step by step, every step that is added must turn out to be ones that bend to the right. If you were going to build a spiral staircase with your eyes closed and you start out with an equal number of left and right handed steps, you could never build the spiral. Impossible.

Here is one very famous case of chirality in life. Do you remember the drug Thalidomide? It "is a sedative drug that was prescribed to pregnant women, from 1957 into the early 60's. It was present in at least 46 countries under different brand names. 'When taken during the first trimester of pregnancy, Thalidomide prevented the proper growth of the fetus, resulting in horrific birth defects in thousands of children around the world'. Why? The Thalidomide molecule is chiral. There are left and right-handed Thalidomides, just as there are left and right hands. The drug that was marketed was a 50/50 mixture. One of the molecules, say the left one, was a sedative, whereas the right one was found later to cause fetal abnormalities. 'The tragedy is claimed to have been entirely avoidable had the physiological properties of the individual thalidomide [molecules] been tested prior to commercialization." [5]

Another example is the artificial sweetener, Aspartame, which is more than a hundred times sweeter than sucrose. However, the mirror image molecule is bitter.

Not only is all DNA right-handed, but proteins are all left-handed. There are 20 different amino acids needed in your body to sustain your life. They are the building blocks for an estimated two million proteins in your body. Your DNA acts like the "designer" for the proteins. It links molecules together along its length by a type of hand-clasping or matching. This is why when the proteins are formed, they are all left-handed when they separate to go about their important functions in the body.

In 1953, Stanley Miller and Harold Urey did an experiment with a mixture of methane, ammonia, hydrogen, and water vapor by passing it through an electric discharge. A few amino acids resulted and the newspaper headline was "Life in a Test-tube." Don't be fooled. Sure amino acids make up proteins and proteins are important for life, but a few amino acids are not life any more than a few auto parts laid out on your driveway make a car, especially if the parts are all left-handed. By the way, it turns out their experiment was discredited anyway because their mixture of ingredients is no longer believed to be the original formula for the primitive atmosphere of the earth. [6]

Your body is a walking miracle every instant in time. The chirality of all the amino acids and nucleotides proves it.

There must be God.

Chapter #41 The First Living Cell

Let's take a couple of minutes to think about the origin of life in the very, very first living cell. Many people think about the beginning of life as something that just happened easily and naturally. One small, tiny, simple cell just spontaneously and accidentally happened. A bunch of chemicals in some goo formed into a blob. No big deal.

If you think that first living cell was just a blob of goo, then it doesn't seem like much of a stretch from pond scum or murky soup of chemicals to a little tiny cell. Some bolt of lightning or other source of energy zapped the chemicals and voila, suddenly life started.

Believers in Evolution do not (and cannot) begin to apply their theory until after life exists and has started reproducing. Mutation and Natural Selection, the processes of Evolution, cannot operate until there is already life reproducing itself. The Theory of Evolution does not explain where everything before life came from or how life itself got started. (It's obviously therefore a sort of religion requiring faith.)

But for right now, let's think about that first living cell a little more deeply given what we now know about living cells. If we can't get the first living cell without there being God, then the Theory of Evolution is doomed because it never functions until there is life.

What are some of the qualities that first living cell had to have in order for life to exist in it? We now know from Biology there are certain basic requirements for life to exist and the whole process is extremely complicated. A single living cell is now considered more complicated than a Cray supercomputer. [1]

Suppose you laid all the individual parts for an automobile out on your driveway, can you now imagine any possible scenario that could take place in the next billion, billion years where those parts get organized by some natural (i.e. no intelligence added) process into a fully functioning car that you could someday drive away? There could be lightning bolts, hurricanes, floods, windstorms, asteroids, whatever, but nothing is going to assemble anything.

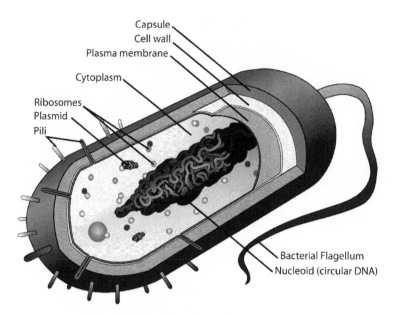

Image 10. Single cell bacteria.

With all the microscopic research done in cell biology, we now know that even a single tiny little cell is like a busy little city. [2] It is much more complicated than an automobile. Even if you had all the chemicals necessary for life in one place like a swamp or deep ocean setting, getting it organized into some form of first living cell is on the order of complexity of simultaneously assembling all the different cars in America.

Here is a short list of some of the attributes that would have been necessary for the first living cell. There are others that you can find in the research if you want to go into more depth. I'll expand on some of these later on after the list.

1. Reproduction and Inheritance.[3] The first living cell had to be able to reproduce a second living cell or there would never have been any more life. It also had to pass on its genetic characteristics by some mechanism such as DNA.

2. Cell Membrane. [4] There had to be a wall around the contents of the cell to hold in the material. Otherwise, it would drift away or be destroyed by other chemical processes. The Cell Membrane also has to be permeable to let chemicals go in and out. It must also be able to grow in size.

96

3. Digestion for Energy. [5] Life requires a process to get energy. There had to be a system for breaking down chemicals and converting it to get energy out of them.

4. Protein Production. [6] There had to be a system for making proteins and enzymes or it could never reproduce itself. There are 20 basic amino acids that are necessary for all the known life forms.

5. Repair capability. [7] All DNA and RNA molecules are subject to harmful mutations and damage from other chemicals. There had to be a process of repairing them when they are multiplied.

6. Elimination of Waste. [8] There would need to be a process for getting rid of used up chemicals.

7. Respiration. [9] Most life forms take in oxygen in some way. Scientists are still debating if the first living cell would have required a process of taking in oxygen.

So this is a very, very amazing list of abilities required for life. I might also have included growth as the eighth property and a ninth property might be sensing and responding to the environment. [10]

To go from a goo of chemicals to a fully functioning living cell that meets the above requirements without any intelligence applied seems a lot less likely than assembling an automobile. You might be able to imagine how one or two of the above processes or systems could have happened, but all of them is not reasonable or logical.

Let me quickly mention a couple of famous headlines about scientists creating life in the laboratory. First is the Miller–Urey experiment in 1953. They put the hypothesized original chemicals in a test tube and hit it with a bolt of electricity. The result was the formation of some amino acids (less than 10), the so called building blocks of life. Even though this experiment is still found in a lot of science textbooks, it has been fully discredited because the early earth's atmosphere was not like they hypothesized and put in their test tubes. [12] And even if they got some amino acids, it takes 20 to build a protein. That's like getting only some of the simplest car parts on your driveway, it's not a functioning car.

Second, on May 20, 2010, Craig Venter, a pioneer in human genome research was able to synthesize a living bacteria. [12] It was hailed as "creating life". What they did was figure out the DNA of an already living cell. They were able to synthesize a genome of over a million DNA base pairs sequence using very complicated processes and millions of dollars. One part of the process required yeast to help copy the DNA because a machine cannot do it.

At one point there was a mistake of a single base pair missing and it wouldn't work. It took them 3 months to find the error and then make the copy correctly. They then inserted this DNA back into an already living cell with its DNA removed. If you call that "creating life," you have to ignore the fact that all they really did was COPY the DNA of "life" that already existed. Even then they had to put the DNA they copied back into a previously living cell for it to function. The cell of cytoplasm where they put the DNA already had a cell membrane and the systems required for cellular tasks like carrying sugars, copying DNA, removing wastes, converting energy, regulating production speeds, communicating with the environment, and so on. [13]

This is an amazing accomplishment to be sure and I don't want to minimize it, but look at all the intelligence that has gone into it. It has taken some really, really smart people 15 years to get this far and they've barely started. So how much intelligence will it take before they can "create life," if ever? Will they still try to claim life happened accidentally with no intelligence behind it? That would be laughable.

Okay, back to the list of requirements for life. **Requirement Number 1, Reproduction.** Think back to Biology class in school where you learned about mitosis and cell division. The first living cell had to be able to do that all by itself the very first try. Otherwise there would be no second living cell. We know that all reproducing cells contain DNA, a very complicated molecule. [14] It is the mechanism that inherits the characteristics of the cell to the next generation.

The simplest life forms must have a DNA molecule of thousands of base pairs. [15] It would have to somehow decide to split in half and make an exact perfect copy of itself. Then the two strands would have to separate into two different areas of the cell and the cell membrane would surround each one and split into two new cells.

Evolutionists have to believe that the DNA pre-exited the first living cell. It could not logically have formed accidentally at the same time as the cell membrane formed or after the cell already existed. However, DNA is too complicated to last outside a cell. This idea has basically been deemed unlikely because DNA cannot exist for long without protection from harmful mutations and serious breakdown from contact with oxygen and other chemicals and ultraviolet light.

Number 2, Cell Membrane. There has to be a cell membrane to surround the cell, otherwise you don't have a cell. But a cell membrane is an extraordinary boundary. If you have ever seen an animation of what's happening all the time with the membrane that surrounds a living cell, you will be amazed. [16] You probably did science experiments in school with osmosis. Well, osmosis is going on all the time with nutrients, water, oxygen, wastes, and other chemicals passing in and out of the cell through the membrane. Just where did the membrane around the first living cell come from? Could something like that have been floating around in the soup too at the same time as all the perfect chemicals and scoop them up and then close the whole thing like a fishnet?

I think this is getting too long. But as you can see, each well-established attribute of a living cell that is listed above would require more intelligence than we currently have in the world of science.

There must be God.

Chapter #42 Bats and Echolocation

We are all somewhat familiar with bats. But when I took some time to research them more seriously, I was astonished by their abilities.

Some bats can reach a top speed of 60 miles per hour. They come in all different sizes and live almost everywhere. There are 1,240 species of bat identified which is about 20% of all mammals classified.

The most astounding feature of bats is that they can fly around in total darkness very quickly without ever hitting another bat, some tree branch, or a wall. In darkness, they can locate a mosquito or moth that is flying, then track it down, catch it, and eat it.

Scientists have discovered that bats have the ability to do this by using sound and what they call "Echolocation". It means that they make a loud noise and then by listening for the echoes that come back they figure out all the landscape and other animals around them.

There are tremendous challenges that had to be overcome in order for this system to work.

1. The sounds they make have to be loud enough to echo back to their ears and be detected. Imagine how much sound is going to echo off a flying mosquito? Not much. As you may remember from science class, sound energy dissipates at the rate of the square of the distance from the source. Bouncing off a mosquito back toward the bat, it is again going to be dissipating as the square of the new distance. Some bats make noise as loud as 140 decibels. Luckily for us the sound waves are above our ability to hear them (ultrasonic). We experience pain at 125 decibels.

2. Their eardrums must be extremely sensitive to detect mosquito echoes, but how do they not blow out their own eardrums when they make a 140 dB noise. It seems they have muscles in their ears that act to muffle or disconnect the tiny little "hammer" and "stirrup."

3. The sound cannot be continuous or else the echo also would be continuous and interfere with interpreting the "data" and causing confusion. They make a "clicking" sound at a rate of about 10 per second when they are cruising but reaching up to a maximum of 200 per second when chasing a prey. The sounds may also be varied like a whistle or changed depending on the prey they are chasing or some other need.

4. The sound of each individual bat has to be unique. Bats might roost in a colony of 1,000's. How come their noises don't interfere and cause confusion and collisions with other bats all making loud noises at the same time?

5. The bat brain has to make calculations which take into account the Doppler Effect. Sound waves change pitch if the source of the noise is moving away (lower) or coming closer (higher). You may have experienced a train whistle sounds lower after it has passed you by. Imagine the complicated computer programming that would be necessary to duplicate what a tiny bat's brain can do when chasing a moving mosquito.

6. The sound waves used must be the shorter ones. Longer sound waves would not be useful for accurately identifying tiny little objects that are just millimeters in length.

7. Sound waves travel faster in warmer air than in colder air so they will travel out and back faster on warmer days. Bat brains have to take this into account.

8. Different surfaces reflect sound differently. Water, wood, metal, plants all must be echoing back sound waves that are slightly distorted based on their surface properties.

9. The bat brain has to be really fast. Think how fast that mosquito is moving and in all different directions. The bat brain has to get the information from the ears and calculate how fast to move and in which direction quickly enough to catch the mosquito.

10. The bat brain has to interpret all objects in its environment. The bat has to figure out the difference between a swarm of mosquitoes and a tree branch or another bat instantly.

11. Bats also have to be able to recognize the opposite sex in the dark. Otherwise they can't find a mate and reproduce. Infants have to be able to locate their own mothers in order to get milk.

There are other things going on as well, but that should be enough to amaze anyone.

When my kids were young, they used to play a game in the swimming pool called "Marco Polo". One person closed his eyes and tried to catch others who would shout out "Marco". That was hard enough because they would move after they shouted out. But suppose they didn't have to shout and the person with his eyes closed made all the noises and tried to locate the others by the echoes he heard.

Darwinian evolution requires gradual incremental steps of development over many generations. Bat echolocation is far beyond the design capabilities of human beings although we have some understanding through developing Sonar. Echolocation is a capability that needs to be functioning almost instantly at the beginning of the species because you will never catch a mosquito gradually. If a bat is flying in the dark and his echolocation is not working, he'll soon crash into something and seriously injure himself.

Flying is a phenomenal ability for a mammal. Flying in the dark is many times more amazing. Natural Selection would quickly kill off the bats that tried flying in the dark without echolocation. Bats with good eyes flying in the daytime would surely outlive bats with bad eyesight or those trying to fly at night. Echolocation has no chance to develop over many generations. The odds of flying and echolocation developing simultaneously by evolving over many generations are astronomical.

Speaking of odds, scientists have also found echolocation used by whales and dolphins. These species and bats are totally unrelated. To have both accidentally "evolve" this phenomenal ability is beyond common sense. There must have been a cosmic designer that created both species using a common pattern.

There must be God.

Chapter #43 Sucking and Breast Milk

I think you know that all mammal babies are born with the innate instinctive sucking ability. How could that ability have evolved slowly, simply, gradually over millions of years and many generations?

If a baby doesn't come out of the womb knowing how to suck already, then within a matter of hours it will be dead. There is no trial and error over many generations. There is no survival of the fittest because there is no survival. It's life or death at birth.

The Theory of Evolution is very seductive because they always use words like "simple," "easy," "slow," "gradual," "many generations," "great periods of time," etc. But behind it all is only faith and assumptions. Evolution of higher ordered species from lower ones has never been scientifically observed nor demonstrated in a laboratory. The Theory of Evolution is a religion of faith in lifeless chemicals.

If you have had children and you breastfed them, you were certainly amazed that the baby immediately knew how to start sucking. There was no learning process. We even have pictures from inside the womb of a baby sucking his/her thumb.

The process of a mother producing milk for a new born baby is a miracle in itself. The appearance of milk and the baby sucking it was definitely designed by an intelligent being.

Most of her life a female mammal does not have any milk to give no matter what she might try. Through a miraculous process of hormonal changes triggered by interactions with the growing fetus, the production of breast milk gets started at just the right time.

When the baby is born, milk is ready to start flowing when the baby starts sucking.

How could a slow, gradual process over may generations produce milk at precisely the moment when the infant starts sucking? It has no special survival benefit for the mother, only the baby. How does mutation or natural selection account for producing breast milk? The whole process makes the mother much more vulnerable to predators.

If the milk comes at the wrong time, the baby dies. If the baby does not suck, it will die. There doesn't seem to be any room for trial and error. It's success or death. Many generations of developing breast feeding over millions and millions of years cannot cut it. There are too many obstacles to be overcome.

The very first creature to exist of each mammal species had to have this ability. It could not have developed separately over long periods of time on each branch of the evolutionist so-called tree of life.

The whole process of milk being produced and baby sucking is very, very complicated and has to work out simultaneously and be successful at the birth of the very first baby of each species.

Scientific research is also finding out some amazing benefits of breastfeeding babies. Some of the health benefits for the baby that have been determined are: fewer illnesses and stronger immune system; less constipation and diarrhea; better stools and digestion; less allergies; lower diabetes risk; antibodies that protect against infection; all the nutritional needs of the baby during first 6 months; stronger vision; protection against ear infections; better mental development, higher IQ and less antisocial behavior; better mouth formation for less speech problems; less eczema; improved bone quality; healthier hair; increased independence and emotional stability; eases frustrations and daily stresses.

Amazingly enough, there are also great benefits for the mother as well. Here are some that researchers have discovered: stronger bones for later in life; lower risk of osteoporosis, anemia, and arthritis; lower risk of breast cancer; lower risk of cardiovascular disease; lower risk of ovarian cancer, uterine cancer, and endometrial cancer; natural bonding and closeness with the baby; helps the uterus return to normal size in a timely manner.

All these extremely valuable benefits must have been working from the very first baby that sucked.

Every father and mother knows that the mother's body went through all kinds of complicated and miraculous changes when she was pregnant. She had no control over that. If she was the smartest woman in the world, could she have told her body all the right things to do so that baby could be born and survive? Absolutely not. It was all controlled by a much higher intelligence.

There must be God.

Chapter #44 Murphy's Law

I'm sure you have heard of Murphy's Law. It goes like this: "If anything can go wrong, it will."

Over the years it has been easily accepted and adopted by people as a popular truism. [1] Even many similar sayings have been added to it. Here are a couple of my favorite "corollaries". "If two things can go wrong, the one that will cause the most damage will go wrong." "If something can go wrong, it will go wrong and at the worst possible time."

I even own two books about Murphy's Laws.

The more complicated something is, the more likely it will break down or malfunction. Isn't this our experience in life? Isn't this our intuitive understanding of the laws of nature? That's why we can laugh and accept Murphy's Laws. If something is complicated, it's therefore more difficult to build it, install it, and maintain it, because it's more likely to break down.

Think about complicated computer programs. We are getting updates from Microsoft all the time to fix "bugs". Imagine buying something at a store that needs to be assembled when you get home. The more parts there are and the more complicated the instructions are, the more chance there will be a problem putting it together.

If you are a painter and are going to put a couple thousand brushstrokes on a canvass, how many mistakes are you going to make?

Now let's think about Evolution where believers have faith that millions upon millions of times a more complicated living being developed from a less complicated one without any intelligence being involved. All the wondrous beauty and awesomely complicated systems of life developed from nothing. I'm sorry, even with our best human intelligence it's not just hard to do that, it's impossible.

Evolution Theory says that over a lot of time, more and more complicated systems develop and better and better functioning parts happen by natural laws. I don't experience any natural laws like that. Things that are complicated are more likely to break down and it takes a lot of effort and intelligence just to maintain them.

Evolution Theory says that dumb chance does better than applied human intelligence. And dumb chance is not just a little bit smarter, it's billions or trillions of times smarter. Human beings cannot duplicate a simple blade of grass! But dumb chance has accidentally produced all of the estimated 8.7 million species on earth. [2]

Evolutionists place unshakeable faith in natural selection. They believe this force keeps everything moving forward and upward. But natural selection never even begins to operate until there is the process of reproduction functioning successfully. They never allow questioning about where the ability to reproduce came from. Nothing about the process of reproduction is simple in any way. And where did life come from before it is reproducing? Life could not have originated by natural selection. All the attributes of life had to be in place before reproduction could take place, for example, DNA, RNA, proteins, respiration, digestion, cell membranes, repair capability, waste elimination, and much more. [3]

If Murphy's Law operates even once in a while, then evolution is impossible. If something can go wrong, it will … eventually. So therefore "given enough time" (as the evolutionists like to say) things will not develop greater and greater complexity, they in fact will go "wrong".

There must be God holding it all together.

Chapter #45 The Eye

The eye is a wonderful proof for God. The more you know about it, the more impossible it could come into existence without God, a supremely intelligent being, having created it. Just follow along with me for some of what it does and how it does it.

This is going to be my longest chapter because there is so much information and research done on the eye and it is so astounding. I have read maybe 100 articles about the eye and this post is hardly going to scratch the surface of the awesomeness of all the different types and abilities of the eyes in creation. I'm not even going to cover many of the amazing parts. I hope you can read to the end of this. I tried to make every paragraph succinct and educational.

The human eye can detect 7 to 10 million colors. That's more than any machine known to man. All the colors we see are all within only 1.5% of the entire light spectrum. [1] By such an amazing accident (for evolutionists) or incredible design (for religious people) our eyes see exactly the wavelengths of light where the color is and not the others. Those colors that we are able to see happen to be truly marvelous.

Photoreceptor cells in our eyes can catch photons of light and send a signal to the brain which interprets what color it is and distinguishes various objects. Evolutionists talk about some "original" light sensitive cell like it was simple. Just read about "Signal Transduction in the eye" [2] and how receptors are chemically turned on and off instantaneously if you want to get an idea of how tremendously complicated it is to activate a photoreceptor.

Evolutionists also never talk about all the millions of colors. Did photoreceptors recognize just one color in the beginning and then "gradually over time" accidentally become able to tell the difference in all the millions of colors. That's a hard one to believe because the ability to see any color at all is extremely complicated. [3]

Even if some first creature developed a photo receptor cell, so what? It would be pointless for survival unless it was somehow connected to a brain that was also connected to a muscle system to provide movement.

Evolutionists talk about the eye evolving to help the creature escape predators. Excuse me. If this is supposed to be the first eye to develop, then there are no predators with eyes yet. What are they escaping from?

Also, even having a photo receptor cell is not valuable for survival unless there is some way to tell which direction the danger is coming from so you can escape in the other direction. There are way too many logical holes in these evolutionist faith statements. Their faith in evolution is blind. They don't even ask simple questions.

The retina of the human eye is made up of an average of 120 million rods and 6 million cones, each with their own neuron that carries messages to the brain. (Birds have 10 times that number.) The rods see in black and white for night vision and the cones see all the different colors. There are 3 types of cones that perceive different wave lengths. The retina is further divided into the macula, a small central area giving central vision, and the fovea, a small depression at the center of the macula which gives the clearest vision. In the fovea the blood vessels, nerves, and ganglion cells are all displaced for better vision. The area in the macula is 100 times more sensitive than the rest of the retina.

Does Natural Selection really explain how this could have developed gradually step by step with each step over sequential generations being better able to survive and pass on its genes? It would take millions of generations. There's not enough time. Humans all have eyes the same, so all 7 billion of us and all humans in history must have descended from an original ancestral couple that had eyes like we all have now. And eyes have never evolved since. And not one of all the millions of supposedly intermediate stages of eye is still around. Not one older stage ever shows up in random individuals either. Every other kind of eye or intermediate stage has disappeared completely. This all stretches even our imagination.

All eyes have a lens made out of a transparent protein substance found nowhere else in the body. This lens must necessarily be formed out of a flexible substance and it must have muscles to change its shape so it can alter the path of the incoming light and constantly re-focus it on receptor cells. If you can't focus the light, you can't see anything.

There are 12 muscles on the outside that move the eyeball around in the socket, including one that uses a pulley mechanism to swivel the eye (the Superior Oblique muscle, please look up a diagram of eye muscles). Eye muscles come in pairs to move your eyes up and down, left and right. If the muscles only turned your eyes to the right, they would be stuck there until many generations later when a muscle developed to pull them back left. The same is true if you only had a muscle to pull them up but not one to pull them back down.

Tilt your head and your eyes adjust so you can still see well.

Evolution hypothesizes that blind chance mutations have the amazing ability to come up with these changes so they can be selected for by natural selection. That's total blind faith. How could the lens material and all those muscles happen accidentally, without any intelligent design at all? One small change at a time will never produce a continuously workable eye.

Recent discoveries have revealed that the muscles surrounding your eyes are amazing. They "jitter" at the rate of 30 to 70 microscopic movements per second all day every day. If the muscles did not do this, you would not be able to focus as well because your brain's programming of the incoming signals removes any unchanging image. [4] These jitter motions come in 3 types, called drifts, tremors, and saccades. The ones named "tremors" move the cornea and retina about 0.001 millimeter (about 1/70th the width of a piece of paper). Our eyes do all this automatically. [5]

Here's a fact you probably learned in grade school, the lens inverts all the images coming through so it hits your retina upside down. Your brain automatically turns it right side up. If your brain didn't do that, you'd have a hard time escaping from any predators. The brain is taking upside down images from both your eyes, inverting them, and putting them together. Evolutionists don't talk about that.

Another necessary part of the eye is the iris which opens and closes to let in varying amounts of light. Too much light and you are blinded. You are probably not aware of how much work your iris is doing all day long because it's totally automatic. That sure is a nice ability to have or you might be blinded or in the dark most of the time.

And then there are also your eye lids, some pretty useful pieces of skin with their own sets of muscles. Each eye has over 50 glands in the eye lids for secreting oil for lubricating the eyes.

Everybody has tear ducts that come in mirror image sets for each eye. How does something like that happen by accident? Like every other detail of your eyes, you will find your tear ducts are like a miracle if you read up on the research to understand what they do and how they do it. Not only do you cry when something gets in your eye, but your tear ducts also work when you are emotionally moved. How do evolutionists explain that?

Another essential ingredient to being able to see is the optic nerve. This statement is from Wikipedia:

"Each human optic nerve contains between 770,000 and 1.7 million nerve fibers, which are axons of the retinal ganglion cells of one retina. In the fovea, which has high acuity, these ganglion cells connect to as few as 5 photoreceptor cells; in other areas of retina, they connect to many thousand photoreceptors." [6]

On top of everything else that happened by accident for evolutionists, you also have to add the accidental development of an optic nerve which would have no purpose unless there were photoreceptor cells on one end and the brain on the other. Of course, there is an optic nerve coming from each eye, thus doubling the number of nerve fibers to the brain which interprets the signals.

Even if the eye developed and then for some reason started sending electrical impulses to the brain, probably the most remarkable achievement of all is how the brain translates those impulses into "seeing" colors and then translating those colors into shapes and giving them meaning?

Darwin himself recognized that the unbelievable complexity of the eye was a problem for his theory, but then he went ahead and ignored it and assumed evolution anyway. "The eye to this day gives me a cold shudder." [7] The idea of natural selection producing the eye "seems, I freely confess, absurd in the highest possible degree." [8] Today, after all the scientific discoveries since Darwin, I think his comment about his natural selection theory to be "absurd in the highest possible degree" has been substantially proven.

There are lots of diagrams you can find of the supposed evolution of the eye, but they are pure imagination (emphasis mine). If you read the explanations carefully, you will always discover that they are a hypothesis… in other words complete conjecture. There is absolutely no fossil evidence for these diagrams. The diagrams are always described as "likely," "probably," or "possibly". In other words they are pure speculation and totally from the artist's imagination. They ASSUME evolution before they even draw the first stage. Evolutionists always talk like it's the "gospel". But it's blind faith.

If you look at an evolutionist's diagram imagining how an eye could evolve, you'll quickly see how they make huge leaps and changes in the design because they know where they want to get to. But all you have to do is use the old "slow and gradual" argument that they themselves espouse and think about the real world.

Every single minor change means a significant number of changes in DNA. How many generations need to live and die between the changes in the pictures? Remember these are animals with only partial eyes that have to find a mate somehow. They have to pass the "improvement" to the next generation and not lose it. That means both the male and female have to have it AND it has to pass to all future generations and never get weeded out. If Natural Selection really works, it works both ways. Not only does it improve things, it should also eliminate unnecessary, non-functional parts, or those that are a hindrance.

Even if one eye could evolve, which is an unbelievable stretch, how do you account for two eyes right next to each other. That's got to be statistically hundreds of times more difficult. Most evolutionists make up an explanation for one eye and then stop. They still have to explain how did we get two so perfectly connected and coordinated eyes working in harmony and also connected into the brain in order to give us parallax vision and 3-dimensional mental images?

Evolutionists have two main techniques to try to explain eye evolution. Logically they fall apart because both techniques assume evolution before they start their explanation. This is called circular reasoning, using evolution to prove evolution. The most common is to notice other eye-like structures in nature and assume they were one of the steps in a long process that has never, ever been seen. A helicopter may look like an intermediate step from a car to an airplane, so what? Applying true logic reveals the false assumptions.

Just because simple eyes exist and complex eyes also exist in nature, that is no proof that complex eyes evolved from simple eyes. Cars did not evolve from soap box racers or skate boards just because there are design similarities.

Secondly, evolutionists look in the womb and see the eye develop in stages which they call evolutionary stages. They may say that a seed growing is evolution, but it's not. Why is the growth process in the womb necessarily the explanation of the process that took millions of years? Also, a seed already has the full complement of DNA structure. It's not evolving, it's fulfilling instructions which are already there.

Evolutionists like to use what I'll call "magic words". They sound nice but they are totally unscientific and no respectable scientist uses them. Here are examples that you'll find all the time: "selective pressures," tinker, suggest, at some point, scenarios, hypothesizes, diverging, proliferated, arose, favored, modified, emerged, developed, etc. And the biggest one of all is "may have". Those are not words used by real scientists with solid evidence. Passive, unthinking processes cannot do intelligent things. Evolutionists are really only telling a story that they already believe. They can make it up as they go along whenever there is an obstacle.

Another problem that evolutionist believers have is their so-called tree of life where all species developed from a single cell. Since mammals, fish, birds, insects, amphibians, etc. all have different types of eyes and are on different "branches" of the tree, therefore the evolution faith requires that all the different types of eyes "evolved" independently of each other. The Wikipedia article states that complex eyes have evolved between 50 and 100 separate times in evolution. [9] Imagine the mathematical odds against that, can you? Evolutionists are forced to believe that eyes not only evolved one time in history but 50 to 100 separate times. To make it even more impossible, almost always the animal developed exactly two of them.

Wikipedia quietly admits that "Since the fossil record, particularly of the Early Cambrian, is so poor, it is difficult to estimate the rate of eye evolution."

If you read their article with a critical "eye" for logical and rational challenges, you'll be amazed at the continual leaps of faith they espouse.

You should know the truth. The fossil record only shows eyes already developed, never a partial eye.

> "The oldest eye in the fossil record, that of a trilobite, is a very complex faceted compound eye that 'dates' back to the Cambrian, conventionally dated about 540 million years ago." [10]

Did you get that, the oldest fossils with eyes (trilobites) already have a fully developed eye, in fact a very complex one at that.

Another way that I could put it is that there is no fossil record at all to support evolution of the eye. Or you could also say that any evolution of the eye is pure speculation because there is zero existing evidence for it.

Here is another statement admitting that evolutionists have no idea how an eye could evolve.

> "The curious thing, however, about the evolution of the vertebrate eye is the apparent suddenness of its appearance and the elaboration of its structures in its earliest known stages." [11]

They just DO NOT know where eyes came from or how, but they admit that eyes appeared suddenly. That is not evolution, by the way.

Remember, I've only covered some of the amazing aspects of the eye.

The eye was awesomely designed, but Evolutionists just won't accept it.

There truly is God.

Chapter #46 Ants

As a result of my studies, I have come to believe that every plant, animal, insect, and fish are proofs for God in and of themselves. There are hundreds of thousands of such proofs everywhere you look for "he who has eyes to see and ears to hear."

Pick any one that you like and research it extensively. You can go on and on and on being more and more astounded. Each is so marvelous that the only possible conclusion, if you are willing to accept it, is that it was designed by a super intelligent source.

Let's talk about ants for a while…tiny creatures with a brain no bigger than a pinhead. There are over 12,500 cataloged species of ants, with estimates of perhaps 22,000 in existence. [1]

Evolutionists have their creation story for how all these different ants came into being. The story always starts with knowing the conclusion and figuring out the path of how blind and accidental processes might have arrived at that end. It's pure fiction. When you analyze each supposed step with logical questions, you'll have to believe in miracles to accept that it could really have happened.

There isn't any real proof that can be observed, so in the end you have to decide what story you are going to believe in. Did all of these astounding capabilities of ants just come about accidentally? Or is there a God behind it? Either way, you are a still just a believer. There is only faith.

Here is a quote that shows what I mean. In the considered opinion of biologist Jochen Zeil of the Australian National University.

> "I think that every animal we look at [including the ant] is a more competent, more robust, more flexible, more miniaturized and a more energy-, material-, sensor-, and computation-efficient agent than anything we have ever built." [2]

I would agree with him, but his conclusion is different than mine. He thinks that it all happened by accident and he chooses to believe in evolution. His faith is that there was no invisible God behind it.

Ants are everywhere in the world. Have you ever taken the time to watch them? Probably you studied them in school somewhere and you were very impressed at what they can do. A functioning colony of ants may contain millions and millions of ants and some colonies may be as big as a house. Scientists have poured cement into ant colonies and then dug them out to see what they look like. There are amazing passageways and chambers for many purposes.

How big in size is an ant brain do you think? But amazing things are going on inside there. Researchers have concluded they are doing math as complicated as the programmers who built the Internet so that billions of tiny packets of information run smoothly along channels and through nodes and switches to get to their final destinations. Here is a quote about ant math and food supplies and storage:

"The algorithm relates at least three critical variables: the rate of outgoing foragers, the amount that the rate increases with each returning ant, and the amount that the rate decreases with each outgoing ant. Researchers discovered that this ant algorithm closely matches the one that programmers wrote to regulate Internet traffic. The algorithm uses two formulae:

1. $\alpha_n = \max(\alpha_{n-1} - qD_{n-1} + cA_n - d, \alpha)$, $\underline{\alpha}_0 = 0$
2. $D_n \sim \text{Poisson}(\alpha_n)$ [3]

Here is another type of math. Researchers Chris Reid and Associate Professor Madeleine Beekman experimented with ants and changeable mazes. [4] They discovered that ants can adapt well enough to create an optimal solution to a maze, something few computer programs can do.

This was called the "towers of Hanoi" puzzle. [5]

"The game involves transferring disks of tapering size from one of three stacks to another without placing a larger disk on top of a smaller one. For the ants, though, researchers transposed the different stacking options onto a maze of hexagons, where the shortest route to food corresponded to the best solution to the puzzle. Of course, the ants solved it. They even reworked new solutions to overcome blocked tunnels. In addition, the pioneer ants that solved the puzzles somehow explained the correct route to their relatives." [6]

Ant colonies of necessity have incredible systems to function as they do with effectiveness and efficiency. All the food coming in and being stored and used up needs to be accounted for, measured constantly, and maintained. There are systems for heating and cooling the food, systems for disposal of wastes, systems for hygiene and disposal of dead ants, systems for caring for eggs and the newborn, systems for protection and survival in case of floods or invasions.

114

"An ant colony has several entrances, leading to a variety of subterranean chambers. Each chamber has a specific use. Some are for food storage. The queen has her own room. In another chamber workers tend unhatched eggs. A deeper room serves as a nursery for larvae and cocoons. In the replete gallery are the worker ants whose expanded abdomens contain surplus food for the colony. In another room, worker ants are digging a new chamber." [7]

Scientists believe ants have a sophisticated guidance system like GPS and also that they are able to count and remember how many steps they have taken away from the nest so that they can return. They can also communicate through a number of different chemical signals to other ants.

"Distances travelled are measured using an internal pedometer that keeps count of the steps taken and also by evaluating the movement of objects in their visual field (optical flow). Directions are measured using the position of the sun. They integrate this information to find the shortest route back to their nest. Like all ants, they can also make use of visual landmarks when available as well as olfactory and tactile cues to navigate. Some species of ant are able to use the Earth's magnetic field for navigation. The compound eyes of ants have specialized cells that detect polarized light from the Sun, which is used to determine direction. These polarization detectors are sensitive in the ultraviolet region of the light spectrum." [8]

Stop a minute and meditate on what an ant can do with its teeny, tiny brain. I'm flabbergasted that people can believe an ant could have evolved slowly over time.

Just think about how complicated the ant eye mechanism must be to accomplish what it does. Please read about The Eye in my previous proof for God. But the ant uses other really complicated systems as well like smell and touch and muscles all integrated into their tiny brains.

Ants have been observed to be moving in pairs where one seems to be teaching the other one. I think one should conclude that they are passing on information which strongly indicates intelligence rather than accidental origins.

Evolution hypothesizes that the process of natural selection is at work. This normally involves a male and a female parent. Ant mating and reproduction can be very different from that. Here is a statement from Wikipedia:

"A wide range of reproductive strategies have been noted in ant species. Females of many species are known to be capable of reproducing asexually through thelytokous parthenogenesis and one species, Mycocepurus smithii, is known to be all-female."[9]

That seems like some big issues for evolutionists. Maybe there are no male and female in some ants. Sometimes an ant egg becomes one or the other. Also they go through a metamorphosis stage like caterpillars and butterflies.

"The life of an ant starts from an egg. If the egg is fertilized, the progeny will be female (diploid); if not, it will be male (haploid). Ants develop by complete metamorphosis with the larva stages passing through a pupal stage before emerging as an adult. The larva is largely immobile and is fed and cared for by workers." [10]

If males are "haploid," it means they only have 1 set of chromosomes, not two to offer for more chance of mutation to work. Secondly, metamorphosis could never be a process that could have resulted from evolution (see my Proof on Metamorphosis, Chapter #19 on that).

Each colony has several different types of ants within the same species, e.g. workers/drones, soldiers, queen, and males. Evolution cannot account for how they accidentally came to exist and then could continue to be produced by the observable ways they are. Typically the food they receive or chemicals around them determine what type of ant they become. Scientists don't really know that much about this subject.

Some ants in a colony can fly, but others cannot. How can that be explained adequately by accidents?

Various ant species build amazing things besides nests. Some make bridges and some can make rafts. Tell me no intelligence was involved in an elaborate construction, it was all by accident, and then let me suppress my laughter.

"Solenopsis invicta, a common species of fire ant, originates from the rain forests of Brazil, where heavy precipitation can cause flooding to occur up to twice daily. In order to stick together as a colony during these deluges, the fire ants hook their legs and mouths together to create a living, breathing waterproof material that floats for hours, or even weeks, if necessary, until floods subside." [11]

In conclusion, there are thousands of different species of ants with incredibly complex systems of organization on a massive scale. It takes a lot of faith in chance and denial of intelligence to believe all this evolved by chance. Remember there are over 20,000 known species of bees, 100,000 species of wasps, and 4,000 species of termites. All of these live in highly developed colonies just like ants. There must be God.

Chapter #47 Gratitude

I just recently celebrated the American holiday of Thanksgiving where we get together with loved ones and spend the day being grateful for our many blessings. Several people that I spoke to during the following week remarked how it was now their favorite holiday. They have a lot of quality time with loved ones and feel so appreciative afterwards. Christmas on the other hand has become so overly commercialized and materialistic. Thoughts are about what I don't have, what I need, what I want, what can I get, and how much I have to spend on others. There is such a vast contrast in the two holidays and the kind of feelings that come out.

Science now can tell us why. Research that has been done on the energies of the heart and the brain has been able to demonstrate which types of thoughts are beneficial and which ones are harmful. [1]

Energies of the heart are now able to be detected up to 6 to 8 feet from the body. And those energies are also able to be picked up by other people near you. Those energies can affect others positively or negatively.

Researchers are even looking into ways of reprogramming our DNA by positive energies and thoughts. [2]

Feelings of gratitude are at the very top of the list for creating what is being called "heart coherence". This energy is healthier for all of the organs of your body. You perform better at physical tests. You have more energy. You are more creative. And you make better decisions.

What is gratitude and where does it come from? Why would this kind of energy have all those benefits? Why does being generous and thinking good thoughts about others lead to wonderful benefits for you as well.

No matter how great your accomplishments are, you don't feel gratitude to yourself. Gratitude can only be felt in relationship with someone or something outside of yourself. Most often it is toward a person or persons for a benefit they have provided you.

In fact, to go one step further about these energies, if you harm another person, there are negative energies created that eventually are harmful to you also.

If some benefit that comes your way is the result of what seems to be just "blind luck" or pure accident, then the gratitude you feel is minimal if at all. You can't be grateful to nothing.

That's why the origins of gratitude cannot be explained by evolution and materialism, which are just blind accidental forces. You do not feel gratitude from a random mutation. "I was so grateful that I accidentally was born." It doesn't happen.

Believers in a Creator are able to experience one of the most profound feelings in the depths of their souls, namely gratitude to God. Think of the last time you experienced a feeling of profound gratitude. This probably inspired a natural desire to share the feeling with others and generously give out from the abundance you experienced.

Non-believers cannot experience gratitude in a relationship to their source of life and all creation. Therefore, they are denied in their soul an energy vibration that is very healing and healthful.

There exists research that shows that believers are happier people and they are healthier people and they get along better with others. Naturally it is controversial and disputed by non-believers. So I don't claim it's a scientific proof, just a lot of anecdotal experience....someday it may be fact. [3]

How you view your own origins makes a huge difference in how you view the world. Did you come from a loving, caring, extremely intelligent, and parental source? Or did you come along accidentally starting from rocks and chemical soup and amoebas?

The energy of gratitude and generosity and the laws they follow are invisible, universal, and eternal. They did not accidentally arise at some point along an evolutionary timeline. They existed from the beginning. Where did they come from? How could they exist if there was no original designer that put in place laws of mutual benefit and relationship?

If "survival of the fittest" were a true law, then research on energy would show that struggle and conflict would produce good health, but they don't. It's just the opposite.

There must be God.

Chapter #48 The Nitrogen Cycle

There are many complex ecosystems that exist all around us. All of them could become proofs for God in themselves.

Let me tell you some of the basic points of the Nitrogen Cycle and let you see that there must be an invisible creative genius behind it.

We all learned in grade school that the atmosphere we breathe is 78% Nitrogen. This is very important because if that percentage were to vary even 1%, we would probably all die.

Nitrogen in the atmosphere is in the form of N_2 molecules which have a very strong bond and are basically useless to living creatures in that form.

However, every living creature requires Nitrogen. It is required in all the DNA and RNA in our cells. It is also required in amino acids and proteins.

The only way we can get usable Nitrogen is by a process which breaks the N_2 bond and it is called "fixation". Most of this is done in nature by several types of specialized bacteria. They convert the N_2 into other molecules such as ammonia (NH_3), or nitrites (NO_2), or nitrates (NO_3). If chemical evolution were true, it is an incredibly lucky accident that all those very sophisticated bacteria exist. Otherwise, we wouldn't.

A God who designed the system makes a lot more sense.

Even more amazing is that those bacteria are not able to convert the N_2 into other molecules if there is ANY Oxygen present at all. It interferes with the process. Where on earth is it possible to find a naturally occurring place with no Oxygen? Miraculously, plants provide little chambers in their roots called nodules and there is a protein called leghaemoglobin which is there and carries away the Oxygen.

Do you see the problem for evolutionists? There are so many miracles that had to happen for this system to exist and none of them involved their two basic tenants of mutation or natural selection. Without there first being plants with nodules, there would be no place for the Nitrogen fixation to take place converting it to a usable form. But without there first being Nitrogen in a usable form, there could be no DNA or RNA to build a plant.

The Nitrogen ecosystem, however, is even more complicated and unlikely than already explained. If the only existing bacteria converts Nitrogen all in one direction, then eventually the Nitrogen in the atmosphere becomes depleted. This would cause serious problems and eventually extinction. Well happily there also exist other types of bacteria which convert the other Nitrogen molecules back into N_2 to replenish the atmosphere.

If you do an Internet search for "Nitrogen Cycle," you will see many, many, many diagrams of the whole Nitrogen ecological system. If you are interested in more information, check out this series of animated diagrams by the PBS Learning site which is very detailed. [1]

Evolution Theory which depends on time and slow, gradual development cannot explain a large ecosystem where all the fully developed living beings that are a part of it must suddenly exist simultaneously or the whole system fails.

There must be God.

Chapter #49 The Moon

Everybody likes the Moon, right? Have you ever met anyone who had bad things to say about the Moon?

The Moon is associated with love and romance. Songs, poems, and art describe it all the time. We think of it as our friend. Sometimes after a really struggling time or when we are feeling especially lonely, we look up in the sky and are surprised by a full Moon. Then the feeling comes over us, "At least God loves me."

All throughout history the Moon has provided light in the night. It has been of incalculable value to our ancestors. Even today many peoples of the world have to depend on the light of the Moon at night. If it were just an average moon in our Solar System it would be 10 times smaller and give off only 1/20th the light, which would be virtually worthless. [1]

How many wonderful memories do you have over your lifetime that include the Moon?

The cycles of the Moon help us tell time and the passing of months and seasons. Many cultures celebrate festivals centered on the Moon. Our own bodies have emotional cycles that correspond to 28 - 29 days, known as biorhythms. Women of course have a fertility cycle of similar length.

No other known planet in the whole Universe has a moon like it. (Read that again.)

That's all really wonderful stuff. That is almost enough proof for God by itself. Such a truly sentimental rock existing up in the sky that moves our hearts so much is very, very unlikely to happen by accident.

However, I need to tell you more about the Moon. Without it, we would all be dead. We could not survive on the Earth if there were no Moon.

The Moon stabilizes the Earth on its axis. If not for the Moon, the Earth would swing back and forth on its axis up to about 90 degrees instead of just the few degrees it varies now. [2] This would cause unbelievable chaos in the temperatures, climate conditions, volcanoes, oceans and more. Nothing would be stable and we could not live here.

The Moon is primarily responsible for the ocean tides. This constant churning, up and down twice a day, is what cleans and refreshes the oceans and shorelines keeping them from getting stagnant. It stirs up the nutrients in the oceans providing the food sources needed by the tiniest of sea creatures, algaes, and oxygen-providing microbes. [3] All life in the sea depends on them. [4] So we depend on them too. Ocean tides are now also being studied as a potential source for clean renewable energy.

The Moon plays a role as a protector in the sky shielding us from such things as asteroids and cosmic dust. Look at all the pock marks on the Moon from collisions. One crater is 8 miles deep and 1,500 miles across, the largest known in the Solar System. [5]

Scientists have been able to learn a lot about the Sun and the Universe only because of the Moon. It is exactly 400 times smaller than the Sun and 400 times closer. What a coincidence! It also revolves around the Earth in the same plane as the Earth revolves around the Sun. This is very unusual and not a single one of the 150 other moons in the Solar System does it. [6]

Because of all this, the Moon is able to eclipse the Sun. Especially valuable to scientists is the total solar eclipse which allows them the only time they can possibly view the Sun's Corona and take measurements on it. This has led to untold leaps in knowledge in fields such as astronomy.

Gravity is another amazing fact of nature that we learn more about with the aid of the Moon. Sir Isaac Newton was trying to understand the Moon's rotation when he discovered gravity. Here is an amazing fact. If you had to replace the strength of gravity between the Earth and Moon with a long steel pole, you would have to get a pole that is 531 miles in diameter. Think about that! It's hard to even imagine an invisible force that strong. It is estimated at 70 million trillion pounds.

OK. Here comes the best part of all. Scientists don't know where the Moon came from! [7] That's right. As long as they exclude God, they have no viable theory for the origin of the Moon.

There have been a number of theories over the years, but we have sent 12 men to walk on the Moon and they've brought back 842 pounds of rock and dust samples. [8] All those theories fell apart. Known laws of physics and geology would have to be violated if they were true.

Godless theories for the source of the Moon fit into three areas: (A) formation from the earth (or fission, somehow a chunk of earth broke off), (B) formation independent of the earth (capture, the moon was passing by), and (C) formation simultaneously with the earth (condensation, from a dust cloud). For a brief consideration of each and how it fails to explain the origin, see the sources in the footnotes. [9] [10] [11]

The latest theory which is what they will try to tell you in textbooks and on websites is about how a Mars-sized planet slammed into the Earth and ended up creating the Moon. But if you read all the way down the page you can find where they mention the arguments against this theory. For example, it's almost impossible that such a collision could happen. Secondly, even if it did, the Moon would certainly NOT be made of the material that is in the rocks that were brought back.

Think that over.

Those textbooks might as well spell it out more clearly like this. "Here's the truth about the origin of the Moon. It resulted when a planet crashed into the earth. BUT the rocks retrieved from the Moon say that is impossible. Anyway, believe us because we're scientists. It's the truth."

I'm sorry, but in my world, the real world, that is not the definition of truth. And it's not scientific either. If the odds are only 1 in a million that it is true, I would simply call it false, and not risk my credibility on it. Scientists who promote lies should have their funding cut off.

Here's a funny description of their state of affairs by one scientist. "The best explanation [for the existence of the Moon] was observational error — the Moon does not exist." [12]

The Moon was created by God. There aren't any other options.

There has to be God.

Chapter #50 Scientists Are Wrong A Lot Of The Time

If you think back over the history of science, you will recognize that many, many times the scientists have been wrong. One might even be able to make the case that they are usually wrong.

Do they think they are wrong at the time? No. They think they are right with almost absolute certainty, just like today. The scientists who thought the earth was the center of the universe not only believed they were right, they violently opposed Galileo when he said the Earth revolved around the Sun. Why did they do that?

To have some fun and surprises you might check out some of the websites about major mistakes that scientists have made in the past: 20 of the Greatest Blunders in Science in the Last 20 Years [1], Top 10 Disproven Theories [2], Why Most Published Research Findings Are False [3], Most Scientific Theories Are Wrong. [4]

For some more fun, check out these websites for some of the more famous quotes by science and world leaders who were wrong on my different topics: It'll Never Work [5], Incorrect Predictions [6], Predictions-Quotes.[7]

Try naming any scientific breakthrough that was not strongly opposed. In fact, I would make the case that the strongest opposition usually comes shortly before the new idea gains wide acceptance because that is when the opponents fight the hardest to stop it. Check out the history of the locomotive, electricity, automobiles, airplanes, television, radio, and computers to name a few.

Do you think that scientists all jumped on board with Einstein and instantly accepted the theory of relativity? Maybe there was no heated debate and angry words. Wrong. That's not how it works.

Einstein himself admitted that he had made a big mistake after refusing for years to accept that the universe is expanding. He even went so far as to fudge his formula to avoid the new truth and account for data outside his pet theory. In the end he called this his "greatest mistake". Here is a reference to a book about Einstein's 23 biggest mistakes. [8]

Have you heard that the sum total of knowledge in the world is doubling every 12 months (and on its way to every 12 hours)? [9] Incredible.

Obviously we don't know it all, do we? Ask any honest scientist and he/she will admit that there are a lot of things they don't know in their chosen field...maybe even more than they think they already know.

We tend to think that we know it all today, the full and complete truth. Only those people in the past were ignorant, but not us. Not even close.

We tend to think that truth is always accumulating in a straight line and always going upward, new truth gets added on top of old truth and they always agree with each other. Nope. New truth will often turn out to be significantly opposed to the old truth. New truth will contradict the old "truth" because the two are incompatible.

One of the "most influential philosophers in science of the 20th century" is probably someone you never heard of. His name is Thomas S. Kuhn [10] and in 1962 he wrote a book called The Structure of Scientific Revolutions. He is the one who popularized the term "paradigm shift".

> "According to Kuhn the development of a science is not uniform but has alternating 'normal' and 'revolutionary' (or 'extraordinary') phases. The revolutionary phases are not merely periods of accelerated progress, but differ qualitatively from normal science."

> "...anomalies are ignored or explained away if at all possible. It is only the accumulation of particularly troublesome anomalies that poses a serious problem for the existing disciplinary matrix. A particularly troublesome anomaly is one that undermines the practice of normal science." [11]

He explained historically how science only progresses in a straight line for periods of time and then a revolution takes place when there is growing uneasiness with the "truth" because it doesn't explain the new data.

This is exactly what is happening to the Theory of Evolution. The theory is not able to explain the data very well any more.

> "Like all other scientific theories, Darwinian evolution must be continually compared with the evidence. If it does not fit the evidence, it must be re-evaluated or abandoned--otherwise it is not science, but myth." [12]

> "If the icons of evolution are supposed to be our best evidence for Darwin's theory, and all of them are false or misleading, what does that tell us about the theory? Is it science, or myth?"[13]

99.9% of all known fossils have been discovered since the time of Darwin, but his "missing links" have never been found. (See Chapter 18) The same goes for the two forces of mutation (See Chapter 27) and natural selection (See Chapter 35). They are failures at experimentally producing any new species. Now we see the Theory of Intelligent Design emerging in opposition. We also see it is being almost violently opposed. Adherents of Evolution want Intelligent Design people to shut up and are trying to get their jobs taken away. [14] They vilify esteemed atheists who change their minds. (See Chapter 17.)

I predict Intelligent Design will win the battle because it better explains the data.

If you look on the horizon, you can see other revolutions in thinking and "truth" that are coming. For example, look at all the books being written by very distinguished and credible people who have lived through and returned from a "near death experience". (See Chapter 10) Many others are now coming forward to testify to their own experiences of life after death. It is showing up more and more on television and in movies. Eventually it will be undeniable.

Another example is in the fields of psychology and medicine. Research is making amazing advances in alternative methods of healing that are more successful. Most people are unaware of what is happening below the surface and out of the public media. Individuals like Mahendra Trivedi are popping up around the world. Over 4,000 scientific experiments have verified his energy healing abilities. [15]

Once it is established that there is life after death, a huge paradigm shift will take place in the world and how people live their lives. Perhaps it will be gradual but the world will change tremendously as people adjust to the idea that they will live forever and the way they act in this life will determine what happens to them in the next.

These developments and discoveries are not random. There is an invisible, intelligent force at work behind the scenes working with the people who are making these discoveries. That Being is the origin of this knowledge and is helping it be revealed to the world.

There is God and He will eventually be known by all of us, even a reluctant scientist.

Chapter #51 Pollination

We are all familiar with pollen, but I think most of us don't know much about the pollination process, nor have we thought about it deeply in the context of Evolution vs. Creation. I sure didn't until recently.

In reading a number of articles I quickly discovered that the process is extremely complicated. One amazing thing that I did not know is that in the vast majority of plants pollination is required BEFORE a seed is able to be produced. No pollination, no seeds.

Only about 10% of plants are pollinated by wind or water. The other 90% require some animal or insect to be involved to transport the pollen. [1] This is very complicated and difficult to imagine how any evolutionary process over time and small changes could possibly work. We are supposed to believe that wonderful harmony and mutual benefit came about accidentally. Humans have a really hard time producing it on purpose. It's even harder to imagine when you learn that some plants do not have random pollinators, but have specialized to the point that only one particular insect is allowed to do the pollination.

Pollen has been around for millions of years. It is known to have remained virtually the same for 120 million years. No changes. How could evolution stop completely for that long (if it was ever working at all)?

Every individual type of plant has its own uniquely shaped pollen. That is amazing in and of itself. No repeats. Pollen is so unique and unchanging that it can be used in a court of law to determine exactly where an item has been if it contains a certain pollen.

You may have heard about the famous Shroud of Turin, touted as the burial cloth of Jesus. Interestingly, scientists know by the pollen in the fibers some of the exact areas in the Middle East where it must have traveled at one time. [2], [3]

Through many amazing adventures, pollen eventually arrives at its destination, then many phenomenal fertilization processes begin taking place. The pollen contains the male gamete (like sperm) that must fertilize the female part of the plant. In many cases it is very difficult to get to the female gamete and the pollen will actually grow a long pollen tube that deposits the male nuclei into the egg.

Actually there are usually 2 male nuclei in the pollen. One will fertilize the egg and the other will unite in a different way and produce the section of the seed that contains the nutrients for the later growth of the seedling plant. If you are interested, I really encourage you to look up pictures of this process.

Every one of the complex stages of pollination shows God's intelligent design. If you try to imagine how a totally random process that works slowly over many generations and small incremental changes could produce such magnificence, forget it. The gaps are too impossible. The probability is too great that even one plant species could do it, let alone the hundreds of thousands of plants all being able to accidentally do it. Add to that the fact that many of the plants do it in different ways so somehow each would have had to "evolve" separately.

Here's a good question of those of the Evolution faith. Did pollen come first or did the plant come first? If pollen somehow came first, since this is the male part, how could the female part have accidentally evolved at the same time and in the same location so there could be fertilization?

Fertilization is really, really complicated. Check out this "Plant Fertilization" tutorial [4] for a fairly simple to understand explanation.

If they somehow met up, how could they have the exact matching DNA? What are the odds? How many times would that process happen before the right sequence of changes takes place so a seed will result with its own nutrients included within the seed shell?

Even if you had a seed, how did the instructions get in the seed to produce a plant that would grow up and produce more of the exact pollen you started with? Even if you had one plant, you would still need another plant with the same DNA nearby for cross-fertilization.

Cross-fertilization is very important to understand. Some plants cannot fertilize themselves with their own pollen. This probably helps with plant immunity, but how could that be attributed to "survival of the fittest" when it's so much harder than self-fertilization. The vast majority of plants require cross-fertilization and there are incredibly fascinating mechanisms that different plants have to prevent self-fertilization and facilitate cross-fertilization. Some plants hide away their female parts until all their pollen has been removed. Some plants have the male and female areas in separated places. Some plants only allow a certain type of insect, for example, to get to their pollen and transfer it. In some cases, scientists don't know how a plant's own pollen is recognized and rejected.

Speaking of insects and other pollinators, just read up on some of the intricate processes that plants have to attract insects or animals to come near. Do plants have brains that thought up the idea of manufacturing sweet nectar to attract a bug? How did that happen? That nectar is providing food for the insect but no benefit to the plant itself. The plant is amazingly generous to give away all that good stuff and not use it for itself somehow. How could a plant have been pollinated before the development of the sweet nectar? How could the nectar evolve over many generations to just the correct sweetness formulation? If only one plant had nectar, why would the insect go to the next plant carrying the pollen? The pollen won't fertilize just any plant, it has to be exactly the same species and a DNA match.

It seems inconceivable that any evolutionary process could start with only pollen. But it's also just as inconceivable that if you start with a plant and follow the principles of evolution that you could ever develop a system like pollination in a slow and gradual way over many successive generations.

Scientists don't know where plants came from.

"The ancestors of flowering plants currently remain a mystery, and scientists aren't sure what kind of events or conditions might have spurred their origin.

> "'So far, no direct ancestors of flowering plants are known," Hochuli said. "Some groups of plants are suspected to be closely related. But the evidence is weak, and most of these groups are thought to be too specialized to be at the base of the flowering plants.'" [5]

In this scenario, you would have to start with a plant that could fertilize itself somehow. But starting there, how did it suddenly develop pollen grains that have two male nuclei? Even then, what good is male pollen unless there was also the female ovule accidentally developed at the same time on the same plant? Even if you had that, how would you eventually get to two separate plants that both require cross-fertilization? The odds of two plants appearing spontaneously and being a matched DNA pair is astronomical. If randomly a plant grew that required cross-fertilization from another plant, how could it ever become dominant? [6]

Plants make so many kinds of seeds, nuts, and fruits. Could it have just accidentally happened that most of these are good for birds, animals, and even humans to eat? No way.

Could it be accidental that these foods are mostly nutritious and not totally worthless or even poison? No way. Could it be accidental that they all taste so good? No way. It's beyond obvious that it was designed.

There clearly is God.

Chapter #52 Garbage In, Garbage Out (GIGO)

In the early days of computers about 1963 a certain phrase arose as a caution against blindly believing whatever results would come out of a computer. [1] Too much faith, like blind belief, in a machine could easily lead to false results and disastrous decisions. That phrase was "garbage in, garbage out" and it meant that everyone should be super vigilant against assuming something was true just because a computer model said it.

It was based on the obvious truth that even the most perfect computer program in the world would produce garbage if given faulty data as input. Computers do not "do the right thing" as much as we would hope. They do only and precisely what they are programmed to do.

There is a corollary as well. Even if you were to put the perfect, infallible data into a computer, if the software program has a bug in it, then again the results will be faulty.

I once owned a calculator that worked just fine almost all of the time. But it must have had a minor short somewhere in its circuitry because when doing one particular calculation, it always got the wrong answer. I discovered it by accident because my spreadsheet was giving me a different answer. It was so hard to believe at first. That was a pretty faith breaking experience. My "faith" in that calculator being correct on other calculations was destroyed and I ended up throwing it away.

My contention is that if you are looking for the "origin of species" (Darwin) or for that matter the origin of anything else, you cannot leave out intelligence as a contributing factor. A purely mechanistic model doesn't make rational sense from the entirety of our experience of life.

We are all familiar with the process of creation by humans. An artist for example first has an idea in his mind. The idea is invisible and insubstantial, but it has a "reality" to it. No one would deny its existence. Nor would anyone deny that there was intelligence at the source of the idea. Without the intelligence first, then the idea next, there would never be the artist's painting.

Order and complexity originate from an invisible idea. Randomness and chaos do not become ordered unless acted upon by a force that originated with an invisible intelligence and an idea. In fact, we know that randomness and chaos tend toward greater and greater randomness if left alone (see Second Law of Thermodynamics, Chapter 31).

To try to explain order and complexity, not to mention life itself, by purely mechanical or mechanistic causes, totally ignoring any invisible intelligence, is "Garbage In". All the observed processes of nature are being violated. "Garbage Out" is to be expected no matter how good your program/explanation is.

Imagine some pictures of archeological excavations of ancient ruins. Suppose I decide to believe that it was impossible for human beings to have existed in the place where the ruins were found. I would have to come up with an explanation that excluded intelligence for the formations right before my eyes.

Let's call it the "Theory of the evolution of ancient ruins". Random storms and winds and earthquakes must be the cause. Maybe we have to add in bacteria and small animals too. These forces have left behind complex rock formations that look designed but certainly could not have been designed because there was no intelligence involved. We can only talk about natural forces and not supernatural or invisible ones. Surely we would get deeply caught up in the processes of the storm systems and the flow of water, how winds form patterns on sand dunes, and how earthquakes shear off rock surfaces.

Are you seeing the "Garbage In"?

We combine all the forces together and tell a wonderful story about how it all "must have happened". We even still recognize the odds are millions and millions to one that it could have happened. But there it is right there in front of our eyes, so we know it happened. Just given enough time and the odds somehow worked out so that it must have happened the way we imagined.

Our story of how it happened took a lot of intelligence to come up with, but we "are certain" there could not have been any intelligent force working to create the ruins. We're certain of that because we decided it at the beginning. These explanations are the best we can come up with using all our scientific abilities in this age, so they must be correct. We don't need to resort to some idea of intelligent designer or god. Sure there are some gaps, but they will be worked out by future scientists. Besides that, we are all in agreement, minus a few religious fanatics and ignorant peoples.

Garbage out.

Any rational person looking at those pictures of ancient ruins, as simple as the design and order are, immediately concludes that there was an intelligent source. The more complex and complicated the ruins become, then the greater intelligence is assumed for the creators. The complexity of a single cell is many orders of magnitude more complicated than these ancient ruins and yet some people insist a cell could come about by random mutation. Garbage out. Intelligence is invisible, but it is still real.

There must be God.

Chapter #53 Rules

Everywhere around you are thousands of rules you follow every day. They are all invisible, but they none-the-less exist and are real. We human beings will come and go, but the rules will continue indefinitely.

There are rules of the road for driving, rules for cooking our food, rules for the games we play, rules for the structure of the sentences I'm writing, rules for social interactions at home and at work, rules everywhere all day long.

The so-called natural world, untouched by the power of human beings, has hundreds of rules. Think of all the rules of mathematics. Did you ever take a class in chemistry or even have a chemistry set as a kid? Lots of rules there. Physics too has lots and lots of rules. Simple things like gravity and magnetism control our lives by their rules.

Most of the rules are very beneficial to us. Can you imagine a life without rules? How much longer would it take you to drive somewhere if there were no rules?

Often there are consequences involved if you don't follow the rules. In our games you get a penalty for breaking the rules. In our society you get a punishment for breaking the rules which might even mean getting thrown in jail. If you break the rules of good health, you are likely to get a disease.

All these rules are invisible. They exist in our minds and in the laws of nature. Where did they come from?

The rules of games were obviously created by the inventor of the game. Rules for driving are established by the people in authority in the government. Rules for good manners are set up by the leaders of a society. All the rules come from intelligent sources.

Here's a question. Can rules come into existence spontaneously from nowhere? Have you ever seen that? Do rules create themselves? Hardly. If we recognize rules, we can be pretty certain that they originated in an intelligent source.

What about the rules of nature? Look at the very basics of the Periodic Table, its order and symmetry. There are so many rules in chemistry. Look at the rules of motion and force in physics. Where did they come from?

Scientists used to tell us that the universe always existed. That's just the way things are. There was no beginning. But it's now generally accepted that the universe did have a beginning at a certain point in time. So if everyone clearly accepts that there are rules, then where do they say that those rules came from?

Who made the rules?

We already concluded that the rules did not make themselves. What does an atheist say at this point? It just happened. I don't know. It's a mystery.

Most of us have a somewhat rebellious nature where we like to break the rules once in a while to see what happens. That's when we find out what the penalty is. If we break some of the more serious rules, then the consequences are more serious, not only for ourselves, but for others.

The most important rules to follow are the rules of love because that is the pathway to happiness and peace. Why do we want to be happy? Why is love important? Scientists will eventually find the source of the rules if they keep studying. It will be undeniable. The source is invisible. It is intelligent. It is loving.

Because there are rules, there must be God.

Chapter #54 Trophic Cascades and Wolves

Here is a very eye-opening story about a relatively new discovery in research on ecological systems.

Scientists used to believe that conservation efforts to restore ecosystems must follow the pattern of evolution. In other words, you had to start at the bottom in the lowest "trophic" levels. The term, "trophic," refers to different levels of the food chain, for example plants, insects, etc.

A "cascade" is like a stream falling down a waterfall and breaking into more and more streams with each rock it splinters against.

The concept of "trophic cascade" describes when a large carnivore at the top of the food chain has a cascading effect down to all the lower levels and it spreads out in many, many directions and has many diverse, even unexpected impacts.

The most stunning example to date comes from Yellowstone National Park in Wyoming. There had been no wolves in the park for 70 years until they were re-introduced in 1995 to 1996. If you have 4½ minutes to watch this video, I think you will be astounded: "How Wolves Change Rivers." [1]

My synopsis of the video: Wolves kill some species of animals for sure, but we now know they give life to many others. Elk populations had built up in Yellowstone until by grazing they reduced much of the vegetation to almost nothing. The new wolves killed some of the elk and it radically changed the behavior of the elk. They started avoiding certain parts of the park where wolves could kill them easily, especially the valleys and gorges. Vegetation in those areas started to regenerate immediately. The heights of some of the trees multiplied 5 times. In just 6 years aspen, willow, and cottonwoods came back. Birds then started moving in. Songbirds and migratory birds moved in. Beavers started to increase because of the young trees. Beavers built dams in the rivers and provided habitats for otters and muskrats, ducks and fish, reptiles and amphibians. When the wolves killed coyotes, the number of rabbits and mice increased. Then came the hawks, weasels, and foxes to eat those prey. Also badgers, ravens, and bald eagles came to feed on the carcasses left by the wolves and other available small prey. Bears came back too. Bears also killed some of the elk and reinforced the impact of the wolves. Even more amazingly, the wolves changed the behavior of the rivers. Because of the new vegetation, the rivers meandered less. The river banks had been stabilized and collapsed less often. The channels were straighter and became deeper. There was less soil erosion. Pools formed for all the wildlife to drink from. [2], [3], and [4]

The ecosystems we are seeing are definitely not "survival of the fittest" or a "dog eat dog" world. Even the main prey of the wolves, the elk population, was not harmed. As a whole they were hardier and more disease free. The old and sick were culled out. They were forced to get stronger to survive.

All of the species benefitted: the plants and trees, the insects and birds, small, medium, and large animals, even the fish and amphibians. Even the rivers and streams benefitted.

Scientists following evolutionist models got it wrong. All aspects of nature fit together harmoniously. They believed an ecosystem was built from the bottom up and so tried unsuccessfully to introduce plants.

Just as I explained about how the intricacies of the First Living Cell (Chapter 41) had to have been designed, we can see this interconnectedness and co-dependency of all creatures at higher levels of nature must have been designed as well. Chance and blind mechanisms could not create such complexity, especially not in such a top-down cascade model.

The wolves in Yellowstone are a marvelous example of an intricate ecological system that is impossible to conceive could have happened randomly or even by Natural Selection. (See my chapter on how the mechanism of Natural Selection, Chapter 35, loses variability not gains it.)

When something is designed by intelligence, the final goal is known and all the building block steps support the end goal. In this case, the wolf at the top of the mountain of the trophic cascade was already conceived of before all the other creatures ascending up the food chain were put in place. Otherwise the benefits cascading down would not exist.

Scientists are now discovering more and more trophic cascades besides wolves. [5] Every time a new one is discovered it reinforces the evidence for a designer by new orders of magnitude. It is exponentially more difficult to create two trophic cascades than one.

"When we try to pick out anything by itself, we find it hitched to everything else in the Universe." – John Muir

There must be God.

Chapter #55 Jigsaw Puzzles

I'm sure you must know what a jigsaw puzzle is. Probably you have put together many in your life starting from really simple ones with maybe only four pieces when you were a child.

Some of the most challenging jigsaw puzzles can get up over 1,000 pieces or more and take hours and hours to put together.

Piece by piece you put them together. For the whole puzzle there is only one way to put it together. The two pieces that are supposed to fit together next to each other must be arranged that way or the whole puzzle will not be correct. No two pieces are interchangeable. Every piece has exactly one other piece that fits on each side.

Once the puzzle is completely put together, then you can see the whole picture. There is a total uniqueness of each of the individual pieces, but they make up an intricately interconnected whole design.

When they assemble a jigsaw puzzle, most people look at the picture on the box. Why? It's because it helps them to know the overall design and get an idea of where certain features and pieces go. This makes the assembly easier. Imagine how much harder it would be if you never ever saw the picture on the box and didn't know what you were making. It would be a lot harder.

Now imagine how much harder it would be if there were no picture glued on the pieces to start with. In other words, all the puzzle pieces are the same color or blank. That probably makes putting the puzzle together 10 or even 100 times more difficult.

Now let's go another step even more difficult. Take 5 or 6 different puzzles with no pictures and mix up all the pieces. How much longer would it take you, an above average intelligent being, to correctly assemble all those 5 or 6 puzzles?

Here's the point. The Theory of Evolution is essentially saying that in the beginning there are only pieces of the puzzle. There is no big picture. Somehow, magically the pieces are assembled into this amazingly interconnected, complex universe.

Please refer back to my chapters on DNA (#21 and #30), I talked about how the human genome has 3 billion characters. Every living being has its own genome with hundreds of thousands or billions of characters uniquely arranged.

In my chapter on Trophic Cascade, #54, I talked about the intricate interconnectedness of every living creature in nature from the top of the food chain down to the organisms in the dirt. In my chapter on the Moon, #49, I talked about the incredible precision of its placement in the sky and so many beneficial effects on the Earth. Those are just some examples and there are hundreds, thousands more.

Now think of a jigsaw puzzle with 3 billion pieces that you are trying to assemble. It would take a while wouldn't it, especially if there were no pictures on the pieces? But, now the most important part, try to subtract any and all intelligence before the assembly starts. Without any intelligence, how long will it take to assemble the picture?

We know that just in nature on Earth alone there are way more than 3 billion pieces of complexity. That's not to mention the rest of Universe. There are between 8,000,000 and an estimated 100 million species of living beings which each have their own DNA. All of those millions of species are intricately connected within their local ecosystems which also magnifies the complexity in quantum leaps.

Evolutionists believe all of this came about without any intelligence anywhere to be seen.

Someday maybe they'll step back and see the big picture. When you see an amazing design, you know there must be a designer, even if you don't see him.

There must be God.

Chapter #56 Snowflakes

This past Tuesday was five days after the start of spring. Still we received two inches of snow and it's been freezing cold. In fact, snow has been a regular weekly occurrence this whole month. This winter has been one of the coldest on record in the last 100 years where I live.

So this chapter will be a tribute to the lowly snowflake. May I not see another one until next winter!

In reading the Wikipedia article on snowflakes, it says that scientists aren't really sure how snowflakes get made or what holds them together.

"In warmer clouds an aerosol particle or "ice nucleus" must be present in (or in contact with) the water droplet to act as a nucleus. The particles that make ice nuclei are very rare compared to nuclei upon which liquid cloud droplets form; however, it is not understood what makes them efficient. [1]

It's amazing that something as simple as some frozen water is a mystery to today's scientists. Whoever claims that scientists have discovered all the truth is either not digging deep enough or intentionally deluding themselves.

The exact details of the sticking mechanism remain controversial. Possibilities include mechanical interlocking, sintering, electrostatic attraction as well as the existence of a "sticky" liquid-like layer on the crystal surface. The individual ice crystals often have hexagonal symmetry. Although the ice is clear, scattering of light by the crystal facets and hollows/imperfections mean that the crystals often appear white in color due to diffuse reflection of the whole spectrum of light by the small ice particles." [2]

Snowflakes are absolutely fascinating and beautiful. Pause here and go look at some amazing photos of snowflakes to remind you of what they can look like. This footnote will take you to a famous snowflake photographer. [3] This footnote will take you to photos from CalTech. [4]

Here is a reference link to some time-lapse photography of snowflakes being formed. It is almost like they are alive. [5]

Your typical snowflake has about 10^{19} (10 quintillion) water molecules.[6] Since there is an unbelievably huge number of molecule combinations going into a snowflake, it pretty much guarantees that old saying that "no two snowflakes are identical."

When you looked at snowflakes in pictures, did you get some type of feeling in response? What is that feeling? Do you have any thoughts about where such amazing patterns could have come from? Do you marvel at the intricate details? Do you think, "Wow, what an amazing accident!!! What an amazing accident!!! What an amazing accident," over and over and over again every time you look at a different snowflake? Hardly.

Scientists may not be able to explain it yet, but one thing we can be sure of is that the ability of water to turn into snowflakes has been a property of water since the very origin of water. It could not be something that was added or "evolved" at a later time.

Long before there was life on earth and long before any inkling of "evolution" existed, there was water. And surely that water had the capability to make snowflakes.

If there is a creator of water, that intelligent being endowed it with the capability to make snowflakes long before we came along to look at and appreciate them.

If there was no creative intelligence, then it must have all come from NOWHERE. All of it. Then, of course, there is no purpose to anything? Without a purpose, what value is there? When you look at something that has no value, it does not inspire you. Think of a piece of junk. You don't feel inspiration or amazement.

The joy that is experienced from the beauty of a simple snowflake is almost universal among human beings. We all feel it. How could that be? That we all have a reaction of awe and wonder at snowflakes is not accidental or a mistake. There was no ancient "natural selection" for only people who could appreciate snowflakes and they were the only people able to survive.

There is an overall design built into human beings so we can appreciate the precious gifts around us, all the way down to the lowly snowflake. Even one scientist, Dr. Masaru Emoto from Japan, goes so far as to proclaim that humans by using thought energy can change the patterns of ice crystals. [7] Very interesting research (but controversial of course). His photos are really interesting. He was featured a movie, What The Bleep Do We Know. [8]

Not just snowflakes, but all of the tiniest particles of the universe are awe inspiring. DNA is a beautiful spiral staircase. At the other extreme are the largest entities of the universe which inspire awe as well. The amount of beauty we can discover is mind boggling, even infinite.

There must be God.

Chapter #57 The 17-Year Cicadas

How many animals can count? Probably you have seen dogs and horses count, maybe even elephants. Of course they were trained by intelligent beings (namely humans) to do that. Also they are considered among the "higher animals". But have any of them counted up to 17. You probably would not ever think than an insect can count, let alone count up to 17.

Even people might have a little trouble counting up to 17 if you counted so slow that it took you 17 years. That's a little more difficult because you have to remember your place for a whole year before adding 1.

Well, let's talk a little about the 17-Year Cicada. There are over 2,500 species of cicada that have been described and they are still counting new species. [1] Different cicada species emerge on different schedules. Some species come every year. Some every 13 years. But the most famous and largest "brood" comes every 17 years to the eastern part of the United States and may number 1 trillion individuals. As many as 1.5 million cicadas of this species may emerge from a single acre of land.

They are 1½ inches long and basically harmless, just annoying. The adults which emerge do not eat at all. They will climb a tree, molt/shed their skin exposing their wings, then fly around to find a mate.

Within 6 weeks the females have all laid their eggs in a slit they carve in a tree and they have all died. When the eggs hatch, the larvae drop to the ground and burrow in, never to be seen again for 17 years.

By the way, the cicada emerge when the ground temperature is exactly 64 degrees. Also, the males emerge first and are out there with their very loud mating calls when the females come out. Females do not make noises. They all have two big red eyes and 3 smaller black ones. Each species has a distinct mating call which is made inside the male abdomen by "clicking" parts while a type of echo chamber magnifies it. The sounds can get as loud as 120 decibels, among the loudest of all insects. Wikipedia has some sample sounds. [2]

17 years is a really long lifespan for an insect. Even more amazing about Cicadas is that each generation only mates once, and it's at the very end of their life after 17 years. If evolution were true, you would only have 6 generations every 100 years, so only 6 chances to get a beneficial mutation (which I have already detailed very rarely happens). In Chapter 27 on "The Truth About Mutation," I wrote how scientists have mutated fruit flies (on

141

purpose using intelligence) for over 40 years and thousands of generations without ever producing a new species. If the scientists were studying the 17-Year Cicada, there would only be 2 generations in that same 40 years.

How did the 17-Year Cicada learn to count to 17? Have you ever heard of any case where a number sequence emerged when there was no intelligent origin?

Let's also remember that you have to have a male and a female for mating purposes to get a next generation. The male and female also have to both be alive in the same 6 week window and in the same vicinity on earth to be able to meet and mate. If one or the other stays in the ground longer by just 6 weeks in 17 years, then they can't mate. If there is a mutation of the genome for the time the species stays under the ground, it has to be simultaneous in both male and female so they can still come out at the same time. How is that possible to be coordinated?

Not only would the mutation in both the male and female have to be in the same direction (longer time or shorter time), but it would also have to be of exactly the same length of time in weeks. I suppose you could say there are billions of them and enough randomly could meet up for mating. But somehow you still have to get to the end point of all of them staying in the ground exactly 17 years at the end of the evolving.

Another problem is the temperature of 64 degrees. How could the male and female have mutated separately but still somehow decided jointly on that exact temperature and never mutate away from it?

And here is an even bigger problem. How do they know what the temperature is? Are you able to tell me what the temperature is right now or can you tell me when it hits 64 degrees? We all know the Cicadas stay underground for 17 years and then when the temperature hits 64 degrees, they come out. Oh and by the way, the males come out first.

Also only the males have a mechanism for making a gigantic noise, which the females don't do. So if you believe in evolution, you have to believe this is all accidental mutations and natural selection for them to have different body mechanisms, but the same timing.

What if the females didn't like the sounds that the males make? Then they would ignore them.

Of course, we all know that males and females of all species are astoundingly different in body parts. New research is showing they are even more different than was thought in the past. There is no possibility that they could have evolved slowly in incremental changes because they would have to have made complementary changes in the same generation and live in the same vicinity of each other, meet, and mate. (See Chapter 1 on Male and Female.) The Theory of Evolution should have been debunked at its beginning.

How does an insect tell that the temperature is 64 degrees above the ground when it is below the ground? How did that kind of mechanism evolve? Even if you somehow had an organ to tell the temperature, it somehow has to be wired to the brain and send a signal. Once the signal arrives in the brain that the temperature is 64 degrees, so what? Somehow the brain has to figure out that it now has to dig upward, climb a tree, shed its skin, find a mate, copulate, and then die all within 6 weeks.

When an insect can do something that no human can do, even the greatest genius among us, there is no way to convince me that this evolved from nothing.

There must be God.

Chapter #58 The Cambrian Explosion

We have all been taught by the Theory of Evolution that all species came into existence by small incremental changes over a long period of millions of years. Diversity came about over time from the beginning as various mutations created many new species. The various species branched out over time creating more and more phyla or groups of species. Diagrams of Evolution therefore appear like a giant tree and get the nickname, "Tree of Life."

This "tree of life" structure is Darwin's prediction that all species evolved from one original life form.

Would it surprise you to know that the fossil record is not like this at all? Would you feel betrayed by the scientific community and media if you found out that the truth is totally different?

Here are diagrams of what the actual evidence in the Fossil Record looks like. All the major phyla appeared in less than 1% of historical time. Since that time a number have gone extinct, exactly the opposite of Darwin's prediction.

There is no Darwinian Tree of Life in the fossil record. The true record looks like the below diagram which shows just two sample phyla out of the many phyla that exist. Each phyla appears suddenly and without any connection to other phyla.

Darwin predicted there should be a tree trunk and many branches leading to many other branches. NONE of this has ever been found. His predictions cannot be verified in the fossil record, so therefore I must conclude that the theory must also be wrong.

The best fossil records available on earth actually show that the majority of phyla suddenly appear, FULLY FORMED, within a very narrow period of time and with no precursors. It all happened about 540 million years ago. There are no developmental stages or slow changes in the fossil record. All fossils are fully formed species and basically no changes occur over time except for variations within a species. For example, horses may get bigger or smaller, but they are always horses.

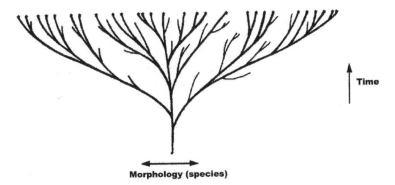

Morphology (species)

The evolutionary "tree" — which postulates that all today's species are descended from the one common ancestor (which itself evolved from non-living chemicals). This is what evolution is really all about.

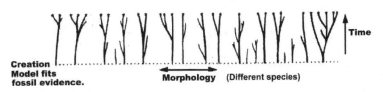

Creation Model fits fossil evidence.

Morphology (Different species)

The true creationist "orchard" — diversity has occurred with time within the original Genesis "kinds" (creationists often call them **baramin**, *from Hebrew* **bara** = *create, and* **min** = *kind).*

Image 11. Tree of Life vs. Orchard
©1999 Jonathan Sarfati.

The name given to this phenomenon, sudden appearance of all the phyla, is literally an "explosion". It happened during the Cambrian Age and hence it is the Cambrian Explosion.

Time magazine called it Evolution's Big Bang. "New discoveries show that life as we know it began in an amazing biological frenzy that changed the planet almost overnight." [1]

"The fossil record - in defiance of Darwin's whole idea of gradual change - often makes great leaps from one form to the next. Far from the display of intermediates to be expected from slow advance through natural selection many species appear without warning, persist in fixed form and disappear, leaving no descendants. Geology assuredly does not reveal any finely graduated organic chain, and this is the most obvious and gravest objection which can be urged against the theory of evolution." [2]

Time magazine calls this an "objection" that can be "urged" against the theory of evolution. I'd call it total demolishment.

Suppose you make a time line from the beginning until now and convert it to a 24 hour clock. On that clock almost all of the species on earth appeared in their early forms, each with their unique "body plans," all within just a 2 minute span of the clock. That should forever debunk Darwin's slow and gradual in my opinion.

Scientists have discovered the major fossil beds with the finest fossils in locations all over the globe. The beds in Chengjiang, China, include extremely well preserved soft-tissue specimens. All the fossil beds exhibit the same explosion of species in the Cambrian Age, during the same time frame. The period is 0.14% of the time clock mentioned before. This is absolutely NOT slow and absolutely NOT gradual change. There are various calculations about how big that window is ranging from about 5 to 10 million years out of billions.

The Theory of Evolution is totally disproved based on the evidence in the fossil record. However, if you are a true believer, you deny the evidence shows what it clearly shows. You either make up a story of why you are still right or try to destroy the messenger.

"Yet, here is the real puzzle of the Cambrian Explosion for the theory of evolution. All the known phyla, except one, along with the oddities with which I began this discussion, first appear in the Cambrian period. There are no ancestors. There are no intermediates. Fossil experts used to think that the Cambrian lasted 75 million years. But even that seemed to be a pretty short time for all this evolutionary change. Eventually the Cambrian was shortened to only 30 million years. And if that wasn't bad enough, the time frame of the real work of bringing all these different creatures into existence was limited to the first five to ten million years of the Cambrian. This is extraordinarily fast!" [3]

Evolutionists have been grabbing at straws to hold on to their theory for years despite the clear evidence from the Cambrian Explosion. Some of their typical excuses cannot stand up to thoughtful examination.

1. Not enough fossils have been discovered yet. Darwin used this reasoning too. "The explanation lies, as I believe, in the extreme imperfection of the

geological record." That was back when we had just 1% of the current fossil record. Unfortunately for them, every time new fossils are discovered, it just further substantiates the evidence of the existing fossils and the Cambrian Explosion.

2. Missing links and the precursor species didn't fossilize. How could that possibly be true all over the world? It is a gigantic mystery. It's especially problematic since there are existing fossils of many species from BEFORE the Cambrian Explosion WITH soft bodies and EVEN single-celled animals.

3. Punctuated Equilibrium. This idea basically says that all the necessary evolving of each of the different species must have taken place in tiny, isolated groups. No records can therefore be found or maybe we just haven't found them yet. It says everything went along for millions of years without changing, then suddenly there was a burst of change. Totally upside down from Darwin.

Oh, please!

So they won't give up. The new explanation of the fossil record is to say that changes take place in spurts separated by long periods of no change. Hence it is called "punctuated" (spurt) and "equilibrium" (stays the same for a long time). Therefore they are really saying, "We admit that we just can't find the right fossils predicted by Darwin, so it must be that evolution takes place very rarely and in extremely isolated places. That's why we haven't found the fossil evidence." They know the evidence exists somewhere. However, the proof remains only in their minds.

During the Cambrian Explosion almost all species suddenly came existence. Clearly this is a repudiation of Darwin's idea of slow and gradual. Punctuated equilibrium admits to the truth. Darwin was wrong.

Punctuated Equilibrium believers have no clear explanation of why or how change happens in spurts. But they are undeterred.

Actually, this idea has been proven false by statistical analysis. To get the very large number of changes that are required to evolve all the different species, you must necessarily have huge numbers of mutations. There must be enough individuals reproducing in order to account for all those mutations. This model has nowhere near enough reproducing individuals in their populations.

The paleontologists have all the evidence right before their eyes, but they won't take the "leap of faith" away from accepted dogmas. You can lead a horse to water, but you can't make him drink.

Verbalizing publicly that the fossil evidence is totally against the Theory of Evolution is likely to get a professor fired or his/her funding taken away.

When scientists have a hidden agenda, truth suffers. They will not go where the evidence leads them. They are not being true scientists. And we are all the worse for it. Think what amazing discoveries await us once scientists stop wasting energy pursuing and/or defending a fraud and devote that same energy to discovering more about the true loving source of all things and the amazing creation.

There is truly God.

Chapter #59 Invisibility

You may have heard someone say at some time that "God cannot exist because no one has ever seen God." In this chapter I'm going to discuss invisibility and why that does not disprove God. In fact, God has to be invisible.

Let's think about some things that are invisible. Just because something is invisible does not mean that it is not real.

In my Proof for God Chapter 45 on The Eye, I noted that our eyes cannot see any light outside of a rather narrow "visible spectrum". The visible spectrum is only 1.5% of the whole range of light rays that exist. We cannot see most of the ultraviolet or infrared parts of the spectrum. There are some animals that can see things that we cannot see.

Some people have the ability to see auras, which are energy fields that most people cannot see. There are many discoveries in the field of Kirlian photography that show life/energy forms that cannot be seen with the naked eye. Some people seem to have the ability to see and communicate with the spirits of the deceased which are invisible to the rest of us. I think most of us will admit that there are limitations to what our physical eyes can see and therefore being visible to our eyes is not a prerequisite to a substance being real.

There are lots of ordinary things that are very real but you can't see them. How about a glass window? You can see very clearly right through it, but we know how solid it can be. There is even such a thing as bulletproof glass, which is very solid.

Air cannot be seen, but where would we be without air? However, if you have ever stood in a strong wind, you know it could blow you over. Wind can move huge ships and tornadoes cause tremendous destruction. That's a very powerful force, but you can't see it. Every child loves a balloon, but there is nothing visible inside of it.

There are other amazing forces like gravity and magnetism that scientists don't know where they came from. They are invisible, but very powerful.

Other things you can't see are carrying amazing amounts of intelligent information. Think about the radio and television signals all around you. If you tune into one of these invisible channels, you can get sounds and videos from possibly tens or hundreds of channels for music, news, sports, or movies. All of that is somewhere in the air around you right now, simultaneously, but you can't see it, touch it, taste it, hear it, or smell it in any way.

You probably have a cellphone that allows you to carry on an intelligent conversation with another being somewhere else on the planet. That person is invisible to you, but you don't question whether he or she exists. Smartphones allow you to watch a movie or even live events like sports. You can't see the game with your own eyes. How do you know it really exists?

Who knows, maybe someday someone will invent a "hotline" to God.

What about all the people in history? How can you be sure your great, great, great, great grandfather really existed? You've never seen him and neither has anyone else alive. You have to conclude that he must have existed because you exist. Maybe there are photographs of him, but not before 1814. If your ancestors didn't exist, you are the product of a miracle conception at some point.

Just because you may have never seen God, does that mean that no one else has ever seen God either? Hardly. That would be a pretty foolish thing to conclude. Most people have never seen God. But they obviously have not seen everything that could be seen. Millions, if not billions, of people claim to have experienced God and some insist they "saw" God in some form. Those who have had a "Near-Death Experience" often relate an experience like seeing God.

Testimonies of God are written down in every language all over the world and all throughout history. It's pretty hard to discount all that evidence and call it categorically false just because no scientific experiment, based solely in the material world, can verify it. It doesn't matter how intellectually brilliant a scientist may be if he/she is looking in the wrong place. To say that you know for sure there is no God is a staggering declaration that you know the truth beyond all these other people who must therefore be ignorant or deceived.

Here's something else that is invisible but still very real... ideas. They are very real and provide driving forces in people's lives: freedom, truth, goodness, honesty. People are willing to give up their lives to gain freedom. Then there's the greatest motivating force of all, love. It cannot be seen. You recognize it by its effects, by what is created by its power and what lengths people will go to in order to possess it.

If God were visible, that would put physical limitations and boundaries on Him. Can we put boundaries around love and truth and freedom? Clearly not. By definition, God is the one who created the whole universe. He created time and space, and ideals. So He would necessarily be "beyond" or "outside" of time and space. Or maybe "throughout" is a better explanation. God should not be inhibited by having to be in one place. He needs to be in all places simultaneously and thus be available to every person who wants a relationship with Him. No matter where you go, you can have access to God. No matter who you are among all the people in the world, you can have access to God. If God is love, and support, and comfort, how wonderful for all of us.

Of course, if you believe God is mean and nasty or repulsive, then you don't want that kind of God anywhere near you. That would be a horrible reality and you would fight against it. If God is more powerful than Santa Claus, then He can "see you when you're sleeping and know when you're awake." If you do something wrong, then He can see you, judge you, and punish you. That needs to be rebelled against, right?

God has to be real. Everywhere around us is the evidence. People have been experiencing God throughout history. All of nature is a testimony to God because we can't even dream of how to duplicate such beauty and complexity.

In our lives, the most valuable things are not our worldly possessions, but are all the invisible and intangible things like love and freedom. It is impossible that those invisible things originated from rocks and chemicals by random accident.

There must be God.

Chapter #60 Water

Of all the treasures that we could talk about on earth, the number one most valuable substance is water. Every living being requires water. As a matter of fact, every living cell requires water.

The water molecule is so unique and special among all substances. It is so finely tuned and ideally suited to foster the existence of life that it is impossible to rationally conclude it was a cosmic accident. It is much easier to accept that it was miraculously designed.

A water molecule is totally different from the normal properties that would be expected from the patterns of similar compounds in the Periodic Table of Elements. Its freezing temperature and boiling point are way too high. It should be a gas at room temperatures. It should turn from ice to liquid at around -100°C (instead of 0°C) and then from liquid to gas at around -80°C (instead of 100°C). This would mean almost all the water on Earth would not exist (and neither would we).

Uniqueness of Water in relation to similar compounds

Table 1. Melting and boiling points of hydrogen compounds vertical to oxygen on the Periodic Table of Elements. (All others turn to gas quickly, but water doesn't.)

	H_2O	H_2S	H_2Se	H_2Te
Boiling Point °C	+100	-59.6	-4.2	-2.0
Melting Point °C	0	-82.9	-6.4	-4.8

Table 2. Melting and boiling points of hydrogen compounds horizontal to oxygen in the Periodic Table of Elements. (All others turn to gas quickly, but water doesn't.)

	H_4C	H_3N	H_2O	HF
Boiling Point °C	-161.4	-33.4	+100	+19.4
Melting Point °C	-182	-77.7	0	-8.3

Water is everywhere on Earth, covering 71% [1] of the Earth's surface. "Earth is the only known planet to have bodies of liquid water on its surface." [2] No other planet in the known universe has even the tiniest fraction of this much water. Think about the implications of that truth and the specialness of our "home" in the vast universe.

This much water allows for gigantic numbers of species to live in the water, especially the tiny life giving organisms like algae and plankton which produce a lot of the oxygen and nutrition for most species. "It is estimated that marine plants produce between 70 and 80 percent of the oxygen in the atmosphere." [3]

What is the origin of water? It is so absolutely essential to all life that without water there could never have been any life. The properties of water are so chemically unusual and yet so absurdly complementary and coordinated with life that it is impossible to conceive that this is an accidental relationship. The most rational conclusion is that water and life were designed.

All of your needs for Oxygen, down to the last cell, are provided by the water in our blood. The way you get rid of Carbon Dioxide is provided by water. Water does the same thing for plants, but in reverse.

Even the smallest variation in any of the properties of water would be the end of us. It is all functioning miraculously on the tiniest cellular level.

> "If the angle between hydrogen atoms in the water molecule were different, there would be no complex life-giving molecules, and no life on earth." [4]

The following property is one of my favorites. When water freezes, it expands. Only a small handful of other substances do that. But because it does that, frozen water, i.e. ice, floats. The density of ice is almost ten times lighter than liquid water. If water were a normal compound, its frozen form would sink.

But imagine if ice were to sink, then in winter when all the lakes would freeze, then the ice would sink to the bottom. Then new water on the top of the lake would freeze and sink to the bottom. Soon the whole lake from the bottom up would be frozen solid, killing all the fish and plants. When could it ever thaw out? It would take a really long time if ever with the sun only melting the ice on the surface. But fortunately that's not what happens because of how water is designed. The ice floats and actually provides a protective layer against the cold for all life under the surface. Doesn't that sound like it was designed by a brilliant, loving intelligence that was concerned for the life it created?

You probably realize cooler water sinks. This creates what is called "stratification". You might have noticed this when swimming in a lake, that the water down deeper is colder. However, when water becomes ice it rises to the top. This causes a churning effect in the spring and fall that circulates and oxygenates the lake waters. That effect is very beneficial for plant and animal life in the lakes. Also because the warmer water stays on top, the sun's heat cannot penetrate so deeply that it would harm the animal and plant life below.

Another important property of water due to hydrogen bonding is called "cohesion". The hydrogen atoms are constantly bonding and breaking bonds in tiny fractions of a second.

"Cohesion due to hydrogen bonding contributes to the formation of waves and other water movements that occur in lakes. Water movements are integral components of the lake system and play an important role in the distribution of temperature, dissolved gases, and nutrients. These movements also determine the distribution of microorganisms and plankton." [5]

Water has a high degree of surface tension. This also creates a protection effect, not only for lakes and oceans, but even in our own bodies. "Water has a greater surface tension than all other liquids except mercury." [6] That surface tension is what makes water drops take the shape of spheres. Water falling from the sky takes the shape of drops. These can act like little bullets to penetrate and refresh plant life and the earth. They can dissolve and wash away toxins. It mixes up soils and fertilizes. It erodes rocks over time, making soil. It churns the oceans, benefitting fish and plant life.

Water rains down to the earth to nourish all life. It then flows towards streams and rivers to the sea where it evaporates and goes back into the atmosphere to repeat the cycle. The unidirectional flow of water in the evaporation/condensation cycle enables water all over the earth to continuously cleanse itself and renew the earth and all forms of life.

When water is heated in hot climates, the water vapor can carry large amounts of heat energy away to cooler locations and then release it in the form of rain. This cools the hotter climates and warms the colder ones, while at the same time refreshing and oxygenating the atmosphere.

"Water is called the 'universal solvent' because it dissolves more substances than any other liquid. This means that wherever water goes, either through the ground or through our bodies, it takes along valuable chemicals, minerals, and nutrients." [7] This allows water to carry nutrition throughout your body to every one of your approximately 100 trillion cells (other sources say 40 trillion). It also allows the water to extract the waste products from your cells and carry them to the organ that is designed to eliminate them.

Colloidal action is another special property of water. The inherent vibration by the H_2O molecules pushes around any dissolved substances so they are evenly distributed throughout the water.

Capillary action and surface tension are also important properties. This means that water goes into the tiniest of cracks and crevices automatically. This makes your life so much easier because your heart does not have to provide huge amounts of force to get your blood to circulate through all the tiny capillaries to supply all your cells. Blood carries nutrients to every cell in the bodies of all animals and then removes waste products. Water in the sap in trees and plants carries nutrients for their life.

> "Water also has the ability to pass through cell membranes and climb great heights in plants and trees through osmosis and capillary force. Osmotic pressure and capillary action enable water to climb hundreds of feet to the tops of the highest trees. The mystery of osmosis enables plants to feed, and plants and animals to carry on a multitude of life processes. Osmosis enables marine creatures to absorb fresh water in an increasing salt-water environment." [8]

Water has the highest heat capacity of any liquid, [9] meaning it can absorb relatively huge amounts of heat. This means it is slow to increase in temperature and to eventually boil. It also releases heat very slowly. Our whole planet and everything on it benefits from this. The sand on the beach can get so hot you can't walk on it, but the ocean stays cool and doesn't turn to steam.

The oceans keep our entire environment from getting way too hot and conversely from getting way too cold. Water makes a "womb" for all life, a protective habitat. It's almost analogous to the female womb that lovingly supports the growth of new life. If you live near a large body of water, the winters are warmer and the summers are cooler.

Because water can absorb great amounts of heat and our bodies are mostly water, it means our body temperature is much easier to regulate and there are not huge swings to deal with. Our body even has a mechanism to release sweat that will evaporate from our skin taking heat with it and keeping us cooler.

> "More energy is required to evaporate liquid water than most other substances. To evaporate each gram of water at room temperature, about 580 calories of heat are needed, which is nearly double the amount needed to vaporize a gram of alcohol or ammonia." [10]

Water remains a liquid over a very large range (0°C to 100°C, 32°F to 212°F). Most other substances have a much shorter range between solid and gaseous states. This range allows life to exist over a large spectrum of temperatures.

One source noted that water has "at least twenty-three anomalies, properties that the laws of chemistry and physics say it should not have." [11]

This chapter doesn't cover all the amazing properties of water, but let's get to the point. Does this prove that God exists? Suppose every morning when you wake up, you go outside your front door and there waiting for you is exactly all the food and water that you will need for the day to live. The next day the same. The day after that the same. It never fails. All your essential needs are provided for in exactly the right proportions. If any of the ingredients were to vary slightly, you would starve or die of thirst. Could this be just a cosmic accident? The odds are so infinitesimally small as to be non-existent.

There must be God.

Chapter #61 Muscles

If you are a fan of any sport, I'm sure you are amazed by what human beings can do. How strong and how fast they are and how coordinated they can move is astounding. It is almost incomprehensible that their eyes can see a ball moving over 100 miles an hour and through the brain coordinate their arms, legs, and hands to catch or hit that ball with precision. Also, I'm sure you know that many animals are capable of feats that humans cannot begin to duplicate.

All of these movements are accomplished by specialized cells called muscles.

If you do an Internet search for "evolution of muscles," you will come up with almost nothing. The articles have totally speculative statements or are just a description of a supposed sequence of development, but there is no explanation.

If they are honest, they will admit they have no idea of the origins of muscles. For example, "The structure and function of vertebrate striated muscle, which can be contracted at will, has been studied in detail, but its evolutionary history remains obscure." [1] Here is another, "While the structure and function of muscles, especially of vertebrates, have been intensively studied, the evolutionary origin of smooth and striated muscles has so far been enigmatic." [2] Even Wikipedia, which is pro-evolution, admits this with a disclaimer at the top. "This article has multiple issues." [3]

The tiniest movements we make, like the "jitter" of each eye over 30 times a second (See Chapter 45, The Eye), like every beat of your heart, like large jumps with your legs, are all accomplished by many muscles. Every time your mind wants your body to do something, it calls on specific muscles to accomplish it.

Not only movements, but our minds have so many emotions they need to be able to express. So our faces are designed with all the muscles we need for that. Why would all those facial expressions we can make be necessary in order to be the fittest to survive as evolutionists claim?

I like this description from How Stuff Works.Com.

> "Because muscles are so crucial to any animal, they are incredibly sophisticated. They are efficient at turning fuel into motion, they are long-lasting, they are self-healing and they are able to grow stronger with

practice. They do everything from allowing you to walk to keeping your blood flowing!" [4]

Many things inside your body happen automatically to keep you alive, but they happen without you having to think about it. Muscles move your food down your esophagus, through your stomach and intestines, and all the way out. Your lungs suck in air. Your heart beats almost every second. This is all done by muscles.

Wikipedia has a list of 642 "skeletal muscles" which are the ones controlled by our consciousness and the list includes their location in the body and their purpose. [5] But some other sources may count muscles differently and come up with as many as 850.

Muscles exist in 320 pairs. According to Wikipedia's sources, "almost every muscle constitutes one part of a pair of identical bilateral muscles, found on both sides,..." [6] Remember this point. It will be important later.

There are 3 distinct types of muscles.

Skeletal muscles, also called "voluntary," are ones which can be controlled by the mind. These are the 642 mentioned above.

Smooth muscles, or "involuntary," are ones which we cannot control. They are contained in our digestive system (esophagus, stomach, intestines), blood vessels, bladder, bronchi (lungs), arrector pili (skin), and, in females, the uterus (childbirth).

Cardiac muscle is found only in the heart and is very unique. The cells are specially designed and connected so they can all contract at the same time at the command of cells called "pacemaker" cells in the heart.

42% of a man's body mass is muscle. For women it is 36%. While we are on the subject, it could be noted that men and women have many differences in their muscle systems, particularly in the reproductive area. If you want some fascinating reading sometime, check out how the uterus works.

The Skeletal muscles can be further subdivided into "slow twitch" or "fast twitch" muscles. The slow twitch muscles contract for a long time but with little force. The fast twitch muscles can contract rapidly and with strong force. The fast twitch muscles are even subdivided into 3 more categories.

Muscles are made up of many, many muscle cells which are arranged together in bundles inside a sheath called a sarcolemma. Furthermore, many of these sheaths are again bound together in a large bundle which is surrounded by another sheath called a fascicle. Then again many fascicles are bound together in another sheath called an epimysium. This reminds me of the steel cables used to make the Golden Gate Bridge. This design gives amazing strength.

Inside every muscle there are numerous arteries and veins to bring blood with oxygen and nutrition and carry away waste products. There are also many nerve endings coming all the way from the brain that initiate contractions. There are also many mitochondria in the cells to process oxygen, fats, and carbohydrates as fuel for energy.

The whole process of chemical reactions and how a muscle is able to contract and relax is super complicated and over my head. But you can research the details yourself if you are interested.

Common sense will tell you that our muscles were designed by a super intelligence. The abilities of man-made robots are miniscule in comparison.

Remember I noted that muscles all come in pairs. If you put your arm out, you need a complementary muscle to pull it back. If you look up, you need a complementary muscle to pull your eye back down. If you step forward, you need a complementary muscle to keep you from falling over.

If there is no God, and all muscles came about by accident, mutation, and natural selection, how can you account for complementary pairs of muscles? Mutation would have to guess right 340 times. Suppose you evolve a muscle (which isn't easy) that will move your arm out. What good is that? How many generations will it take with all people having their arms hanging out until some individual evolves a muscle to bring his arm back in. If it's a man, he has to wait for a woman to also evolve that same muscle to pull in her arm, find her, marry her, and have children. Then they become the Adam and Eve for all mankind because we all have both those muscles. All the people without both those muscles have died out. Oops, I almost forgot that we have to repeat that process 339 more times to account for all the other muscle pairs in our bodies. And that's just the voluntary muscles. How we could possibly evolve the cardiac and involuntary muscles is still not accounted for.

Remember evolving a muscle is not going to be simple. You have got to also evolve the nerves (connected to the brain) and arteries and veins (connected to the heart) inside the muscle and then surround it all with 3 layers of sheathing. You also have to evolve the tendons to connect the muscles to your bones. This is not even in the realm of possibility.

Natural Selection would theoretically prevent the evolution of muscle pairs anyway. Survival of the fittest would eliminate single muscles before their complementary muscle could evolve. You can't close your eyes and not be able to open them. If you stick out your arm and can't bring it back, you would not be one of the fittest that could survive.

I've already discussed in other chapters the explanations of how mutation (Chapter 27) and natural selection (Chapter 35) have never been shown to be processes that can produce new species. So too, they are not processes that can even begin to explain how muscles originated either.

We discussed human muscles above, but every other species of mammal, fish, birds, and insect has muscles as well. Most all of those muscles are in pairs. We're talking about several million species that would have had to evolve their own unique muscles to accommodate their unique skeletons.

All those species also have hearts and involuntary muscles as well. Those would all have to evolve separately too inside every animal species. This is astronomically impossible.

Think about involuntary muscles for a minute. If evolution were true, then at some point before our lungs worked automatically we would have to think "breath in, breath out," all the time. Ridiculous. Before our esophagus evolved to automatically push our food down, we would have to think about it. At what point after many generations of evolution did we have to stop telling our stomach to move the food along and our lungs start breathing on their own? Equally ridiculous. It was all in place from the beginning or we would have died out as a species.

What about the cardiac muscle in the heart? How did that muscle accidentally "evolve" and start beating. At what point did the arteries and veins get connected and then blood was created to move around the body or up to the lungs for oxygen and back again?

The masterpiece of the human body is not the result of ad hoc, random additions over many generations. It was designed from the beginning.

There must be God.

Chapter #62 Common Sense

All people have what is called "Common Sense" (to a greater or lesser degree it seems). This is the ability to organize our experiences in life and our observations into a coherent understanding of how things work.

This definition is from Wikipedia:

> "Common sense is a basic ability to perceive, understand, and judge things, which is shared by ("common to") nearly all people, and can be reasonably expected of nearly all people without any need for debate. ...a type of basic awareness and ability to judge which most people are expected to share naturally, even if they cannot explain why." [1]

You've probably heard the expression "That doesn't make sense". This is based on our ability to judge our environment and make rational order of it. This is part of our intelligence. It can only exist because there is genuine order in the world around us and not chaos. There is a natural order of things and there are universal laws and principles.

Let's take a statement like, "Rocks turned into people". Your reaction would probably be "that doesn't make any sense". Yet that is a basic conclusion you would have to draw from so-called "scientific theories" that don't include God.

Atheists must necessarily believe that given billions of years, starting from rocks, eventually through purely chemical processes, then life accidentally started. Then came bacteria, and from bacteria life kept getting more and more complicated until humans came about.

Common Sense pretty much would tell you that life didn't come from rocks no matter how long you waited, even billions upon billions of years.

If I tell you that there is absolutely nothing in a certain place, then suddenly for no reason there was a huge explosion and after that there were huge stars and planets everywhere, what would you say? "That doesn't make any sense." Precisely. If there was nothing, what exploded? And why?

At the same time as the Big Bang exploded and produced gigantic amounts of matter, it also produced universal laws of physics and chemistry. It also produced time and space. Does that make sense?

161

How about this? There was a huge explosion, then after a while, tiny particles began to move closer together. Eventually they turned into rocks, which became huge. Then they started to spin and they got hotter and hotter. "That doesn't make any sense." You're right. Our experience tells us that after an explosion, matter is far apart and does not come back together on its own.

There are a lot of stars in the Universe, at least 11 trillion for every person on earth. Starting from Nothing, Nothing exploded and created huge amounts of dust which then violated physical and chemical laws by coming together trillions upon trillions of times to make stars out of the dust. Sorry, this doesn't make sense.

Where did the energy for that explosion come from? It was an extreme amount of energy to be sure. We were taught in school that energy is "neither created nor destroyed, it just changes forms". Does that make sense...energy from no energy?

By the way, scientists say that the Big Bang produced ONLY the elements of Hydrogen, Helium, and maybe Lithium in the first 10 seconds to 20 minutes. [2] and [3] Somehow those 2 or 3 elements eventually became all of the 100 plus other elements of the Periodic Table all by themselves in a process taking tens of thousands of years. I'm having trouble. This is not making sense.

You've probably heard that scientists do not believe in "Spontaneous Generation," the concept that life can spring up from non-life. Aristotle synthesized the concept and it was believed for 2,000 years. [4] and [5] Atheists must necessarily believe in Spontaneous Generation. Clearly there was no life at one time and now there is. If it wasn't spontaneously generated, then where did it come from? Common Sense is against spontaneous generation.

Or how about the idea that if you take lots of different rocks and rain on them for a long time until you have soup, out of the soup comes life. The goo became you. This violates the principle that all particles in water become dispersed, not organized. Probably many other laws are violated as well.

So what if you zap the soup with a lightning bolt? Our Common Sense will tell us that the energy added from a lightning bolt creates more chaos, not complex order. Have you ever seen a tree that was hit by lightning? Adding energy creates an explosion, not life. (See Chapter 41 on the First Living Cell.)

Do you believe that over a long, long time everything got more complex all by itself? Doesn't make any sense to me. Over time everything rusts, decays, or falls apart.

Do you believe that adding energy in the form of sunlight will cause more complexity and organization? That doesn't make any sense. Adding random energy actually hastens decay. Think about leaving your tools or car out in the yard for many years. What's going to happen?

Only by adding energy PLUS adding intelligence can you create something better organized.

Intelligent scientists trying for 40 years could not mutate a fruit fly into anything else but a fruit fly. Do you believe if given enough time that it could randomly happen WITHOUT intelligence? Doesn't make any sense. (Check out Chapter 27, The Truth About Mutation)

If I told you, "My house built itself over thousands and thousands of years. There was no creator. It happened slowly and gradually, one small piece at a time." You didn't see what happened over thousands of years and you're not a scientist, so how do you know the truth? A house is not all that complicated, especially when compared to a human body, so maybe "It could have happened." The odds are against it, but it could have happened. The house got there somehow, obviously because it's there. I'm sorry, folks, no. It didn't just happen. Even billions of years is never enough time for my house to build itself. It had to have a creator.

Here's my point. I'm not denying that the Big Bang happened. But I am denying that it could have happened without God. Common Sense will also tell you that every step of the way from the Big Bang to human beings, adding more and more complexity, going against the laws of chemistry and physics, would never have happened UNLESS there is an outside force with intelligence acting on the system.

Atheists might say we are really, really lucky to be here. We won the Cosmic Lottery by accident. We beat the odds. It was one in a million chance, but it happened. Let me ask one final question for your Common Sense. If the odds are 1 in a million (actually millions times millions) that life came about accidentally, what is the explanation that accounts for the reverse odds?

There seem to be just two choices, namely (A) life came about accidentally from materialistic causes or (B) it didn't. If the odds are one in a million that proposition A is correct, then obviously the odds are 999,999 in a million that proposition B is correct.

That proposition is that life was designed and came from an intelligent source. That's common sense. And that's proof there must be God.

Chapter #63 Skin

Before you ever came out of your mother's womb, you had developed a fully functioning and amazing organ covering your entire body. It is called skin and it accomplishes at least six functions that keep you alive. Without any one of these functions not one of our ancestors would have survived.

Is it even possible to imagine how skin could have evolved in a slow and gradual process taking thousands of generations? If human ancestors evolved from fish with scales, then those scales had to become skin. Looking at skin for a little while in this chapter should convince you that scales did not turn into skin in a godless process.

The following functions of skin are all necessary for us to survive. Just try to imagine how any one of them could have evolved one at a time over many generations? [1]

Barrier to water and nutrient loss. Our skin actually keeps us from losing moisture to the air and anything that we touch such as our clothes. It also keeps nutrients in that the cells could lose if exposed.

Healing. Skin has amazing immunization and healing functions. It protects us from permanent damage and blood loss. (See Chapter 70 on Healing.)

Protection against pathogens. Our skin prevents bacteria and viruses from entering our bodies. The top layer of our skin is actually dead cells which are constantly sloughing off.

Barrier to toxins and harmful chemicals. Our skin protects us from most harmful chemicals in our environment, shielding us against any damaging effects of what we touch or what touches us.

Shield and protection against damage. It is the first line of defense against injuries.

Organ for excretion of salts, urea, and toxins. Our skin actually releases a number of toxins for us. It secretes sweat to keep us cool and lubricate the skin.

Temperature regulation. Our skin helps regulate our body temperature. When we get too hot, it allows blood closer to the surface to give off heat and sweat glands release fluids to cool us through evaporation. When we get too cold, blood vessels contract to keep blood away from the surface. Muscles in the skin contract so that we shiver in order to generate heat.

Are you remembering to try to imagine how these functions could "evolve" over many generations?

Blood pressure regulation. Mechanisms in our skin increase or decrease the flow of blood in capillaries to regulate our blood pressure.

Sense of touch and pain. Everywhere on the surface of our skin we can experience touch. Imagine trying to live without being able to feel anything. We are extremely sensitive to our environment, from the lightest touch of the spring breeze to the heavy thud of a hammer on our thumbnail. (See Chapter 87 on Pain.)

Sense of hot and cold. What if you put your hand on a hot stove and couldn't feel it? What if you took a hot shower but couldn't tell how hot it was? What if you couldn't tell if it was a cold day or a hot day?

Friction grip. Our skin on our palms and fingertips is specially designed with thicker skin and ridges so that we can grab things and hold onto them. What if your glass of milk kept slipping out of your hand?

Identification. Not only your fingerprints are unique and useful for identification, but your face is totally unique because of your skin. Take the skin off our faces and we'd all look pretty much the same.

Synthesizes Vitamin D. We all need Vitamin D to survive. Our skin makes that for us when we get enough sunlight.

I recently watched a DVD of a scientist, Dr. David Menton [2], who talked for two hours just about details of the skin. He hardly "scratched the surface" as they say. It was totally amazing and way beyond what I want to cover in this chapter. All of the above functions are very, very complicated processes involving very specialized cells in the skin. How anyone could imagine, let alone believe, that this all came about by accident is dumbfounding to me.

Let's just talk about hair for a minute, as just one example of the complexity of different aspects in the skin. When you are born, you already have every hair follicle you will ever have. There are 3 types of hair on your body and the hair follicles are able to change themselves so that they can grow each of the different types of hair.

Lanugo hair is the type you have in the womb. It falls out before you are born.

Vellus hair is short, fine, light-colored, and barely noticeable hair that develops on most of a person's body from his/her childhood. It grows to a certain length and then stops. Eventually a totally new hair starts to grow underneath and the old hair falls out. Most of our body is covered with this type of hair as well as most animal bodies, although it is darker on animals.

Terminal hairs are thick, long, and dark. This is the kind that keeps growing continuously like on your head and in a man's beard. Humans are almost the only animal that has this type of hair. Poodles are one of the very few other animals that have it.

Each hair follicle on your body has a small muscle attached to it. (Refer to Chapter 62, Muscles. Nobody knows how muscles could have "evolved". Well, they didn't.) So for example, if you get a chill, that muscle will get a signal from a nerve and make the attached hair stand up. If evolution were true, how does this make sense?

Also, each hair has a nerve connected to it that connects the hair to your brain. So when the wind blows your hair, you feel it because it registers in your brain. I'm sure you've noticed the wind blowing even though it is invisible. This is certainly a wonderful ability to have which makes us very sensitive to the people and the world around us.

Hair follicles have sebaceous glands [3] which secrete oils which lubricate and waterproof the skin. Specialized sebaceous glands secrete tears to help lubricate our eyes. Our hands and feet do not have these, which is a nice design feature so we don't slide all over the place or lose our grip. There are a number of different types of sebaceous glands in different areas of the body. Very, very interesting if you want to look it up.

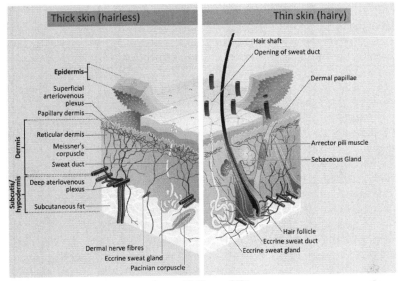

Image 12. Types of Skin.

Another amazing fact about our hair is that in some specific areas of our body there is a sweat gland which is attached to the hair follicles in that area. For example, when your body gets overheated, sweat comes out of the hair follicles in your arm pits, which helps cool you down quicker. Only one other animal sweats like humans, the horse. No evolutionist believes that we evolved from horses or that horses evolved from people, so how can they explain that we both have this amazingly complicated function in our skin. What are the odds that totally unrelated species could develop this same complicated mechanism in their skin?

Each hair follicle is also connected to arteries and veins to supply oxygen and nourishment and also to carry away wastes. Without these incredibly complex connections for blood, each hair could not survive.

Did you ever see a woman in the circus hanging by her hair and wonder why it doesn't pull out and she falls? This is because each hair has a sheath around it which has a zigzag or ratchet pattern that is exactly matched by the surrounding hair follicle. It holds the hair in sort of like Velcro. But amazingly the hair can still grow.

OK, so I have just talked about hair so far and it's just a very small proportion of what's in your skin. But this chapter is getting pretty long so let me finish up quickly, but strongly note that the following, equally amazing properties of skin could all be talked about just as much as hair.

Our skin is composed of 3 layers: epidermis, dermis, and hypodermis. The very outermost layer, the epidermis, is composed of many layers of only dead cells. They are arranged in a complicated interlocking pattern like patio tiles. There are even small hook-like structures keeping them attached to each other. When a top layer of cells falls off or gets rubbed off, it gets replaced from the bottom. A layer of cells dies in the dermis and all the cells move up toward the surface. What an amazing design for replenishing the skin!

Think how amazing this is. As cells are lost on the surface, how do the cells below know to die in just the exact quantity to replace the lost cells? If your skin did not have this ability, then maybe too many dead cells would build up and clog the surface. Or maybe too few cells would be produced and all your epidermis would be rubbed off exposing the dermis where all the blood vessels and nerve endings reside.

That layer of dead cells, the epidermis, is about the thickness of Saran Wrap and yet it is totally essential to your survival. It holds in moisture so you don't dry out. It keeps toxins and chemicals out along with bacteria and viruses.

Blood is carried into every tiny square millimeter of your skin by an incredible network of capillaries. Look at a picture sometime of the capillaries in your skin. There is no way this came about by random incremental changes.

Your skin has millions of nerve endings everywhere. These are all connected to your brain and sending signals about your environment. Is it hot or cold? Are you being touched lightly or strongly? They can tell the texture of substances, whether they are soft or abrasive.

There are actually two types of skin. "Thick skin" is on your palms and feet. It is hairless but contains specialized nerve ending so it is much more sensitive to touch. "Thin skin" is everywhere else and contains hair.

Your palms and fingers have more specialized touch sensitive nerve endings. The name for the ending of those nerves is Meissner's Corpuscle. [4] They are responsible for sensitivity to very slight touch. How amazing that just where you need it the most, your skin provides super sensitivity. Try to imagine if your palms and fingertips were not as sensitive as they are. Read up on this type of corpuscle and how it works and tell me this is not a miracle.

You know what pain is. Do you know how miraculous it is that you can feel it? Everywhere in your skin are specialized free nerve endings called 'nociceptors' or 'pain receptors' that only respond to tissue damage.

"In nociception, intense chemical (e.g., chilli powder in the eyes), mechanical (e.g., cutting, crushing) or thermal (heat and cold) stimulation of sensory nerve cells called nociceptors produces a signal that travels along a chain of nerve fibers via the spinal cord to the brain. Nociception triggers a variety of physiological and behavioral responses and may also result in a subjective experience of pain in sentient beings." [5]

Notice that nociceptors have a special connection to the brain and even can trigger "automatic" muscle reactions to pain themselves, not initiated by the brain. Think about your "reflexes" and how quickly you pull your hand off of a hot stove.

This is just the proverbial "tip of the iceberg" about how fantastic your skin is.

Imagine that you could not experience physical pain from your skin. You would never know if you had damaged any part of your body.

The skin on your face is what makes you look like you. We would all pretty much look alike without our skin. In fact the skin on your face has lots of embedded muscles whose sole purpose is to outwardly express your inner emotions. No other animals have anything like it.

All of us actually have the same color of skin. It is only because of different amounts of a chemical called melanin released in our skin that makes some skin black, brown, yellow, or red, or whatever. This too is an amazing process.

The idea that all these functions of our skin were not designed by a superior intelligence but happened accidentally over a few million years is impossible. I have only been describing the incredible functionality of human skin. What about all the other animals that have skin as well? Some skin allows their owners to live in amazing environments, very, very cold or hot, wet or dry places. There are probably as many different types of skin as there animals. This multiplies the probability against evolution exponentially. The only thing that makes rational sense is that there must be a master intelligent designer.

There must be God.

Chapter #64 Missing Links

I'm sure you have heard of the term "Missing Link" and understand that it refers to missing fossils in the fossil record that would show the transitional stages between certain species according to the Theory of Evolution. The theory predicts which species are the ancestors of other species and that there was a slow and gradual transition with many intermediate generations.

Did you ever stop to think deeply about how many Missing Links there truly must be? Even just a rough guess? If you look at the imaginative drawings made by evolutionists, you might suppose that there are just one or two Missing Links. But that could not be further from the truth. I intend to show you in this chapter that there would necessarily be billions of Missing Links if evolution were true. Thus it isn't true and God is behind the creation of each species.

There are so many countless Missing Links that honest scientists should have discarded the Theory of Evolution a hundred years ago for that reason alone. But they have clung to a God denying ideology while still claiming to be scientific against all the evidence.

I suggest you refer to the Wikipedia page of Missing Links which they call Transitional Fossils. [1] Many of the so-called missing links are just drawings. Get that? There is no proof they existed. There is no fossil. How could an honest scientist call a drawing a "transitional fossil" if it has never been found?

A drawing is not a fossil and it certainly is not a missing link and it is not scientific. They base these drawings mostly on their imaginations because all they have are a few bones and no complete skeletons. Go down the page of so-called missing links, take out the illustrations, and then count how many are incomplete, inconclusive, speculative, or controversial. That is not evidence and it is not good science.

Let's take a simple example of "evolving" from a monkey foot to a man's foot. Evolution is supposed to take place by slow gradual mutations over many generations and Natural Selection acts on the results to weed out the new species or feature that is "fittest". I previously wrote chapters on the Truth about Mutation (#27) and Natural Selection (#35) and showed these processes are a FAIL and will not work. But let's just suppose for the sake of this chapter that they did work as theorized. What would you get? I contend there would have to be millions upon millions of fossils we don't have and therefore these are Missing Links. There are just too many Missing Links everywhere. We can't call evolution a reasonable theory.

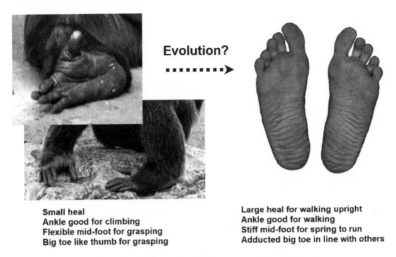

Evolution?

........▶

Small heal
Ankle good for climbing
Flexible mid-foot for grasping
Big toe like thumb for grasping

Large heal for walking upright
Ankle good for walking
Stiff mid-foot for spring to run
Adducted big toe in line with others

Image 13. Changes from Chimpanzee to Human Feet.
©2016 Jim Stephens

Using a slow and gradual transition, exactly how many intermediate foot shapes are needed to get from an ape foot to a human foot? The exact number is certainly higher than 10 or 20, don't you think? Note that the shape of the feet are different. The toes are different (especially the big toe). The heels are different. And the ankle has to have changed a lot because a human walks upright. For each small change in the foot according to evolution theory there was a living being with that type of foot who produced descendants. It seems there would necessarily have been a male and a female at each incremental stage. Also, very likely, there had to be more than one generation for each small change. Every one of those living beings with a transitional foot could have been fossilized like any ape or human that did get fossilized. So where are they? None have been found. Therefore, they must all be considered Missing Links, right?

Just considering the foot alone, there have to be many generations of Missing Links. Now think about other parts of the ape body transitioning to the human body. Consider the pelvis. [2] and [3] There are many, many intermediate stages to transition through in the pelvic area to be able to walk upright. This is also true for the neck. There are major changes to the skull, the chest, the arms, the hands, the spine, and just about every other part. For an ape ancestor body to be modified into that of a human, there are going to be thousands upon thousands of changes. Therefore, there are thousands upon thousands of generations of Missing Links, not just one or two individuals.

Here's another equally important point to consider. According to evolution, mutation produces many variations of a given species and then Natural Selection weeds out the fittest one to survive. Think about how many variations existed but did not advance as the "chosen" one. Random mutation by definition must have produced hundreds if not thousands of "mistakes" or "mutants" that lived and died but were not on the direct line from ape to human. These beings supposedly lived and died but they were not part of the "fittest" which were selected by natural selection and eventually resulted in humans.

All those mutants lived. Maybe they didn't reproduce much, but they could have been fossilized. Where are they in the fossil record? These beings are all Missing Links also. So how many more Missing Links should be added to our estimate? Well, we surely have to assume that for every mutation that "got it right," the Theory of Evolution predicts that many, many would have "got it wrong" and thus have died out.

So for each and every direct-line transitional step (Missing Link) from apes to humans, there must have been tens or hundreds of mutations off the direct line. These beings were just as likely to have been fossilized just like the apes or men that did get fossilized. Let's call these Missing NON-Links. They are definitely missing, but they are not on the "direct chain or lineage" from apes to humans. A wild guess would be that there are thousands upon thousands of these Missing NON-Links, just going from apes to humans, which is a short distance on the so-called evolutionary "tree of life".

So far I have talked about Missing Links and Missing Non-Links between apes and humans. But evolution supposedly explains the transition from every species to every other species. Because there are something like 800,000 species, we have to conclude that there are hundreds or thousands of Missing Links and Missing Non-Links for every one of those other species of plants, insects, birds, fish, amphibians, mammals, etc. Otherwise evolution is not true.

How many Missing Links are there? I originally said billions. Can you see where I got that estimate?

Darwin thought the problem of Missing Links would be solved once they discovered more and better fossils. But his problem has only gotten worse. Of all the known fossils today, 99.9% of them have been discovered SINCE Darwin. In other words, we have 1,000 times more fossils today than at Darwin's time. The more fossils that are discovered and the better preserved they are, the less Darwin's theory is supported. Missing Links are not being found. Claims of Missing Links exist but in a tiny fraction of the number compared to predictions.

Another problem concerning Missing Links is that there have been many fakes. Unscrupulous scientists wanting fame and fortune have trumpeted their "discoveries" of the Missing Link to prove evolution. Either they were unscrupulous frauds or else they had to be totally incompetent, which is less likely.

> "Professor Reiner Protsch vn Zieten lied about the age of Neanderthal skulls and artifacts for 30 years. A university panel exposed his frauds and he resigned February, 2005. Protsch had dated the "Bischof-Speyer" skeleton at 21,300 years but testing at Oxford showed them to be 3,300 years old." [4]

As an example, the **Nebraska Man** was "reconstructed" from a single tooth. In the end it was discovered to be the tooth of an extinct pig.

The Piltdown Man was falsified with a human skull and an apelike jaw. [5]

Heidelberg Man has long been controversial, coming under a lot of skepticism more recently. [6]

Peking Man was pieced together from a collection of bones and fragments.

> "From 1921 to 1966, unearthed Peking Man fossils were six nearly complete crania or skullcaps, 19 large fragments of skulls, numerous small fragments of skulls, 15 incomplete mandibles, 157 isolated teeth, three pieces of humerus, one clavicular, one lunate, and a tibia." [7]

Here's another argument that should be considered. Suppose someone someday does claim to have dug up another Missing Link. How can they prove it is our ancestor? All you have are some bones. If I went to a cemetery and dug up some bones, what could be proven from looking at those bones? We could know if it was human, if it was a male or female, its size and approximate weight. We could guess at its age and maybe a bunch of other things. But how do you know he/she had any children? You could get DNA off of real bones, but not off of a fossil. You don't know if this was the ancestor of anybody. You don't know if their descendants reproduced. Could a fossil woman in Africa really be the great-great grandmother of a fossil woman in China?

All of the so-called Missing Links from apes to humans really are only pieces of a skeleton. Look at pictures of the famous "Lucy" skeleton. Contrast any picture of the actual bones that exist with the drawing you'll see that was created from someone's imagination. There is no full skeleton. Lucy had no hands or foot bones, but artists just draw human hands and feet anyway.

One individual can't be our ancestor because there had to be male and female and many generations. There should be a whole lot of individuals in a particular group of beings, even whole tribes for any evolution to feasibly work. One very isolated individual can't logically be an ancestor.

If all scientists have are pieces of a skeleton, how do you know for sure what the rest of it looked like? How do they know all the pieces belong to the same individual being? They are only guessing. And we know we can't trust that because of all the hoaxes that have already be passed off as real. If these pieces were really human fragments and they truly survived for millions of years, how come there are not thousands of other pieces that also survived those millions of years.

The earth should be covered with human remains and Missing Links. Bones found in England, China, and Indonesia are supposedly millions of years old. However, they were found in damp earth, which is scientifically controversial because they should have decayed.

Look at real human skulls from various races. They are very different, yet they are all human. Can you tell if one is the ancestor of another one? Impossible.

Something else, as well, evolutionists are guilty of confusing differentiation within a species with transition between two different species. In the Wikipedia article already mentioned the writers make the mistake of categorizing as Transitional Fossils, fossils that are clearly not intermediates between two different species. They are simply developments within the same species.

Horses have changed over time. Dogs have changed over time, as have most species. But this is NOT evolution between species. No creation scientist or proponent of Intelligent Design denies that there has been differentiation within species. Horses have changed. That's undeniable. But what is denied is that one species becomes another species, which is the essence of the Theory of Evolution. Apes are not the ancestors of humans.

If you take out the faked Missing Links and then the controversial ones between apes and humans, all you really have left are apes and humans with nothing in between but someone's imagination.

Image 14. All Links are Missing.
© 2016 Nari Hanna

The Theory of Evolution has so many "holes" in it (to coin a phrase) that it should have been debunked 100 years ago. In claiming to follow the "evidence" they have refused to accept the very obvious fact that millions of fossils that should be there are not anywhere to be found. And they have denied its implications.

One final point. Let's imagine way, way in the future that you go to a fossil bed and dig up a whole lot of rather simple fossils. Then you arrange them in an order that makes sense to you, putting them into a rational sequence. You find a whole series of antique cars, old cars, and modern cars and you put them in order. Or maybe you find a whole bunch of telephones to put in order from old dial up phones, to push button phones, to cordless phones, to cell phones.

What is the meaning of the sequences? Did evolution take place? The objects in the sequences are much, much less complicated than living animals. However, absolutely no respected scientist would claim that these rather simple series of devices could have evolved without the input of higher intelligence. Therefore, it makes no rational, scientific, or even logical sense for someone to decide that there was no intelligence involved in the development of all the former beings which became the actual historical fossils that we have today.

There must be God.

Chapter #65 Mitochondrial Eve and Y-Chromosome Adam

Genetic scientists seem to be in general agreement that we are all descendants of one woman and one man. This research was fairly recent, starting about 1978. They, of course, do not believe in the creation story of Adam and Eve in the Bible, but their conclusions are getting closer and closer.

In case you have not heard about this, it makes very interesting reading. But I think it raises a number of profound challenges to the Theory of Evolution.

The scientists base the above conclusions on the known facts of human reproduction, specifically on properties of the sperm and egg.

Mitochondrial Eve

What are mitochondria? They are membrane-bound organelles found in the cells of all plants, animals, fungi, and many other forms of life.

> "Mitochondria have been described as 'the powerhouse of the cell' because they generate most of the cell's supply of adenosine triphosphate (ATP), used as a source of chemical energy." [1]

Every person inherits his or her mitochondria for every cell in their body exclusively from their mother. The father contributes only a sperm cell to the developing fetus. But a sperm has only a small amount of mitochondria in the tail that gets used up in propulsion or else destroyed after fertilizing the egg.

Researchers sampled the DNA from the mitochondria in 147 people from all the major racial groups of the world. From this DNA they concluded that we all descended from a single woman. They think she must have lived between 99,000 and about 200,000 years ago in Africa. [2] It's a theory and has its opponents, but it has gained a lot of support. The theory is interesting, but a little complicated. I encourage you to read up on it if you would like to. Scientists believe there were other women alive at the same time, but their line of descendants died out or does not include all living humans today.

This common female ancestor of all anatomically modern humans alive today was nicknamed "Mitochondrial Eve".

Y-Chromosome Adam

What is the Y-Chromosome? Probably you learned about it in school.

"The Y chromosome is one of two sex chromosomes (allosomes) in mammals, including humans, and many other animals. The other is the X chromosome. Y is the sex-determining chromosome in many species, since it is the presence or absence of Y that determines the male or female sex of offspring produced in sexual reproduction." [3]

Females do not have a Y-Chromosome in their cells. Only males inherit Y-Chromosomes and they always come from the father only. Therefore researchers can study the Y-chromosomes of men all over the world and can then theorize that all men are related and in fact descended from one man long ago. This is based on certain changes to the DNA in the Y-Chromosomes. By theorizing about the rate of mutations or types of changes to the DNA itself, they can make predictions about a common male ancestor. It is believed that many generations ago the ancestor of all men came from the same tribe, and finally a single great-great-......-great-grandfather.

The conclusion is this, that we are all descendants of one male ancestor and he has received the nickname of "Y-Chromosome Adam". [4] He lived by various estimates between 120,000 and 338,000 years ago. And by analyzing the divergence of DNA in earthly populations, it was determined that he also likely lived in Africa.

This is a nice coincidence because most religious groups also believe that all humans are descendants from one man and one woman. Scientists have not concluded that they mated with each other, but they do put them in Africa and within a few thousand years of each other. Religious people believe that God miraculously created the first man and woman. Secularists and evolutionists believe that there were many other humans around at the same time as Mitochondrial Eve or Y-Chromosome Adam, but their lineages did not result in an unbroken line to all humans alive today.

So let's now look at some of the contradictions and challenges that the evolutionists have to deal with.

First off, scientists say that roughly 200,000 years ago (plus or minus 100K) a male and a female existed that were anatomically JUST LIKE US. Over the 200,000 years until today, although there have been mutations in their genes, they are still humans just like us.

This means there has been no evolution or species change for 200,000 years. There has been no evolving since that couple. There is no slow and gradual change that Darwin predicted for the last 200,000 years! Think about that for a minute. If there has been no observable change in the last 200,000 years, how can we be so sure that there was any change the previous 200,000 years? Or how about the 200,000 years before that? If there has been no evidence in genetic research of evolution in 200,000 years, why assume evolution is true at all? They are building their case on faith, aren't they?

Secondly, 200,000 years is a long time without significant change. The human body is extremely complicated and the time frame is just too short for evolution to be true. Current scientific belief is that humans diverged from apes about 5 to 7,000,000 years ago.

> "A new study of genes in humans and chimpanzees pins down with greater accuracy when the two species split from one. The evolutionary divergence occurred between 5 million and 7 million years ago, an estimate that improves on the previous range of 3 million to 13 million years in the past. Modern chimps are the closest animal relative to humans." [5]

There are some very major changes that had to take place in the body structure of apes to turn them into humans. Remember also that both female humans and male humans had to evolve from ape-like creatures. Presumably both the male and the female had to evolve thousands of similar changes at very nearly same time for Natural Selection to be working. Imagine if women evolved but men didn't. Then the men would still walk around and be shaped like chimpanzees.

Very little if anything has actually changed in human bodies in the last 200,000 years according to genetic scientists. Where is the slow and gradual change predicted by Darwin? 5 million is only 25 times 200,000. If almost nothing changes in 200,000 years, then how could there be millions of dramatic changes in the previous 4,800,000?

It doesn't make sense. How could there be rapid change from an ape shape to a human shape and then no change? The Theory of Evolution predicts slow and gradual change. Scientists say there is no difference between humans today and 200,000 years ago. In order to get humans from monkeys in 4,800,000 years there has to be a lot of rapid changes and that violates the Theory of Evolution.

Thirdly, genetic scientists are accepting that we all are descendants of one man and one woman. This makes sense because it's not likely that mutation could have produced identical advances or genetic advantages in two different and distinct lineages, nor in very distant locations. All of us have 3 billion codes in our DNA makeup, so random mutation will never produce the same mutated human beings in two different locations.

But if we are all descendants of one male and one female, how could a supposed evolutionary change take place in one individual and then that new trait be spread throughout the whole population of humans? The only way that can work is if all descendants WITHOUT the new trait die off and only descendants WITH the new trait survive. Therefore, a new common ancestor would be needed every time a new trait emerged. And it would take not just a new Eve, but it would presumably require a new Adam for each change.

Let's try to think of how we humans could evolve from today. Then I think you'll see this is impossible. I would maintain that it would be equally impossible to have happened in all the populations in the past.

Let's just suppose that someone was born who had mutated hugely in one generation (not the Darwinian slow and gradual) so that this person would clearly be the fittest to survive. (Think of the X-Men movie.) Just to pick an example, let's say this person has a super-Einstein brain. You can make up your own mutated trait if you like for your own example to imagine.

Let's call him Xavier (X-Men again) for reference purposes. (Also we could use She-xavier if you prefer an example using women.) Our goal is that all human beings at some point in the future have this new mutated trait, super-Einstein brain. That would mean that Xavier must become the ancestor at some point in the distant future of all the humans alive on the planet. Those without the new trait (super-brain) must become extinct. What would have to happen? How long would it take?

This mutated characteristic (super-Einstein brain) would have to able to be passed on to Xavier's children. Not all mutations can be inherited so the odds are challenging. Also Xavier would have to somehow marry a spouse who is compatible with his mutation being inherited. He might not mate at all of course. Not all spouses would necessarily reproduce the mutated trait with him even if they mated. The odds of all this are not good. But let's keep going. Suppose all of their children had super-brains. Still they would also have to intermarry with "normal" humans without super-brains. There aren't any other humans with the super-brains. The genes for super-brains would have to be dominant or they would die out quickly.

There are 7 billion people in the world having children. How long would it take, if ever, before all people in the world would have a super-brain? That would mean that all people were descendants of Xavier.

We would also have to get to the point that all children being born would have super-brains and the genes for non-super-brains are totally gone from the gene pool. Otherwise, some children might be from parents that still carried the non-super-brain genes and the result could be that their children might have ordinary brains.

179

One other major problem is that the human race is spread all over the globe and onto every tiny island. If the mutation occurred to Xavier in Africa say, how could it possibly spread all over the globe to all the other human groups?

This seems so absurdly complicated to me that it is impossible. And this is just for one change. If we came from monkeys, we had to go through thousands of changes if not millions. (Read Chapter #12, Chimpanzees, for more information on the millions of DNA differences between apes and humans.)

Fourthly, the idea behind Natural Selection and Survival of the Fittest is that EACH time there is an advance, then it somehow becomes universal among all members of that species in later generations. So for every small advance through the evolution process, and there have been thousands of them, there would have to be an Xavier and a She-xavier to start the species all over again with the new trait.

The corollary of course is that all the other members of the species without the new advantage are going to die out and leave no descendants. Once there are millions of members of a species, how could there be continuing evolutionary changes that spread to the entire population and don't leave behind a single individual? We know that the DNA of every individual of a species is basically identical. Evolutionists want you to believe that the DNA of some advantageous mutation can be spread exactly as it is to the DNA of every individual in a species at some point in the future. But think about it practically.

If mutations were that powerful (which they aren't), there would be total chaos in the DNA of every species. Millions of individuals would mean millions of mutations all vying to change the DNA of the whole species.

Fifthly, as we can see it becomes impossible to explain how such a process (mutated super-Einstein brains) could evolve a new human race. However, evolution has a tremendously bigger problem. Evolution is supposed to apply to every other one of the 800,000 species (insects, birds, fish, plants, animals, and even bacteria). Because evolution works magically only when there is reproduction, therefore new traits have to start with an original male and female in every case. So once any significant change takes place, you would have to start all over again with another original male and female who mate with each other or at least somehow become a common ancestor of the whole species later on.

There are so many major changes between species that this process of starting over with a new couple would have to be repeated hundreds and hundreds and hundreds of times. (See Missing Links, Chapter #64) All birds, fish, animals, and all living beings would have to evolve by this process, not some magic. That doesn't make sense. There is not enough time in history. There is no such fossil record.

The only theory that is workable is that God created each species, a male and female, as unique originals at a point in time and from there came many variations within the species but not between species.

There must be God.

Chapter #66 Arrowheads and Stone Bowls

I'm sure you must know what arrowheads are, right? But have you ever thought deeply about the implications of arrowheads. If you find a rock somewhere and you get all excited proclaiming it is an arrowhead, what are you really saying?

What you have is materially only a rock, but it has a particular shape which you think means it is something more. You believe that the current shape is "not natural," i.e. it could not exist accidentally. You believe without a doubt that an intelligent being, certainly a human being not a chimpanzee intellect, made that rock into that shape.

Why do we think like that?

Is it that you have faith that Nature does not create arrowheads? Or do you know it's a fact, a scientific truth, that Nature does not create arrowheads?

How about another example, ancient stone bowls? Probably you believe that Nature does not make and cannot make those bowls either. It takes a being with intelligence to create even such a simple bowl.

Evolutionists believe that rocks (given enough time) became human beings without the intervention of any intelligence. They believe rocks became a primordial soup and later that came alive, and then it eventually became people.

If rocks can't even become arrowheads or bowls without intelligence acting on them, then evolution cannot be true. It's all faith, not fact. Some intelligent being must exist that caused it. Even though we cannot see the actual intelligent being who created an arrowhead, we believe that he or she absolutely existed based on the evidence of the existence of only the arrowhead.

What is the nature of that evidence? There are basically two aspects, order and purpose. We see an order that is not found in Nature even though nature is orderly. We also recognize a design and a purpose in the arrowhead. The purpose is invisible, but nonetheless it is very real. The purpose clearly does not emerge from the physical object itself but from the designer of the object.

When there is purpose and design, there is a designer.

There must be God.

Chapter #67 Blueprints for the Empire State Building

I'm sure you know what blueprints are and have seen them from time to time. Even a simple building takes pages and pages of blueprints for every aspect of the construction.

For this chapter I want to talk about the Empire State Building in New York City and think about its blueprints. Then I want to compare that building to the human body.

No sane person would ever assert that the Empire State Building happened by accident. It clearly was designed. Just imagine all the blueprints that must have been required in order to construct that building. Floor by floor, it was built from a hole in the ground up. There must have been thousands and thousands of pages.

Tremendous planning and organization were involved. They had to have plans for putting in the duct work to circulate the air for people to breathe. They needed a system for air conditioning in summer and heating in winter for every floor. They had to supply water for drinking and plumbing pipes for toilets and sinks on every level. They had to run electrical wires for lighting and power. They needed telephone lines throughout. They needed systems for trash removal, elevators and stairs for people to move up and down. There had to be freight elevators for bringing in desks, furniture, and machinery. It was tremendously complicated.

Now ask yourself, which is more complicated, the Empire State Building or the human body.

The human body has similar systems but even more complicated. The body has lungs for breathing, a water distribution system, a plumbing system, a circulation system for nutrients, a nerve system for communication, a heating and cooling system, a waste disposal system, and many others. It has all the component systems of the Empire State Building and then many more.

I'm sure you've noticed that the Empire State Building does not move around, but the human body can. The Empire State Building does not eat food and digest it. Its energy source is electricity from the outside.

Another thing, the Empire State Building does not grow. It didn't start off as a little Empire State Building and grow bigger and bigger each year until it reached its current height of 1,250 feet. The human body grows and changes, so if blueprints were to be made for a human body, there would have to be blueprints for the newborn size, a one year old size, a two year old size, all the way up to adult size.

Here's another big difference. The Empire State Building cannot reproduce. It can't have babies. Think about that. How complicated would the blueprints have to be for a reproductive system? Would we have to have male and female buildings?

If the Empire State Building absolutely could not come into existence without having really intelligent designers, even if you wait billions upon billions of years, there is no conceivable way that the human body could have come into existence without an intelligent designer.

There must be God.

Chapter #68 Symmetry

In this Proof for God, let's take a look at "Symmetry" and think about all the symmetry in the world and whether or not it could have come about by randomness.

The dictionary definition of Symmetry is "the correspondence in size, form, and arrangement of parts on opposite sides of a plane, line, or point; regularity of form or arrangement in terms of like, reciprocal, or corresponding parts." [1]

Everywhere you look, there is symmetry. The vast majority of things created by humans (intelligent beings) contain symmetry. Our vehicles, our furniture, our art, even our foods usually contain symmetry. Go into any type of retail store you can find and walk up and down the aisles and calculate the percentage of items that exhibit symmetry. It's clearly a very high percentage.

Nature too is full of symmetry. Almost every animal, bird, fish, insect, and even plant that I can think of contains symmetry.

You have two eyes, two ears, two nostrils, symmetrical teeth, two arms, two hands, two legs, two feet, and on and on. Even you have a lot of symmetry inside your body under your skin. All the way down to the microscopic level of the chemicals in your body, there is symmetry.

So here's the big question, how could all of this totally dominant and overwhelming amount of symmetry come about if the original cause is random mutation. Start with something like an ameba in your mind and then imagine randomly adding appendages like arms or legs. The odds are very, very small that this process would produce any symmetry. That's by the definition of "random".

Now imagine the odds of getting exactly two arms in exactly symmetrical locations on both sides of the body. The odds are huge against getting exactly the two arms, but now you have to get two fully symmetrical hands at the end of those arms. Then you have to get two legs in symmetrical positions. That multiplies the odds exponentially. But we are just barely beginning. We still have to get two symmetrical eyes, and ears, and on and on. For each new symmetrical pair, multiply the odds exponentially higher.

The odds are impossibly high for getting just one eye. (See Chapter #45 The Eye) But in order to get two eyes randomly in exactly symmetrical positions on your face is astronomically more difficult. Why not imagine an eye randomly growing on the palm of one of your hands? Why couldn't that happen within the principles of the Theory of Evolution? If Natural Selection were really in operation that might just be a more ideal location than on your face.

Evolution says everything developed gradually over great lengths of time. Then that must mean that one eye grew before the second eye grew, right? Two eyes (two arms, whatever) could not have suddenly appeared simultaneously because that is not slow and gradual.

Why not grow three or four arms? Wouldn't that allow us to survive better? Why have arms just on the sides? Why not have an arm in the front and an arm in the back too?

Some animals ended up with exactly four legs (no arms and hands). Think about the odds of growing one leg, then a second leg, a third leg, and finally a fourth leg over many generations. Slow and gradual would mean one leg at a time and then we would have to wait at least a generation or two (or a hundred) before we could grow another leg. You can't suddenly get four legs in one generation, can you? Doesn't that seem to violate the Theory of Evolution. And also remember that the front legs are symmetrical side to side and so are the back legs, but they are usually not symmetrical front to back.

How about all the insects with six legs or spiders with eight legs? How does the slow and gradual process explain eight legs and the symmetry that is there? Why stop there? What about centipedes and millipedes. The record for most legs is the millipede which has 750 legs, all of them in symmetrical pairs.

Let's think about birds. In the slow and gradual process of evolution, one arm or leg had to turn into a wing before the other one did, right? Birds could not have gotten two wings at the same time, in the same generation. Maybe it was many generations that birds had one wing and one leg before that leg started to change into a second wing in exactly the symmetrically opposite position on the other side of the body. If that second wing was misplaced by even a little bit, the bird would not be able to fly. It would just flop around generation after generation until both wings could balance each other out and could be coordinated so the bird could figure out how to fly with these two feathered appendages. That's so silly.

But evolutionists must believe some version of the above scenarios. And they must believe that these impossibly complicated scenarios repeated themselves over and over again in hundreds of thousands of animals' bodies, birds' bodies, fish bodies, and insect bodies.

If random mutation were really the process by which all living species came into existence, then we would be looking all around us at way more craziness. There would not be much order at all. There would be very, very little symmetry.

If fact, what we see all around us is order. Thesaurus.com says that order is the opposite of random. Some antonyms (opposites) for the word "random," are "methodical, planned, systematic, definite, particular, and specific." [2]

As I explained in Chapter #27 on Mutation, intelligent scientists have tried for 40 years to mutate a fairly simple species like a fruit fly into another species and they have not been able to do it. And they were trying on purpose. Smart people have been trying to do it, but without success. Therefore, it seems impossible to believe that beneficial mutation which smart men have never been able to cause ON PURPOSE could happen accidentally and end up producing all the incredibly complex species in the world.

The most simple and logical conclusion is that living species were designed by a super intelligence to be exactly the way that they are AND to NOT be able to be changed.

Scientists are constantly discovering new species never before seen and they estimate there are hundreds of thousands more, but never have they observed one species changing into another one. Surely they have been looking long and hard. Doesn't it tell you something when the evidence is not there? Zip. Nada.

Another aspect of symmetry that needs to be mentioned is the inherent "Beauty". Humans have an intellectual and spiritual ability to recognize order, harmony, and beauty in the universe. When we design things ourselves, we purposefully invest the qualities of order and beauty. Almost no one designs something on purpose that others would call ugly. It would never be appreciated as art or beauty.

One of the most essential attributes of beauty is symmetry. So when we observe Nature and recognize the awesome symmetry and beauty that exists, it triggers in our mind and heart and appreciation of the designer of that beauty. That is a natural instinctive process.

If a person is unable to appreciate beauty, we would consider them to be handicapped in that way. We would feel sorry for them. Their life would seem dull, grey, sad, joyless, even "lifeless," and pitiable. That's what it must be like for those who sense the beauty around them but cannot appreciate the "heart" of the creator behind the beauty. For them everything came from nothing and randomness. There is no meaning and purpose bigger than themselves. How sad.

Symmetry is absolutely everywhere. Randomness is not everywhere; it's even difficult to find.

There has to be God.

Chapter #69 The Archerfish

All over the world there are hundreds and thousands of animals, fish, insects, and plants that refute the Theory of Evolution. I've already shown that neither mutations nor natural selection is a process that can lead to a new species (Chapters #27 and #35). But let's spend a few minutes talking about a certain fish called the Archerfish that lives in Asia. After I describe its astounding abilities, involving the solutions to complex problems of physics, you'll be convinced there was an intelligence behind its design and existence. It didn't come about by accident.

The Archerfish has the amazing ability to shoot a jet of water out of its mouth and knock bugs and lizards off of low hanging branches so it can eat them.

Recent research was completed and published which reveals that its abilities are way more remarkable than they seem at first, although they are very impressive indeed at the beginning. [1] and [2]

As I describe what the Archerfish is able to do, please try to imagine what Darwin would say is the process for the development of this species. Remember Darwinian progress is slow and gradual, taking place over many generations.

Researchers measured the distance the Archerfish could shoot its stream of water and it is a maximum of 6 feet 6 inches. Note that the average Archerfish is only about 6 inches long. They have a unique shape to their mouth and tongue and their gills squeeze the water out at high speed. How far can a human spit do you think? How accurate is the human? And remember that the Archerfish is shooting up.

This footnote has a link to three videos of Archerfish in action. [3]

The unique tongue and mouth shape allow the Archerfish to channel the water and control the stream driven by powerful gills. Since no other fish has anything like this ability, there is no clue about another species it could have come from.

There are no fossils either to indicate a slow and gradual development. One quarter or one half of this ability is obviously useless. Natural Selection, if it were true, would not select for any of the intermediate steps.

Even more amazing is that researchers have discovered that the Archerfish can make adjustments according to the target it is shooting at. For example, it can judge the distance to the prey and shoot closer or farther bursts of water. Due to the shape of its mouth, the water in the stream tends to gather at the tip of the stream into a glob so there is a greater mass to knock the bug off the branch.

The Archerfish seems to be able to adjust the amount of water depending on the size of the bug.

Obviously some bugs are farther away, so the Archerfish has to be able to adjust the distance it shoots. But this presents a very complicated problem of physics. As the shot of water travels through the air, gravity pulls down on it causing it to curve downward. The Archerfish has to be able to aim in a way that gravity is taken into account and perfectly adjust the angle and force to shoot the water over the distance required.

Here's another problem the Archerfish overcomes. If you have a fish tank, you know that looking from air through the water surface causes "refraction" of the light, making the contents of the fish tank appear to be displaced from where it actually is located. [4] This also occurs looking from inside of the water to out of the water. Somehow the Archerfish can account for the refracting property of the surface of the water and still aim accurately enough to hit its target on the tree branch.

How could the brain of the Archerfish ever evolve slowly over many generations to be able to do this without the whole species going extinct from lack of food? Just think of the odds of one single Archerfish mutating and acquiring this ability. That's astronomical odds already. Then somehow that Archerfish has to mate and produce descendants that can do the same thing. This ability has to work correctly or it is useless. It cannot develop in slow stages over many generations.

The Archerfish somehow uses its tongue and a channel in the roof of its mouth to make a nozzle that gets the stream of water to gather together at the tip of the stream, making a bigger glob to attack the prey. Researchers calculated that the force of the water is about ten times the bug's ability to hold on to the branch. The Archerfish is able to adjust the size of the glob to the size of the target.

> "Furthermore, the time needed until water assembles at the jet tip is not fixed. Rather, it is adjusted so that maximum focusing occurs just before impact. Surprisingly, the fish achieve this by modulating the dynamics of changes in the cross-section of their mouth opening, a mechanism that seems to not have been applied yet in human-built nozzles." [5]

You are an intelligent being. Just imagine what effort and practice it would take you to learn how to spit like this. Could you get good at it? Now can you imagine a fish brain learning to do it all by accident if their survival depended on it. I can't.

There must be God.

Chapter #70 Healing

A couple weeks ago I was working in the garage and I scraped my arm on the corner of a sheet of wood. As would be expected, I started to bleed because I had scraped off the surface layer of skin about 3/8 inch across. For the next couple of weeks, I have been watching my arm heal, which is one of the most amazing abilities inherent in all living organisms. Living beings can repair themselves from damage.

Healing is such an amazing process, even more astounding when you research all the stages that your body goes through in that process. There are literally hundreds, if not thousands, of processes involved for a healing to take place. The ability to heal could not have developed in a Darwinian process that is slow and gradual. Half stopping the bleeding is not enough.

Let me share just a summary of a few of those processes with you, but first, here is a quote that I found that shows scientists really can't explain the whole process very well at all.

"Despite the advances in understanding the science of wound healing, many more steps have yet to be discovered and elucidated.

"Although seemingly basic in concept, advances in molecular science have allowed modern medicine to gain a true appreciation of the complex interplay between the cells involved in the phases of wound healing." [1]

Note that it is still too complicated for them to understand. How can they believe it happened by chance? They just assume no God and make up theories from there.

To continue, scientists vary as to whether there are three or four phases to the healing process, but regardless of how many, they agree that there are distinct phases that happen.

"When your skin gets cut, your body springs into action to heal the wound. First, the body works to limit blood loss by reducing the amount of blood flowing to the wounded area. Proteins in blood, such as fibrin, work with the blood platelets already in place and plasma to form a protective covering called a scab. While your skin regenerates underneath the protective layer, the scab protects the wound from outside infection." [2]

Notice that your blood vessels leading to the wound constrict at first to limit the blood loss. Wounded cells release thromboxane A2 and prostaglandin 2-alpha which cause the vessel constriction. Once blood loss stops, then the blood vessels expand to allow more white blood cells to accumulate and get rid of infection, bacteria and debris. They do the opposite of what they did before. How is that possible?

"Platelets (triggered by enzymes leaked from the torn blood vessel) rush to the scene. These sticky blood cells clump to each other and then adhere to the sides of the torn blood vessel, making a plug. Clotting proteins in the blood join forces to form a fibrin net that holds the platelet plug in place over the tear, and in just a few seconds or minutes (depending on how bad the scrape is), BLEEDING STOPS, thanks to coagulation! The fibrin plug becomes a scab that will eventually fall off or be reabsorbed into the body once healing is complete." [3]

The scab makes a dry, temporary crust which protects the damaged area during healing.

The blood contains lots of platelets for just this purpose. Platelets only exist in animals. They are produced in a totally different location in your body from the skin, namely the bone marrow. A healthy adult produces about 1,000,000,000,000 platelets a day and they only circulate for about 8 to 9 days before being removed by the spleen and liver. Platelets are so tiny they are only 1/5th the size of red blood cells. Note carefully this quote:

"Complicating any verbal description is the fact that at least 193 proteins and 301 interactions are involved in platelet dynamics." i.e. the making of platelets. [4]

If this process evolved in a slow and gradual way, the body would bleed to death and die before it could reproduce. Think of all the times you get injured and bleed during your lifetime.

Of course evolutionists would probably say that the healing ability was developed long before humans came along. But the problem for simpler organisms is even more complicated. They are much more likely to die from a simple wound than we are. The odds are less they could ever reproduce. The healing process is extremely complicated. Therefore, it could never evolve in one generation according to the Theory of Evolution. And what about platelets only existing in animals? They must have been created by God or the first animals would have bled to death before they could "evolve".

The second phase of healing is Inflammation. The blood vessels that previously constricted to stop blood loss now dilate to bring more blood to the area. The area swells up and the extra blood brings the white blood cells which engulf and kill bacteria and remove debris. Fibroblast cells also gather at the site and start producing collagen which gradually fills up the wound under the scab and creates new capillaries.

Skin cells around the edges of the wound thicken up and gradually stretch under the scab into the center of the wound, meeting skin from the other side. This takes about 3 weeks. This tissue forms a scar which gradually becomes stronger as more collagen is added, taking up to 3 years to complete the healing.

Here is a description of the next phase, called Proliferation.

"Proliferation (growth of new tissue): In this phase, angiogenesis, collagen deposition, granulation tissue formation, epithelialization, and wound contraction occur. In angiogenesis, vascular endothelial cells form new blood vessels. In fibroplasia and granulation tissue formation, fibroblasts grow and form a new, provisional extracellular matrix (ECM) by excreting collagen and fibronectin. Concurrently, re-epithelialization of the epidermis occurs, in which epithelial cells proliferate and 'crawl' atop the wound bed, providing cover for the new tissue. " [5]

That's a lot of different processes going on involving all kinds of different specialized cells and chemicals. Healing doesn't work if any of these processes are not functioning. So how could evolution by slow and gradual changes possibly create such an intricate system?

We're not done yet. Wound contraction takes place next by cells called myofibroblasts contracting like muscles and shrinking the wound. Then unneeded cells die off, somehow knowing they are not needed.

The last phase is Maturation and Remodeling where cells realign themselves like the original skin and unneeded cells die off.

"Increased collagen production and breakdown continue for 6 months to 1 year after injury. The initial type III collagen is replaced by type I collagen until a type I:type II ratio of 4:1 is reached, which is equal to normal skin. Also, fibroblasts differentiate into myofibroblasts, causing tissue contraction during this phase of wound healing." [6]

How do the cells know what the original skin looked like and then be able to replace it?

This information and description are extremely simplified. Read up on it a little more if you are interested. If not, take my word for it, healing ability is no accident. ... There must be God.

Chapter #71 Fruit

Everybody loves fruit. But have you ever done any research on "fruits"? I tried to find out how many different kinds of fruits there are in the world, but I could not find an answer. Nobody knows. Clearly there are thousands. (For fun go to Top 20 Fruits You Probably Don't Know [1] or 20 More Fruits You Probably Don't Know [2].)

> "Although it is not known exactly how many types of fruits exist in the world, the answer numbers in the thousands. Agriculturalists constantly cultivate new varieties of fruits; for instance, at least 1,600 varieties of bananas exist as of 2014." [3]

Imagine a life without fruits. Eating would be much more boring, but also we would be much more likely to have nutritional deficiency diseases, maybe even become extinct.

What do evolutionists say about where fruits came from? Not much actually, I did an Internet search for it. They say of course that slowly over great lengths of time, random mutations somehow produced a sweet fruit. Animals and insects liked them so much more than other plants that they ate a lot of them and spread their seeds all over the place by pooping.

Let's think about this a little more seriously and try to imagine the step by step processes that would have had to be involved.

I want to discuss particularly two of the most astounding features of fruits: (A) they taste so great and (B) they carry many, many health benefits for humans. There are others, but I think these two will show that fruits clearly defy the concepts of evolution.

Even with all of our creative genius and intelligence as human beings, we cannot create even one fruit that is better than the ones in nature. Doesn't that tell you something? Not just a few, but all these thousands of wonderful fruits just accidentally happened without any intelligence involved. That means that random accidents are smarter than all the combined human intelligence because randomness comes up with better food for us than we can make on our own. Not only did it happen one time, but it happened over and over again thousands of times. So the smartest scientists are like dummies compared to random mutations.

Evolutionists have a faith in randomness that goes beyond blind faith if you ask me.

So in the course of historical time, what came first, the fruits evolving on the plants or the animals to eat them? Evolutionists say animals spread the seeds that grew in the fruits. So that means that fruits came into existence after there were already animals. But if there were no fruits for the animals to eat, how did they get all the nutrition that they needed to survive. It's kind of a catch 22. So they would have had to evolve simultaneously, right? But that doesn't make so much sense either, because if the fruit were only partially developed, why would the animal eat it?

Think for a minute of what is necessary in the way of changes in a plant for it to go from a plant that has no fruit to one that bears fruit. There would have to be thousands of chemical and biological changes in the plant. Usually the fruit is an integral part of the reproductive organs of a plant. This means that the male and female parts of one plant or else both a male plant and a female plant would both have to make evolutionary changes that completely corresponded to each other simultaneously. If not, then the plant would not be fertilized correctly and there would be no next generation.

Plants have a life cycle. Starting from a seed, it can take many years for a plant (fruit tree) to reach maturity and be able to bear seeds of its own. Standard apple trees take at least five to eight years to bear fruit and cherry trees take longer. [4]

So if a tree is one that does not bear fruit and experiences a simple mutation so that it can bear fruit, it is probably going to take some five years before that mutation could be passed on to another generation of trees by the fruit.

Remember also that scientists tell us that most mutations are detrimental or neutral and very few are positive. (See Chapter #27 Mutation) How many of the seeds would actually carry the mutation when it happens? Certainly only a tiny, tiny fraction of the seeds would have any mutation at all, but an even much smaller fraction of those would have a mutation going toward producing a partial fruit. Now among all the seeds that a tree produces each year, what percentage do you think will grow up into another mature tree? I'd be willing to bet that percentage is very low. I remember my aunt and uncle had this huge old cherry tree that used to produce so many cherries that the ground would be covered with them. But not many new trees sprung up.

If a plant somehow mutated enough to make a fruit, (a big if) how did it get the taste just right to be so satisfying to humans, or even animals? How many possible mutations are there that taste terrible? There isn't enough time since the Big Bang for a plant to mutate all the combinations of tastes in order to get just the right one. And you can't please all the people all the time. Some people like apples and some don't. Some people who love apples love the Delicious but not the Granny Smith. The seeds of the apple won't get spread for the magic of the evolutionist process if the people (or local animals) don't like the taste.

Now here's another incredible difficulty for evolutionists. They may talk about the great taste of fruits as the reason they are here according to natural selection, but they still have to take into account that fruits each have many, many health benefits. How did that come about? People might eat the fruit because it tastes so great, but what if it poisoned them. No more evolution. How can evolutionists explain that fruits contain many wonderful nutrients for humans? The nutrients don't particularly help the plant or tree itself. Did the plants mutate again and again until it somehow got exactly the right combination of nutrients for humans (animals, or insects, etc.) and also the right taste too? That would mean thousands of millions of new chemical and biological processes. That doesn't make much sense because there are so many other plants and trees that are doing just fine and they don't make any fruits that are edible.

"The total number of plant species in the world is estimated at 270,000. Approximately 1,000 to 2,000 species of plants are edible by humans. About 100 to 200 species of plants play an important role in world commerce, and about 15 species provide the majority of food crops. These include soybeans, peanuts, rice, wheat and bananas." [5]

What is more difficult to evolve, a great taste or great nutritional benefits for humans? It seems to me that the chemical and biological processes to produce great taste would be easier and also more likely to get the fruit eaten and the seeds spread. But it is going to be way more complicated for the fruit to become full of healthy nutrients. Even if the plant had wonderful nutrients, humans and animals won't eat it if it tastes terrible. Here are some sample references of the amazing benefits of just four fruits.

25 Powerful Reasons to Eat Bananas [6]
Bananas: Health Benefits, Risks & Nutrition Facts [7]
The Health Benefits Of Bananas Are Numerous [8]
5 Health Benefits of Apples [9]
15 health benefits of eating apples [10]
10 Reasons To Eat Pineapple [11]
13 Health Benefits of Oranges [12]
Etc., etc., etc.

Once again we could ask, which came first, the nutrients in the fruit or the animal to eat the fruit. If the animals are not there to eat and then spread the fruit seeds, how do the seeds get spread? If the nutritional fruits are not there for the animals, how do they survive without it? What good is the fruit if it has no nutrition? If you believe they evolved side by side at the same time, fruit evolving nutrition and taste and animals evolving, you have a scenario that takes more blind faith than any religious person has.

Here's another very interesting point. You have surely noticed that oranges come in segments inside the peel, usually ten. Another fruit like bananas however grow in a totally different way, on a huge stalk in a big bunch, inside peels.

The banana peel comes off rather easily and the banana can actually be divided into three sections. What does evolution have to say about fruit being conveniently packaged for human and animal consumption? Could ten segments in an orange have developed by some slow and gradual process of natural selection? And why is that feature selected as the "fittest" over some other simpler system?

I love fruit. Because there is fruit, I conclude there must be God.

Chapter #72 The Superb Lyrebird

Most birds have one or two sounds that they can make or "songs" that they "sing". The fact that any animal can make such sounds at all is a phenomenally complex accomplishment involving their ears, brain, syrinx, beak, mouth, and lungs all working simultaneously. It is so amazing that it would "impress the great composers". [1] (I highly recommend this webpage reference as an introduction about bird sounds and the messages they are communicating. It will really inspire you about birds. See the footnotes for some sample passages.)

> "The vocal skill of birds derive from the unusual structure of their powerful vocal equipment. The syrinx is the sound-producing organ in birds. It is the equivalent of the human sound box. The syrinx contains membranes which vibrate and generate sound waves when air from the lungs is passed over them. The muscles of the syrinx control the details of song production; birds with a more elaborate system of vocal muscles produce more complex songs." [2]

The Lyrebird in Australia gets even more complicated by a whole new order of magnitude. Not only is it considered by many to be the loudest bird in the world, but it can hear, remember, and then somehow imitate extraordinarily complex sounds and sequences. Check the footnotes for some links to videos on YouTube where Lyrebirds are videotaped reproducing sounds such as a chainsaw, the hammering in of a nail, sawing on wood, a camera shutter, a motorized drive on a camera shutter, a radio broadcast, and even a man cursing.

This excerpt is from an article in Wikipedia that I highly recommend for more information.

> "The lyrebird's syrinx is the most complexly-muscled of the Passerines (songbirds), giving the lyrebird extraordinary ability, unmatched in vocal repertoire and mimicry. Lyrebirds render with great fidelity the individual songs of other birds and the chatter of flocks of birds, and also mimic other animals such as koalas and dingos. The lyrebird is capable of imitating almost any sound and they have been recorded mimicking human caused sounds such as a mill whistle to a cross-cut saw, chainsaws, car engines and car alarms, fire alarms, rifle-shots, camera shutters, dogs barking, crying babies, music, and even the human voice." [3]

Please go to my footnotes for a list of additional videos on YouTube of the Superb Lyrebird. (I guarantee you will be amazed.) [4]

> "In the wild, males will not only flawlessly imitate some 20 different species of birds, but multiple calls from each. They're particularly fond of imitating Australia's famous laughing kookaburras, and Dalziell has heard them mimicking the wing beats of small birds jetting through the forest understory. Up to 80 percent of a lyrebird's song can consist of such mimicry, according to Dalziell..." [5]

The Superb Lyrebird can imitate other birds so well that they are completely deceived into believing it is one of their own. [6]

Scientists who study the Lyrebirds say they have fossils dating back 15 million years ago.

The Lyrebirds get their name from the beautiful tail feathers on the male that grow when he is three or four years old. There are 2 species of Lyrebirds (Superb and Albert's), but only the Superb species has these amazing tail feathers.

Evolutionists have quite a number of problems trying to explain how this ability could have developed slowly and gradually in the Lyrebird. They never actually discuss how changes in the brain or vocal mechanisms take place. They refer to some generalized explanation of sex appeal in the male making him more attractive to the female AFTER he has evolved. That's just a distraction because there is no evidence of HOW he could anatomically evolve. Describing an ability is not demonstrating evolution. Don't be fooled.

One big problem for evolutionists is, "What was the order of development of the needed parts?" Imagine the brain of a Lyrebird and how it evolved. Did it first evolve the ability to hear, record, and memorize a very complex sequence of sounds slowly and gradually? How would that be a benefit to survival? Then many generations later its lungs, syrinx, and beak changed so it could make all those sounds it had already remembered.

What about the other way around? Did the mouth, throat, syrinx, and lungs slowly and gradually evolve to this level of specialization and then the brain evolved after that? Could all these complex mechanisms have evolved all on their own without the brain? Note that the anatomical mechanisms evolving slowly over many generations would have to conveniently evolve piece by piece without any designer until the whole thing would suddenly work. Once the "musical instrument" existed, then the brain has to be able to "play" it. The brain would have to evolve so it could eventually learn how to take the stored memory of a sound and reproduce it. Did this take many generations?

Maybe when you were a kid someone made for you a flute out of a hollow bamboo reed. [7] You blew in one end and were shown that by covering different holes you could make different sounds. So far so good. But how long was it before you could play a song on that flute? Not easy was it? And you were a pretty smart kid! Learning to play even a simple musical instrument is not easy.

The other possibility for evolution is that all these complicated, interconnected systems developed simultaneously. First they were one tenth developed, then one quarter developed, then one half developed, and so on. In this case, it doesn't seem like anything will work very well until it is all finished. There seems to be very little survival benefit at each of the intermediate stages along the way. So how could evolution like this be realistic? Besides that, the chances of many interconnected mutations happening nearly simultaneously is non-existent.

Evolutionists believe that the Lyrebird accidentally developed a very sophisticated vocal mechanism (way more complicated than a homemade flute). The Lyrebird can create thousands of sounds compared to a few on your flute. That bird brain also accidentally figured out how to instantly remember various complicated sounds that it hears and then somehow learned to reproduce the exact sounds and sequences using its amazing vocal apparatus (way beyond some simple flute).

That bird brain had to have accidentally developed not only "perfect pitch" [8], but also "perfect rhythm/timing/beat" in order to repeat a series of sounds. Furthermore it would also have to have a "photographic memory for sound". If a human being could accomplish something like this, he/she would be considered one of the "wonders of the world".

The Lyrebird could not have evolved. It was designed.

There must be God.

Chapter #73 Punctuated Equilibrium

Many people have never even heard of The Theory of Punctuated Equilibrium. It has been around since 1972 and it spells the end of Darwinism as you know it.

As I have explained fully before in Chapter 18 (The Fossil Record), Chapter 58 (The Cambrian Explosion), and Chapter 64 (Missing Links), there is no evidence in the fossil record for Darwinism, the slow and gradual emergence of new species from previous species by passing through transitional forms.

Even Darwin himself recognized this, but he blamed an inadequate fossil record. Ever since Darwin, as more and more fossils were discovered without any transitional forms, evolutionists found this only an uninteresting observation not disproof, if they acknowledged it at all. Certainly they kept it an unspoken secret knowing it could damage belief in Darwinism.

Here are two quotes from Newsweek Magazine back in 1980.

"The missing link between man and the apes, whose absence has comforted religious fundamentalists since the days of Darwin, is merely the most glamorous of a whole hierarchy of phantom creatures. In the fossil record, missing links are the rule: the story of life is as disjointed as a silent newsreel, in which species succeed one another as abruptly as Balkan prime ministers. The more scientists have searched for the transitional forms between species, the more they have been frustrated." [1]

"... Evidence from fossils now points overwhelmingly away from classical Darwinism which most Americans learned in high school:...Increasingly scientists now believe that species change little for millions of years and then evolve quickly, in a kind of quantum leap...The theory is still being worked out" [2]

You didn't know that Evolutionists don't believe in Darwinism any more, did you? They are trying to work out a new theory.

Darwinism actually began to die out among paleontologists even earlier in 1954 when Ernst Mayr published his paper, "Change of genetic environment and evolution". [3] He showed that Darwin's theory of slow and gradual evolution could not work in real life if there were large numbers of a given species. He proposed "Allopatric speciation" as the process of evolution and it was generally accepted by 1972.

"Allopatric speciation suggests that species with large central populations are stabilized by their large volume and the process of gene flow. New and even beneficial mutations are diluted by the population's large size and are unable to reach fixation, due to such factors as constantly changing environments. If this is the case, then the transformation of whole lineages should be rare, as the fossil record indicates." [4]

After 120 years of observing the fossil record, the evolutionists finally recognized, and publicly admitted that any given species does not change much, if at all, for millions upon millions of years.

Have you seen that in your textbooks yet?

True believers that they are, this didn't stop them. Darwin's Theory of Evolution had predicted that there would be slow and gradual changes upward over time resulting in many new species. This never showed up in the fossil record. Rather than say that the Theory of Evolution was wrong, they decided that the slow and gradual must have been wrong. (Isn't that the same thing?)

They didn't think to tell every school teacher after about 1954 that what they are teaching kids about slow and gradual evolution is false. The evolutionists let the teachers go on teaching Darwinian evolution that they themselves no longer believe and have recognized as false.

"In 1972, paleontologists Niles Eldredge and Stephen Jay Gould published a landmark paper developing this theory and called it punctuated equilibria. Their paper built upon Ernst Mayr's theory of geographic speciation, I. Michael Lerner's theories of developmental and genetic homeostasis, as well as their own empirical research. Eldredge and Gould proposed that the degree of gradualism commonly attributed to Charles Darwin is virtually nonexistent in the fossil record, and that stasis dominates the history of most fossil species." [5]

Let me add my own emphasis to double the impact: Darwinian gradualism is "virtually nonexistent," i.e. THE SAME as nonexistent.

The Theory of Punctuated Equilibrium states that a species will stay almost exactly the same for millions of years, i.e. in stasis or equilibrium, until there are sudden "punctuated" changes of a huge degree and a whole new species emerges in a very short period of time.

The original species will probably continue to exist but a new daughter species will spring up suddenly in some isolated location from a small population. Only a small group of individuals could change so radically in a short geological time frame into a new species.

Here is an astounding statement which is found in Wikipedia in the Punctuated Equilibrium article, the section called "Stasis".

"Before Eldredge and Gould alerted their colleagues to the prominence of stasis in the fossil record, most evolutionists considered stasis to be rare or unimportant." [6]

Darwinism predicts there is slow and gradual change over time and yet Wikipedia exposes the fact that nothing was changing over time and yet the scientists thought it was unimportant!

This admission and the new theory obviously turns Darwinism on its head. However, evolutionists, even if they don't see any evidence, still believe it is the truth. Evolution is still true even if they can't find any evidence YET. Besides, they concluded, there was never any real requirement that the changes be slow and gradual.

"...at a conference in mid-October at Chicago's Field Museum of Natural History, the majority of 160 of the world's top paleontologists, anatomists, evolutionary geneticists and developmental biologists supported some form of this theory of "punctuated equilibria." [7]

Let me say that more clearly for you. A majority of the world's top scientists agreed in 1980 that Darwinism as it was taught to you in school is false. Hence my conclusion, Darwinism has died.

Therefore for teachers to teach that scientists believe in Darwinism has been false since at least 1980, 36 years and counting.

Punctuated Equilibrium accounts for the fossil record much better than Darwinism. But you are probably asking yourself, "How could such massive changes evolve a new species in a short period of time if it hasn't happened over millions of years?" The new theory explains this by saying that the massive changes take place in small fringe populations that get isolated from the larger populations. The huge changes take place in a short geologic period of time, i.e. a few thousand years through processes something like inbreeding and major environmental shifts.

This is very helpful because it explains why there are no transitional fossils, no missing links. The populations were isolated and also there were relatively few individuals, therefore they were less likely to leave fossils in the record.

It's also very helpful for evolutionists because it actually predicts that you won't find any proof that it is true. The fossils you need to prove it's true don't exist. So, conveniently, you won't be able to find any evidence that the theory is false either.

Many philosophers of science accept a definition of a valid scientific theory as one that is based upon (A) repeatable observations, (B) one that is subject to testing and making accurate predictions, and (C) one that is "falsifiable." The "punctuationists" clearly have some problems having a valid scientific theory.

Random Mutation and Natural Selection cannot be shown to create any new species even over very long periods of time, so the best new theory evolutionists have come up with is that it must happen over a very short period of time. Their theorized descriptions come off sounding very scientific and very complicated, but the bottom line is that there is no evidence that the process actually works or could work.

Here is an astounding statement by an evolutionist.

> "The core observation that once most species show up in the fossil record they exhibit hardly any change at all – not uncommonly remaining essentially static for millions of years – was made 150 years ago and was known to Darwin, but little was made of it until comparatively recently." [8]

The Theory of Evolution predicts slow and gradual change over time. However, they have made the "core observation" for the last 150 years that this was NOT happening and yet "little was made of it." Do they really call themselves scientists?

> "Now we admit that evolution is more of a fits-and-starts affair than we used to think. This hardly seems to be the stuff of revolution." [9]

That quote is from Niles Eldredge, who came up with punctuated equilibrium. He can say it is no big deal, but it means traditional Darwinism is dying out, if it's not already dead. To me that is certainly VERY revolutionary. Why, because all the schools teaching Darwinism need to stop it right now.

Probably, it will take time, but the handwriting is already on the wall. Darwinism is dead. What you and I learned in school and what is still being taught today is FALSE and they know it. And they don't have any viable proof for their latest theory either, just blind faith and hope they can find some other mechanism in the future to make the theory come true without God.

205

I thought you should know what many of the scientists have admitted to themselves since 1972.

We believers can see that evolutionism is pure faith, not science, even if they can't.

Actually their faith is less scientific than someone's faith that there is a Creator God. The theory of a Creator better explains the scientific facts. Maybe if evolutionists keep researching, they'll eventually find God, but only if they are willing to go where the evidence leads them.

The only truly scientific conclusion is that there must be God.

Chapter #74 Proteins

Most people are familiar with proteins, as in "be sure you eat enough proteins." However, proteins are far, far more significant than that. In fact, if you took all of the water out of your body, what would be left would be 75% proteins. The total number of different proteins that are estimated to exist in the human body is around 50,000.

Proteins are especially troublesome for the God-deniers. This is because thousands of proteins are necessary for even a single cell to exist. However, there is no known process for producing proteins without the DNA from an already living cell. It's a real "Catch-22". Without proteins there is no life, but without life there are no proteins.

"The common bacteria, E-coli, is predicted to have a total of 5,000 organic compounds of which 3,000 are proteins." [1]

The sum of proteins in biological organisms exceeds 10 million, but nobody actually has any accurate count.

Proteins are very complicated molecules. If a simple bacteria requires 3,000 in order to live, then it's impossible that a simple bacteria occurred by accident because you cannot get even one protein by accident, let alone 3,000.

It is estimated that the human body has the ability to generate two million different types of proteins. However, the Human Genome Project concluded that there are only 20,000-25,000 genes, i.e. sections of DNA, used to make proteins. How is this possible? The human body clearly is not using 1 to 1 coding to make the proteins from genes. Some process way more complex and intelligently designed must be at work.

Proteins are made up of amino acids, the building blocks, linked together. There are about twenty different amino acids commonly found in plants and animals. A typical protein contains 300 or more of those 20 amino acids. Especially important to note is that each protein has its own specific count and sequence of amino acids. One mistake in the sequence and it doesn't work, or even worse causes disease.

Yeast proteins are on average 466 amino acids long. The largest known proteins are a component of the muscle fibers with a total length of almost 27,000 amino acids. Do you really think that the thousands of proteins that exist could have accidentally formed with the correct number and configuration of amino acids? Even the simple yeast protein has exactly the right 466 amino acids (of a possible 20 choices) in exactly the right place in the sequence.

Proteins are long chains of molecules, but they are "folded" around on themselves many times making specific, unique 3-dimensional shapes that allow them to do the work they do. [2]

Once a protein is formed, it only exists for a certain period of time and then is degraded and recycled by the cell's machinery. They can exist for minutes or years, having an average lifespan of one to two days in mammalian cells. Abnormal and or incorrectly folded proteins are degraded more rapidly.

Proteins are essential elements for growth and repair, good functioning and structure of all living cells. Hormones, such as insulin, control blood sugar levels. Enzymes are a type of protein crucial for digestion of foods. Antibodies, another type of protein, help us fight infections. Muscle proteins allow for their contraction. Otherwise muscles would not work. Hemoglobin, an iron containing protein, transports oxygen via the bloodstream.

Here is another list of protein functionalities from a science website:

Protein has a range of essential functions in the body, including the following:

- Required for building and repair of body tissues (including muscle)
- Enzymes, hormones, and many immune molecules are proteins
- Essential body processes such as water balancing, nutrient transport, and muscle contractions require protein to function.
- Protein is a source of energy.
- Protein helps keep skin, hair, and nails healthy.
- Protein, like most other essential nutrients, is absolutely crucial for overall good health. [3]

Every one of the above processes is almost a miracle of design in itself. For example, every single cell needs nutrition to exist, but the cell membrane is impermeable to food particles. How does a cell eat? The cell membrane has thousands of proteins actually embedded right in the wall. These types of proteins are called "receptor proteins" because they have an exact shape that fits a particle of nutrition that comes along. When that particle fits into the protein, the protein becomes something different and absorbs that particular nutritional element into the inside of the cell. It's awesome! Clearly it acts more like a designed machine than a random accident.

Here is another additional and more gigantic problem for the God-deniers.

"A cell needs over 75 'helper molecules,' all working together in *harmony*, to make one protein (R-group series) as instructed by one DNA base series. A few of these molecules are RNA (messenger, transfer, and ribosomal RNA); most are highly specific proteins." [4]

Think about that. Just to make a protein in the first place, you have to have 75 other proteins and specialized molecules already there in place and available to play their role. Try to get that to happen accidentally. Any type of evolution is impossible.

All those 75 "helper molecules" must be present in the right places at the right times in the right amounts and with the right structures or else cells cannot make proteins by using the DNA's base series coding. If all those requirements are met, then the cell can line up the amino acids at the rate of about two per second. It takes a living cell only about four minutes to "crank out" an average protein (500 amino acids) according to the DNA coded specifications. Wow.

Now I'll give you one more last insurmountable problem for the God-deniers concerning proteins. For over 50 years, even aided by the super-computers of today, researchers have what is called the "protein folding problem". They are able to determine easily what is the amino acid sequence inside a long chain protein, but every protein is a folded up three-dimensional shape. The problem is they have failed to find the location of the instructions for the folding. They can't crack the coding that does the folding. It does not seem to exist in the physical, material realm. [5]

There are all kinds of issues associated with protein folding. Why does the protein fold the way it does? Where are the instructions, i.e. the code? What is the mechanism for the folding process? How can they fold so fast? Is there any way to predict how they will fold? The ongoing research is getting better at describing what is going on in the mechanism and the orderly arrangement of the molecules, but the big secret that they are not talking about is that this totally exhibits characteristics that had to be designed. It's impossible to have occurred without an intelligent guiding force.

One parting shot. You may have heard about Stanley Miller and his experiments in a spark chamber creating what the media called "building blocks of life" or "life in a test tube." Many school textbooks even proclaim his experiments. Please read up on the latest truth as explained by Prof. Gary Parker in his article "The Origin of Life." Here's the summation of what scientists now know about Miller's experiments. "He had the wrong starting materials, used the wrong conditions, and got the wrong results." [6].

There must be God.

Chapter #75 Hospice Workers

If you wanted to know what happens when you die, who would you talk to? Who are the experts? How about a chemist, or a biologist, or a psychology professor? Would you seek out a theologian or a minister? Let me recommend that you talk to a hospice worker. These people belong to a relatively new branch of nursing and have a special calling in life.

Definition of Hospice: a system of care coordinated by an interdisciplinary team in a comfortable home setting to meet the physical, emotional and spiritual needs of the terminally ill.

Hospice came to America from England, opening the first facility in 1971 in Connecticut. Hospice focuses on pain management, emotional, and spiritual support for the terminally ill. They provide counseling for both the patient who is dying and their loved ones who will be left behind.

Hospice workers see it all. Every day they take care of the dying individual and also their loved ones. They care for all ages, from very young children to teenagers, adults, and of course the elderly who are terminally ill.

Maggie Callanan, a hospice nurse for 27 years, has witnessed more than 2,000 deaths. She is an author and speaker on death and dying. She co-authored the book **Final Gifts: Understanding the Special Awareness, Needs, and Communications of the Dying** which is all about the striking similarities of what people experience as they pass from this life. She said:

> "Wouldn't you like to learn what dying is like, since you're going to do it? Our patients are talking while it's happening. It's like you're standing there watching a preview of coming attractions." [1]

In 2014 there were more than 8 new books published (see Amazon.com) on Hospice workers experiences. Now's the time in history that the world is destined to learn about life after death from those workers who intimately experience it every day. Watch for it and you will see more and more stories being told publicly.

Trudy Harris wrote a book in 2008, **Glimpses of Heaven, True Stories of Hope & Peace at the End of Life's Journey**, about her experiences with 44 patients who died.

> "In the beginning when my patients were explaining these experiences to me, I was very skeptical. I began to hear the same stories over and

over and over again.... After twenty plus years of caring for hundreds and hundreds of patients and hearing the same scene played out over and over and over again, the skepticism went away." [2]

Elissa Al-Chokhachy, author and speaker, wrote **Miraculous Moments: True Stories Affirming Life Goes On**. This book contains 88 stories she has collected from medical professionals and educators. She writes about the experiences of doctors and family members after a person dies.

After a death, their loved one comes to them through sight, sound, touch, smell, or a sign.

"Originally, I thought it was really rare that people had these experiences of loved ones after they die.... I can now say it's quite common, but very few people talk about it. They don't want people to think they're crazy, and they're not even sure it's real or not."

"The more I work with the dying, the more I believe in life after death, I know there is life after death because there are so many affirmations." [3]

In **Death-Bed Visions: The Psychical Experiences of the Dying**, William Barrett says: "If these otherworldly visions were simply hallucinations, how could countless patient stories match? In fact, there have been several sightings of angels by dying children who were surprised to find their holy guides arrived without wings." Hospice workers and doctors' reports of their dying patients' visions from Europe, Asia, and the United States were found to have eerie similarities. Aside from minor religious differences, the deathbed visions of these patients were consistent.

Here are some more words from Trudy Harris:

"I began to see a pattern in my work. The closer my patients came to dying, the more their eyes and spirits seemed to open to a reality I only glimpsed dimly. One after another, patients recounted not just visits from absent loved ones but an extraordinary awareness of God's presence.

"Sins they'd agonized over for years suddenly felt forgiven. Grievances they'd spent a lifetime nurturing vanished in a rush of reconciliation. Even unbelievers unaccountably yearned for God, questioning or arguing with me about my faith, until all at once they began praying. [4]

If there is life after death and all indicators say that there is, then there must be God.

Chapter #76 - 200 Parameters for Life

As scientists learn more and more about the world around us and the universe, they are learning how incredibly synchronized, interconnected, and interdependent every little aspect is.

In fact, some are saying that according to the laws of physics and chemistry, we shouldn't even be here.

In 1966, astronomer and famous promoter of science, Carl Sagan announced that there were two requirements for life to be possible on a planet. He said you had to have a certain type of star like our Sun and you had to have your planet a certain distance from the star. Given there were 10^{27} stars in the universe that would mean there were about 10^{24} planets where life could exist. Surely we were not the only life. Our planet was just a "pale blue dot" according to Sagan, tiny, and insignificant. Humans were insignificant in any scheme of things.

But since that time, scientists have kept discovering more and more parameters that are requirements for life to come into existence. The number of parameters required went up to 10, then 20, then 50. One Christian apologist, Dr. Hugh Ross, an astrophysicist, has compiled 154 parameters in 2004 [1] that must be met by any planet that could possibly support life such as us. That was over 10 years ago. The list has grown since then.

What started out as 10^{24} possible planets for life, kept shrinking and shrinking and shrinking until it hit zero, zip, nada. Then it kept right on going! In other words, the probability that any planet at all, even ours, could exist and support life became more and more impossible. We shouldn't even be here!

For some great reading, look up this resource for a long list of the necessary parameters including detailed explanations.

"Does Life Exist On Any Other Planet In The Universe? Another Look At SETI" [2]

Let me give you some examples. It turns out that not any old galaxy could allow life to exist. Actually it will have to be a spiral galaxy. It will have to be a certain size, not too big, and not too small. It will have to be a certain age, not too old and not too young. These facts would eliminate an estimated 90% of galaxies as candidates for a planet that could support life.

Next, some more parameters about the necessary star were discovered for life to be supported. It would have to be situated in the right location in the galaxy. It has to be located in a narrow region between the spiral arms of the spiral galaxy. If it is too close to the center, it will be destroyed because it will travel too fast and run into one of the spiral arms. If it is too far away, it will travel too slow and be destroyed as well. It can't be in one of the spiral arms either.

There is a nice name given to all these amazing coincidences: the "Goldilocks" parameters, as in "not too hot, and not too cold, just right."

The star has to be a single star. 75% of the stars in our galaxy are double stars or multiples. So they get eliminated. A planet can't exist for long unless the star is single due to the irregular gravity. Also, the star has to be the right size, and the right mass, and the right age. It can't be too hot or too cold. It can't burn erratically and send off varying amounts of energy. The star has to be formed at just the right time in the history of the galaxy or the right chemicals for life won't exist.

The planet that can support life must be in a very narrow zone around the star. It can't be too close or it will get sucked in or burned up. It can't be too far away or it will be too cold. It also has to be tipped on its axis approximately 23 degrees to allow for seasons and the right climate for life to grow in a large habitable zone.

Since life first began on earth, the sun's luminosity has increased about 15%. Normally this would destroy all living things, but because life was growing and absorbing CO_2 and other greenhouse gases, it was perfectly synchronized. Life was able to flourish. A very life supporting temperature has been maintained as life developed and exactly because that life was developing. It never got too cold or too hot. Going too far in either direction would have started a chain reaction leading to destruction of life.

Most stars as they revolve around the center of their galaxy also oscillate up and down. This is bad for life because the center of a galaxy sends off lots of radiation. It is extremely fortunate for us that there are lots of cosmic dust clouds to shield our sun from the radiation coming from the center of the Milky Way and also that our sun does not oscillate up and down too much. If it did, we'd die from radiation.

Obviously we need lots of water for life. If the earth moved just 2% closer or farther from the sun, there would be no more water.

The gravitational pull of the earth is exactly right for keeping water vapor trapped, but also amazingly and precisely right for letting methane and ammonia escape from the earth. These gases would be deadly. A few percentage points change in that and we all die.

The earth rotates on its axis every 24 hours. This is perfect. Any slower and we would be frozen or toasted, depending on which side you were on. Any faster and the winds would blow us away.

The earth is tilted on its axis 23.4 degrees. This is again perfect. More tilt and the climate would go crazy. Less tilt and the amount of livable space would be very small.

I wrote a whole proof for God on the unique qualities of our Moon, Chapter 29. It has many, many significant parameters that are just right. For example, if it was not an abnormally large size for a moon or the exact distance which it is from earth, we'd all be dead.

Did you know that you owe your life to the planet Jupiter? It is estimated that Earth would be struck by large meteors 1,000 times more often if not for Jupiter, obviously resulting in huge catastrophes and death. Jupiter is just the right size and in the right position to protect the Earth. If it were bigger, it would suck us away from the sun. If it were smaller, it would not shield us as well. Jupiter and Saturn have very nice smooth orbits which is to our benefit. If their orbits were a little more erratic, they'd pull us out of our orbit and you guessed it, we'd die.

All the gases in our atmosphere, oxygen, nitrogen, carbon dioxide, etc. seem to be in exactly the right proportions to sustain life. A little more oxygen and we could never put out all the fires.

The Earth has so many "Goldilocks" parameters that it is really mind boggling. The tectonic plates are necessary. The molten core is necessary for life. The earthquakes are necessary. The correct ratio between oceans and land masses is necessary.

This goes on and on and on. Up to 200 parameters have been identified already and that was 10 years ago. I'd be willing to bet that in the future even more parameters are going to be discovered, thus making it more impossible that we are alive by accident. If you want to get into more of the details, I highly encourage you to go to the two resources I have referenced above or other resources that exist. Here is a third from the Wall Street Journal in December, 2014: "*Science Increasingly Makes the Case for God.*" [3]

So you can decide for yourself of course what you are going to believe, but you certainly have to admit that the odds of all these factors occurring so that life could emerge are almost infinitesimally small. Dr. Hugh Ross put the odds at 1 in 10^{42}. There are an estimated 10^{27} stars in the whole universe. Let

me   write   those   odds   out   for   you;   1   chance   in
1,000,000,000,000,000,000,000,000,000,000,000,000,000,000. He also said
that was an optimistic estimate because he was generous when assigning the
odds to each parameter.

If one chance in 10^{42} is the chance we are here and it all happened without
God, then the reverse chances represent the odds that there is God.

Could we really be so lucky to beat the odds of one in 10^{42}? Here's my
conclusion.

There must be God.

Chapter #77 God of the Gaps

If you start to share with people some of the recent scientific evidence that points to God or a master designer, you may hear the rebuttal from someone that your evidence is just a "God of the gaps" explanation. It might even be said with some condescension.

There is no need to fear the "God of the gaps" slur and I'll tell you why. But first, what is "God of the gaps." The term was actually invented by Christian theologians who were trying to identify a certain strategy for proving that God exists which they assumed is doomed to failure.

If you try to argue for God scientifically by saying that scientists have no answer for something, therefore it must be God behind it, eventually science may discover a materialist process that explains it. If they do, then God is pushed out. Centuries ago, people did not understand thunder and lightning and concluded that it must be the gods fighting in the heavens. Once thunder and lightning were understood, poof, no more gods.

200 years ago, people assumed there must be God because the world was so complex and highly organized that only design could explain it. Then Darwin came along with a materialistic based theory that sounded pretty logical and scientific, and poof, many people who didn't want a master designer anymore could base their rejection of God on evolution theory and so-called science, accepting a faith that says it could all happen randomly.

"Because current science can't figure out exactly how life started, it must be God who caused life to start." That makes perfect sense to a believer, but to a God-denier and even your average scientist that is a "God of the gaps" statement. They have faith in a different place. They believe that scientists will eventually discover how life started and additionally of course there will be no need for God.

If you are a believer, you will be happy to hear this news. Over the last 50 years of research you would think that the "gaps" would be disappearing one by one and that scientists are slowly proving the case for the materialists. That's even the way the materialists might be preaching it.

However, actually the "gaps" are getting bigger and bigger. What once seemed to be a small "gap" in materialistic explanations has often, after newer research, turned out to be an even more complex and complicated problem to explain materialistically. Also new "gaps" are being discovered

216

all the time which scientists cannot explain. The evidence for a master designer is getting stronger, not weaker.

Here is a totally mind blowing fact I heard just today. I'm sure it's going to be very controversial for years to come. It is totally beyond my understanding of how such a calculation could have been made, so I'm only reporting this new research. Here it is. Astrophysicists at UCLA have calculated that the total density of the mass of all the particles in the whole universe is so absolutely precise that changing the density by a single grain of sand would have caused the whole universe to cease to exist.

Read that again, will you. Go to the book footnotes for the reference. [1] My mind is blown thinking about it. That's a pretty big "gap" to explain without a designer. That reference contains a chart showing what happens if you vary the density of the universe.

The density of the universe was so precise at one nanosecond after the Big Bang (447,225,917,218,507,401,284,016 gm/cc) that a variation of 0.2 grams would mean no universe. Just 0.2 grams more and the universe would have imploded after 15 billion years. Exactly 0.2 grams less and there would be no stars or planets, just dust.

> "Thus the density 1 nanosecond after the Big Bang was set to an accuracy of better than 1 part in 2,235 sextillion (i.e. 10^{21}). Even earlier it was set to an accuracy better than 1 part in 10^{59}!" [2]

Here is a different example in another field. Biologists thought for a long time that most of the DNA was useless, left over mistakes along the evolutionary trail. They called it "Junk DNA". Maybe you have heard about it. But have you heard the latest? They have found that there is no such thing as "Junk DNA." In fact, all the DNA seems to be used in the best, most efficient way possible to create living beings.

They further discovered that some DNA does even double duty in two different processes. One amazing section does triple duty. A new "gap" was discovered. A really big one for evolutionary biologists! There is no known materialistic explanation for how this type of DNA could have evolved because it performs two essential processes for life.

There's more. The "gap" for a materialistic explanation for the formation of a single living cell is growing bigger also. The odds of a single functional protein happening randomly are put at 1 in 10^{180}. Scientists currently estimate that 265 to 350 proteins are the minimum requirement for life [3], but more likely it will take at least 500 to 1,500. Still those estimates are only for parasites that live off other living cells.

So the estimate for a self-existing and reproducing cell is probably between 1,500 and 1,900 genes for making proteins. So the odds of producing just the proteins for life by random chance are now something like 1 chance in $10^{40,000}$. [4]

Gaps are not disappearing as predicted. They are getting wider. And new gaps are being discovered all the time. Take another example from astrophysics. My previous Chapter, #76, 200 Parameters for Life, lists a few examples from the 200 known requirements for a planet to be hospitable for life. It was first thought there were only 2. It's a known fact that 200 number will never decrease. Most likely it will continue to grow. These are not "gaps" anymore. They are proven scientific facts.

Calculations against natural forces alone being able to create a habitable planet like ours have been increasing. Hugh Ross optimistically put the odds at 1 chance in 10^{215}. [5] Remember there are only 10^{80} atoms in the universe. [6]

All the evidence in the world will not convince some people who don't want to be convinced. But when the evidence becomes so overwhelming, what can you say about the person who won't accept it?

Here is an example that I'm borrowing from Richard Swinburne. [7] There was a man who was kidnapped by a madman who was intent on killing him. The madman rigged up ten machines from a casino that are used for shuffling cards and dealing out one at a time. Each machine had a regular deck of 52 playing cards to shuffle. The madman set explosives all around the man and he calibrated each machine so that it would send a signal to set off the bombs if any card were drawn except the ace of hearts. Only one card from out of 52 in each machine would save his life, the ace of hearts. And all 10 machines had to produce an ace of hearts. If any machine dealt a different card, he would die. The madman goes a long way away and activates the shuffling machines. No explosion. He comes back to the room and there is the man safely alive and each machine has dealt an ace of hearts. The man totally cannot believe his good fortune. He is alive. How could it have happened? Was it an act of God?

The odds of his survival were impossible. He had one chance in 52x52x52x52x52x52x52x52x52x52 = approx. one chance in 144,555,000,000,000,000. He states to the madman that surely there is a God or this could not have happened. The kidnapper says that there is nothing remarkable or surprising about this at all. It happened. He would not be alive to observe it if it hadn't. No big deal. Any other result and he would be dead and not able to see it.

The mathematical calculation of the odds of our being alive in this universe is far, far less likely than the man surviving the bombs above. To those denying a God, our existence is no big deal. The only reality to consider is physical matter. They have decided that science must be limited to material processes only and they have faith it will eventually find all the answers there.

Whether they realize it or not, their beliefs and assumptions are based on faith. Faith in miracles unexplainable by current science and often violating the well-known laws of nature identified so far. As each new "gap" in materialistic explanations is discovered, it makes the odds of us being here by accident less and less likely.

There must be God.

Chapter #78 Icons of Evolution

Suppose you are a high school or college science student and you walk into class on the first day. They hand you a brand new science book. You open it up, but inside is the textbook from 50 years ago. The President of the United States is Lyndon Johnson. No Internet, no cellphones, VCR's are not available yet, DVD's have not been invented. A minicomputer cost $18,000. There are no personal computers.

How much credibility would you place on the material in that textbook?

What if I told you that current science books are still publishing the same information as 50 years ago about the Theory of Evolution, without any updating with new research? The truth is some of the information has been known to be false for 50 years and yet it has never been removed. One drawing that was known to be false 100 years ago (Haeckel's embryo drawings) is still being included as truthful. Young minds of today are not being told the accurate scientific truth. Why not?

This Proof for God is going to talk about the explosive truth contained in a book titled, **Icons of Evolution** by Jonathan Wells. [1] This is not a religious book. It's a science book about truth. Textbooks in school are supposed to tell the truth, right? Taxpayers are footing the bill to have their kids educated not indoctrinated. We should be collectively outraged if Dr. Wells is correct, and he thoroughly documents that he is.

In the back of the book, the author analyzes 10 popular high school textbooks and lays out a clear procedure for giving out grades on the scientific accuracy of the material covering the Theory of Evolution. Seven of the 10 textbooks rated an "F". Two graded out at "D-". One got a "D+". This is sickening.

Dr. Wells even called them "massive distortions and even some faked evidence." [2] The book states, "An 'F' indicates that the textbook uncritically relies on logical fallacy, dogmatically treats a theory as an unquestionable fact, or blatantly misrepresents published scientific evidence." [3]

The book was published in 2002 and to be fair, some of those textbook publishers have probably altered their publications. Nonetheless, we now have a great grading system thanks to Dr. Wells in order to judge the truth or falsity of a lot the material that we learned as kids that supposedly proved evolution was true. Wells spends a chapter each on 10 different examples used in textbooks which are false or misleading at best. If you have kids, I hope you will enlighten them about their 50 year old text books.

The worst lie is Haeckel's drawings from back at the time of Darwin. He tried to show that embryos of many very different species are very similar and thus closely related in an evolutionary tree of life. Even 100 years ago it became known that he faked the drawings and that the real embryos are not that similar.

People who have indoctrination in mind understand very well the purpose of having an "icon" or picture that people can easily relate to and thus swallow a complicated concept uncritically. True seekers of truth, which is the supposed calling of scientists, would have protested these drawings for the last 100 years and they would not be in textbooks today. But people with a set faith always bend an inconvenient truth to fit their own ideas. They make a drawing and claim it as fact when it is not.

Here are the 10 "Icons of Evolution" from the book of the same name. All of them are massive distortions or deliberate falsifications. See if you remember any of them from your science classes.

Icon 1: The Miller-Urey Experiment. This experiment in 1952 supposedly showed how life could have originated in an early earth gas mixture that was struck by lightning. Scientists as early as 1960 began to doubt that the elements in the test tube were the actual elements on the earth at the time of the origin of life. Even if the elements were correct, all it did was create a small number out of the many amino acids required for life. That is still light years away from creating a protein. Hundreds of various proteins are required in order for even a single cell to exist.

Icon 2: Darwin's Tree of Life. It supposedly showed how all life originated from a single cell and branched off into all forms of life in later generations. No fossil evidence has ever been found to support Darwin's tree of life and over 99.9% of the fossils we now have were discovered since Darwin. It's a drawing from his imagination. He made it up.

Icon 3: Homology in Vertebrate Limbs. Because the combinations of bones of various animals seem to be similar and used similarly, this supposedly proves they all descended from a common ancestor. This is obviously a logical fallacy and doesn't prove anything about ancestry. Cars looks similar but they don't reproduce, they are created by intelligence. Bats and whales have the same ability of echolocation, but do they come from the same ancestors? No one thinks that.

Icon 4: Haeckel's Embryos. Already I discussed how this has been a known fake for 100 years and yet we can't get rid of it. Do some research and find a picture of the real embryos when compared to Haeckel's drawings.

Icon 5: Archaeopteryx-The Missing Link This fossil was first discovered in 1861 and was touted as the missing link between reptiles and birds, thus "proving" evolution. There should be millions of missing links but people were satisfied enough to believe in evolution once they could point to this one fossil. Actually a total of 8 of them were found, parts of them anyway, and they were even called "holy relics" and "unimpeachable evidence" by evolutionists. Most paleontologists today, however, do not believe it is the ancestor of any modern birds. There went the missing link.

Icon 6: Peppered Moths. This supposedly showed how moths "evolved" because the darker ones would get eaten less if the trees they landed on were dark trees. Note that changing color may be an adaptation, but it is NOT macro evolution. It was also discovered that the original researcher faked his data by gluing the moths on the trees. They don't really land on those trees.

Icon 7: Darwin's Finches. The beaks of finches got bigger in dry seasons when food was less plentiful. This supposedly showed evolution, but it doesn't because when the rains return, the beaks return to a smaller size. Even if there were a permanent change, they are still finches. That's not evolution.

Icon 8: Four-Winged Fruit Flies. Intelligent scientists in a laboratory bred fruit flies so two small appendages grew into the size of extra wings. You can't prove evolution by applying intelligent breeding. Fruit flies in the wild never develop extra wings. Even for the ones in the lab, the wings were useless and would have been selected out by natural selection as a disadvantage.

Icon 9: Fossil Horses and Directed Evolution. This goes all the way back to a drawing from Othniel Marsh in 1880 supposedly showing the straight-line evolution of small horse fossils to large modern day horses. It turns out the fossil record is not a straight line and it really can't be used as evidence for or against evolution or intelligent design either.

Icon 10: From Ape to Human: The Ultimate Icon. This drawing/icon is especially caught up in the minds of people for several generations. There is no scientific evidence behind this drawing at all. My Chapter #1 Male and Female is all about the impossibility of this drawing because it does not show women evolving simultaneously. My Chapter #64 on Missing Links goes into the fact that there is no fossil evidence for anything between the chimpanzee and the man.

If the Theory of Evolution rests on these icons for its evidence, it should have been in the dust bin of history already 50 years ago. They are just pictures and drawings. There is no science backing them up.

If this is all the evidence they have for evolution, if this is the best they can do, then game over right now.

A number of evolutionist believers reviewed Dr. Wells book and called him essentially ignorant, stupid, or wicked. He responds to them very adequately in my opinion with scientific evidence. If you are interested in all the arguments, please go to his response: "Critics Rave Over Icons of Evolution". [4]

Once people realize they have been duped by clever marketing using false icons and rabid character assassination of anyone trying to teach the truth, then the Theory of Evolution will be quickly shown to be like the Emperor's new clothes, nothing there.

The only ultimate explanation after it all is over will be that life came from a non-material, but unbelievably intelligent source.

There must be God.

Chapter #79 The Heart

Here is a major miracle that you experience every second of your life...your heart.

About three to four weeks after the sperm and egg united and got started to make you, there were a couple of blood vessels that suddenly started pulsing in a very regular beat. Those vessels grew together, enlarged, and twisted around each other to form your heart in only about two weeks. A swirling pattern of muscles formed around a bulge which then split into the four chambers of your heart. It continues to beat about every second for the rest of your life.

In the womb, the heart is responsible for the very development of that fetus into you.

The average heart is about 10 ounces and the size of a fist. Through an amazing process the electric pulses cause the top part of the heart to beat first, followed by the lower part.

It beats an average of 72 times a minute. It beats 1,000 times in 14 minutes. It beats 10,000 times every 2.3 hours. It beats 103,680 times a day, every day, your whole life. It beats a million times in less than 10 days. That's a pretty amazing muscle.

The average heart pumps about 2.4 ounces of blood (.073 liters) each heartbeat. It pumps about 1.3 gallons of blood (5 liters) per minute. That is 1,900 gallons a day (7,200 liters). That would fill an Olympic sized swimming pool in a year. It would fill a couple super-size oil tankers in your lifetime.

All the veins in your body are dumping blood into your heart which sends it to the lungs to pick up oxygen before sending it back out through arteries to capillaries and every cell of your body. The blood takes nourishment to your cells and withdraws waste products. There are 60,000 miles of blood vessels in your body. End to end they would reach around the world at the Equator 2.5 times.

That's not all. That's just the very basics. Modern research is learning a lot more about the heart.

For example, there is more information being carried by your nervous system from your heart up to your brain than from the brain down to the heart. Some research is even showing your heart perceives things milliseconds before your brain does.

The energy field of the heart can actually now be measured up to 8 feet away from your body. Other people are constantly picking up on that energy intuitively and being affected by it. We influence each other on an invisible energy level.

Our hearts, to a much larger extent than we realize, affect our emotions, our physical bodies, our relationships, and our health.

> "The heart generates the largest electromagnetic field in the body. The electrical field as measured in an electrocardiogram (ECG) is about 60 times greater in amplitude than the brain waves recorded in an electroencephalogram (EEG). The magnetic component of the heart's field... is around 5,000 times stronger than that produced by the brain" [1]

Although our hearts are nearly autonomous, there are still nerves that run from our brain to the heart that can speed it up or slow it down according to what is going on in our consciousness. Is that really a lucky evolutionary accident?

When people get a new heart through a heart transplant, they find themselves with habits and memories from the previous owner of the heart. Research is showing that there are sections of memory cells in the heart exactly like the memory cells in the brain.

If you believe that all of this came about by accident through mutations and natural selection over many, many generations, how did it happen? Did the beating start first in some random muscles and then many generations later a heart accidentally formed? Or did the heart accidentally form and then some generations later it started beating accidentally in exactly the pattern necessary to push the blood in the right directions.

When did the valves and the chambers inside the heart form? Even if the heart was beating and pushing blood in the right directions, where did it push the blood before the arteries, veins, and capillaries were accidentally mutated into place which must have taken many generations?

Blood is made in the marrow of our bones. When did blood accidentally start being produced? How did the hemoglobin cells that carry oxygen evolve over many generations? Toxins are cleaned from the blood by the liver. Food and water are inserted into the blood stream by the intestines to be sent to every cell of the body. When did the lungs get accidentally connected to the heart

225

arteries so they could start supplying oxygen that the cells needed (before they all died)?

I'm having an impossible time seeing how small changes over many generations could accidentally put all these complicated systems into place. Oxygen, food, and water are essential for life to exist from the very first cell and the systems need to be in place at the beginning of the very first organism. Waste products and CO_2 need to be removed in the very beginning. The very first human cannot live without all these systems in place right at the start. You can't wait generations for them to develop by mutations one at a time.

All cultures have expressions like "from the bottom of my heart" and "follow your heart." Our very existence is a miracle and at the center of it all is the biggest miracle of all, our heart. It is our constant, trusted and faithful companion. "Be true to your heart" because it is being true to you. It is symbolic of something much bigger than yourself. It is symbolic of your relationship with a Creator and helps remind us about our own spiritual essence.

It's not in your brain, it's in your heart where you will find that there must be God.

Chapter #80 Four Fundamental Forces

Scientists say that in the whole vast universe that there are exactly four types of forces. Yes, only four. Pretty amazing since the universe is so unimaginably huge. Over 13.7 billion years old and variously estimated to be between 27 billion and upwards to 156 billion light years across (NASA says no one knows). And in all the universe there are only four forces.

This discussion will examine these forces and argue that they must have all had their origin BEFORE the universe began and OUTSIDE OF the universe. Therefore, this discussion will attempt to show that there must be God because these forces pre-existed the universe and came from some source greater than the universe.

The four types of forces are (A) gravity, (B) electromagnetic forces, and two forces inside of atoms, (C) the strong nuclear force and (D) the weak nuclear force. [1]

Refer to this footnote for a Chart of the forces with explanations. [2]

Gravity you are familiar with. It holds everything together. There is no known limit to how far it reaches. How much you weigh is a measure of the force of gravity between the earth and your body. The strength of gravity between the Earth and the Moon is estimated at 70 million trillion pounds. If you had to replace it with a long steel pole, you would have to get a pole that is 531 miles in diameter. Think about that! It's hard to even imagine an invisible force that strong. Another amazing thing about gravity is that it is impossible to make a shield against it. Gravity is felt completely right through any known object.

Electromagnetic force is the force that exists between all particles with an electric charge. It is the basis for about every modern invention and convenience in life. It's hard to think of anything we use that did not have electricity involved in its creation. Also the very energy that makes up your body and the nerve impulses that move everything, including your heart and brain are all electromagnetic.

The strong nuclear force holds everything together in the nucleus of atoms, the protons and neutrons. It dominates in nuclear reactions and decaying. Relatively speaking it is the strongest of all the forces, however, it only operates over a very short distance within atoms.

The weak nuclear force is responsible for certain types of nuclear decay of particles.

Note there are very, very precise differences in strength between the forces. If any of them were to vary by the tiniest of strengths, the whole universe would fall apart.

Let's ask where did these four forces come from and when. Is the Theory of Evolution any help? Absolutely not. It doesn't even get a chance to apply until life has already started and gotten to the stage where it can successfully reproduce using DNA.

Did these four forces come about after the origin of the universe? Nope. Most scientists accept the "Big Bang" as the starting point of the universe. But without the four forces, there could be no universe. Therefore, the four forces had to exist before the universe when there was nothing. We could try to say they came about at the same instant as the universe exploded into being, but we still have to conclude that the four forces were "there" somehow BEFORE the explosion.

Gerald Schroeder, doctorate in physics from MIT, points out these facts in a video referenced in this footnote. [3]

Omnipresent is a word usually used in the theological context, as in God is omnipresent. Note that the four forces all could be said to be omnipresent. There is no known place in the universe where they don't operate. They are absolutely everywhere, except possibly a vacuum where there are no particles, but even in a vacuum, gravity could still be there. The four forces are not physical or material, but they operate ON the physical.

All the four forces are also invisible. We can experience or see the effects of the forces but we cannot see the forces themselves. The universe contains time, space, and matter. The four forces are "outside" of time, space, and matter, which is very hard to comprehend since we are "inside". They operate "on" or "over" the universe, but are not affected by the universe.

I could also make a case that the four forces are "all powerful." No matter what you do, you cannot break or change the forces, go around the forces, or get outside of the forces. We are, in a way, "dominated" by the four forces. We are subjects to the Laws of Nature that exist. But that's a good thing. Without them we'd be dead.

How about eternal? Are the four forces eternal? It's more than likely that they are not going to change as long at the universe continues to exist and they've certainly been existing since before the universe. That's about as eternal as you can get by definition. The four forces seem to be very god-like.

How about infinite? The strong and weak nuclear forces operate over very short distances. But scientists believe that gravity and electromagnetic forces are infinite.

God is often called "unchanging" or "immutable". Are the four forces "unchanging?" BINGO.

We could even say that the four forces are "just" and "fair". Everyone is treated equally. You cannot get any fairer than that.

I have been describing some of the laws of physics that are outside the realm of materialism and beyond the universe. I believe that you cannot explain these fundamental forces without resorting to there being a creative designer as the cause. The essence of all things is not within this material universe.

There must be God.

Chapter #81 The Definition of Impossible

We have all heard the expression that "anything could happen" and we typically accept the proposition without thinking about it too deeply. If you then add in the concept of huge amounts of time or even infinity, well then "anything could happen." This is typically part of the argument for evolution.

I want to take a deeper look at what might really be possible and what is in reality impossible by trying to construct a useful definition of what is impossible.

I give credit for this idea to a mathematician named William Dembski in his book, **The Design Revolution**. He clearly put a lot of deep thought into what is possible and what is impossible and why.

He devises a number which he calls a "universal probability limit." This is a number limit that no reasonable person, certainly no person of science or math, could ever argue with. The number is 10^{150}. The working definition is that if the likelihood of some event is less than one in 10^{150}, it is beyond the universal limit and will never happen and could never happen.

I am henceforth going to call that number "the definition of impossible."

Where this number comes from is very important. First you take the number of all the protons, electrons, and neutrons in the universe. That is 10^{80}. Next you multiply that number by the number of seconds since the universe started at the "Big Bang." That is 4.0×10^{17} seconds. Now, lastly, you multiply that by what is theoretically the smallest unit of time, the Planck Unit. There are 10^{43} Planck units in a second.

You have to practically be a PhD in mathematics to understand a Planck unit, but look that up if you are interested. It's something like the time it takes the speed of light to pass a proton.

Now if we multiply those three numbers together, we get $10^{80} \times 4.0 \times 10^{17} \times 10^{43}$ or approximately 10^{140}. Just for good measure, let's multiply this by ten billion more and we get the number 10^{150}. This is how Dembski got the "universal probability limit" or what I'm calling the "definition of impossible."

If the likelihood of an event is 1 in 10^{150}, or anywhere close, and especially anywhere exceeding that, then it is impossible.

The probability of just one DNA arranging itself by chance has been calculated to one chance in $10^{119,000}$. The entire visible universe is 10^{28} inches in diameter. This is from the book, **In The Beginning** by Walt Brown, page 12. [1]

Let's take a fairly simple example of coin flipping. There are only two possibilities for random flipping of a coin, either heads or tails.

What is the possibility that you can flip the coin and it will land on heads 1,000 times in a row? It would be ½ x ½ x ½ ....on and on up to 1,000. There is one chance in $2^{1,000}$. That converts to one chance in 10^{301}.

The conclusion is that it is impossible if we use the "definition" we just established.

So think of it this way. Even if you had one person for every proton, electron, and neutron in the whole universe and they were flipping coins AND they could do 1,000 flips every Planck unit of time since the beginning of the universe, they wouldn't even come close to an outcome of all heads. They have hardly gotten started. Conclusion, it's impossible. The chances are just too small for it ever to happen by accident.

We now have a more realistic understanding of "anything can happen." Actually, as you can see for yourself, it can't.

Did I lose you? Let's go one more simple step and see if that helps. Suppose instead of flipping a coin, you are rolling a die that has six sides and want to get the side with the "one" mark on it to come up 1,000 times in a row.

You can see that is way "harder" than getting 1,000 heads in coin flipping. It's way more impossible, right?

The odds of getting a "one" would be 1/6 x 1/6 x 1/6 ... on and on up to 1,000. This is a much, much bigger number, i.e. $6^{1,000}$. Totally impossible. Are you with me?

And now the final point to show that life did not happen by accident. It is totally impossible to a much, much greater degree than flipping coins or rolling dice.

There are 20 to 22 different so-called "standard" amino acids required by all life forms, even the very simplest living cell. [2]

And those amino acids have to be perfectly arranged in a long chain in an exact order to make a functioning protein. [3] (See my Chapter #74 Proteins.)

Chapter #81 The Definition of Impossible

The really simple proteins are made up of 300 amino acids in a precise order. Once the long chain is created, then it folds over and over again on itself in another exact pattern. Then proteins interact with other proteins.

So the number of possible arrangements for the very simplest protein is 20^{300}. That's because there are 20 to 22 possible amino acids and you have at least 300 amino acids to make the simplest protein.

In a human being the average functional protein has about 450 amino acids, again in a very precise order. That would be one out of 20^{450} random possibilities. That's the average human protein, but the number of amino acids in a single protein can go as high as 34,350 according to one source. [4], [5]

The human body contains approximately 100,000 different, unique proteins [6] but there are estimates up to 2 million. [7] Every different protein has a precise arrangement of the 20 to 22 amino acids.

By the definition of impossible that I have proclaimed, even one single protein is impossible to occur randomly. But we know there are 100,000 or more different proteins (possibly 2,000,000) in the human body.

The most abundant life source on earth, blue-green algae, is also one of the simplest. However, as simple as it is, it still requires about 2,000 genes that each produce different proteins. [8] Any single protein is impossible by randomness and blue-green algae requires 2,000 proteins.

Life is not an accident. The simplest life form could not have occurred randomly. I have shown that it is impossible by definition. Not only that, I have shown it is orders of magnitude more impossible than 1,000 heads in a row by flipping coins.

There must be God.

Chapter #82 The Chicken Or The Egg

You have probably heard the question before about, "What came first, the chicken or the egg?" Everybody knows that chickens come from eggs, but we also know that you don't get eggs unless you have chickens first.

So we have a puzzle that goes around and around trying to figure out the origin of life question. In fact Wikipedia says the chicken versus the egg question goes way back in history to ancient philosophers, even including the writings of Aristotle 350 years before Christ.

Evolutionists would probably follow Wikipedia in saying that the egg came first because mutations would occur in the reproductive process of some other species and the resulting egg when hatched became a modern day chicken.

That's not very satisfactory to me since I see quite a few more chicken or the egg issues that are hiding inside consecutive layers inside of other layers of the chicken and the egg question.

If you have read Chapter #27 on Mutation, then you know that decades of scientific research on mutation has never been shown to produce any viable new species. That's just one challenge.

Think about another fact. No chicken hatches from an egg if the egg is not fertilized by a rooster. So there is another important half of the egg to consider, the male input. Scientists now know that the fertilization takes place way inside the hen and that the egg forms from a protein that is not found in any other animal.

Suppose the impossible could happen and there is actually a mutation of the pre-chicken species that evolutionists claim led up to the chicken. Did the mutation take place before, during, or after fertilization by a necessary type of male component?

Let's designate the pre-chicken female parent's sex chromosomes as the standard XX and the pre-chicken male parent's sex chromosomes as XY. Then the egg coming from the female will have one X chromosome. The male parent contributes either an X or a Y.

If there is a successful mutation in the X chromosomes of the female, call it X*X*, what are you going to get in the next generation? After the contribution from the male, it will be either X*X or X*Y, neither of which is yet really a chicken. That's because the male pre-chicken contributed a non-mutated X or Y. Natural selection will typically weed out mutations like this. So it won't survive to reproduce.

However, let's keep going. Suppose it did. Continuing to the next generation you will have pre-chickens with X*X and roosters with X*Y chromosomes. What do they contribute for the fertilization process? The chicken (female) will provide either X or X*. You will get sperm from the rooster that are either X* or Y.

The odds are only 50-50 that the X* in an egg from the female would be passed to the next generation. The male contributes a X* or Y. The Y is not mutated and neither is one side of female contribution, X. So the next generation will have either, XX*, XY, X*X*, or X*Y.

Only one out of four has the mutation from the original mutated hen.

Can you recognize from this that there also has to be a corresponding "rooster-mutation," from the male side? Otherwise the mutation won't take hold in the lineage. However, even if the rooster mutation occurred somewhere on the earth, it is useless if there is not a successful mating of the two individuals, the mutated pre-hen and the mutated pre-rooster.

Even if you somehow got a mutation that lead to X*X* which could be a hen (female chicken), you are still a long, long way from an X*Y* chromosome set in order to get a rooster (the male chicken). Until you have a female and a male, there will never be a new species.

The odds of any one such mutation occurring are already impossible (again see Chapter 81 Definition of Impossible), but it is even more impossible that both mutations occur within the same generation and those two individuals mate with each other.

As I think about it, almost every aspect of an animal's body poses more chicken or the egg, which came first, problems. Here are some examples:

Which came first, the heart or the arteries and veins to circulate the blood it is pumping?

Which came first, the heart or the lungs to oxygenate the blood that the heart pumps?

Which came first, the muscles throughout the body or the nerves connecting them to the brain to make the muscles work at all?

Which came first, the eyeball or the optic nerve connecting the signals to the brain for interpretation?

Which came first on birds, the wings or the feathers?

What came first, the stomach or the mouth it is attached to?

What came first, the left leg or the right leg?

Which eye came first, the right eye or the left eye?

What came first, the arm or the hand on the end?

Which came first, the male or the female? What about the sperm and the egg? They both had to emerge simultaneously it seems to me. One or the other all alone doesn't make any sense.

The Theory of Evolution is all about slow, gradual, and incremental changes over many generations. So I think it is a very fair question to ask, "Which came first"?

If you allow for an intelligent designer, as I do, then there is no problem with what came first. Think about designing a car. What came first, the wheels or the axles? What came first, the axles or the drive shaft? What came first, the drive shaft or the steering wheel? You could ask hundreds of questions like that and in the mind of the designer there would be answers to what the thought process was. But all the designing was done in the mind. It was all invisible before any prototype was ever created.

Without the invisible design being created first, nothing ever happens in the material world. The material world is the world of effect, not the world of cause.

Once something has been brought into existence in the material world, then further modifications can be made on it.

This, in fact, pretty accurately describes the fossil record. (See Chapter #58 The Cambrian Explosion and Chapter #64 Missing Links for more elaboration.) Most species that appear in the fossil record will appear suddenly and they will be fully formed when they do.

The Theory of Evolution cannot adequately explain the fossil record, cannot show scientific examples of any species mutating into another species even with the help of intelligence/scientists, and cannot explain where the very first life came from to name just three of its major flaws.

Chapter #82 The Chicken Or The Egg

We are all very familiar with the process of creating something. It first starts in the mind where it is invisible. The artist does not put blob after blob of paint on the canvas randomly and end up with a recognizable image of anything. The artist starts with an invisible image in his/her mind as the goal or end product. Then energy, information, and forces are added to bring it into existence.

That's how the world works. That's how the world was created.

There must be God.

Chapter #83 RAS (Reticular Activating System)

This proof is about one of the most important parts of your brain. It may be the answer to the question of why some people cannot accept that there is a God while for others it is as plain as the nose on your face.

In a previous chapter, #16, I wrote about how miraculous and astounding our brains are. This chapter is about just one part of the brain which is about the size of your finger. It is located at the top of the spinal column at the base of the brain stem.

Its job is like a gatekeeper for the signals that are coming in to your brain. As you can imagine, you have millions upon millions of nerve cells that are reporting every second to your brain about sounds, smells, tastes, touches, or sights from whatever they are connected to, like your fingertips, your stomach, your leg muscles, your bladder, well…everything.

Your conscious brain can only handle an estimated 130 messages per second in any meaningful way, so it absolutely needs some way to sort out what is important and prioritize those millions of messages coming from your body. Your RAS is what limits the messages down to the manageable flow.

That's the purpose of the RAS, the Reticular Activating System. Most nerves run through the RAS and then get sent out to various other parts of the brain for the interpretation of their signals.

"The ability to filter out information from external sources and focus on one particular fact, detail, or thought is controlled by this brain region. If it weren't for this circuitry, our consciousness would be overwhelmed and flooded with all sensory information, leading to an inability to make decisions. The system helps in prioritizing information and controls what appears in the mind's eye, at any point of time." [1]

As a simple example of how the RAS prioritizes, think about when you get pain. It immediately gets sent to the front of the consciousness so it can be analyzed and responded to.

But that's not all the RAS does. It is able to learn from the conscious mind what to look for in the environment. Look at this picture and see how quickly you can find one of the two letter "L's" in this diagram.

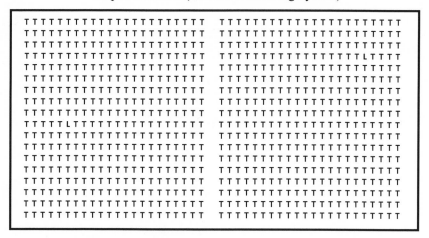

Probably you did not have to look at every single letter one by one.

Have you ever looked for your spouse or child in a huge crowd of people? You found them quickly by scanning. This is what the RAS does.

Here's one more to try. See if you can find the 6 in under 10 seconds.

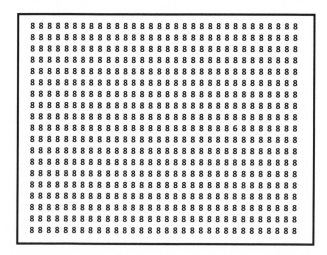

Thus the RAS, as it turns out, is the major goal seeking mechanism in our brains. We can tell it what to look for and it will help us find it. In fact once your RAS is instructed what to look for, whether told consciously or even unconsciously, your RAS will be seeking without you even knowing it.

I'm sure you have heard of the "Law of Attraction". The RAS is the brain mechanism that allows it to work. It sorts through all the inputs from your environment and brings to your attention what you are looking for.

You've also heard of a "Self-Fulfilling Prophecy". What you are looking for is what you will get because you have unconsciously programmed your RAS to find it.

The other thing the RAS does, which we are usually unconscious of, is ignore information and input that we don't want. We think we are seeing "objective truth," but it is already filtered before it gets to our conscious brain. The RAS prevents you from "seeing" information that you don't want to see.

Hence, an evolutionist has set his RAS to reject any information that supports creationism and to only perceive "facts" that support evolution. He doesn't even see evidence contrary to his beliefs because he has told his RAS that he doesn't want to see it. It becomes a "blind spot".

One additional comment I want to add, but there are actually a lot more, is that some researchers believe that whether you are an introvert or an extrovert depends largely on the amount of nerve fibers which are developed in your RAS. [2]

I encourage you to learn more on your own about this amazing part of your brain, the RAS.

So back to the purpose of this chapter. Is it possible for the RAS to have evolved, or is it clearly evidence of design by God?

According to the Theory of Evolution, in some ancient low level species, totally by random accident, a mechanism developed that could sort out differences between incoming signals from nerves. This mechanism gets passed from generation to generation until another random mutation occurs. This mutation allows the mechanism to recognize a certain signal as really important for survival, i.e. pain for example. And then it somehow is able to prioritize that signal over any others.

This is good, so natural selection keeps it going for generation after generation. Then another random mutation somehow recognizes a different nerve signal as hunger. It randomly figures out how to prioritize pain as more important than hunger. This beneficial mutation gets passed down generation after generation.

Eventually this mechanism is able to differentiate millions of nerve signals into which ones are really urgent, which have high priority, and so forth down to low priority. Note that there are about 100 billion neurons in the brain and each one has up to 10,000 connections to other neurons. Also each typical neuron fires about 5 to 50 times per second. [3]

Then, the mechanism randomly mutates again, and again, and again so that it lets only 130 signals pass each second.

Then all the other organisms that don't have this ability die out so that this is the only one that keeps reproducing. Since we all have RAS in our brains, we have to assume we all came from the original ancestor species (even an original couple) that first mutated a fully functioning RAS.

In fact, since most animal species have this RAS ability, the mutations effected all "branches" of the tree of evolution.

Bunk.

No process of mutation over generations has ever produced a viable new species (See Chapter #27, The Truth about Mutation), let alone a complex development of differentiation and prioritizing of nerve impulses that could result in the RAS.

There must be God.

Chapter #84 Homing Pigeons

I've always felt a fascination with the concept of a homing pigeon. There is something somehow very noble about "returning to your home." One of the most famous movie lines is "ET, go home!"

We all somewhere deep in our hearts have a yearning to "go home." Buried deep in our souls, the essence of our being, something is flickering. We want to "return home." What is that? For me it means returning to the God who created me. I believe we have all been separated from our source, and the original love. Okay, on to Homing Pigeons and Proof #84.

I'm sure you have heard of them. Maybe you don't know that they are actually a huge worldwide sport. Millions of people train them and have big races with them for big prizes.

"Pigeons are incredibly complex and intelligent animals. They are one of only a small number of species to pass the 'mirror test' – a test of self-recognition. They can also recognize each letter of the human alphabet, differentiate between photographs, and even distinguish different humans within a photograph." [1]

"Researchers in England devised incredibly complex devices to test the intelligence of all types of birds. Pigeons came out on top." [2]

"Pigeons have strong muscles used for flying. They can fly at the altitude of 6,000 feet. Pigeons can move their wings ten times per second and maintain heartbeats at the rate of 600 times per minute, during a period of 16 hours. Pigeons can fly at the speed of 50 to 60 miles per hour. The fastest known pigeon managed to reach a speed on 92 miles per hour. Because of their incredible speed and endurance, pigeons are used for racing. The Winner of a 400 miles long race can earn a million dollars." [3]

About 5 such races are held each year somewhere in the world.

"In modern times the pigeon has been used to great effect during wartime. In both the First and Second World Wars the pigeon saved hundreds of thousands of human lives by carrying messages across enemy lines." [4]

Pigeons have been carrying messages for humans as far back as 500BC. New evidence suggests they were domesticated by Egyptians some 12,000 years ago. [5]

Pigeons trained for racing often fly about 700 miles in a day. [6] The longest distance ever recorded was in the late 1800's for a homing pigeon that flew over 7,000 miles back home, going from Africa to England, taking over 55 days.

How can the Theory of Evolution (or any other theory without God) explain the development of this ability of a simple bird to find its way home? Even more so, how could this have developed over a slow and gradual process taking generations and generations of mutations and natural selection?

Birds have to find food each day to survive regardless of where they happen to be. Why not just stay there? How does natural selection choose a place far, far away as more beneficial? What's the benefit? Especially if they have never been to that other place before, it could not be selected. And if they started out in the other place, how did they get so lost?

Travel over a long distance is dangerous and risky. It's not likely to be a choice of some unintelligent law of natural selection when compared to staying in one place if there is food. What other criteria could exist for unintelligent selection, perhaps shelter or reproduction? Neither is likely to cause the "homing" ability we are discussing to be able to develop.

Another issue is concerning the exact mechanism that allows them to be able to "go home." Various theories exist but no one really knows for sure! Not yet anyway.

Researchers originally thought they had some "map" in their brains and they relied on the magnetic fields of the earth. But scientists have been able to design ways to shield them from the magnetic fields and also to disable the parts of their brains that are sensitive to it. Still they could "go home." So that may be a dead end.

> "Although magnetic effects on pigeon orientation provide indirect evidence for a magnetic 'map', numerous conditioning experiments have failed to demonstrate reproducible responses to magnetic fields by pigeons." [7]

The latest approach is focused on their ability to smell their way home. No kidding. I have a hard time comprehending the ability of a bird to smell its way for hundreds, if not thousands, of miles. I believe God can create some amazing creatures, but they didn't come into existence by accident.

"The researchers saddled a group of homing pigeons with GPS tracking devices, placed a rubber plug in either their right or left nostrils, and released them 25 miles outside of their home in Pisa, Italy. Pigeons with their left nostrils blocked had a little more trouble navigating than clear-nosed pigeons, but eventually made it home. Birds with their right nostrils blocked made it back, too, but they stopped more often and took an even more circular route than the others. The researchers believe that the birds needed time to gather more smells and construct a map based on odors in the wind. And the finding that the right nostril is the better sniffer suggests that the right and left hemispheres of bird brains have different functions." [8]

Other scientists believe pigeons have ears that can hear the sound of wind over mountains hundreds of miles away. This may be of help in guiding them. Research shows they do actually hear sounds 11 octaves below middle C which is in the range to detect earthquakes and electrical storms. [9]

To believe that pigeons accidentally evolved such a homing mechanism which is so complicated that research scientists cannot understand it takes astounding faith. Think about what is going on in that pigeon's brain for a few minutes. (Recommended reading for more understanding: "For Everything a Reason: Why Ants Walk Crooked and Pigeons Circle Around" [10]).

If a pigeon brain is using smells or hearing or the earth's magnetic fields, it must be able to (A) differentiate very tiny, tiny variations. And it must be able to (B) assign meaning to the differences. Then it must be able to (C) make a decision how to prioritize the data. Then finally the pigeon brain must be able to (D) initiate its own actions based on its analysis. Wow.

All the above arguments should be convincing enough that God created pigeons, but I have one last, and I think, best argument. Think about this: Pigeons in the wild never use a long distance "homing" ability. They never get lost.

They don't need this ability in the wild. Why not? They live, eat, grow old, and die in the areas where they are born. Natural selection cannot explain the development of an ability that is never used and has no survival value.

Homing pigeons don't get lost hundreds of miles from home and then have to search for home. This only happens because of interference by men and women. Amazingly, homing pigeons somehow have incredible capability that they would never normally use in the wild. They only use it when they receive training from people who have learned how to train them.

Homing pigeons must be trained step by step. [11] You first have to train them by acclimating them to the desired "home" or roost. You must keep them locked up for at least four weeks. Then gradually take them farther and farther away and see if they can make it back home. Some do, some don't. If you attach a GPS tracker and let them go at the same distant location many times, you will see that they take many different routes home, but gradually get better and better at it.

Pigeons in the wild never needed to develop the ability to "go home" by natural selection or mutation or any other reason because they were always already home. So how could they ever develop an ability that was never put to use in any way. There is no survival value in it. Pigeons in the wild don't ever wander hundreds of miles from their home AND GET LOST. The ability is useless to them in the wild, but nonetheless they have this ability. That it would or could develop by evolution does not make any sense.

Natural selection requires that an ability get passed from generation to generation because of being selected by survival of the fittest. If the "go home" ability is never used, how could it get passed from generation to generation by natural selection? There is no survival value.

I have faith that the homing ability of the pigeon is a creation of God that is a teaching tool for us. It shows us what we have in our own souls. We have an innate, undeniable, un-erasable desire to "go home." Where is home? It is back to God.

There must be God. God is our home and we are all going there.

244

Chapter #85 Spontaneous Generation

It's funny that I remember learning about Spontaneous Generation way back in grade school or middle school because I don't remember much else from those days. But I remember the teacher saying that people used to believe that if you put an old shirt outside with some seeds in it that in a few weeks you would spontaneously create mice out of the shirt and seeds. How foolish they were. I was laughing inside that we are so much smarter these days.

As a matter of fact, Spontaneous Generation is known to have been believed as far back as the 4th century BC and up until the middle 1800's. It was famously explained by Aristotle.

> "So with animals, some spring from parent animals according to their kind, whilst others grow spontaneously and not from kindred stock; and of these instances of spontaneous generation some come from putrefying earth or vegetable matter, as is the case with a number of insects, while others are spontaneously generated in the inside of animals out of the secretions of their several organs." -Aristotle, History of Animals, Book V, Part 1 [1]

Spontaneous Generation is the belief that life can be created in a very short period of time, almost spontaneously, if given the right conditions. Here are some examples.

> "For example, a seventeenth century recipe for the spontaneous production of mice required placing sweaty underwear and husks of wheat in an open-mouthed jar, then waiting for about 21 days, during which time it was alleged that the sweat from the underwear would penetrate the husks of wheat, changing them into mice. Although such a concept may seem laughable today, it is consistent with the other widely held cultural and religious beliefs of the time." [2]

> "Many believed in spontaneous generation because it explained such occurrences as the appearance of maggots on decaying meat." [3]

> "Crucial to this doctrine is the idea that life comes from non-life, with the conditions, and that no causal agent is needed (i.e. Parent). Such hypothetical processes sometimes are referred to as abiogenesis, in which life routinely emerges from non-living matter on a time scale of anything from minutes to weeks, or perhaps a season or so." [4]

It was not until 1859 because of an ingenious experiment by Louis Pasteur that science began to realize that life does not occur by Spontaneous Generation. In 1864 Pasteur came up with his declaration that "all life is from life". It has become known as the Law of Biogenesis.

"The law of biogenesis, attributed to Louis Pasteur, is the observation that living things come only from other living things, by reproduction (e.g. a spider lays eggs, which develop into spiders). That is, life does not arise from non-living material, which was the position held by spontaneous generation. This is summarized in the phrase "all life [is] from life." A related statement is "all cells [are] from cells;" this observation is one of the central statements of cell theory." [5]

"For more than one hundred years, biologists have taught that spontaneous generation of life from non-living matter was disproven by the work of Redi, Spallanzani, and ultimately Pasteur. This work was so conclusive; that biology codified the "Law of Biogenesis," which states that life only comes from previously existing life. Although, this doesn't prove absolutely that life couldn't ever have generated itself from non-living matter because it is impossible to prove a universal negative. However, the Law of Biogenesis is just as solid as the Law of Gravity. (emphasis added by this Author.) Even though we accept the law of gravity, we cannot prove that if you continued to drop apples forever, that at one point, one apple may not fall." [6]

"Spontaneous generation is the incorrect hypothesis that nonliving things are capable of producing life." [7]

Well, well, we seem to have a dilemma. Evolutionists want us to believe, as they do, that a long time ago, life suddenly and spontaneously sprang from chemicals. That would seem to contradict the Law of Biogenesis and all established science since the 1850's.

Atheists and Evolutionists are clever folks of course and they know they have a problem, namely there is no such thing as Spontaneous Generation, even on the bacterial level. So what do they conclude when all scientific evidence is against them? They conclude there really was Spontaneous Generation a long time ago and Pasteur didn't really disprove it. Besides that, Darwin wasn't really talking about the origin of life. Others have taken care of that argument, or not, sort of.

Here are some of the kinds of things they say.

"So we must ask - what did Pasteur prove? Did he prove that no life can ever come from non-living things? No, he didn't, and this is because you cannot disprove something like that experimentally, only theoretically, and he had no theory of molecular biology to establish this claim. What he showed was that it was highly unlikely that modern living organisms arose from non-living organic material. This is a much more restricted claim than that primitive life once arose from non-living non-organic material." [8]

"1. Pasteur did not disprove the origin of life by natural means, and the saying "all cells from cells" was not intended to cover the initial period of life on earth. Darwin did not propose a theory of the origin of life in the beginning.
2. Evolutionary theory was not proposed to account for the origins of living beings, only the process of change once life exists. However, many have thought that the theory of evolution logically requires a beginning of life, which is true. Of those, many have thought that a natural account of the origin of life is necessary, and some have proposed models which have borne up or not as research proceeds." [9]

So what did Darwin really "prove," huh, using this reasoning? Did rocks come alive? The Theory of Evolution does require a beginning of life and it does NOT provide an explanation. Also in fact no scientific experiment has ever shown that one species can evolve into a different one

Scientists agree there is no Spontaneous Generation. "All life is from life." I say so too. Evolutionists won't say it however.

God is alive and God generated life. It didn't happen accidentally from chemicals or non-living matter.

There must be God.

Chapter #86 The Tongue

One of the most amazing and powerful muscles in the human body is the tongue. Without it we would hardly be able to speak and communicate, let alone something like singing.

Besides that, our tongue greatly facilitates our ability to eat because it moves the food around in our mouths while chewing. Try eating without using your tongue sometime.

It also just so happens that our tongue contains all of our taste buds which send signals to our brain letting us know if our food is sweet, sour, salty, bitter, or umami (now being intensely studied). Imagine your life without your taste buds. Every meal every day would be tasteless and every snack in between.

Evolutionists do not have an explanation for the origin of the tongue. They also have a hard time explaining how a somewhat similar organ accidentally developed in many, many totally unrelated species on the so-called "tree of life".

Reptiles have long tongues for snatching their next meal out of the air. Snakes have a forked tongue that also allows them to smell. Butterflies have a proboscis that unfurls and gets inserted into flowers to suck up nectar. The Blue Whale has the biggest tongue, weighing in at almost 6,000 pounds. [1] It certainly looks like there was some intelligent planning going on.

The human tongue is composed of eight different muscles. How wonderful that they decided to work together in harmony. If you refer back to my Chapter #61 Muscles, you will read that scientists have no explanation for where muscles could have originated. Muscles are that unusual and amazing.

Four of the eight muscles are attached to bones. They are called "extrinsic" [3]. These muscles allow you to move your tongue out and then back in, and side to side and back again to the middle. It certainly is a wonderful accident (for atheists) that we developed a muscle that pulls the tongue back in after we stick it out. Otherwise we'd be stuck with our tongue out all day. I'm sure the muscle that pulls the tongue in must have evolved second. If the tongue never sticks out, there would be no benefit for developing a muscle to pull it back in.

The other four muscles in the tongue are called "intrinsic".

"These muscles alter the shape of the tongue by: lengthening and shortening it, curling and uncurling its apex and edges, and flattening and rounding its surface. This provides shape, and helps facilitate speech, swallowing, and eating." [2]

The astounding property of these muscles is that there are no other muscles like them in the human body. Wow. Scientists don't know where they came from and don't know much about how they work either. The only similar muscles like them are found in the legs of an octopus.

"'The human tongue is a very different muscular system than the rest of the human body,' Khalil Iskarous, an assistant professor of linguistics at the University of Southern California who is helping to lead the research, said in a prepared statement. 'Our bodies are vertebrate mechanisms that operate by muscle working on bone to move. The tongue is in a different muscular family, much like an invertebrate. It is entirely muscle — it's muscle moving muscle.' Both move by compressing fluid in one section of a muscle, creating movement in another part. But we know little about exactly how that movement is initiated and so finely controlled.'" [3]

If you look at the underside of someone's tongue, you will see lots of blood vessels. These are needed to constantly supply the muscles of the tongue because it is always working. Even when you are sleeping your tongue is working. You wouldn't have a tongue without those blood vessels, so how do evolutionists explain the accidental mutations that had to evolve both the muscles and blood vessels simultaneously.

"When we swallow, we stop breathing, and a stiff little flap attached to the back of our tongue covers the top of the trachea, so that food slides down and into our stomachs and not into our lungs. That flap is called the epiglottis." [4]

Can evolutionists explain the process of slow and gradual development of the epiglottis? If you don't have the whole thing in place from the beginning, you would constantly be choking on your food.

You have of course heard of fingerprints. Well, you also have a 'tongue-print' that is totally unique to you among all human beings. [5]

"Your mouth is a jungle, home to bacteria, viruses, fungi, and protozoa. When you open wide a fresh supply make their way inside. Most are harmless, taking advantage of the wonderful hospitality inside you. Let's looks at some of the many types of bacteria found in your mouth, tongue and elsewhere....Of all the types of microbes living in your mouth, bacteria are the most numerous. It has been estimated that there are over

100 million in every milliliter of saliva from more than 600 different species." [6]

I imagine that atheists must feel very grateful for the extremely long series of fortuitous accidents that allows them to be able to talk. In an astounding coincidence to the evolution of a tongue, we also evolved the larynx right at the top of the tube going to our lungs where air could be exhaled over it to make various sounds. The mouth also evolved into a very convenient shape that allows the three, working together, to make a tremendous variation of sounds. Those sounds get accidentally heard by the ears of other humans, who luckily evolved ears.

All those variations of sounds could be repeated and repeated until the other person began to figure out that they actually meant something intelligent. Atheists refuse to see any intelligent planning behind all this. They insist that for every small incremental and accidental mutation at the DNA level there must have been some benefit to the new DNA so that it was "selected" by a natural (i.e. godless) law. This DNA won out over all other DNA patterns until the next slight change. Either the larynx, tongue, and mouth developed simultaneously or they developed sequentially, but in the end we could talk and others could listen.

As you can probably tell by now, I'm having trouble taking the Theory of Evolution seriously.

What is the explanation for how taste buds evolved? They are so small you can't even see them.

"Each taste bud is made up of taste cells, which have sensitive, microscopic hairs called microvilli. Those tiny hairs send messages to the brain, which interprets the signals and identifies the taste for you." [7]

The average tongue has between 2,000 and 10,000 taste buds. Each taste bud has about 15 receptacles that send the signals about taste to your brain. Every 10 to 14 days, your taste buds die off and are replaced with new ones. [8]

Let's thank God or cosmic accidents for that DNA mutation!

It's really wonderful that taste buds accidentally would evolve on your tongue rather than your toe, or your fingertip, or your elbow. In fact, they are mostly found on the top side of your tongue with a few others underneath your tongue, on your lips, or in your cheeks.

There are five different kinds of taste buds. Now how did that evolve? And miraculously they all happen to be on or around your tongue. How great is that?

None of your taste buds work unless they are in a moist environment. That's a nice coincidence too because your mouth is a moist environment. In fact, the tongue is covered with a mucous membrane and even has saliva glands to keep the tongue moist.

By doing just a little research on the chemical process that happens between the chemicals in our food and their stimulation of our taste buds, we find that the whole process inside the receptors is incredibly complex. I think evolutionists have a problem explaining this too.

If you put something sweet in your mouth, the taste receptor for sweet gets triggered and sends an electrical signal all the way to a specific location in your brain. Luckily there is a really, really long chain of nerves that accidentally connects your taste receptor to your brain. It's really lucky or we would never know what sweet is. (I'm being facetious of course.)

I'm guessing that sweet taste buds would have had to be the first to evolve because they are our favorite. Then after tens of thousands of years there was an accidental mutation and another and another and finally we had a new taste, maybe "salty" or "sour". I'm pretty sure "bitter" would come last. Then it happened again, and again, and again until there are finally five different tastes. Wow. Is that believable? Not really.

How wonderful and amazingly lucky that we have all those taste buds or else eating would be mighty, mighty dull. Also it's a fantastic coincidence (for atheists) that it just so happens that the food that evolved out there in the world just happens to trigger the taste buds that evolved and we end up with delicious tastes. Not only delicious but nutritious too. If the food out there tasted terrible and wasn't healthy for us, we would never eat it and hence never have energy to keep on living and evolve. Then we wouldn't be here.

This is just too many lucky accidents for me to believe in.

Conclusion, there must be God.

Chapter #87 Pain

Thank God for pain...nobody ever said.

However, you are about to learn why we can in fact recognize that a loving God created us because we have the incredible ability that allows us to feel pain.

There are about twenty documented cases of American children born with a genetic defect called "congenital insensitivity to pain." It makes them unable to feel any pain at all. This becomes one continuous nightmare for their parents.

> "Congenital insensitivity to pain (CIP), also known as congenital analgesia, is one or more rare conditions in which a person cannot feel (and has never felt) physical pain.... It is an extremely dangerous condition." [1]

In my footnotes I reference a video of a little girl on the Oprah Winfrey show.

> "She poked out her own eye, chewed her skin raw and bit her tongue until it bled. Five-year-old Gabby Gingras feels no pain. As someone who has no nerves to carry the pain signal from her skin to her brain, she's one of the rarest little girls in the country." [2]

There is also Ashlyn Blocker.

> "Ashlyn walked over and put her hands on the muffler. When she lifted them up the skin was seared away. There was one story about the fire ants that swarmed her in the backyard, biting her over a hundred times while she looked at them and yelled: 'Bugs! Bugs!' There was the time she broke her ankle and ran around on it for two days before her parents realized something was wrong." [3]

Here is a footnote reference to the story of Isaac Brown. [4] He broke his pelvis and did not know it. One day he was found pounding on a door with a piece of broken glass. No pain. He once put his hand on a hot stove burner. No pain. He had to be taught that "blood is bad".

Dr. Stephen Waxman, a leading researcher on this condition, blames the problem on mutation and says that probably just one gene out of 30,000 has been messed up. [5] Evolutionists should listen to themselves if they say a mutation is what causes this horrendous problem. And then watch them try to say with total belief in Evolution that mutation is the miraculous process that gave us all good things.

At the beginning of May in 2015, I hurt a vertebrae in my spine and was in bed for two and a half weeks with excruciating pain. During that time, I was not thanking God for pain actually. But I did think a lot about pain. You would think that with two and half weeks in bed that I could get a lot of reading and such done. Not actually. I could only think in a straight line for a few seconds at a time. Then the pain would return and the only thing I could think of was how to adjust my body to alleviate some of the pain. I spent most of the time thinking about how to get out of pain. When you are in pain, it overrules everything else.

Our ability to feel pain is phenomenal in its complexity. It is unbelievable in its accuracy. The sensitivity to the damage, vicinity, and seriousness of an injury is way better than you could imagine if you designed it yourself.

There are several different pain receptors, but they, in fact, work together to report the intensity and severity of the damage that has been done.

> "Your pain receptors are the most numerous. Every square centimeter of your skin contains around 200 pain receptors but only 15 receptors for pressure, 6 for cold and 1 for warmth." [6]

Think about that…200 receptors for pain in a square centimeter. Each one of them connected to your brain.

There are two different types of nerve cells lined up end to end that report pain to your brain. They even use completely different types of pathways to get to your brain. Two different centers in your brain do the interpretation of the pain signals.

> "The conscious perception of pain probably takes place in the thalamus and lower centers; interpretation of the quality of pain is probably the role of the cerebral cortex."[7]

In other words you have more than one system in your body for reporting pain. Think about how two systems to accomplish the same function could have possibly evolved separately and accidentally. You have a backup system.

> "Pain travels through redundant pathways, ensuring to inform the subject: 'Get out of this situation immediately.' Without these attributes, the organism has no means to prevent or minimize tissue injury." [8]

253

"Pain from the skin is transmitted through two types of nerve fibers. A-delta fibers relay sharp, pricking types of pain, while C fibers carry dull aches and burning sensations. Pain impulses are relayed to the spinal cord, where they interact with special neurons that transmit signals to the thalamus and other areas of the brain." [9]

Wikipedia writers believe in Evolution and make this statement in their article, "human awareness of painful stimuli is an evolutionary necessity to avoid injury and death." Well, duh.

Since it is necessary, then it must have evolved due to necessity. That's wrong because mutation and natural selection are not driven by necessity (an intellectual concept.)

But just exactly HOW does the Theory of Evolution describe the development of your pain recognition system? I did not find any answers to my question, only a lot of descriptions of the history of pain research. Evolution says there must have been a slow and gradual process of random mutations that were beneficial. So somehow a receptor for pain accidentally mutated into existence and that was beneficial enough to spread all over our bodies and then be inherited to all mankind.

But it's more complicated than that. It must have taken millions of more mutations before the nerve chain (of hundreds or thousands of nerves) developed to get the signal to our brains which then somehow learned to recognize the signal as pain.

How could pain receptors somehow mutate everywhere, completely covering our bodies? But somehow they did not cover our bodies equally since certain areas have more receptors than others. Luckily the most pain receptors are in exactly the places where we need them most.

But the story is much more complicated yet again. There are actually four different types of pain receptors in the skin. How could that evolve?

"Skin nociceptors (i.e. pain) may be divided into four categories based on function.

The first type is termed high threshold mechanonociceptors or specific nociceptors. These nociceptors respond only to intense mechanical stimulation such as pinching, cutting or stretching.

The second type is the thermal nociceptors, which respond to the above stimuli as well as to thermal stimuli. (i.e. hot or cold)

The third type is chemical nociceptors, which respond only to chemical substances.

A fourth type is known as polymodal nociceptors, which respond to high intensity stimuli such as mechanical, thermal and to chemical substances like the previous three types." [10]

There is a great amount of research and information available if you want to continue to study about pain. For example, scientists have been able to distinguish 22 degrees of "Just Noticeable Differences" in applying heat to our skin. This article, as you can see is just scratching the surface.

Also it's a fact your body has pain receptors everywhere, not only on your skin, but also in all of your joints, your arteries, and inside your body connected to all your various organs. There are different types of pain sensors in these areas as well. Did all this evolve slowly and gradually? Not likely.

"The distribution of pain receptors in the gastrointestinal mucosa apparently is similar to that in the skin; thus, the mucosa is quite sensitive to irritation and other painful stimuli. Although the parenchyma of the liver and the alveoli of the lungs are almost entirely insensitive to pain, the liver and bile ducts are extremely sensitive, as are the bronchi and parietal pleura." [11]

Let me highlight one more amazing ability we have which defies Evolution, our reflexes. If you put your hand on a hot surface, you will pull it off immediately, even before the signal gets to your brain. Similar reflexes exist connected to all of our pain receptors. The neurons from our pain receptors to our brains all go through our spinal cord. But there is a short circuit process if the pain is intense. There are nerves directly from the spine to our muscles that make them pull away from any pain source. Our brain is bypassed. Is there really a way for this to evolve slowly and gradually?

Nobody likes pain, but what an incredible blessing it is that we have the ability to feel it. If not, we would be constantly injuring ourselves in terrible ways and have really shortened lives. When we experience pain, we are strongly driven to do something about it and to get it to stop. Looking at the whole pain perceiving ability, it totally testifies to having been designed.

For a related chapter, read Chapter #70 Healing. The process of healing is another total miracle that had to be designed.

There must be God.

Chapter #88 The Waggle Dance of Honeybees

I think you are probably familiar with the game of Charades where one person tries to act out a phrase while other members of his/her team try to guess the meaning.

Let's suppose that the message you are given to act out is the exact location of tonight's dinner for your team. It so happens the dinner is a couple of miles away.

Remember, you cannot speak and you cannot write. It's pretty important that you can convey this information or you might all go hungry and eventually die.

Oh, and just to make it a little more tricky, let's just say that we shrink your communication ability down to the level of a honeybee and similarly for those receiving the message.

Sounds really, really difficult, right? Well, just how do bees do it successfully all the time?

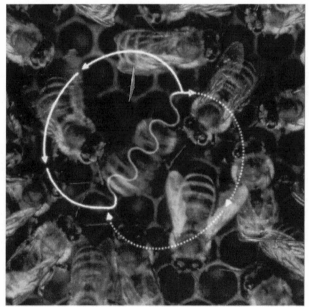

Image 15. Honeybee Waggle Dance.

Please go to the footnoted reference and watch this National Geographic video (less than 2 minutes) to see a great summation of how they accomplish it. [1] As you might have guessed from the title, they do a little dance.

The Theory of Evolution might say that given millions of years and thousands of generations, the precise method to communicate where the food is located had to (A) accidentally get acted out one day by one honeybee in some way that was (B) correctly understood by another bee. The second one who understood the message, (C) flew off in the right direction and (D) to the right distance and found food. Somehow this accidental communication of information (E) was passed on to other bees in the hive and then (F) passed on to the next generation and ultimately (G) to all honeybees in the world.

I'm having a little trouble imagining that this could happen (sarcasm intended).

Around 40 years ago a scientist, named Karl von Frisch, a professor of zoology at the University of Munich in Germany, discovered the communication technique of honeybees. He set up a very ingenious experiment. He created two honeybee feeders and set them in totally different directions and distances from the hive. Then when bees eventually arrived at the feeders, he painted little spots on them so he knew which ones visited that feeder. He was able to film their actions inside the hive. That is when he discovered what has been named the Honeybee Waggle Dance. He was later given the Nobel Prize for Medicine in 1973 for his work.

Wikipedia says,

> "Waggle dance is a term used in beekeeping and ethology for a particular figure-eight dance of the honey bee. By performing this dance, successful foragers can share, with other members of the colony, information about the direction and distance to patches of flowers yielding nectar and pollen, to water sources, or to new nest-site locations." [2]

Von Frisch discovered that the honeybee will do a short wiggling dance in a straight line, then stop wiggling. It will swing around to the right and circle back to its original starting point for the dance and then do it all over again. However, the second time when it gets to the end, it will swing around to the left and circle back to the beginning point.

Von Frisch was able to determine that the precise axis the bee is traveling during the dance section tells the other bees the direction to fly in. He also discovered that the number of waggles during the dance was communicating the distance that they should fly.

"While running the straight-line course of the dance, the bee's body, especially the abdomen, wags vigorously from side to side. This vibration of the body produces a tail-wagging motion. At the same time, the bee emits a buzzing sound, produced by wingbeats at a low audio frequency of 250 to 300 hertz or cycles per second." [3]

But it is much more amazing than you might first think, although this is totally amazing already. The bee hive is usually built vertically. However, the direction that the bees have to fly will be a horizontal direction. Somehow the bee doing the dance has to be able to take the horizontal direction and distance information and convert it in her brain before she does the dance on a vertical surface. Also, the bees receiving the information have to be able to convert it in their brains back into the original information horizontally.

Von Frisch discovered that the dance being done on the vertical hive surface was using gravity as a reference point and that straight up represented the location of the sun and straight down represented 180 degrees away from the sun.

Here is a footnote reference to an outstanding animated video from Georgia Tech College of Computing (7.5 minutes) that illustrates the experiments of Karl von Frisch and demonstrates how bees communicate. [4]

If the axis of the waggle dance was 30 degrees off of the vertical to the right, then the other bees were able to understand that they should take the position of the sun and then fly exactly 30 degrees to the right. Amazing that they can know the exact angle, right?

"The distance between hive and recruitment target is encoded in the duration of the waggle runs. The farther the target, the longer the waggle phase. The more excited the bee is about the location, the more rapidly it will waggle, so it will grab the attention of the observing bees, and try to convince them. If multiple bees are doing the waggle dance, it's a competition to convince the observing bees to follow their lead, and competing bees may even disrupt other bees' dances or fight each other off." [5]

Now if you are really thinking, you'll realize a big problem...namely the sun keeps moving all day long. Even more challenging is that the arc of the sun is not the same every day but changes in the sky according to the seasons. If the bees live south of the equator, you have to flip things over.

Not only does the sun moving in the sky make it difficult, but sometimes it is so cloudy that we can't see the sun. Astoundingly, the bees are able to see ultraviolet light, which penetrates the cloud cover.

So they can see the sun at all times. Not only that, but even more bewildering for a non-believer is that the honeybee's eyes polarize the sunlight like polarized sunglasses. That means they can even more accurately identify the exact direction of the sun.

The bees have a finely tuned internal clock (Where did they get that?) so a dancing bee who has been in the darkness of the nest for a while somehow calculates where the sun is going to be when their fellow bees head off from the hive. The axis of its dance has to change because the sun moved in the sky.

Not only that of course, but those leaving the hive are going to be continually calculating changes to the direction they should fly according to the amount of time that has elapsed and the change in position of the sun.

Here is another video. This one is loaded with film footage of bees at work and what their eyes are really seeing. (5min, 18sec.) [6]

The bee also communicates a second very important piece of information…the distance to fly to get to the food source. This is done by either the number of waggles or the length of time waggling. Researchers now estimate that one second of waggling equals one kilometer of distance. If the food source is close, there is no waggling at all, but just a circling around motion.

> "While several variables of the waggle dance relate to distance (such as dance "tempo" or the duration of buzzing sounds), the duration of the straight-run portion of the dance, measured in seconds, is the simplest and most reliable indicator of distance. As the distance to the food source increases, the duration of the waggling portion of the dance (the "waggle run") also increases. The relationship is roughly linear. For example, a forager that performs a waggle run that lasts 2.5 seconds is recruiting for a food source located about 2,625 meters away." [7]

But note that scientists have observed that if there is a strong headwind coming from the direction of the food source, the bee will have to fly a longer time to reach the destination. The waggle dance will last longer. This leads scientists to believe that the bees are not measuring the distance to fly but the amount of energy it takes to get to the food source.

The forager bees who do the waggle dance also bring back on their legs and abdomen some of the food source that has been discovered. So the other bees are able to sample what their goal is at the distant location.

So smell may also be a strong component of the communication. Pretty amazing.

Scientists know the waggle dance is real, so bees really in fact can do this. However there is controversy about how much it is effectively used by other bees, with estimates as low as 10% of other bees actually using the data.

The simplest and most elegant explanation for the waggle dance is that it was designed by the Creator of the Universe, an unimaginably superior intelligence. If you decide against there being a Creator, then you have to posit some other explanation which must be based on pure accident and random happenstance coming together in a fortuitous way. Then another random accident brings another fortuitous result. This pattern repeats itself again and again, thousands or more accurately millions of times. Notwithstanding that this violates the laws of nature and probability, you must imagine and try to believe that's how it happened because, voila, the truth is that scientists have now discovered these facts of how bees communicate using the waggle dance.

I'll stick with, there must be God.

Chapter #89 Earthworms

Did you ever stop to think that we might not be around if not for worms? At least we would not be as healthy as we are.

"In 1881 Charles Darwin wrote: 'It may be doubted whether there are many other animals which have played so important a part in the history of the world, as have these lowly organized creatures.'" [1]

"They are the main contributors to enriching and improving soil for plants, animals and even humans. Earthworms create tunnels in the soil by burrowing, which aerates the soil to allow air, water and nutrients to reach deep within the soil. Earthworms eat the soil which has organic matter such as decaying vegetation or leaves. Plants cannot use this organic matter directly. After organic matter is digested, the earthworm releases waste from their bodies called castings. Castings contain many nutrients that the plant can use. Some people even use earthworm castings as garden fertilizer." [2]

I'm sure you have at least a passing encounter with worms. Maybe you dissected one in a school biology class or you went catching nightcrawlers for fishing.

Earthworms range in size from one millimeter to over six feet long in Australia. [3] The world record is 22 feet long from South Africa. Most worms live in the upper one meter of the earth, but have been known to exist as deep as five meters (16.5 feet). [4]

It is estimated that there are between 250,000 and 1,750,000 worms per acre (i.e. between 62 to 432 per square meter). The mass of all the worms actually outweighs the animal life on the surface. [5]

This amazing creature makes it very hard to believe in Evolution. Go read a few articles with details about the earthworm's body structure or benefits to nature.

Clearly they benefit insects, birds, amphibians, plants, and humans, but what good are they for their own benefit? What explains why Natural Selection or survival of the fittest would choose worms to prosper and not die out?

If a bird eats a worm, the bird survives, but not the worm. Clearly the bird is the fittest to survive. If the worm eats dirt and dead leaves and poops a nice nitrogen fertilizer for plants, that's good for the plants, but what does the worm get out of it?

Wikipedia states "earthworm casts are five times richer in available nitrogen, seven times richer in available phosphates, and 11 times richer in available potassium than the surrounding upper 6 inches (150 mm) of soil. In conditions where humus is plentiful, the weight of casts *(poops. Author)* produced may be greater than 4.5 kg (10 lb.) per worm per year." [6] Wow!

Earthworm populations consume two tons of dry matter per acre per year, partly digesting and mixing it with the soil.

Worms also use chemicals for digestion called drilodefensins.

> "A world without drilodefensins would be a very different world, according to the researchers. Dr Bundy, from the Department of Surgery and Cancer at Imperial, said: 'Without drilodefensins, fallen leaves would remain on the surface of the ground for a very long time, building up to a thick layer. Our countryside would be unrecognisable, and the whole system of carbon cycling would be disrupted.'" [7]

Earthworms break up thatch which is a rough, dense layer of matter on the surface composed of dead grass, stems, and roots. Thatch blocks the flow of water and nutrients to the soil.

There are 6,000 to 7,000 different species of worms. Remember now that the definition of a species is that only members of the species can successfully inter-breed. So if two worms are from a different species of worms, they cannot inter-breed. Unless there is breeding, there is no Evolution. So each worm has to find another one of its own species before it can breed. It would seem pretty hard to find a mate if you are living and burrowing underground most of the time.

Worms have no eyes, another problem in finding themselves a mate. But they don't need eyes if they are in a dark hole anyway. Luckily for worms, they are hermaphrodites. This means they have both male and female genitals. But they can't fertilize themselves, so they must encounter another worm of the same species.

> "Special ventral setae *(bristle like hairs. Author)* are used to anchor mating earthworms by their penetration into the bodies of their mates." [8]

When two worms meet and copulate, both worms get "pregnant" and each produces an egg cocoon which will contain between one and 20 eggs. [9] The babies when they hatch look just like the parents but very tiny and will grow to full size in about 12 months.

Let's think for a minute about the problem that Evolution would have trying to explain hermaphrodites. What came just before the first worm? Was there an original worm with both genders within itself? Then we would have to explain how the male and female parts differentiated into separate organs in separate locations on the worm. Did it suddenly mutate both male and female parts in the same generation? That's extremely unlikely. Remember that Evolution is slow and gradual. But if the female part develops first without the male part, no fertilization or reproduction can take place.

Even if you suddenly had one worm that mutated with both male and female genitals, you'd still need a second one to fertilize it. Maybe we could imagine that two worms from the same cocoon both had the mutation. But they have to grow up for months before they can mate and then they have to find each other to do it. But instant genitals which are male and female couldn't be called evolution, slow and gradual.

Worms are all over the world. They are mostly all the same, so they had to have originated with one "Adam/Eve worm" whose descendants have spread all over the world. Where are all the precursors of this first ancestor worm if it really did evolve? (See my Chapter #64 Missing Links) They must have all died out because there is no evidence of them. If any intermediary worm type beings before the first ancestor worm existed and they had descendants, then all those descendants died out without a trace.

If we theorize that in the beginning there were male worms and female worms, we need to inquire how they originated by mutation and evolved separately. Did the male worm evolve one day from an egg of some non-worm animal? That doesn't work if there is no female nearby. He would die without reproducing. Male and female would have had to evolve simultaneously and within the same dirt pile, within a few feet from each other.

Hermaphrodite reproduction by worms is very, very interesting and complicated. Slow and gradual evolution is impossible to explain it. After mating, a worm makes a slime tube and fills it with fluid. It then crawls out of the slime tube depositing eggs and then sperm into the tube as it passes by. The tube then becomes an egg cocoon. Baby worms emerge in two to four weeks.

"The earthworm will move forward out of the slime tube. As the earthworm passes through the slime tube, the tube will pass over the female pore picking up eggs. The tube will continue to move down the earthworm and pass over the male pore called the spermatheca which has the stored sperm called the spermatozoa. The eggs will fertilize and the slime tube will close off as the worm moves completely out of the tube. The slime tube will form an "egg cocoon" and be put into the soil." [10]

Let's turn to other thoughts about the "first worm". Could it have evolved under the ground where they live now? That's not likely. It must have developed from an above ground animal. Developing reproduction processes under ground seems almost impossible.

If the "first worm" mutated into existence above ground, what would lead it to start eating dirt? The whole digestive system front to back has to be in place before it can eat dirt. The mouth has to be there along with the stomach, the circulatory system, even the excretory system.

Also, the earthworm has special adaptations so that it can live underground. It either slithers through soft dirt and dead leaves, pushing with a force ten times its body weight, or else it eats its way through hard ground. But how did it evolve the ability to move its various segments in order to slither. That takes major coordination so a brain and nerves are necessary.

A worm also has tiny hairs sticking out of its sides that help hold one part in place while another part creeps forward. How does mutation explain the existence of tiny hairs all over a worm's body?

"The earthworm is made of about 100-150 segments. The segmented body parts provide important structural functions. Segmentation can help the earthworm move. Each segment or section has muscles and bristles called setae. The bristles or setae help anchor and control the worm when moving through soil. The bristles hold a section of the worm firmly into the ground while the other part of the body protrudes forward. The earthworm uses segments to either contract or relax independently to cause the body to lengthen in one area or contract in other areas. Segmentation helps the worm to be flexible and strong in its movement." [11]

Circumferential and longitudinal muscles on the periphery of each segment enable the worm to move. Similar sets of muscles line the gut, and their actions move the digesting food toward the worm's anus. [12]

It's a fact that the excrement from worms is a fertilizer for plants. How could that be a random mutation that gets selected by survival of the fittest? Why would the worm's survival depend on the value of its excrement to plants.

The worm has a highly developed digestive system that creates usable nitrogen and other elements for the plants. It even uses tiny grains of sand to help grind up the dirt. That would take hundreds, if not thousands, of mutations of a worm's DNA to produce.

"Food enters the mouth. The pharynx acts as a suction pump; its muscular walls draw in food. In the pharynx, the pharyngeal glands secrete mucus. Food moves into the esophagus, where calcium (from the blood and ingested from previous meals) is pumped in to maintain proper blood calcium levels in the blood and food pH. From there the food passes into the crop and gizzard. In the gizzard, strong muscular contractions grind the food with the help of mineral particles ingested along with the food. Once through the gizzard, food continues through the intestine for digestion. The intestine secretes pepsin to digest proteins, amylase to digest polysaccharides, cellulase to digest cellulose, and lipase to digest fats. Instead of being coiled like a mammalian intestine, an earthworm's intestine increases surface area to increase nutrient absorption by having many folds running along its length. The intestine has its own pair of muscle layers like the body, but in reverse order—an inner circular layer within an outer longitudinal layer." [13]

Think about all those incredible chemical reactions that are going on inside the lowly worm.

Scientists believe that worms have a sense of touch and taste. That takes an amazing nervous system.

Worms have blood and a circulatory system. How could that evolve and what keeps the blood moving?

"The aortic arches function like a human heart. There are five pairs of aortic arches, which have the responsibility of pumping blood into the dorsal and ventral blood vessels. The dorsal blood vessels are responsible for carrying blood to the front of the earthworm's body. The ventral blood vessels are responsible for carrying blood to the back of the earthworm's body." [14]

Earthworms are very unique creatures. They are amazingly adapted to do what they do, burrowing through dirt and leaving fertilizer, air and water passages for plant growth behind them. They have a brain, digestive and excretory system, nervous system, movement ability, reproductive system, touch and light sensitivity. All this is proof of design and purpose.

There must be God.

Chapter #90 Copying Degradation

Most of you who have ever worked in an office are probably aware that when you make a photocopy, it is not an exact copy of the original. If you then make a photocopy of the photocopy, and you continue to repeat this process always making a copy of the last copy, then pretty soon you will be able to really notice the difference between the very original sheet and the latest copy. The discrepancies become really obvious after a while.

There is always a slight degradation with each new generation of copying. This is what I mean by "Copying Degradation."

In my office we have a tremendous copy machine that does color copies, double-sided, folded, stapled, and even hole-punched copies. It cost over $20,000. But it cannot make a perfect copy and is subject to the same rule as above. Every once in a while, we have to call the technician to repair it and re-calibrate it.

If you talk to computer hardware people, you will also learn that the same is true for digital copying inside a computer. The computer is based on the binary system, meaning all information is stored as "0's" and "1's". Computers are, of course, vastly more accurate at copying, but sooner or later there is a mistake. You know this because sometimes your computer locks up for no reason and you have to restart it to make it work. Every modem and Wi-Fi system has a built in error correction system or "protocol" that checks constantly to be sure the data being transmitted and received is identical.

So if Copying Degradation is a universal truth in the real world, what is the result that it yields? Do we ever end up with something that is better than the original? We know we never end up with a photocopy that is better than the original, especially after many generations. For data copying in computer programs, an error in copying data, or worse yet the program software, is most likely to cause a malfunction and very, very, very unlikely to result in a better program.

Let's think about DNA. Rather than a binary system like computers, it is based on four possible "base pairs" and two are used on any given rung of the ladder. What do you think keeps happening as the DNA gets copied over and over? This is a question that scientists can now investigate.

The Theory of Evolution predicts that given time and many small incremental and accidental changes to the DNA coding, along with some natural selection, the end result is a totally new species that is fully functioning.

Evolution predicts that DNA copying has made copying mistakes millions upon millions of times and that this has successfully increased functioning complexity. Starting out with something akin to an amoeba, we have advanced all the way to the millions of varied species and to the human body and brain.

According to my Internet search, the latest scientific estimate is that there are approximately 8,700,000 different species on the earth. The Theory of Evolution says that all 8.7 million species started out from a single cell with DNA. By repeatedly copying that DNA over and over, mutations occurred so that the 8.7 million new species eventually arose.

That's a phenomenally huge statement of faith if you ask me.

Those who believe in God have many varied ideas of how God did it, but it's still a very big mystery. They do however admit that their beliefs are based on faith.

However, there is some agreement among the believers who are also scientists that God created according to "kinds". This means that God created an original model or body plan of a species and then there was tremendous variation from that original. Take for example the "dog kind". God somehow created the original male and female dog and then all the different breeds eventually could emerge by natural selection or mankind's active intervening in the process.

Dogs actually have 78 chromosomes in their genome which allows for tremendous variations. By comparison, chimpanzees have 48 chromosomes and humans have only 46 chromosomes.

These facts seem to show the opposite from the Theory of Evolution model. More complicated life has less chromosomes (comparing humans and dogs). Evolution starts with a very simple set of DNA that branches into more and more complicated forms of life.

Creation theories start with a very complicated original "kind" and predict that over time DNA changes lead to loss (not gain) of DNA complexity and the differences and variations within a species are the result of the loss of information in the DNA code.

So here we have two profoundly opposite predictions and we should be able to do scientific experiments to observe which of these two processes is taking place in nature.

If evolution is true, then we should see the DNA of species getting more and more complicated and gradual improvements in the code which eventually can lead to a new species. After all, that's how they believe we got the 8.7 million species.

But if the DNA copying from one generation to the next shows that there is copying degradation, then our scientific conclusion will have to be that evolution is false. That will only leave us with one of the alternative theories that involves a Creator being.

Well, folks, the scientific research has been done. The results are in. There is in fact copying degradation at the DNA level which is taking place. DNA degrades over time. It does not get more complex. Is this surprising, not really? It's the same in life everywhere you look.

> "My own work with 35 protein families suggests that the rate of destruction is, at minimum, 8 times the rate of neutral or beneficial mutations...Simply put, the digital information of life is being destroyed much faster than it can be repaired or improved. New functions may evolve, but the overall loss of functional information in other areas of the genome will, on average, be significantly greater. The net result is that the digital information of life is running down." [1]

It is statistically impossible for evolution to be taking place because it could not overcome the disadvantage of 8 harmful errors to every one possibly beneficial or neutral error.

Durston, author of the above quote, goes much further, even saying the human genome is running down.

> "First, the digital information for the bacterial world is slowly eroding away due to a net deletional bias [2] in mutations involving insertions and deletions. A second example is the fruit fly, one of the most studied life forms in evolutionary biology. It, too, shows an ongoing, genome-wide loss of DNA [3] across the entire genus."

Even human DNA has been shown to be degrading.

> "Finally, a consideration of the long-term consequences of current human behavior for deleterious-mutation accumulation leads to the conclusion that a substantial reduction in human fitness can be expected over the next few centuries in industrialized societies unless novel means of genetic intervention are developed." [4]

> "We continue to discover more examples of DNA loss, suggesting that the biological world is slowly running down. Microevolution is good at fine-tuning existing forms within their information limits and occasionally getting something right, but the steady accumulation of

deleterious mutations on the larger scale suggests that mutation-driven evolution is actually destroying biological life, not creating it." [5]

Here is another important fact. Scientists have discovered that there are as many as three processes within a cell that actually repair DNA when there is a mutation. These are (A) damage reversal, (B) damage removal, (C) damage tolerance. [6] Cells do not like copying mistakes. Another name for mutation in cells is cancer.

> "As a major defense against environmental damage to cells, DNA repair is present in all organisms examined including bacteria, yeast, drosophila, fish, amphibians, rodents and humans. DNA repair is involved in processes that minimize cell killing, mutations, replication errors, persistence of DNA damage and genomic instability. Abnormalities in these processes have been implicated in cancer and aging." [7]

As far back as scientists have known about DNA, there is no known example of a new species arising out of another species. Believe me, they have been trying to find one. As mentioned in Chapter # 27 The Truth About Mutation, scientists have tried unsuccessfully to mutate fruit flies for 40 years and could never produce a new species.

If you have a theory and you derive logical predictions from that theory, but those predictions are totally false, then the only conclusion is that the theory is false and worthless for further study. That's where we stand today if we accept the scientific evidence.

The Theory of Evolution is scientifically falsifiable.

As we have seen throughout history, faiths and beliefs die slowly even after they are proven false. But rest assured, the Theory of Evolution is dying. Many don't know it yet, but scientific evidence will put the nail in its coffin.

Therefore, there must be God.

Chapter #91 Spider Webs

I'm sure you must be familiar with spider webs. Every one of us has seen them and most of us have gotten tangled in one from time to time. Most of us would be just fine if we never had anything to do with a spider or its web again.

We try to avoid encountering them or even thinking about them, but a spider's web is an engineering marvel that most of us could not begin to figure out how to create even if we had the resources. Scientists don't even know how spiders do it.

Most spiders have three different "spinnerets" that are organs in their bodies to produce the three different types of silk that go into making a spider web. They have both sticky and non-sticky silk. Most of the silk threads in a spider web are the "sticky" type which catches insects for them to eat.

As you have probably heard, the silk of spider webs is stronger than steel for its size, but it is way more elastic.

Did you ever wonder why spiders don't get all caught up in their own webs? They have special legs, claws, feet, and hairs that help them not get stuck. They also spin the type of silk that is "non-sticky". When they run across their web, they stay mostly on the non-sticky silk threads.

Reading about spider webs is a fascinating education.

There are so many elements that come together to create a spider web that most rational people who study about the details have to conclude that it is a total miracle of engineering. Only blind faith can assert it happened by mutation and natural selection through slow and gradual changes as predicted by the Theory of Evolution. If you are going to have blind faith, why not pick one that is so much simpler and more elegant, namely, there is a super-intellect designing it all.

I want to go through the article in Wikipedia.Org on Spider Webs and point out some questions that you should ask yourself if you have any doubt about God.

> "When spiders moved from the water to the land in the Early Devonian period, they started making silk to protect their bodies and their eggs."
> [1]

The writer says that spiders just "started making silk." Now if you learn what they are really doing, you'll see this is a miraculous performance. It's not like they decided to put on a jacket or something. Spiders somehow developed a special organ in their bodies that they never had before. This brand new organ actually makes a long continuous strand of silk that is stronger than steel for its size. Somehow they realized that this string coming out of themselves would be good to wrap themselves or their eggs in for protection.

That's a miracle or it's a design.

> "Spiders gradually started using silk for hunting purposes, first as guide lines and signal lines, then as ground or bush webs, and eventually as the aerial webs that are familiar today." [2]

Each sentence is taking one or more gigantic leaps that defies logic. It feels like a bedtime story.

The kind of silk that was produced to wrap themselves or their eggs must have been the "non-sticky" silk. Otherwise, they'd be in a total mess. So in order to use any silk for hunting purposes, they would need the "sticky" type of silk. This is not produced in the same bodily organ, or spinneret. They need a totally different type of spinneret to produce the "sticky" silk. So they have to grow a whole new organ.

Next, you might also ask yourself, "How did they learn to hunt with sticky silk?" Imagine that you grow an organ to produce sticky silk and it starts oozing from your abdomen. How do you figure out what to do with it? Since it is sticky, it will get all over you, sort of like duct tape gone wild. Remember it is stronger than steel at your level of size. Somehow you have to learn to turn it on and off. Then next, over many generations of getting all stuck to yourself, you evolve special hairy arms and hands with special cells so you can deal with the sticky silk.

Remember the concept of Natural Selection says that every slow and gradual step along the way was an advantage to survival so it was preserved. I'm having a hard time imagining myself wrapped in duct tape and thinking I could survive better that way.

Ok, let's skip ahead. You've got this long strand of sticky silk emerging from your body that you have managed to get under control. How does it become useful for hunting? The author claims it must have been used "first as guidelines and signal lines". I guess the spiders must have laid it out across the ground and realized that if food got stuck to it, then they could reel it in like on a fishing line. That seems like a possibility until you think of getting some double-sided duct tape and laying it out across the ground. You're not going to catch anything but dirt. Even if you laid it up the side of a tree, you're probably only going to catch tree bark.

Maybe they hung upside down from a tree branch and dangled the sticky silk strand in the air. They might accidentally catch a bug for dinner. Odds are not so good. They also might catch a bird and get carried away. I just don't see this as an improvement on survival abilities. There are more bugs on the ground to eat than they could catch in the air.

Then we learn that spider spinnerets have glands that produce different types of silk thread like for trapping prey or wrapping them up. This is an amazingly complicated development for evolution, but it is glossed right over.

Some spiders can even produce eight different types of silk. Naturally we could ask how evolution accomplished all that.

Obviously, each type of gland is unique and so there had to be a lot of DNA changes in both male and female spiders. If only one gender mutated, then it would have only spiders who had not mutated to reproduce with. Each contributes a sperm or egg but one of them would not carry the mutation. A new trait is not likely to get passed to the next generation. That's Genetics 101.

The article says that it is more energy conserving for a spider to wait until some food is caught in the web than to go chasing it down. However, it later talks about how much energy it takes for the spider to create a whole web from contents made inside its own body. My common sense tells me that the spider is better off chasing down prey and getting dinner rather than building a web and waiting.

How much energy does a spider actually expend to run down an insect as opposed to creating a huge spider web? Which strategy is more likely to lead to survival of the fittest? Seems to me that a spider that runs down some food gets to eat it right away as contrasted to the one that builds a huge nest and waits and hopes.

Remember the spider trying to evolve the web for catching food is not going to get it right the first generation. It has to evolve gradually over many generations. I think they would starve before they evolve the different types of spinnerets and silk and then learn by trial and error how to make a web.

A spider can produce from a gland on its body a thread stronger than steel (relatively) which has much greater elasticity. It has taken human beings with intelligence thousands and thousands of years to produce steel, yet evolutionists believe that spiders accidentally stumbled on the way to

272

produce it from a mutating organ in their own bodies starting from scratch, nothing. This all built up step-by-step, gradually over many generations. Really?

Here's another issue. Scientists know that a spider web is a mixture of sticky and non-sticky silk which allows the spider to walk over his/her own spider web and not get stuck to it. Just how in the process of figuring out how to build a spider web did the spider learn to make a pattern of non-sticky silk to walk on and avoid the sticky silk. Do you think it was trial and error? Going back to the duct tape analogy, the spider would get stuck in his own web many, many times before learning how to engineer the non-sticky silk that he/she could walk on. The strands would have to be in a certain pattern and distance between them so the spider could get anywhere in the web that an insect might get stuck. The spider legs must be able to reach across the gap.

They tell us that a spider takes measurements like an intelligent construction worker planning his next move by using his own body as a measuring stick.

Next I really want you to see the phenomenal way a spider actually goes about spinning a web. Then let's ask ourselves lots of questions of how can this rationally be explained without a master designer.

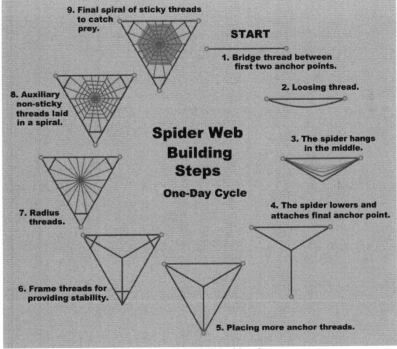

Image 16. Spider Web Building Steps.

"Many webs span gaps between objects which the spider could not cross by crawling. This is done by first producing a fine adhesive thread to drift on a faint breeze across a gap. When it sticks to a surface at the far end, the spider feels the change in the vibration. The spider reels in and tightens the first strand, then carefully walks along it and strengthens it with a second thread. This process is repeated until the thread is strong enough to support the rest of the web." [3]

Think about this for a little while. It's talking about a spider up in the air letting a silk drift in the breeze. (Remember to think about duct tape.) However, the Wikipedia author previously said that webs were created on the ground first. So spiders were merrily making spider webs on the ground until they realized they realized they might be better if they were made up in the air. Then they somehow figured out that they should go up high and dangle a sticky silk to blow in the wind. If it dangles around for a while and doesn't stick on anything, then they should let out some more silk.

Once it sticks to something, they carefully reel it in and try to make it tight. Then they travel down the sticky silk (remember duct tape) without getting stuck in it and without breaking it and falling. They drag some other sticky silk behind them without getting stuck in that and attach it to the end point. Now they have two strands across the gap. But still they repeat this process again to make the sure it can support the whole future web. How they know when they have enough strands is a mystery. With each additional strand of sticky silk (remember think double-sided duct tape) they manage to go back and forth across without getting stuck. How many generations did it take them to learn how not to get stuck.

After they've got that first multi-strand thread, then they make another one that is longer so they can dangle from it. They drop down with a thread and this makes a Y shape. They anchor that and then start to fill in the main spokes of the web. These silk threads are the non-sticky type. Later they add spiral after spiral of the sticky silk to catch a prey.

"The spider easily grips the thin threads with special serrated claws, a smooth hook and a series of barbed hairs on the end of its legs." [4]

Note all those key specializations of the hairs, legs, and claws. Each one of course had to evolve slowly and gradually over many generations. Do you ask yourself how that could happen when you read these accounts of evolution that are supposed to be scientific?

About all I can say to this is WOW what intelligent engineering. I have been daily watching a construction crew put a new wing on the building where I work. Each day is awesome as the scaffolding goes up in a precise and coordinated way, step-by-step. It takes a lot of brainpower to figure out an engineering feat like the lowly spider is accomplishing.

Lastly there is the spider's ability to sense by touching a silk thread that it has caught something. Its brain can tell the difference between the wind blowing or a leaf and true prey stuck in the spider web by touching a silk strand with its claw.

> "The spider might also leave the web, to retreat to a separate nest, while monitoring the web via a connected signal line." [5]

There is no way that all these different types of spiders learned to create different types of webs using several different materials from different organs in their own bodies in a slow and gradual process.

There must be God.

Chapter #92 Emperor Penguins

One of the most amazing documentaries I have ever watched is called "March of the Penguins." I saw it five or six years ago with my family and to this day whenever I think about that movie and Emperor Penguins, the word that comes to mind is "unbelievable". The movie is narrated by Morgan Freeman and is kind of slow moving, but you just cannot stop watching it. I checked Amazon and you can download it for $3.99. I highly recommend you put it at or near the top of your list of movies to see next.

Emperor Penguins are the largest of all penguins standing an average of around four feet tall and weighing around 50 to 100 pounds. They live in Antarctica and when winter starts coming, all of the other penguins start heading north for warmer waters. The Emperor Penguins do the opposite. They march right into the teeth of the worst of winter. Then they breed, incubate the egg through the coldest winter, and even hatch it before spring comes. They are the only Antarctic bird that breeds in the winter. [1]

> "They breed during the depths of the Antarctic winter and in some of the most desolate, coldest, windiest and downright grim places on the planet during the season of 24 hour darkness." [2]

How can evolution explain such behavior? It takes many special adaptations for them to survive which would never be necessary if they just went north to warmer water. They are certainly good survivors, but this is not the easiest way to survive and in fact only about 19% of their chicks do survive. [3]

This chapter is about the amazing abilities they have in order to survive in the coldest place on earth. Surely you will be able to see that they could never develop these abilities slowly and gradually over many generations in minus 40 degrees Fahrenheit. They would all die in the very first generation without having all their amazing abilities present at their very beginning and endowed by their designer.

Emperor Penguins breed in the winter in Antarctica where the temperatures average minus 4 degrees F during the day and reaching minus 40 or 50 degrees F at night. [1] (Another source says minus 80 degrees F.) The wind can blow up to 89 miles per hour or 120 miles per hour depending on your source. Think of the "wind chill factor" in that wind. The females will lay one egg, but they cannot let it touch the ice or be exposed to the outside air temperature. In two minutes it would be dead. They lay the egg on top of their feet and keep it protected by a special fold of skin and feathers called a "brood pouch".

Soon after that, the females very carefully pass the egg to their mate trying not to let it touch the ice. If it does, it is lost. The male keeps the egg on top of his feet for the next three or four months and protects it with his special "brood pouch". The male does not eat during this whole time.

The female walks for the 30 to 75 miles to get to the ocean. She eats a lot of food and stores up as much as she can to take back to regurgitate for her baby chick. The egg will hatch in about 63 or 64 days of sitting on the male's feet. Hatching can take two or three days because the shell of the egg is unusually thick.

She walks all the way back to her mate. This trip takes an average of 115 days round trip. [4] When she gets back to the flock, there are hundreds and hundreds of males. How does she find her mate?

> "As the species has no fixed nest sites that individuals can use to locate their own partner or chick, Emperor Penguins must rely on vocal calls alone for identification. They use a complex set of calls that are critical to individual recognition between parents, offspring, and mates, displaying the widest variation in individual calls of all penguins. Vocalizing Emperor Penguins use two frequency bands simultaneously. Chicks use a frequency-modulated whistle to beg for food and to contact parents." [5]

The chicks are carefully passed from the male to the female. Then the males, now weighing about 26 pounds less than when their mate left, take off walking the many miles to the sea to get something to eat.

To think that Emperor Penguins evolved is preposterous. They could not have evolved the ability to survive in these harsh winters someplace else and then moved there. What individual or group would go into the cold in the first place if walking the other way would be warmer and safer? How could the female and male learn to cooperate like they do? If an egg touches the ice, the embryo dies, first time and every time. No way it could evolve over generations. The male and female both have special "brood pouches" to protect the egg and chick. Where did those come from? How did they develop the special vocalization abilities they have to locate their mates among hundreds or thousands of others?

I can't even cover all of the unbelievable things that they are able to do. They have special feathers and a special layer of fat (up to 3cm) to protect them from the cold. They could not survive without it. It would not "evolve" unnecessarily in a warmer climate and it could not evolve slowly in frigid temperatures because the penguins would die before breeding. It would not need to evolve in the border between cold and warmer climates because the penguin could just walk to a warmer area. All other penguins breed in the spring when warm weather is coming. How could Emperor Penguins "evolve" to breed at the beginning of winter, totally different timing? The answer is that they didn't, evolution is not a plausible explanation.

"Its stiff feathers are short, lanceolate (spear-shaped), and densely packed over the entire skin surface. With around 100 feathers covering one square inch (15 feathers per cm²), it has the highest feather density of any bird species. An extra layer of insulation is formed by separate shafts of downy filaments between feathers and skin. Muscles allow the feathers to be held erect on land, reducing heat loss by trapping a layer of air next to the skin. Conversely, the plumage is flattened in water, thus waterproofing the skin and the downy under layer." [6]

Or check this out. Emperor Penguins can control their body temperature to a great degree. They don't even have to alter their metabolism to regulate from minus -10 to 20 °C (14 to 68 °F). If it gets colder than that, they move around or shiver, but they can also increase fat burning.

Here is another ability that seems impossible to have evolved. And check this out.

"A penguin's normal resting heart-beat is about 60-70 beats per minute (bpm), this goes up to 180-200 bpm before a dive as they load up with oxygen, then as they hit the water, the rate drops to 100 bpm immediately slowing to only 20 bpm during most of the dive so they use the stored oxygen in blood and muscles to the maximum effect. On returning to the surface again, the heart rate goes back to 200 bpm probably to pay back the "oxygen debt" they have incurred during the dive." [7]

Researchers have found that Emperor Penguins can dive as deep as 265m (869 ft.), with dive periods of up to 18 minutes. Even one small female was recorded at 535m (1,755 ft.).

During deep dives there is a very serious problem to overcome, the pressure which can reach 40 times that on the surface. Penguins have special bones that are solid, rather than air-filled like most birds. This way they don't get crushed. How could they evolve such bones?

Here's another fact extremely hard to explain by evolution.

"Eventually, the female returns across the sea ice. This usually coincides with the hatching of the chick. Sometimes the chick will hatch before the female returns. If this happens, it will be fed with a secretion of protein and fat produced by the male from its esophagus, a sort of penguin 'milk'". [8]

Milk produced by the male of the species!!!

All right, here's one last amazing fact. Just exactly how could the following coordinated action of the group evolve over many generations? They would all have died before they were successful at it.

To protect themselves from the extreme cold, the males gather by the hundreds in a very tight group. However, it is not so tight that they touch each other. If they did that, it would compress the air insulation in their feathers.

The juveniles get the inside where there is less exposure. The adult males are on the outside and they gradually rotate around taking turns receiving the brunt of the cold winds.

Did they learn how to do that the very first generation that lived in the Antarctic winter? Evolution would say they developed the ability over many generations. But how could they survive without knowing how to do that?

Again I suggest you watch "March of the Penguins" DVD to get a real impactful understanding of the life of the Emperor Penguins.

Fact after fact after fact about Emperor Penguins defies any slow and gradual mutation/natural selection scenario. Evolution of an Emperor Penguin is impossible.

You'll see. There has to be God.

Chapter #93 Camels

Just as the Emperor Penguin (Chapter #92) could never have evolved in the frigid and desolate Antarctica without dying before evolving, there is an animal specifically adapted by God for the harsh climates in the desert. I'm sure you know that animal is the camel. However, you will be amazed to learn the details about the camel.

For evolution to be true and a camel to evolve all the special adaptations that it has for the desert, it would need to be living in the desert most of the time, otherwise the adaptations are useless so would not be selected slowly and gradually over many generations by Natural Selection. But if you think about it, the camel could not be living in the desert in the first place UNLESS it already has its special adaptations.

> "A camel can go a week or more without water, and it can last for several months without food. It can survive a 40 percent weight loss and then drink up to 32 gallons (145 liters) of water in one drinking session!" [1]

If the camel did not live in the desert, there is no advantage to developing the special adaptations that it has. So Natural Selection would never develop a camel outside of the desert.

Camels have been domesticated for at least 3,500 years. This means that they have been very, very helpful to humans living in the desert areas of the world.

> "Humans have used camels for their wool, milk, meat, leather, and even dung that can be used for fuel. Camel milk is an important food of the desert nomadic tribes. A camel can provide a large amount of meat for these people also. The camel's hump is considered a delicacy in these cultures." [2]

You could easily recognize that this might have been designed because they were so perfect for the job. They even got the nickname "ship of the desert" because they can carry 200 or more pounds about 20 miles a day. They can reach 7 feet tall at the hump(s) and weigh 1,500 pounds. They can run 40 miles per hour for short distances and average 25 mph for long distances.

Camels have two rows of thick eye lashes to provide great protection against sands and winds. They have an inner eyelid which is actually transparent and allows the camel to see though it while protecting the eye. This third eyelid has the special ability to wipe sand and dust out of the camel's eye.

"Camels have three eyelids. Two of the eyelids have lashes and the third eyelid comes from the corner of the eye. The eyes are protected by a double row of long curly eyelashes which help keep out the sand and dust. Thick bushy eyebrows shield the eyes from the desert sun." [3]

The Camel's nostrils are unique. They can be closed at will to prevent sand and dust from entering. They also have a unique lining which captures the moisture out of the air when the camel breathes out. This allows the Camels to preserve moisture in their bodies.

Camels have small ears and lots of hair over their ears to keep out the sand.

Camels have very unique lips. The upper lip is split in the middle and each side can be controlled independently. Each half is tough but flexible. This allows the Camel to put its mouth down close to the ground sideways and chew off low lying vegetation.

The Camel has a very leathery surface inside its mouth. This allows it to eat thistle bushes and cactus and other sharp and strong plants that grow in the desert.

Camel humps do not store water, but they do store fat, up to 80 pounds of fat. This allows Camels to go for weeks and even months on very little food. The fat when metabolized produces energy and also actually releases more than a gallon of water for each gallon of fat. So it is actually a wonderful mechanism for storing water.

"When there is little food and water, the camel's hump fat releases water; 9.3 grams of fat releases 1.13 grams of water, according to research by the University of Singapore." [4]

Another advantage of storing fat in their hump is that camels don't have to store it throughout the rest of their body which would tend to make them hotter in the summer because of the insulating effect of fat.

Camels have very thick coats that reflect sunlight and help keep them from overheating. Their long legs keep them farther from the hot sand.

Camels have an amazing ability to absorb and maintain water in their bodies. Their kidneys and intestines are excellent at holding water. Various sources say they can drink between 30 and 53 gallons of water in a single session. That's twice the amount of liquid that would fit in your car's gasoline tank. That's three times the amount in a normal tall kitchen garbage can (13 gal.).

Scientists do not know where all the water goes. Any other animal that drank that much compared to its size would die.

Conversely Camels can still function if they are dehydrated way past the point where other animals would die. Most mammals would die if they lose 15% of their water (critical loss of water is called dehydration), but a camel can lose 20-25% water without becoming dehydrated.

Camels are unique among all mammals because their red blood cells are oval instead of round. This allows their blood to continue to circulate in their capillaries even when the blood gets thicker due to less and less water content.

Camels can even conserve water by concentrating their urine into a thick syrup. They also extract all the moisture from their feces so that it is almost completely dry. It can be burned as fuel from the moment it is released.

Camels have another totally unique ability. Almost all mammals maintain a constant body temperature and this takes energy. Humans keep a body temperature of about 98.6 degrees. Camels can allow their body temperatures to go down to 93.2 degrees at night or up as high as 105.8 degrees before they begin to perspire. Humans would die at those extremes. Camels can survive temperatures down to -20 degrees in winter and up to 120 degrees in summer. How do they do it? Scientists don't know, nor do they know how it could have evolved in a slow and gradual process.

How about their brains getting overheated in the desert?

> "Maintaining the brain temperature within certain limits is critical for animals; to assist this, camels have a *rete mirabile,* a complex of arteries and veins lying very close to each other which utilizes countercurrent blood flow to cool blood flowing to the brain." [5]

Tell me how something like their cooling system for the brain could possibly evolve by a slow and gradual process over generations. Their brains would be fried by the sun. And what is "countercurrent blood flow"?

Camel feet are specially adapted to walking on sand because they have two large pads on each foot that expand when stepping down and then close up as they are being lifted for the next step. When Camels walk, they walk differently than most animals. Both feet on one side move at the same time so it looks very unnatural. If you've ever seen them run, it looks very funny. But this is a great design for walking in sand, because your feet sink and this makes it easier to get out with less energy.

Camels have special kidneys and intestines. They have special immune systems. But I've gone on long enough.

A person who believes in evolution might be able to imagine how a camel could evolve a couple of these special adaptations, but there are way, way too many of them to be explained like that. Fortunate accidents may happen once in a while, but not repeatedly.

It is therefore clear to me that the Camel was designed and not evolved. Hence, there must be God.

Chapter #94 Whales

Everybody is familiar with whales and we have all been astounded at how big they are. The Blue Whale can get up to 112 feet long and weigh 200 tons, as much as 33 elephants.

But do you know that whales are mammals? That means that they are warm blooded and they breathe air. Their babies are born alive and are fed milk. There are at least 40 different known species of whales.

So if you are a faithful believer in Evolution, you somehow have to find a way to believe that whales started out on land and not water. You already believe life started out in the ocean and then evolved by emerging onto the land and evolving into mammals.

Somehow those highly evolved mammals with four legs ended up going back into the ocean and becoming the largest animals on earth.

Darwin thought it was the bear that evolved into a whale because he saw them swim a lot. Over the years, evolutionists have come up with other mammals that are the ancestral relatives of whales. Their religious faith in evolution requires that some animal evolved into a whale. Even though there is no known ancestor in the fossil record of the whale, evolutionists claim there are lots of relatives along the family tree, and that's enough proof for them. How they decide what is a relative of the whale is always interesting.

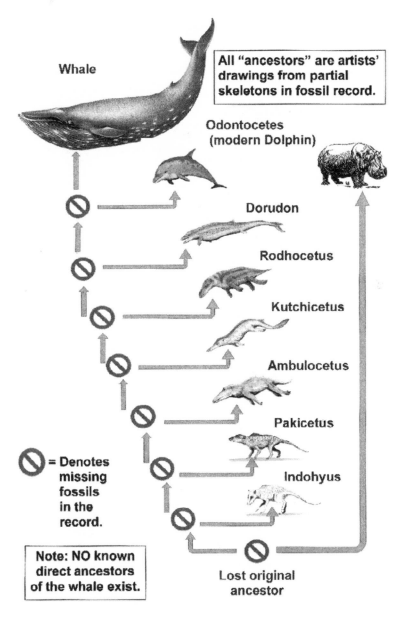

All "ancestors" are artists' drawings from partial skeletons in fossil record.

Whale

Odontocetes
(modern Dolphin)

Dorudon

Rodhocetus

Kutchicetus

Ambulocetus

Pakicetus

Indohyus

🚫 = Denotes
missing
fossils
in the
record.

**Note: NO known
direct ancestors
of the whale exist.**

Lost original
ancestor

Image 17. Missing Whale Ancestors, all of them.
©2016 Jim Stephens

Notice on this chart that the space is blank in every case where there should be a direct ancestor to a whale (the triangles with a question mark in them). All the chart shows are species that supposedly branched off from the main line that leads to whales. If we have fossils of all the animals shown, why is there not one single fossil in the direct ancestral line to the whale? [1]

The current animal getting the most credit for possibly becoming a whale is called Pakicetus and was a wolf-like animal of about that same size, 5 or 6 feet long. Evolutionist proof seems to be all wrapped up in the similarity between the teeth and ear bones of the two species.

Look at the two wolf-like animals at the bottom of my chart, Indohyus and Pakicetus. From those two it is a huge, huge leap to the new body plan of the third one up, Ambolucetus, which I'll mention more in a minute. It is much more adapted to the water.

The Smithsonian Institute has an article titled "How Did Whales Evolve?" which I thought might provide some good answers. It's a very long article and makes some sweeping claims about evolution. But, if you pay attention, you'll see they have to admit that they still don't have any ancestors of whales. The article takes a long time going into the history of fossil discoveries but never answers "How Did Whales Evolve?" which you would have expected from the title. At one point they tell the truth and then lie about what it means.

> "Though not a series of direct ancestors and descendants, each genus represents a particular stage of whale evolution. Together they illustrate how the entire transition took place." [2]

Sure, we know, "It might have happened." That's not science. They don't have any direct ancestors, but something else proves the transition is true for them.

They even admit later that analysis of genes and amino acids refutes this ancestry line and indicates whales are related to hippos. The title and the article are pure propaganda.

Here is another example of an article that is even worse, "How Whales' Ancestors Left Land Behind" from LiveScience.com. The following paragraph is their explanation for "How Whale's Ancestors Left Land Behind." What a joke!

> "The 'first whale,' a creature whose lifestyle (living on land but eating fish from the nearby sea) represented the early stage of this transition into the water, was a wolf-size fish eater...Whereas this creature had a body clearly adapted for land, its relatives began acquiring features better suited to life in the water, such as webbed feet and a more streamlined, hairless shape." [3]

In their religious zeal for evolution, lots of imagination is allowed.

Here is another example. The actual bones discovered for the Pakicetus were only the fragments of a skull and several teeth. The evolutionists produced from those bones a fully developed artist's drawing of Pakicetus. Since this was going to be the ancestor of a whale, it was drawn splashing around in the water and eating fish. It had a long tail and legs beginning to look like webbed feet. But, the story is not over. Later, more bones were discovered. The real bones included parts of two legs, some ribs, and a mammal like tail. This forced the artists to come up with a totally new drawing. Here is an example.

Image 18. Pakicetus Became the Whales?

The moral of this story is that you should always ask to see the actual bones that have been found and not the artist drawing. (See also Chapter #64, Missing Links, the sections on hoaxes and "Lucy".)

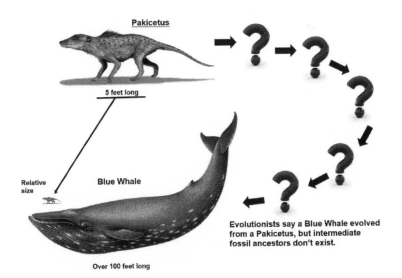

Image 19. Whale Ancestors, Nothing but Missing Links.
©2016 Jim Stephens

So what do we really have?

Pakicetus (wolf-like) > Missing Link > Missing Link > Missing Link > Missing Link > Missing Link > Missing Link > Whale. Just stop for a minute and think about the monumental indoctrination that has to be perpetrated for you to believe something like that. Where's the proof? There is no fossil record that is even claimed to be a direct ancestor at any stage. There are just artist's drawings.

Another animal often named as a side lineage of the ancestral lines of whales is called Ambulocetus. This is another case of evolutionist's great imagination. Looking at the actual fossil bones that were found compared to the artist's drawing, you might not be able to conclude whether it walked or swam primarily. It seems to have a pelvis for walking. Whales have no such structure. What is believed to be the back foot of Ambulocetus was discovered 5 meters above the rest of the fossil.

In a lot of the drawings on whale evolution you will also see a Basilosaurus. But they often leave out the fact that it was 10 times bigger than Ambulocetus and "the serpentine form of the body and the peculiar shape of the cheek teeth make it plain that Basilosaurus could not possibly have been the ancestor of modern whales." [4]

Here is another totally unscientific quote from American Museum of Natural History under the title of "Whale Evolution." It is followed by a drawing from someone's imagination presented as fact.

> "One group of hoofed mammals spent more and more time in the water, living on the abundant food there. Eventually they left land altogether—evolving into the fully aquatic whales. Take a look at a few of these early extinct whales below." [5]

Oh really? "Eventually they left land altogether" how scientific! Are people brain-dead not to question such a statement?

As anyone can easily see, for a wolf-like animal to "eventually" evolve into a whale, there have to be some tremendous, even unbelievable, changes. Let's ask one of the obvious questions. Why? Evolutionists will say that Natural Selection chooses the fittest to survive. So a wolf, being a carnivore, is trying to catch fish. He would be better adapted if he had web feet, so he grew them. Huh? Then he would be better adapted if his tail grew and became useful for swimming and he developed bigger lungs to stay underwater longer. Huh?

288

Which wolf is more likely to survive in your opinion, a wolf that is trying to catch fish or a wolf that tries to catch a rabbit? Even a wolf that is half way to evolving webfeet is worse off at catching rabbits and only very slightly better at catching fish. Since evolution takes many generations, which wolf is going to survive?

No wolf if he gets really hungry trying to catch fish is going to evolve web feet. He is going to go catch a rabbit. Whatever the wolf might want to do, he can't just change his feet.

The same argument applies continuously. A wolf is so absolutely unfit for swimming and living in water that any wolf that tried it would die long before it could reproduce. The fittest to survive are clearly the other wolves out catching rabbits.

Now let me just share a few of the amazing characteristics of a whale. If you are an evolutionist, you would have to come up with some explanation for how each one of these features could evolve slowly and gradually through many generations. All of the intermediate stages in a slow process are poorly adapted for survival.

The Tail. For whales, this is their primary source of power for swimming. There are "flukes" on the end that go out sideways which add more driving force and maneuverability. A wolf tail swings mostly side to side, not up and down, and has very little of the strength needed for propulsion. That would have to evolve. It's a totally different design.

Skin. Mammals have hair and sweat glands. Whales do not. Whale skin has lots of extra fat or blubber. That's very different, right? This is a complete change of skin on the whole body.

Blubber. Whales have huge amounts of fat deposits called blubber, up to 11 inches thick. This serves as insulation in cold water and also protection for the very deep dives that they do.

Lungs. Whales have a huge lung capacity that allows them to stay underwater for long periods of time. They also can slow down their metabolism to increase their dive time. The lungs of a humpback whale can hold about 5,000 liters of air. By comparison, human lungs hold about 6 liters of air.

"Whales are adapted for diving to great depths. In addition to their streamlined bodies, they can slow their heart rate to conserve oxygen; blood is rerouted from tissue tolerant of water pressure to the heart and brain among other organs; haemoglobin and myoglobin store oxygen in body tissue; and they have twice the concentration of myoglobin than haemoglobin." [6]

What an incredible adaptation, rerouting your blood.

Eyes. Whale eyes are specially adapted to be able to see in water which has a far higher refractive index than air. Their eyes also have to be able to withstand the tremendous pressure down deep in the ocean.

Sonar and Hearing. Many types of whales have sonar. This means they have a special organ that can make a sound which goes through the water and bounces back when it hits an object. They also have a receiver to pick up the sound that bounces back, sends signals to their brains, and the brain then interprets what it means. It is similar to what bats can do, however whales have to do it in water using the fatty lipids in their heads. This is very different from doing it in air. (See my Chapter #42, Bats and Echolocation.)

"Odontocetes are known as toothed whales; they have teeth and only one blowhole. They rely on their well-developed sonar to find their way in the water. Toothed whales send out ultrasonic clicks using the melon. Sound waves travel through the water. Upon striking an object in the water, the sound waves bounce back at the whale. These vibrations are received through fatty tissues in the jaw, which is then rerouted into the ear-bone and into the brain where the vibrations are interpreted." [7]

Does there exist a good explanation about how this echolocation ability could arise slowly over many generations? All the parts have to be there from the beginning or the system doesn't work.

"Instead of sound passing through the outer ear to the middle ear, whales receive sound through the throat, from which it passes through a low-impedance fat-filled cavity to the inner ear. The whale ear is acoustically isolated from the skull by air-filled sinus pockets, which allow for greater directional hearing underwater." [8]

So here is another example of a dramatic change from a land animal. Whales have a very different process of hearing.

Blowholes. All known terrestrial mammals have nostrils on the front of their faces. Whales have either one or two blowholes in the top of their heads. Think about all the changes that would be required for your nostrils to migrate to the top of your head. It's not just the hole in your skull that has to move, but all of the muscles, sensory nerves, air passages, nerve channels that connect to the brain, and probably a lot more. All have to change and change drastically. Not only that, your lungs have to change tremendously as well because you would need a gigantic lung capacity to stay underwater for a long time. Changing the size of your lungs requires changes in your ribs and spine and probably your heart and other internal organs.

Flippers. Clearly whales have fins on the sides instead of legs and feet going downward like mammals. How do legs turn into fins? The skin is different. The muscles are different and used differently. This requires rewiring to the brain as well.

Special Rib Cage. What about the bones? Changing from a wolf-like animal would require almost a complete makeover of the skeleton. The pelvis in land mammals cannot be found in whales. How does a transitional species with half a pelvis manage to either walk or swim well?

Whales swim well because of their massive tails and the muscles that move them up and down. Also their well-developed flippers on each side help guide and propel them in the water. This takes a special rib cage adapted to the muscles to move the animal.

A unique characteristic of their rib cages is that the ribs are not attached in the center of their bodies like other mammals. This is very important on deep dives where the pressure is gigantic and would crush their ribs if they were rigid.

Reproduction. Whales somehow have to do it all in the water. Like other mammals, males have a penis and females have a vagina. If they really evolved from wolves, then both the male and female would have to evolve their respective sexual parts at the same time and in the same vicinity in the ocean to locate each other so they could mate. There are videos on YouTube of whale sex. Somehow I have trouble imagining that could come about accidentally. And that's not all the problems they need to solve in order to reproduce.

Here is a fun fact. The penis on the Blue Whale is about 8 to 10 feet long and weighs in at over 400 pounds.

Baby whales come out the opposite of most mammals, tail first. Because they will soon need to breathe once they are born, the head comes out last to keep them from drowning. Try to imagine how evolution turned the babies around in the womb before birth so they wouldn't die.

Mother whales have mammary glands like other mammals. The mother squirts out the milk which is as thick as toothpaste. How did evolution get that right?

The milk has great amounts of fat to speed up the growth of blubber to protect the baby from cold water.

It takes 11 months before the baby finishes up nursing.

Baleen Whales. One of the types of whales is really different. It has huge bristle-like walls in their mouth that act like sieves. Look at pictures of these whales and the structures in their mouth. Think about all the changes in their head size and shape, body, nervous system, eating habits, and much more that would have had to evolve separately over many generations. If their land-mammal ancestors were successful, why make all the minor changes that would be less advantageous to develop this way of eating.

The long plates of baleen strain through tons of water a day to capture food like krill, zooplankton, and small fish. The material is similar to human fingernails.

Sleeping. Here is something you probably don't know about whales. Try to imagine how this could have possibly evolved.

"Unlike most animals, whales are conscious breathers. All mammals sleep, but whales cannot afford to become unconscious for long because they may drown. While knowledge of sleep in wild cetaceans is limited, toothed cetaceans in captivity have been recorded to sleep with one side of their brain at a time, so that they may swim, breathe consciously, and avoid both predators and social contact during their period of rest." [9]

By the Theory of Evolution, every one of these adaptations would have had to evolve over many generations. So try to imagine having 5% of a tail, 10%, 20%, etc. Or how about evolving so half your brain can go to sleep while the other half stays awake. Think over all of the other amazing features listed above one by one. How can any one of these if only partially completed be selected for by Natural Selection? You'd have ridiculous looking deformed beasts that would die out in one generation because they are so poorly suited for the environment they are supposed to live in. Whales are an all or nothing proposition.

There has to be God.

Chapter #95 Archaea

Probably most of you have never heard of Archaea. I had never heard of them either until just recently. In fact, the world had never heard of them until they were discovered in 1977.

Archaea constitute a domain or kingdom of single-celled microorganisms. These microbes are prokaryotes, meaning that they have no cell nucleus or any other membrane-bound organelles in their cells.

Classification is difficult because the majority have not been studied in the laboratory and have only been detected by analysis of their nucleic acids in samples from their environment. [1]

Before 1977 they had always been considered a type of bacteria. But then microbiologist Carl Woese was able to recognize that they were very different from bacteria.

> "He had stumbled on a brave new world of microbes that looked like bacteria to our eyes, but were in fact so unique biochemically and physically that they have ultimately proved to be more closely related to us than to them. He had stumbled on an entirely new form of life, right here on Earth." [2]

Being a believer in the Theory of Evolution, he concluded that back at the beginning of Darwin's Tree of Life, there must have been an early split. Bacteria went one way and Archaea and all other life went the other way. Of course Archaea was so primitive, it had to have branched off from the Tree of Life itself at the very beginning. It doesn't even have a cell nuclei.

So Woese came up with an all new branch and thus there are now three major branches off of Darwin's Tree of Life. Evolutionists don't really give an explanation for whatever it was that came before these three branches.

To get a better idea of some of the differences between Archaea and bacteria, one good website is WiseGeek. Here is just one point of many.

> "Archaea and bacteria are both single-celled microorganisms known as prokaryotes but this is one of the few things they have in common. Even though they both look vaguely similar when viewed through a microscope, each represents a completely different group of creatures. In fact, archaea differ from bacteria as much as humans do, in terms of their biochemistry and genetic structure. Archaea and bacteria have

different cell membranes and cell structures, and archaea are found in extreme environments where most bacteria could not survive." [3]

It turns out that Archaea are totally everywhere on the earth. In fact they make up as much as 40% of the biomass in the open ocean and 20% of the biomass of all living things on the earth even though they are microscopic in size.

"Archaea are particularly numerous in the oceans, and the archaea in plankton may be one of the most abundant groups of organisms on the planet." [4]

They come in all shapes and sizes. Some are totally different from each other and do the exact opposite thing biochemically. Here is an example.

"Archaea carry out many steps in the nitrogen cycle. This includes both reactions that remove nitrogen from ecosystems (such as nitrate-based respiration and denitrification) as well as processes that introduce nitrogen (such as nitrate assimilation and nitrogen fixation)." [5]

See my Chapter #48, Nitrogen Cycle, for more information on that.

"To our surprise, we have found super-sized filamentous archaea almost big enough to see with the naked eye living on mangrove roots. We have found methanogenic archaea that interact with protozoa in the guts of cows and termites to help these organisms break cellulose down for energy. We've even found an archaeon that lives symbiotically with -- of all things -- a sponge." [6]

Archaea play an extremely important role in maintaining all life on earth.

Some scientist have found Archaea are involved in ammonia oxidation reactions which are very important in the oceans and in soil.

Archaea produce nitrite, which other microbes then oxidize to nitrate which is a nutritional requirement of plants and other organisms.

Archaea are required in the carbon cycle also. They play a role in the decay of organic matter for the functioning of ecosystems in sediments, marshes, and sewage-treatment plants.

Different Archaea are active in the sulfur cycle. They help release sulfur from rocks so it can be used by other organisms.

Some researchers believe that we would never have been able to come to exist on the earth without Archaea. Millions of years ago, the earth was covered with methane gas. They think it was the type of Archaea that digests methane that ate it all up or we could never have come along. Even today some scientists estimate that Archaea convert 300 million tons of methane per year into more life friendly chemicals.

"Scientists have discovered a methane metabolizing Archea in the extreme pressures of deep sea sediments. It is estimated that these bacteria-like organisms consume 300 million tons of methane each year, which prevent the Earth from turning into a furnace. According to Kai-Uwe Hinrichs, a biogeochemist at the Woods Hole Oceanographic Institution in Massachusetts and one of the authors of the study, 'If they hadn't been established at some point in Earth's history, we probably wouldn't be here.'" [7]

A tremendous amount is NOT known about Archaea. Nobody knows how many species of Archaea there are. Estimates say there are 18 to 23 phyla, but only 8 have been even studied a little.

"Consequently, our understanding of the role of archaea in ocean ecology is rudimentary, so their full influence on global biogeochemical cycles remains largely unexplored." [8]

But scientists have been able to learn some things about their internal makeup, replication, and the biochemical processes they exhibit.

Let's note here that they do not reproduce sexually. There are no male and female so it is hard to apply the Theory of Evolution. They do not have "parents" to give them two different sets of DNA.

So let's look at some of the questions that Evolutionists are not going to be able to answer.

If you have read any of my previous chapters like Proof for God, #40 Chirality, #21 DNA, #27 The Truth about Mutation, or #35 Natural Selection, then you are probably already asking yourself some good questions.

In the very beginning for Evolutionists, somehow DNA came to exist. In the opinion of many scientists, it would be impossible to come into existence without super-intelligence involved because there is so much order, information, and design to DNA. But let's skip over that discussion for this proof.

Evolutionists were forced to put Archaea and bacteria at the very bottom of the Tree of Life because they are so primitive. But they are so different it is impossible to explain that one was the ancestor of the other, so they don't. They make separate branches of the tree and leave the beginning a mystery.

As an example of their differences, bacteria and archaea use amino acids with the opposite handedness (chirality). These are the very building blocks of their existence. Archaea are more like humans than bacteria.

Phylogenetic Tree of Life

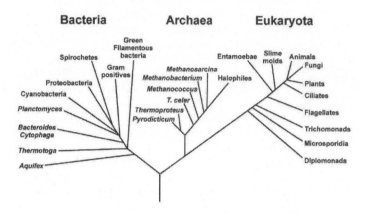

Image 20. Archaea in Evolutionist "Tree of Life."

To mutate from bacteria to Archaea or any other living thing is impossible to conceive of based on the different handedness of their enzymes. Remember DNA is a long, long chain of millions, if not billions, of individual amino acids.

Evolutionists have to believe that enzymes of both left-handedness and right-handedness somehow developed, once to produce Archaea and the plant/animal branch and another time to produce bacteria. The odds are astronomical against an enzyme coming to exist by Evolution even one time. But two independent times is not even conceivable. And then another miracle has to happen to produce the third branch of the Tree of Life (plants and animals).

We could stop there, but let's keep going. Once one Archaea somehow exists as a fully functioning cell, it has to already contain all the necessary DNA to be able to replicate itself. (Please read Chapter #41, The First Living Cell, to learn how difficult that is.)

Here's something else. Archaea hold all the records for being able to survive in the most extreme environments like hot, cold, acidic, or salty.

It there was one very first Archaea, how do you explain such an extreme diversity of Archaea living in every environment on the earth? They are single celled organisms so when they multiply they do not have two parents from which to inherit different DNA. Their DNA somehow makes a copy of itself and then the cell splits into two "daughter cells" having exactly the same DNA.

They just make a copy of themselves according to their existing DNA. I will concede that there might be some mutations during copying, but this is not a process that leads anywhere toward species development. See my Chapter #90, Copying Degradation, and my Chapter #27, The Truth about Mutation.

Mutation is very rarely beneficial. It usually leads to death. There's no hope there for growth and development of many different phyla of Archaea.

Archaea live in many such extreme environments that they could not have evolved there. There are Archaea that are living at 130°C on the ocean floor next to an active volcano. Water boils at 100°C remember.

There is no oxygen there and the heat destroys all other living things. How did they get there in the first place and not get destroyed on the way? How could they adapt to the heat in that environment without being killed first? If the heat didn't kill them, how did they get oxygen and energy? They would have had to evolve the ability to convert compounds in the environment into oxygen and energy after they arrived there. It's pretty clear that they had to be able to survive in that environment before they ever got there not after they arrived. Survival of the Fittest is totally out of the realm of possibility.

How about the type of Archaea that can thrive in a totally acidic environment of pH 0 (zero), comparable to sulfuric acid? All plants and animals die in acid. Since Evolutionists put Archaea on the Tree of Life, how do they explain that some type "adapted" into being able to do this? They could not have adapted once they were in the strong acid environment, no survival of the fittest because there are no survivors. Even bacteria which Evolutionists say came earlier on the Tree of Life are killed by acid.

Different types of Archaea also live in extremely alkaline environments. Some can live in extremely cold environments. Others live in the soil, the ocean, marshlands, even sewage.

There are even Archaea that live in your stomach that help you digest certain types of molecules. We are really lucky that they are there or we might not survive. That's a very acidic environment which dissolves almost everything that comes into it. But not your very own Archaea.

"Methogens such as M. Smithii, the most abundant methanogenic archaeon in the human gut is an important player in the digestion of polysaccharides (complex sugars). Methangenic archaea help to remove excess hydrogen." [9]

Here's a neat little sentence with gigantic implications.

"Like bacteria, archaea cell membranes are usually bounded by a cell wall and they swim using one or more flagella." [10]

How can evolutionists explain one or more working flagellum on an Archaea? That means they have a working tail that motors them around. A tail takes a lot of engineering. A half evolved tail does not work. Evolution cannot explain in slow, gradual steps how you get a flagellum.

Archaea are so tiny that we can't see them and yet there are so many that they make up 20% of living things on the planet. There are so many different kinds of them and they all seem to provide extremely essential chemical processes for our survival. We'd die without them.

There's still a lot more to be learned about them, but just knowing what we know already makes it impossible to believe that they occurred by random chance or natural selection.

No evolutionary explanation suffices. There must be God.

Chapter #96 Blood

I have been reading numerous scientific articles about blood. This information is astounding. There is only one rational conclusion, your body is a walking miracle.

I recommend that those who believe that random chance and "survival of the fittest" can result in such a miracle need to take a step back and examine their motivations. They might ask themselves honestly why they want so badly that evolution be true.

The best current estimate by scientists is that there are 37.2 trillion cells in your body, not counting all the microbes. [1] Inside each and every one of those cells there are approximately 10 million chemical reactions taking place every second of your life. [2] Every chemical reaction requires oxygen and fuel, and then removal of any waste. Let's thank God for our blood, because every cell that does not come in contact with it would die.

And just how does blood get near enough to every cell? It travels through an incredible network of capillaries. Capillaries are so thin that about 40 of them side by side equals the width of a human hair. If you lined up all the capillaries in your body, it would reach 60,000 miles, ¼ of the way to the Moon.

If you believe that life developed slowly and gradually over many generations, which came first blood or capillaries? If blood developed first, was it just sitting there in a pool? If capillaries developed first, what was their purpose if there was no blood to circulate?

The story of blood is phenomenal. About two weeks after a sperm fertilizes an egg, the zygote has gotten so big that the growing number of cells cannot survive. They need a transport system to get oxygen and nutrients. Perfectly on time, some of the developing cells form into tubes that start pumping. (See Chapter #79, The Heart) Simultaneously, capillaries start forming as well as blood.

Red Blood Cells start forming in a temporary "blood forming sac" that grows on the outside of the embryo. By the middle of month two, RBC production will now be taken over by the baby's liver and spleen. By month number five, RBC production is now taking place in the bone marrow of the fetal upper legs and shins. It continues to be made there in children, but eventually it moves again. In adults, most RBCs are produced in the bone marrow of the pelvis, cranium, vertebrae, and sternum.

The fine-tuning of this whole process screams out that it was intelligently designed. Even the few things that I have pointed out so far could not have developed in a slow and linear process over many generations. The organism would never survive.

And this is just the beginning.

Men on average have about a gallon and a half of blood and women a little over a gallon. It is about 45 percent blood cells (nearly half) and 55 percent plasma. Blood makes up about 7 to 8 percent of your weight.

> "The liquid component of blood is called plasma, a mixture of water, sugar, fat, protein, and salts. The main job of the plasma is to transport blood cells throughout your body along with nutrients, waste products, antibodies, clotting proteins, chemical messengers such as hormones, and proteins that help maintain the body's fluid balance." [3]

If you think that is complicated, we are just scratching the surface. But stop and think how a slow and gradual process based on mutation and natural selection over many generations could produce all of those absolutely essential functions of blood one by one and not have the organism die off somewhere along the way, probably at the very beginning. There are too many limiting factors that kill a cell if all those processes are not in place from the beginning. These are mind-boggling chemical reactions. For just a taste, read Chapter #74, Proteins.

Now we'll start to get extremely complicated. There are three basic components in blood that I want to discuss briefly (if possible).

1. Red Blood Cells (also called erythrocytes or RBCs) which carry oxygen to the tissues.
2. White Blood Cells (also called leukocytes) which fight infections.
3. Platelets (also called thrombocytes), smaller cells that help blood to clot. [4]

Red Blood Cells

RBCs are produced in bone marrow and develop from a generic type of cell (pluripotential hematopoietic stem cells) that could also have become a White Blood Cell or even Platelets. It is very difficult to imagine how complicated this is. There are sensors in the body that turn on or off switches that control how much of each type of cell is made. There is a hormone (called erythropoietin) which comes primarily from the kidneys and that is what controls the production of Red Blood Cells. Think about that. A hormone from the kidneys controls production of RBCs in the bone marrow. How many generations does it take to "evolve" that process?

RBCs are really, really unique. They have no nucleus because the cell loses it during growth along with other organelles. [5] They are shaped somewhat like a donut which just happens to be the best design of surface area for absorbing a full load of oxygen in a fraction of a second. They are made from five very specialized proteins that are very flexible. This is vitally important because they are about twice as big as a capillary and need to bend nearly in half to travel down the capillary and then spring back into shape on their way back to the heart.

RBCs are loaded with a protein called hemoglobin that is a fantastic carrier of oxygen and carbon dioxide. There are 250 million hemoglobin molecules in each of your billions of RBCs. [6] Hemoglobin carries 97% of the oxygen that gets from your lungs to your cells.

Your body makes about two million RBCs every second to replace those that die off. [7] In men, there are an average of 5,200,000 RBCs per cubic millimeter and in women there are an average of 4,600,000 RBCs per cubic millimeter. The ratio of cells in normal blood is 600 RBCs to 1 White Blood Cell and 40 platelets.

Amazingly, RBCs do not eat up any of the oxygen themselves as they carry it out to all your cells. Special enzymes provide the power they need. This is another process that precludes evolution and necessitates a master designer. How could Red Blood Cells evolve so they don't need oxygen?

Thankfully, the RBCs also remove Carbon Dioxide from our cells. The RBCs carry a certain enzyme (called carbonic anhydrase) which removes most of the CO_2 (70%) in our cells so it can go back to the lungs for elimination. The enzyme, carbonic anhydrase, speeds up the process of CO_2 combining with water by 5,000 times. [8]

That sure looks like a designed plan also. Enzymes don't form by accident and even if they did, you would still have to get the exact right one in the right place.

White Blood Cells

White Blood Cells are the amazing cells that circulate throughout our bodies to fight disease. They are made in the bone marrow from the same original cells as the Red Blood Cells. WBCs come in the following six main types, with their average percentages:

- Neutrophils - 58 percent. Have faintly blue-pink granules with digestive enzymes to eat bacteria.
- Eosinophils - 2 percent. Have orange-red granules. They kill parasites and have a role in allergic reactions.
- Basophils - 1 percent. Have purple granules. They are not well understood, but they release histamine.
- Bands - 3 percent. These are immature Neutrophils.
- Monocytes - 4 percent. They kill bacteria and also destroy old, damaged and dead cells in the body.
- Lymphocytes - 4 percent.

"Neutrophils and monocytes use several mechanisms to get to and kill invading organisms. They can squeeze through openings in blood vessels by a process called diapedesis. They move around using ameboid motion. They are attracted to certain chemicals produced by the immune system or by bacteria and migrate toward areas of higher concentrations of these chemicals. This is called chemotaxis. They kill bacteria by a process called phagocytosis, in which they completely surround the bacteria and digest them with digestive enzymes." [9]

Our disease fighting immune system is phenomenal, to say the least. The smartest scientists can't come close to copying it, let alone making a better one.

When the WBCs release the granules into the blood stream to fight disease, they last for about 4 to 8 hours before being absorbed into body tissues and sticking around another 4 or 5 days. What an amazing system for fighting disease for you. How can anyone conceptualize how this could have evolved?

Platelets

When you cut yourself, your blood will clot and form a scab. Did you ever ask yourself why your blood does not clot inside your body and turn you into a statue? The smooth inner surface of the blood vessels and a finely tuned balance of chemicals or "clotting factors" keeps that from happening. Evolutionists must believe that we are really lucky that blood clotting worked perfectly the very first time. Otherwise we would have bled out completely on the ground or else frozen solid from internal clotting.

"...platelets are not actually cells but rather small fragments of cells. Platelets help the blood clotting process (or coagulation) by gathering at the site of an injury, sticking to the lining of the injured blood vessel, and forming a platform on which blood coagulation can occur. This results in the formation of a fibrin clot, which covers the wound and prevents blood from leaking out. Fibrin also forms the initial scaffolding upon which new tissue forms, thus promoting healing." [10]

The number of platelets also has to have a controlling chemical process so there is just the right number in your body. Too many platelets and people would be getting strokes and heart attacks. Too few and we'd lose a lot of blood to excessive bleeding. Here again it looks like there must have been a very intelligent designer.

Okay, I'm sure you are getting the idea and are probably tired of reading so I'm going to wrap it up now.

There are different types of Platelets: T-cells and B-cells. The T-cells come in 4 types: (1) Helper T cells, (2) Cytotoxic T cells, (3) Memory T cells, and (4) Suppressor T cells. Each of them has their own unique chemicals and very complex purposes.

And I haven't even talked about the Plasma, which makes up 55% of your blood.

In conclusion, over and over again when you look at your own blood, there must be God.

Chapter #97 The Retina

In doing research for my next proof for God, I came across a quote that blew me away. I had never heard any detail like this about the retina of your eye, even though I had already written one whole chapter about the Eye (#45).

As you know, the retina of your eye is the part that allows you to be able to see this page or anything else. It is full of nerve cells that convert light into electrical and chemical signals that are sent to the brain down the optic nerve.

Your retina is thinner than Saran Wrap, by the way.

I find what it does really hard to imagine. Here is the quote:

> "...it is clear that the human retina's real-time performance goes unchallenged. Actually, to simulate 10 milliseconds (ms) of the complete processing of even a single nerve cell from the retina would require the solution of about 500 simultaneous nonlinear differential equations 100 times and would take at least several minutes of processing time on a Cray supercomputer. Keeping in mind that there are 10 million or more such cells interacting with each other in complex ways, it would take a minimum of 100 years of [1985] Cray time to simulate what takes place in your eye many times every second." [1]

You could quibble and say that this is an old quote, which it is, from about 1985. But even given that computers are a lot faster now, it would still take a super computer (like big in size and needing lots of power) to do what your tiny little retina is doing every second, in each eye of course.

Researchers at UC Berkeley discovered that our retinas form a stack of 10 to 12 different image representations of what we view by using "cross-talk" between different layers of cells in the retina. The images are not very good quality. But they are all sent to the brain and the brain assembles them into the wonderful images we experience. [2]

No person in their right mind who knows what a computer chip is would ever proclaim that it could have evolved. Yet some very sane people refuse to see that there was any super intelligence behind the formation of a retina that is vastly superior to any computer chip. And besides retinas have been around for millions of years.

"The retinal rods and cones are composed of various layers. The human rods have a dynamic range of about 10 billion-to-one. In other words,

304

when fine-tuned for high gain amplification (as when you are out on a dark night and there is only starlight), your photoreceptors can pick up a single photon. Phenomenal sensitivity! Of course the retina does a number of processing tricks on that just to make sure it is not picking up "noise" or false positives, so you don't see static; it really wants at least six receptors in the same area to pick up the same signal before it "believes" that it is true and sends it to the brain. In bright daylight the retina bleaches out and the volume control turns way down for, again, admirable performance." [3]

Take note that your retina can pick up a single photon of light. That's how sensitive it is. But just to be sure there are no mistaken electrical impulses sent to the brain, the retina makes sure by checking around and only sending a signal if six photoreceptors all pick up the same thing.

A retina that sensitive if exposed to sunlight would get totally bleached out and you wouldn't be able to see anything. However, your retina is able to adjust to major changes in the amount of light. Imagine how that could possibly evolve. And remember, all this ability is contained in something thinner than Saran Wrap. Note also that the retina is transparent (you can see right through it).

That's just the tip of the iceberg. Just about everything about your retina is a profound miracle.

I mentioned above that the dynamic range sensitivity of the retina is about 10 billion to one. For modern photographic film we are only talking about a range of 1,000 to one.

Think some more about a computer chip when compared to your retina. Remember that the computer chip was absolutely designed by some very smart people. The retina only occupies 0.0003 cubic inches of space and the power consumption of the retina is about 0.001 watts. The retina has a resolution of about 10,000 by 10,000 pixels. It has about 25 billion equivalent "gates" in it that are like the transistors in a computer chip.

Other parts of the retina are equally miraculous. There are three layers of cells on the back of the retina: the Retinal Pigment Epithelium, the choroid, and the sclera. The Retinal Pigment Epithelium is a multifunctional and indispensable structure. The RPE is a single-cell-thick tissue layer consisting of relatively uniform polygonal-shaped cells. These cells touch the extremities of the rods and the cones (the photoreceptors) with dense microvilli and basal membrane infoldings.

Posterior to the RPE is the vascular choroid layer which is filled with blood vessels that supply oxygen and nutrition, and remove waste.

"The structure of the choroid is generally divided into four layers (classified in order of furthest away from the retina to closest):

1. Haller's layer - outermost layer of the choroid consisting of larger diameter blood vessels.
2. Sattler's layer - layer of medium diameter blood vessels.
3. Choriocapillaris - layer of capillaries.
4. Bruch's membrane - innermost layer of the choroid." [4]

Note that your retina has small blood vessels, medium sized, and also larger blood vessels. These are all necessary for the correct functioning of the eye. It's incomprehensible that this emerged by evolution in a slow and gradual process.

The fossil record constantly shows only animals that have fully formed eyes.

Posterior to the choroid layer is another layer of connective tissue known as the sclera.

Evolutionists like Richard Dawkins, Kenneth Miller, Daniel Dennett, and others have claimed that Evolution is proved because the retina of the eye is backwards. They say this is a "poor design" because the rods and cones are facing away from the direction where light enters the eye. The retina was even called "functionally stupid". Their "proof" is that they know better how the retina should be correctly designed and we would have better vision if our eyes were like squid eyes. Since it's a "poor design," it must have evolved because they know if there were a God, He would not have done it that way. He would have done it their way.

A "flawed design" is their evidence against a creator God and an argument for a random process of mutation.

So, what if scientists, upon further research, can prove it is not a flawed design but actually the best possible engineering? Could we then proclaim that there is a God? Would the atheists be forced to change their minds?

Well, as it turns out that is exactly what has happened. Many researchers have discovered that the design of the retina is actually the best design and that there is no evidence that the Evolutionists' idea of the "best" design would even work at all.

I'm not going to spend a lot more time on this, but I want to point you to a fantastic technical paper that goes into all the details of why the design we have is perfect. If you are interested, read the article: "*Why the Inverted*

Human Retina Is a Superior Design" by Jerry Bergman and Joseph Calkins. [5]

Here is a short list of some of the reasons why the design of our human retina is actually the best design and was clearly designed by an all knowing intelligence.

1. Rods and Cones need a lot of blood. Rods and cones require a greater blood supply than any other bodily tissue. They require close contact with blood in order to receive oxygen and nutrients. Waste products need to be carried away. Vision actually happens because chemical reactions are taking place and sending signals to the brain. Heat is being generated that needs to be cooled by the blood. Photopigments constantly have to be replaced and recycled. Rods and cones (photoreceptors) get used up and have to replace themselves about every 7 days or so. [6]

2. Best location of blood supply. If the retina were designed in the opposite way, where would the blood supply be? You can't put it in front of the rods and cones. If you put it along the sides, it would take up too much space and reduce the number of rods and cones. That would cause poorer vision.

3. Need opaque layer to absorb excess light. The rods and cones need to be close to a dark surface to absorb stray light. Otherwise, reflecting light would distort our vision. The Retinal Pigment Epithelium provides that dark surface.

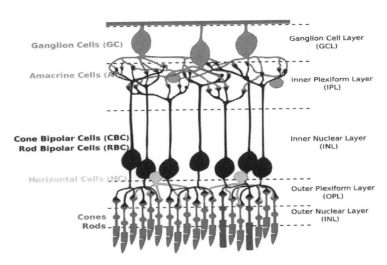

Image 21. Retina of Human Eye.

4. Retinal Pigment Epithelium needed. This layer of cells produces critical enzymes for vision. It also stores Vitamin A for regeneration. The RPE also helps maintain water and ion flow between the neural retina and the choroid, protects against free radical damage, and regulates retinoid metabolism. It is also a barrier to protect the inner parts of the eye.

5. Retina should not be more sensitive than it is. As I mentioned above, the retina can recognize a single photon of light. You cannot get any better than that. Our retina works better than any other design. If there were somehow greater sensitivity, you might see "too much" and get blinded. It might be helpful at night, but not at all during the day. It would cause more eye damage too. Why do you think people wear sunglasses?

6. Müller cells. Recent research has discovered Müller cells in the retina. They are actually like funnels that help carry the light through the retina so it is less distorted. They have the perfect index of refraction to transmit the light with minimum loss and distortion. It's like God invented fiber optic cables thousands of years ago. How about that for design?

7. Light does not get blocked. Amazingly, very little light is actually blocked by the part of the retina the light encounters first. This is the transparent layer of many nerve cells leading to the optic nerve and then the brain. Normal nerve cells are covered with a substance called myelin. But the nerve cells in the retina do not have this covering which would have blocked some of the light. Also the larger blood vessels and nerves inside the eye travel around but not over the area where your focused vision takes place. What a good design.

8. Waste must be carried away. There are waste products from the chemical reactions as well as the dying rods and cones. If the rods and cones faced the front, all the garbage would accumulate inside your eye. The result of that is obvious.

9. Fast recycle time. You know if you drive at night and look into the oncoming headlights you are temporarily blinded. The close blood supply allows a relatively fast recycle time. If your rods and cones faced the other way, you'd be temporarily blinded much longer.

10. Color and much greater detail than squid eyes. Research on squid eyes shows they can perceive shape, light intensity, and texture, but any details are seriously lacking. Squid have only 20 million receptor cells in their retina, whereas humans have 126 million. Squid have only rods, whereas humans have rods and three types of cones, allowing us to see the whole color spectrum. [7]

11. Momentary shadows are a good thing. It turns out that the light having to pass through various cells before getting to the rods and cones is a good thing. Constant light would bleach out the rods and cones, but the momentary darkness gives them a break and allows them to regenerate. Think again about sun glasses.

So we can now conclude that there is no "poor design" here at all. In fact, the design is so magnificent it is beyond our understanding.

There must be God.

Chapter #98 Acacia Trees and Ants

Gardening is thought of as a skill that requires pretty advanced intelligence. Humans in the whole history of evolution did not start to garden until about 12,000BC. [1] So it took humans a long time to figure it out.

This Proof for God is about the symbiotic relationship between certain trees and certain types of ants. In particular I want to talk about the Central and South American Bull-Horn Acacia tree and the Pseudomyrmex ant, which is a genus of stinging, wasp-like ants. But there are other similar relationships.

At least 100 other species of plants and ants exhibit this type of relationship. [2].

> "Many species of acacia tress that are deficient in chemical defenses have developed a mutualistic relationship with stinging ants in which protection is exchanged for nutrients and a home. Acacia trees and their symbiotic partner can be found all over the world in temperate, desert, and tropical regions, especially since some species of acacia trees are highly invasive. They reach sexual maturity typically three years after germination, and the adult trees can be used for industrial or decorative purposes. During development, the acacia trees form symbiotic relationships with ants to promote healthy growth for both the ant and the tree. Not only are the trees vigorously protected, but they also provide ants and their larvae a ready home and available nutrients." [3]

Note how the author of the above quote talks about the plant and ants as if they are intelligently discussing with each other how they are going to form a mutually beneficial partnership. How come we humans can't form a relationship with a plant if an ant can do it? Or how come we can't form a nice relationship with a bunch of ants if a plant can do it?

As I explain below what amazing things scientists have discovered about this relationship, you will see that the Theory of Evolution has no plausible explanation for its existence. Even if one such implausible relationship could have evolved, how could 100 totally distinct and unique types of plant to ant relationships evolve without any connection to each other?

An important point to make in the beginning is that the Bull-Horn Acacia tree cannot survive without the help of the ants. In experiments where the ants were taken off the tree, the tree died within two to fifteen months.

"In studying this amazing relationship, researchers removed the ants from some of these trees. Within two to fifteen months the tree was dead. Without the ants' care, animals eat off all the leaves and surrounding plants overrun it." [4]

So without help from the ants, there could not be any Bull-Horn Acacia trees. So how could the trees ever have evolved without the ants already there to take care of them? But how did the ants learn how to take care of these particular trees before the trees existed? Gardening the trees would have to have evolved too. It would take a long process of learning for the ants, if ants can even learn like that. Taking care of the Acacia trees is very, very complicated as we shall see.

If you have two minutes, check out this National Geographic video about a similar Acacia tree and its ants. I think you will be amazed: https://www.youtube.com/watch?v=Xm2qdxVVRm4

In this symbiotic relationship, let's look first at what the Acacia tree does for the ants. There is a lot of the trademark of intelligence here and if you don't accept that there is a God, then you have to think it is the tree that has intelligence or else it is just some accidental process.

"The mutualistic relationship is established when a newly mated queen is attracted to a tree by its odor and starts nesting inside the large, hollow acacia thorns. She lays 15-20 eggs to produce the first generation of workers. As the colony grows, more thorns become inhabited, and when the colony reaches around 400 individuals, the ants start to protect the plant." [5]

Scientists know that the queen ant can smell an Acacia tree. Think of all the evolution that would have to go into an ant being able to smell, let alone being able to recognize a particular tree as the one that would provide a good place to start a nest.

The Acacia tree provides a wonderful place for ants to build their nests. The ants can drill a hole into the horns of the plant that are hollow inside and this makes a perfect place for a nest. Since the horns are fairly small, the ants will make nests in the horns all over the tree.

The Acacia tree actually has special glands on their stems which secrete a carbohydrate-rich, sweet nectar that is very nutritious for the ants. If that gland evolved through a slow and gradual process and the nectar that is secreted then also had to evolve by a slow and gradual process, don't you think the ants would find a different source of nutrition instead of waiting around? Evolutionists have amazing imaginations, but I'd like to see them point out any actual plant that has ever evolved something like this on its own

311

in the thousands of years that humans have been watching plants. It's never been seen, but still they believe in evolution.

The Acacia tree also produces what are called "Beltian bodies" on the tips of its leaflets. These Beltian bodies are made of a protein-lipid which doesn't seem to have any other use or value except for the ants to feed their larvae. [6] The Beltian bodies seem to be perfect for that single purpose. Look at a picture on the Internet of Beltian bodies and imagine the evolution that had to take place for the tree to produce such a "fruit". Trees live a long time. They would have to produce seeds, which grow up, and then produce new seeds. How many generations would it take in a slow and gradual process of tree after tree until the Beltian bodies were perfected. Remember that the Beltian bodies give no benefit at all to the tree except to attract the ants by providing the perfect nutrients for their larvae. Remember that without the ants, the trees mostly die so getting many generations of trees to evolve implies that the ants were always there.

That's already too incredible for evolution. But now let's take a look at what the ants do for the tree.

If a plant eating animal or insect comes along that will harm the Acacia tree, the ants release a pheromone which is a nasty odor and it sounds the alarm. All of them rush out to attack. They will bite and sting any intruder very severely, usually driving them away.

However, the ants are uniquely selective. If a Praying Mantis or a spider comes along, which actually can benefit the Acacia by eating insect pests, the ants leave them alone. Now how could they have ever evolved that type of selectivity? Ants also will not bother the bees that pollinate the tree.

Another thing that the ants do for the tree is keep away vines and other plants. The ants will chew through any vines that come on their tree or its leaves, thus getting rid of any threat. The ants seem to even know that the tree needs sunlight and will remove leaves of other trees that are obstructing the sunlight.

> "According to Daniel Janzen, livestock can apparently smell the pheromone and avoid these acacias day and night. Getting stung in the mouth and tongue is an effective deterrent to browsing on the tender foliage. In addition to protecting V. conigera (Acacia) from leaf-cutting ants and other unwanted herbivores, the ants also clear away invasive seedlings around the base of the tree that might overgrow it and block out vital sunlight." [7]

And here is a very amazing fact that was discovered recently, the ants actually help prevent bacteria problems on the leaf surfaces. Researchers at the Max

Planck Institute for Chemical Ecology in Jena, Germany, have found that it is likely something on the legs of the ants that yields the antibacterial benefit. Evolutionists are going to have a problem explaining how something like that evolved.

> "Analysis of the surfaces of the leaves revealed that the number of plant pathogens as well as of necrotic plant tissues increased considerably when mutualistic Pseudomyrmex ferrugineus ants were absent. These plants also showed strong immune responses in the form of an increased concentration of salicylic acid, a plant hormone which regulates defense against pathogens. Detailed analysis of the bacterial composition on the surfaces of the leaves suggested that the presence of mutualistic ants changed the bacterial populations and reduced harmful pathogens. Although far less pronounced, this effect could also be observed in parasitic ants.

> How antimicrobial protection is transferred from ants to plant is still unclear." [8]

Is that convincing enough that this relationship was designed and not evolved? How about one more point. Researchers have discovered that the tree secretes some repellent, probably from its pollen, that keeps the ants away temporarily during pollination. This maximizes the reproduction of the seeds of the tree because the ants don't run over them and disturb their growth. But the secretion eventually wears off about the time that the fertilization has already taken place. So now the ants will come around again and they will perform their duty of protecting the leaves and tree. [9]

No human being could design something with this chemical and biological sophistication.

There must be God.

Chapter #99 Complexity, Equilibrium, and Energy Costs

I'm sure you remember the phrase from physics class that a body in motion tends to stay in motion and a body at rest tends to stay at rest. This is known as Newton's First Law of Motion.

This has an interesting application to recent research on evolution. As you can imagine, it takes a certain amount of energy to produce something new and different. And mutating new systems is the essence of how evolution creates new species.

If forces are in a state of equilibrium, then generally there will not be change. Darwinism requires that there be change over time and therefore there must be an input of energy.

Here is the definition of equilibrium.

A condition in which all influences acting cancel each other, so that a static or balanced situation results. In physics, equilibrium results from the cancellation of forces acting on an object. In chemistry, it occurs when chemical reactions are proceeding in such a way that the amount of each substance in a system remains the same. [1]

In a July, 2014, peer reviewed article in the journal Complexity, researchers Snoke, Cox, and Petcher have realized that the Theory of Evolution has a major problem. Their abstract says this.

"A scalable model of biological evolution is presented which includes energy cost for building new elements and multiple paths for obtaining new functions. The model allows a population with a continual increase of complexity, but as time passes, detrimental mutations accumulate. This model shows the crucial importance of accounting for the energy cost of new structures in models of biological evolution." [2]

The bottom line seems to be that whatever cause generated the biological features we observe, unguided Darwinian evolution is not it. Natural Selection requires many different mutations to choose from to get one that is useful. Having enough alternatives for success of Natural Selection would create too much dead weight on the population to be able to continue to thrive. [3]

They used a computational model to simulate the processes that must take place for evolution to be true. The Theory of Evolution says that Natural Selection chooses one from among many variations in a survival of the fittest process. The essential starting point therefore must first be the existence of the many variations for Natural Selection to be able to act on something.

If you don't have many variations already existing, then the odds of Natural Selection working successfully become totally impossible.

In order to get many variations, there is necessarily an energy requirement for each one. The researchers tried different levels of energy as the amount needed to make a new variation and then tested to see what the results would be.

If it takes a lot of energy, then very few will happen. If it takes a small amount of energy, then you can get an abundance of mutations.

There is also another energy cost to be factored in. It takes energy for carrying along useless or redundant systems. The more efficient a living system is the more likely it will be successful. Excess baggage is likely to be dropped.

So in other words, once a good design exists, it tends to be in equilibrium and it will continue. It will not develop other systems because of the extra energy required to develop them. Adding new variations onto an already functioning and efficient system would require extra energy that the organism would tend to select against.

As an example, how do you evolve a human pelvis from a monkey pelvis? The orientation, structure, and strength points are very different because a human walks upright. The monkey pelvis works fine for the monkey. Why would a partially human pelvis and a partially monkey pelvis be remotely a good idea from an efficiency perspective? Walking either way would be difficult.

If you are trying to develop a monkey into a human, you could make the same argument for legs, feet, arms, hands, and on and on.

The model simulation showed that in most cases no changes would take place in a working system. It also showed another problem.

If you plug a number into the model that would represent a low cost of energy in order to make a new variation, then you would indeed get lots of variations. This is necessary for Natural Selection to be able to operate. However, those many variations would tend to be carried forward even if they did not have a functional purpose. This ultimately caused the organism to fail from the burden of useless vestigial systems.

In order for Natural Selection to function, the theory says there have to be a lot of alternatives to choose from. But the modeling based on energy costs demonstrates a big challenge for Darwinism. The model results show that too many of those various new systems would not get discarded because they are not costly to keep maintaining. The organism would eventually have to fail from the burden.

There was no stable energy cost point for getting to the scenario where Natural Selection could work its magic. They either got no evolution or too much useless evolution which Natural Selection could not deal with.

Snoke, Cox, and Petcher found the energy cost of producing variations showed two outcomes, both falsify the Theory of Evolution.

"There are two competing processes. On one hand, the energy cost of carrying vestigial (non-functioning) systems makes them weakly deleterious, not neutral, which tends to reduce their number. Conversely, without stabs in the dark, that is, new systems which might eventually obtain new function but as yet have none, no novelty can ever occur, and no increase of complexity. Thus, if the energy cost of vestigial systems is too high, no evolution will occur." [4]

So here is the big problem. The tendency it turns out is for everything to stay in equilibrium once an efficient system is attained. From there, no evolution occurs. The energy cost of creating many variations so Natural Selection could take place is too high. Thus no new systems tend to develop and no further evolution takes place.

When researchers tested what would happen if only a small amount of energy cost was needed to produce lots of variations. They found that this would produce the many new systems that are needed, however, this would also lead to many left over systems that are useless. Over time, more and more useless systems would accumulate. Eventually that would cause the organism to die out from lack of efficiency.

So getting to a result of having lots of new systems means secondarily that you cannot weed out slightly deleterious traits. Over time unhelpful traits accumulate. Eventually such mutations pile up to an extent that the population reaches a crisis point, and crashes. The junk has become an unbearable burden. The organisms go extinct. [5]

Before there can ever be "survival of the fittest," there has to be "arrival of the fittest" on the scene. Science is now having a problem identifying how systems could even "arrive," let alone be in a position to be selected as survivor.

Many scientists now recognize the insufficiency of the classic Darwinian story to account for the appearance of new features or innovations in the history of life. I already pointed this out in Chapter #29, Mathematics, and Chapter 73, Punctuated Equilibrium.

Scientists are having to turn their focus to other theories to account for remarkable differences between genomes, the sudden appearance of novel body plans, and genuine innovations like the bat's wing, the mammalian placenta, the vertebrate eye, or insect flight. They realize that the traditional explanation of population genetics cannot even account for "the arrival of the fittest," let alone the "survival of the fittest." [6]

Let me repeat the conclusion of that peer-reviewed article. Please pass it on to others so that they too will be aware of what researchers themselves are more and more aware of.

> "The bottom line seems to be that whatever cause generated the biological features we observe, unguided Darwinian evolution is not it." [7]

As research continues, even stubborn believers are going to have to give up on Darwinian unguided evolution. The end has to come sooner or later and it will be scientists who pull the plug on Darwinian Evolution.

There must have been some intelligence far greater than ours to engineer the world around us.

There must be God.

Chapter #100 Quality Control and Error Correction

The Nobel Prize in Chemistry for 2015 was given jointly to three scientists who discovered repair mechanisms in our DNA.

"The Nobel Prize in Chemistry 2015 is awarded to Tomas Lindahl, Paul Modrich and Aziz Sancar for having mapped, at a molecular level, how cells repair damaged DNA and safeguard the genetic information. Their work has provided fundamental knowledge of how a living cell functions and is, for instance, used for the development of new cancer treatments." [1]

"Damages occur to your DNA every day." Sara Snogerup Linse is the chair of the Nobel Committee for chemistry. 'In fact, right here, right now, if all those errors were left uncorrected, your genetic material would have very little resemblance to the original chromosomes in your very first cell. Life as we know it today is totally dependent on DNA repair mechanisms, as have been revealed in molecular detail by this year's chemistry laureates.'" [2]

Think about what these Nobel Prize-winning chemists are actually saying. This is totally anti-evolution. Our DNA repairs itself. Maybe that seems like it is not important, or perfectly natural, unless you think about it for a few minutes. What is DNA repairing itself from? Why mutations of course. DNA does not like mutations and actually has at least three different ways of fighting against mutation, and trying to stop mutation, and repairing against it when it does happen (which is often).

Now evolutionists will have a much more difficult time explaining that their touted mechanism for developing new species is even remotely possible. Scientists have now shown that mutation cannot really be the process for change.

Here is what the Nobel Academy said about Dr. Paul Modrich's discovery of the "mismatch repair mechanism".

"This mechanism, mismatch repair, reduces the error frequency during DNA replication by about a thousand fold," the academy said. [3]

The Nobel Prize was given to three men who have made evolution about a thousand times more difficult. Imagine that. It was already one in a trillion. What will science finally be forced to admit after this? And what might they discover if they look in the right place for the source of life?

Tomas Lindahl, Paul Modrich and Aziz Sancar won the Nobel Prize for having mapped, at a molecular level, how cells repair damaged DNA and safeguard the genetic information from any mutations. It's now a fact that cells repair their own DNA when mutations take place.

Lindahl, a Swedish scientist, discovered that DNA actually has a pretty high rate of decay and that should have prevented any development of life on earth. That led him to search further and discover a molecular machinery, base excision repair, which is constantly working to counteract any collapses in our DNA.

Modrich, an American, was able to show how a cell corrects errors that occur when DNA is replicated during cell division. The mechanism is called mismatch repair, and it alone cuts down from 1,000 errors to only one error in replication.

> "Paul Modrich showed how cells correct errors that take place during DNA replication, every time a cell divides. This mismatch repair fixes some 99.9 percent of the errors that take place." [4]

Sancar, a U.S. and Turkish citizen, discovered another mechanism called nucleotide excision repair. This is the process that cells use to repair UV damage to DNA.

The conclusion of all this means almost 100% of DNA errors are repaired. That makes evolution impossible!

Here is another amazing statement in a report.

> "Towards the end of the 1960s, many scientists considered DNA to be incredibly stable. But working at the Karolina Institute in Stockholm, Dr. Lindahl worked out that there must be thousands of potentially damaging attacks on the genome every day – an onslaught that would make human life impossible." [5]

The Nobel Prize Committee admitted that human life should be impossible because DNA is so fragile. Dr. Lindahl, way back in 1974 (that's 42 years ago) proposed a mechanism to explain how we could even exist despite the fact that our DNA is so unstable. (Note, we shouldn't be here. We are a miracle.)

So scientists on the leading edge of DNA research have known for 42 years that evolution is impossible.

Here is more of the statement from the Nobel Committee.

319

"But many billions more divisions take place on the path to adulthood, until we carry enough DNA in our trillions of cells to reach 250 times to the sun and back. The most remarkable feat is how the genetic information is copied so faithfully. 'From a chemical perspective, this ought to be impossible,' the Nobel committee said.

"'All chemical processes are prone to random errors. Additionally, your DNA is subjected on a daily basis to damaging radiation and reactive molecules. In fact, you ought to have been a chemical chaos long before you even developed into a fetus,' they added." [6]

The chemists admitted that "from a chemical perspective" evolution is impossible. But they didn't say "evolution," they said "life". Obviously, something beyond chemistry must be at work here.

Here's the truth that evolutionists must now face. Their theory about a slow and gradual step by step process for species development must now overcome the newly established chemistry of DNA repair mechanisms. How can evolution claim that mutation is their operating process when it is being reversed 99.9% of the time by these Nobel Prize winning repair mechanisms?

Have you ever tried to go someplace by taking two steps forward and two steps back? The Theory of Evolution starts from very simple organisms and ends up after a long climb at millions of extremely complicated structures. But evolution can never even get started without DNA. Now we find that DNA basically won't mutate because it already has inside itself an anti-mutant mechanism in place.

DNA repair mechanisms are like "quality control" in a manufacturing plant. Here is a definition:

"'Quality control' is a system for verifying and maintaining a desired level of quality in an existing product or service by careful planning, use of proper equipment, continued inspection, and corrective action as required." [8]

The DNA repair systems are truly an example of quality control. Therefore, I can name at least six separate actions that are required. You have to be able to (A) inspect the DNA replications for errors, (B) recognize when there is a copying error or failure and exactly where it is, (C) turn on a repair mechanism, (D) fix the error, (E) turn off the repair mechanism, and (F) check to see if the repair was successful. Sounds a lot like intelligence was required at a very highly sophisticated level that human beings can only imagine. ...There must be God.

Chapter #101 The Messiah

As I was getting closer and closer to my goal of 101 Proofs for God, I began thinking a lot about what should be the concluding Proof for God, number 101. I wanted it to be a more universal one, something more of the heart than the head.

I thought about "good and evil" and "morality" which have been classic proofs for God because they cannot originate inside of the materialistic world. I thought about "free will" and "faith" because those are very real things, but they are definitely not of this material world. No materialistic explanation of our existence (i.e. evolution) can explain their existence.

As I sat down and prayed about it, "The Messiah" came to my mind. That was very satisfying and totally appropriate. After all, what's life and proofs for God all about right now anyway?

The Messiah is the essential crux of human history. For believers, this one person, Jesus of Nazareth, leads us to being able to explain who is God, how the world got messed up, what the solution is, and what kind of world we should be looking forward to.

Just think about the effect that one almost totally obscure man has had on the world since he lived. He lived in a pretty obscure, little country for only 33 years and shared his ideas for only three years. Not only has he had an effect on billions of people for the last 2,000 years, but even today there are billions of people being affected by his life. His ideas affected the founding of our nation, its constitution, and government. Freedom and responsibility have led to the greatest advances in science, medicine, technology, art, and commerce that the world has ever seen.

How do you explain that type of phenomenon from three years of a man's life? He was tapping into something way beyond ordinary lives. Something very supernatural must be going on.

Now, I'm not going to try to convert anybody to anything here. I just want to put forth some facts that might bring a new perspective or two for you.

Let's take a look at the Bible from the perspective of it being just a book and compare it to other books. The Bible is the bestselling book of all time with over five billion sold. (To be accurate, Quotations from Chairman Mao claims over six billion in print, but does not claim they were all purchased. Also, the Qur'an claims billions, but there are not enough accurate records.) [1]

The next best seller at 150 million is Lord of the Rings. The Bible outsells it by 30 to 1.

Back in 2001, records show the number of new Bibles distributed (sold or given away) in the United States was about 168,000 per day. [2]

Could the Bible possibly be just a lie and really worthless to all those people? Are they really that stupid? Could they just be deluding themselves? Could they just be fantasizing their experiences with the God of the Bible?

There is totally overwhelming evidence that God really does exist everywhere you look. See my website,www.101ProofsforGod.Com, or one of the many others. Furthermore and most importantly, you can have a relationship with Him if you decide to. But there is a real catch, you have to decide to by your own freedom and responsibility. A leap of faith is required to have an experience.

Before this last chapter I've put together 100 Proofs for God and if you read all of those and are still not sure if God exists or not, your next step actually is to take a "leap of faith". There are plenty of other proofs I could write about. I could keep going for another 40 years and get up to 1001 Proofs for God.

However, faith in God is actually a gift that comes to you once you accept that God exists and decide to believe in Him. Only after you have received the gift of faith, then you start to build your relationship with God. That relationship is the place you want to get to. That's the part that is wonderful. That's the goal.

Think of people like St. Francis of Assisi or Mother Teresa. They had an amazing personal relationship with Jesus. They had many deep experiences with him as have millions of others down through the years. As you probably know, St. Francis was the first to receive the stigmata, where his wrists, his feet, and his side shed blood in the same place as Jesus' crucifixion. It lasted for two years prior to his death. [3] The stigmata came upon him during a 40-Day fast when he was 43 years old.

This paragraph is from his biographer.

"His wrists and feet seemed to be pierced by nails, with the heads of the nails appearing on his wrists and on the upper sides of his feet, the points appearing on the other side. The marks were round on the palm of each hand but elongated on the other side, and small pieces of flesh jutting

322

out from the rest took on the appearance of the nail-ends, bent and driven back. In the same way the marks of nails were impressed on his feet and projected beyond the rest of the flesh. Moreover, his right side had a large wound as if it had been pierced with a spear, and it often bled so that his tunic and trousers were soaked with his sacred blood." [4]

Many people have received stigmata over the years. But modern science cannot explain it. So what do they conclude?

"Some modern research has indicated stigmata are of hysterical origin, or linked to dissociative identity disorder....There is a link between dietary constriction by self-starvation, dissociative mental states and self-mutilation, in the context of a religious belief. [6]

In essence, researchers conclude that religious people are crazy people. Is that what you want to believe about St. Francis? How about Mother Teresa? You'd have to be a crazy person to spend your life among lepers like she did, right?

Some people may say that the historical Jesus did not exist. (That might be an even better proof for God if somehow all the miracles connected to Jesus for 2,000 years have been done by God without an earthly Jesus.)

But he actually did exist. The evidence for his life is far more substantial than evidence for other ancient figures that everybody accepts as having existed without doubt, e.g. Socrates, Plato, Aristotle, Homer, and others.

Go to this type of resource for a thorough analysis of proof for Jesus: *Is The New Testament Reliable As An Historical Record?* [6] It lays out three tests to apply to historical documents: (A) The Bibliographical test, (B) The Internal evidence test, and (C) The External evidence test. The life and teachings of Jesus of Nazareth pass with high flying colors.

There are some 24,000 copies of the New Testament in existence (5,600 in Greek, 10,000 in Latin, and 9,000 in other languages from wide ranges all over the Middle East.) This compares to "The Iliad" by Homer which is in second place with 643 copies. [7]

There are only about 250 known manuscripts for Plato. [8]

"We have 114 fragments of the New Testament dating back to 50-100 A.D., and 5,366 Greek copies of parts of the New Testament, and over 19,000 manuscripts in other languages, including 250 books containing most of the NewTestament and 325 complete New Testaments within 225 years of their writing and less than 300 years from Christ's Resurrection." [9]

A surprisingly huge number of the New Testament fragments and copies are very close in time frame to their original documents, increasing the likelihood that they are accurate. But for Plato who lived around 400BC, we do not have any copy of his work that was made until 1200 to 1300 years later. So there could be a lot of errors in the copy. For Homer, our existing copies were made 500 years after his originals.

Further evidence for the real life of Jesus is that many people living at his time or shortly thereafter wrote about him and his followers and the New Testament. Writings of later church fathers contain 19,368 citations referring to texts from just the Four Gospels alone. [10]

Another question that people often ask is, "What's the whole big deal about a Messiah, anyway?" For non-believers, Jesus is not a big deal. However, people with a religious inclination know in their hearts there is something wrong with this world. Human nature has good and evil. It's different when compared to the harmony in all of Nature.

Somehow we are separated from the goodness and happiness that we long for in our hearts. If there is a Messiah, a person who saves us from this situation, then that provides an explanation for our plight and a solution to return to the original ideal. There is hope. Also, the existence of the Messiah is proof there is a God acting behind the scenes who loves us and sends the Messiah for us.

There could never be The Messiah if there were no God. In fact, The Messiah necessitates a loving, long-suffering God who is trying to bring home His "lost sheep," His lost children. That is exactly the Heavenly Father that Jesus taught us about. No one else in history taught us that God is our Heavenly Father and forgives us for our sins.

Certainly, Jesus believed in God. If there ever was an "expert" whom we could trust knew what he was talking about, he's the one.

Maybe you think that you know "the truth" better than anyone else. Or maybe you think you get to decide what "truth" is according to what you want it to be. If you know all truth and you decide what truth is, then we should call you "god," shouldn't we?

One day everyone will find the truth, whether it is in this life or the next. Deep inside every person is the inerasable quest for truth. That is the guarantee that we will all keep searching until we find our source.

As I have shown throughout this book, over and over again, there must be God.

Footnotes and Comments

#6 Bigness

[1] NASA: "Ask an Astrophysicist."
http://imagine.gsfc.nasa.gov/docs/ask_astro/answers/021127a.html. Accessed June 11, 2016

#10 Life After Death

Reference Sources on Life after Death:

Proof of Heaven: A Neurosurgeon's Journey Into The Afterlife, by Dr. Eben Alexander, #1 New York Times Bestseller for 39 weeks through 8/4/2013. Famous brain surgeon spends 7 days in a comma experiencing God and the spiritual world. http://www.ebenalexander.com/. Accessed June 12, 2016.

Life After Death: The Evidence, by Dinesh D'Souza
Drawing on some of the most powerful theories and trends in physics, biology, philosophy, and psychology, D'Souza concludes that belief in life after death offers depth and significance to this life.

Life After Death: The Burden of Proof by Deepak Chopra
In Life After Death, Chopra draws on cutting-edge scientific discoveries and the great wisdom traditions to provide a map of the afterlife. It's a fascinating journey into many levels of consciousness. But far more important is his urgent message: Who you meet in the afterlife and what you experience there reflect your present beliefs, expectations, and level of awareness. In the here and now you can shape what happens after you die.

Is There Life After Death? The Extraordinary Science of What Happens When We Die, by Anthony Peake
This book proposes a simply amazing theory - a theory that states that personal death is a scientific impossibility. Using the latest findings of neurology, quantum physics, and consciousness studies, Anthony Peake suggests that we never die. After reading this book you will understand the reason for your life and how you can make it better next time.

The Science of Life After Death: New Research Shows Human Consciousness Lives On, by Stephen Hawley Martin
A lengthy and exhaustive study by the University of Virginia Medical School clearly indicates consciousness continues after death in at least some cases, if not all. This particular study, begun in 1961 and continuing today, was initiated by Ian Stevenson, M.D., a psychiatrist who graduated first in his class at McGill Medical School. Stevenson went to great lengths and much effort to follow scientific protocol in his investigations. Over the years, more than 2,600 of the cases he and others investigated have checked out in terms of the details.

On Life after Death, revised by Elizabeth Kubler-Ross and Caroline Myss
In this collection of inspirational essays, internationally known author Dr. Elisabeth Kubler-Ross draws on her in-depth research of more than 20,000 people who had near-death experiences, revealing the afterlife as a return to wholeness of spirit.

The Afterlife Experiments: Breakthrough Scientific Evidence of Life After Death, by Dr. Gary E. Schwartz
Risking his academic reputation, Dr. Gary E. Schwartz asked well-known mediums to become part of a series of experiments to prove, or disprove, the existence of an afterlife. This riveting narrative, with electrifying transcripts, documents stringently monitored

experiments in which mediums attempted to contact dead friends and relatives of "sitters" who were masked from view and never spoke, depriving the mediums of any cues.

Life After Death: Some of the Best Evidence, by Jan W Vandersande PhD
Renowned physicist Dr. Jan W. Vandersande surveys evidence for an afterlife and finds a lot of the observed physical phenomena both credible and compelling. Intended for skeptics and believers alike, Life After Death condenses more than 100 years of literature and testimony-including the author's own psychic experiences.... . As the book makes clear, the occurrences during such episodes, though fantastical, can't be dismissed as mere fantasy or fraud. Through historical accounts, photographs and personal experience, this engagingly written work adds to a growing body of evidence for the existence of an afterlife that's increasingly difficult to ignore.

Life After Life: The Investigation of a Phenomenon--Survival of Bodily Death, by Raymond Moody
In Life After Life Raymond Moody investigates more than one hundred case studies of people who experienced "clinical death" and were subsequently revived. First published in 1975, this classic exploration of life after death started a revolution in popular attitudes about the afterlife and established Dr. Moody as the world's leading authority in the field of near-death experiences.

Life After Death, by Mary T. Browne
A renowned psychic and spiritual healer with clients all over the world, Mary T. Browne had her first clairvoyant experience at the age of seven. For more than thirty years since then, her visions of the other side and her communication with her teachers, both in spirit and on the earth plane, have helped to form not just her understanding of death, but her philosophy of life.

Thirty Years Among the Dead, by Dr. Carl A. Wickland
It's about the author's experience treating cases of spirit possession. It gave great insight into the realms of the spirits and their rather very serious impact on those living. The departed spirits communicated through an intermediary, medium, his wife. The stories told touched my heart and enhanced my understanding of the nature and character of the spirits.

The History of Spiritualism, Volumes 1 and 2 (Cambridge Library Collection - Spiritualism and Esoteric Knowledge) by Arthur Conan Doyle
Sir Arthur Conan Doyle (1859-1930) is best known for his creation of the character Sherlock Holmes. Trained as a medical doctor, Doyle - like many Victorian intellectuals - became fascinated by spiritualism and its promise of communication with the afterlife. Doyle was a firm believer in the movement, claiming as evidence 'sign[s] of a purposeful and organized invasion' from the spirit world. In 1926, he published this influential two-volume history. Volume 1 covers the background and origins of spiritualism, beginning with Swedenborg before turning to the 'supernatural' events in upstate New York in 1848 that are generally regarded as the beginning of modern spiritualism. It then focuses on key individuals including D. D. Home, and on scientific investigations of spiritualist phenomena. The History provides valuable insights into Victorian and early twentieth-century culture and the controversies generated by spiritualism at that time.

Best Evidence: An Investigative Reporter's Three-Year Quest to Uncover the Best Scientific Evidence for ESP, Psychokinesis, Mental Healing, Ghosts and Poltergeists, Dowsing, Mediums, Near Death Experiences, Reincarnation, and Other Impossible Phenomena That Refuse to Disappear (2nd Edition) by Michael Schmicker
"Best Evidence is indeed one, if not the best itself, of the major books explaining and offering proof that psi phenomena are here to stay whether we like it or not," Fred Alan Wolf, Ph.D, physicist and National Book Award winning author of Mind Into Matter, Taking the Quantum Leap. "My highest recommendation, not just one but a half-dozen

astounding stories, any one of which can change the way we think about the nature of reality," Dean Radin, Ph.D, author of The Conscious Universe: The Scientific Truth of Psychic Phenomena. "For skeptics and cautious believers alike, a splendid introduction to 'impossible phenomena that refuse to disappear,'" Stanley Krippner, Ph.D, Co-Editor, Varieties of Anomalous Experience: Examining the Scientific Evidence. "Hard line skeptics won't be pleased, but Schmicker has done his homework an excellent survey of the strongest evidence," Marcello Truzzi, Ph.D, Center for Scientific Anomalies Research.

To Heaven and Back: A Doctor's Extraordinary Account of Her Death, Heaven, Angels, and Life Again: A True Story... by Mary C. Neal M.D.
A kayak accident during a South American adventure takes one woman doctor to heaven — where she experienced God's peace, joy, and angels — and back to life again.

My Descent Into Death: A Second Chance at Life, by Howard Storm.
Storm, an avowed atheist, was awaiting emergency surgery when he realized that he was at death's door. Storm found himself out of his own body, looking down on the hospital room scene below. Next, rather than going "toward the light," he found himself being torturously dragged to excruciating realms of darkness and death, where he was physically assaulted by monstrous beings of evil. His description of his pure terror and torture is unnerving in its utter originality and convincing detail.

23 Minutes In Hell: One Man's Story About What He Saw, Heard, and Felt in that Place of Torment, by Bill Wiese.
Wiese saw the searing flames of hell, felt total isolation, and experienced the putrid and rotting stench, deafening screams of agony, terrorizing demons, and finally, the strong hand of God lifting him out of the pit--"Tell them I am coming very, very soon!"

Heaven is Real But So is Hell: An Eyewitness Account of What is to Come, by Vassula Ryden.
This book features her amazing encounters with both good and evil forces and reveals profoundly important messages for all humanity, largely hidden until now. Sometimes harrowing, but filled with hope, it answers many of the questions that people have been asking for thousands of years and at the same time offers a glimpse into God's love and justice, and of what is soon to come.

#13 The Infinite Monkey Theorem

[1] Wikipedia.org., "Infinite Monkey theorem," http://en.wikipedia.org/wiki/Infinite_monkey_theorem. Accessed June 11. 2016

[2] Wikipedia.org., "Infinite Monkey theorem," http://en.wikipedia.org/wiki/Infinite_monkey_theorem. Accessed June 11. 2016

[3] Wikipedia.org., "Infinite Monkey theorem," http://en.wikipedia.org/wiki/Infinite_monkey_theorem. Accessed June 11. 2016

#14 Empty Space

[1] Chown, Marcus, "11 Of The Craziest Things About The Universe," May 25, 2011, http://www.huffingtonpost.com/marcus-chown/11-of-the-craziest-things_b_628481.html#s107477. Accessed June 12, 2016.

[2] ScienceIQ.com, "Neutron Stars," http://www.scienceiq.com/Facts/NeutronStars.cfm. Accessed June 12, 2016.

"The electrons themselves take up little space, but the pattern of their orbit defines the size of the atom, which is therefore 99.9999999999999% open space!"

Footnotes and Comments

#15 Computers

[1] Greenemeier, Larry, "Computers have a lot to learn from the human brain, engineers say," Mar 10, 2009, Scientific American, http://www.scientificamerican.com/blog/post.cfm?id=computers-have-a-lot-to-learn-from-2009-03-10. Accessed June 12, 2016.

#16 Your Brain

[1] Newquist, H.P. 2004. The Great Brain Book. New York, NY: Scholastic Inc.

[2] Chudler, Eric. "Brain Facts and Figures." November 1, 2011.

[3] Fishetti, Mark, "Computers versus Brains: Computers are good at storage and speed, but brains maintain the efficiency lead," Scientific American, November 1, 2011, http://www.scientificamerican.com/article.cfm?id=computers-vs-brains. Accessed June 12, 2016.

[4] Disabled World towards Tomorrow website, "Human Brain Facts and Answers," http://www.disabled-world.com/artman/publish/brain-facts.shtml. Accessed June 12, 2016.

[5] Turkington, Carol. 1996. The Brain Encyclopedia. New York, NY: Checkmark Books.

[6] Disabled World towards Tomorrow website, "Human Brain Facts and Answers," http://www.disabled-world.com/artman/publish/brain-facts.shtml. Accessed June 12, 2016.

[7] National Geographic, "Brain," http://science.nationalgeographic.com/science/health-and-human-body/human-body/brain-article/. Accessed June 12, 2016.

[8] Edmonds, Molly. "Do Men and Women Have Different Brains?" http://science.howstuffworks.com/life/inside-the-mind/human-brain/men-women-different-brains.htm,. Accessed: June 9, 2016.

[9] Hawkins, Jeff. "On Intelligence" 2004

[10] "Brain versus Computer," Lucid Pages, http://www.lucidpages.com/branco.html. Accessed June 9, 2016

[11] Guy, Allison, "Replacing Synapses with a Single Switch," June 16, 2012, https://www.nextnature.net/2012/06/replacing-synapses-with-a-single-switch/, Accessed June 9, 2016.

[12] "Drug Addiction: The Synapse and Drug Addiction, BiologyWriter, http://biologywriter.com/backgrounder/drug-addiction/, Accessed June 9, 2016

Additional Reference:

Juan, Stephen. 2011. The Odd Brain: Mysteries of Our Weird and Wonderful Brain Explained. Riverside, NJ: Andrews McMeel Publishing.

#17 Dr. Antony Flew

[1] Francis S. Collins, author of The Language of God. Quoted in the Preface to There Is A God by Antony Flew

[2] Richard Swinburne, author of The Existence of God. Quoted in the Preface to <u>There Is A God</u> by Antony Flew

[3] Flew, Antony, There Is A God, Harper Collins, 2007, New York, NY

[4] YouTube videos search on "Antony Flew" example: https://www.youtube.com/watch?v=VHUtMEru4pQ. Accessed June 12, 2016.

[5] Flew, Antony, There Is A God, Harper Collins, 2007, New York, NY, page 88

[6] John Hick, professor and Fellow of the Institute for Advanced Research in Arts and Social
Sciences, University of Birmingham. Quoted in the Preface to <u>There Is A God</u> by Antony Flew

[7] Michael Behe, author of Darwin's Black Box and The Edge of Evolution. Quoted in the Preface to <u>There Is A God</u> by Antony Flew

[8] William Lane Craig, Research Professor, Talbot School of Theology. Quoted in the Preface to <u>There Is A God</u> by Antony Flew

[9] Flew, Antony, There Is A God, Harper Collins, 2007, New York, NY, page 135.

[10] Dr. Benjamin Wiker: Exclusive Flew Interview, 30 October 2007. http://www.tothesource.org/10_30_2007/10_30_2007.htm. Accessed June 12, 2016.

#18 The Fossil Record

[1] The Theory of Evolution can take many forms. I am referring specifically in this case to the theory that humans evolved from single celled organisms and other common ancestors of other species through some process of mutation and natural selection which also included ape-like creatures.

[2] Darwin, Charles, The Origin of Species, Chapter Six: Absence or Rarity of Transitional Varieties.

[3] Colin Patterson, personal communication. Luther Sunderland, Darwin's Enigma: Fossils and Other Problems, 4th edition, 1988, 88-90.

[4] Denton, Michael, Evolution: A Theory In Crisis. Pages 160-162."

Further Reference DVD: Darwin's Dilemma: The Mystery of the Cambrian Fossil Record, Illustra Media, 2009 for information about Chinese discoveries.

[7] Charles Darwin, On the Origin of Species by Means of Natural Selection, or the Preservation of Favoured Races in the Struggle for Life, 1859, page 158.

#22 Life Spans

[1] Wikipedia. Drosophila melanogaster (Fruit Fly) article. http://en.wikipedia.org/wiki/Drosophila_melanogaster, Accessed June 11, 2016.

[2] Clark, Liat, "Geneticists Evolve Fruit Flies With The Ability To Count," Wired UK, July 12, 2012, http://www.wired.com/2012/07/flies-learn-math/. Accessed June 11, 2016

#23 Children and Parents

Footnotes and Comments

[1] Pobanz, Kerry, Life In Eternity: Human Beings in the Spirit World, ISBN 978-1-105-65604-0. Lulu.Com, 2013.

#24 Pacific Golden Plover

[1] Wikipedia article, "Pacific Golden Plover," https://en.wikipedia.org/wiki/Pacific_golden_plover. Accessed June 11, 2016

[2] Marshall, Tom (June 13, 2011). "Plovers tracked across the Pacific". http://phys.org/news/2011-06-plovers-tracked-pacific.html. Accessed June 11, 2016.

[3] Charles Darwin, The Origin of Species: A Facsimile of the First Edition, Harvard University Press, 1964, p. 189.

#25 New Zealand Long Finned Eel

[1] New Zealand Department of Conservation, "Eels: About the long fin eel.," http://www.doc.govt.nz/nature/native-animals/freshwater-fish/eels/. Accessed June 11, 2016

Additional video reference. Long-finned Eels of Marlborough, New Zealand (YouTube video) http://youtu.be/95nUTKnDIU4. Accessed June 12, 2016.

#27 The Truth About Mutation

[1] Wikipedia article, "Theodosius Dobzhansky," (January 24, 1900 - December 18, 1975) http://en.wikipedia.org/wiki/Theodosius_Dobzhansky was a prominent geneticist and evolutionary biologist, and a central figure in the field of evolutionary biology for his work in shaping the unifying modern evolutionary synthesis. Accessed June 11, 2016.

[2] Alan H. Linton, emeritus professor of bacteriology, University of Bristol (U.K.), in The Times Higher Education Supplement (April 20, 2001), p. 29.

#28 The Lottery

[1] Hoyle, Fred, Evolution from Space (co-authored with Chandra Wickramasinghe), 1982/1984

[2] Wikipedia article, "Fred Hoyle," http://en.wikipedia.org/wiki/Fred_Hoyle, Accessed June 11, 2016, Hoyle was knighted in England in 1972. He is also the originator of the term "Big Bang".

#29 Mathematics

[1] Moorehead, Paul S., Kaplan, Martin M. (eds.), "Mathematical Challenges to the NeoDarwinist Interpretation of Evolution," Wistar Institute Symposium Monograph Number 5 (Philadelphia, PA: The Wistar Institute Press, 1967)

[2] Eden, Murray, professor of electrical engineering at M.I.T. "Inadequacies of Neo-Darwinian Evolution as a Scientific Theory." http://www.examiner.com/article/mathematical-challenges-to-the-neo-darwinian-interpretation-of-evolution. Accessed June 11, 2016

[3] Ulam, Stanislaw M., "How to Formulate Mathematically Problems of Rate of Evolution," in Mathematical Challenges to the Neo-Darwinian Interpretation of Evolution (Wistar Institute Press, 1966, No. 5), pg. 21

"[I]t seems to require many thousands, perhaps millions, of successive mutations to produce even the easiest complexity we see in life now. It appears, naively at least, that no matter how large the probability of a single mutation is, should it be even as great as one-half, you would get this probability raised to a millionth power, which is so very close to zero that the chances of such a chain seem to be practically non-existent."

[4] Schutzenberger , Marcel, "Algorithms and Neo-Darwinian Theory," in Mathematical Challenges to the Neo-Darwinian Interpretation of Evolution (Wistar Institute Press, 1966, No. 5), pg. 75

"We do not know any general principle which would explain how to match blueprints viewed as typographic objects and the things they are supposed to control. The only example we have of such a situation (apart from the evolution of life itself) is the attempt to build self-adapting programs by workers in the field of artificial intelligence. Their experience is quite conclusive to most of the observers: without some built-in matching, nothing interesting can occur. Thus, to conclude, we believe that there is a considerable gap in the neo-Darwinian theory of evolution, and we believe this gap to be of such a nature that it cannot be bridged within the current conception of biology."

[5] Sewell, Granville, "A Mathematician's View of Evolution," (The Mathematical Intelligencer, Vol 22 (4) (2000) pp 5-7),

Sewell notes that there are "a good many mathematicians, physicists and computer scientists who ...are appalled that Darwin's explanation for the development of life is so widely accepted in the life sciences." Sewell compares the genetic code of life to a computer program--a comparison also made by computer gurus such as Bill Gates and evolutionary biologists such as Richard Dawkins. He notes that experience teaches that software depends on many separate functionally-coordinated elements. For this reason "[m]ajor improvements to a computer program often require the addition or modification of hundreds of interdependent lines, no one of which makes any sense, or results in any improvement, when added by itself." "...But just as major improvements to a computer program cannot be made 5 or 6 characters at a time, certainly no major evolutionary advance is reducible to a chain of tiny improvements, each small enough to be bridged by a single random mutation."

[6] Coppedge, James F., Evolution: Possible or Impossible? "Chapter 7: How Large Numbers Can Help You," pp., 118-120. http://creationsafaris.com/epoi_c07.htm. Accessed June 11, 2016

#30 S.E.T.I. and DNA

[1] S.E.T.I. Wikipedia. http://en.wikipedia.org/wiki/SETI, Accessed June 11, 2016

"The search for extraterrestrial intelligence (SETI) is a collective term for the scientific search for intelligent extraterrestrial life. For example, monitoring electromagnetic radiation for signs of transmissions from civilizations on other worlds". Some of the most well-known projects are run by Harvard University, Ohio State University, the University of California, Berkeley and the SETI Institute."

[2] shCherbaka, Vladimir I. and Makubovb, Maxim A., The "Wow! signal" of the terrestrial genetic code, Icarus, Volume 224, Issue 1, May 2013, Pages 228–242. http://www.sciencedirect.com/science/article/pii/S0019103513000791, Accessed June 11, 2016

Footnotes and Comments

Excerpt from the Abstract: "Here we show that the terrestrial code displays a thorough precision-type orderliness matching the criteria to be considered an informational signal. Simple arrangements of the code reveal an ensemble of arithmetical and ideographical patterns of the same symbolic language. Accurate and systematic, these underlying patterns appear as a product of precision logic and nontrivial computing rather than of stochastic (i.e. random - Jim) processes (the null hypothesis that they are due to chance coupled with presumable evolutionary pathways is rejected with P-value $< 10^{-13}$). The patterns display readily recognizable hallmarks of artificiality, among which are the symbol of zero, the privileged decimal syntax and semantical symmetries. Besides, extraction of the signal involves logically straightforward but abstract operations, making the patterns essentially irreducible to natural origin."

[3] Wikipedia: "Icarus (journal)," http://en.wikipedia.org/wiki/Icarus_(journal). Accessed June 11, 2016

"Icarus is a scientific journal dedicated to the field of planetary science. Its longtime owner and publisher was Academic Press, which was then purchased by Elsevier. It is published under the auspices of the American Astronomical Society's Division for Planetary Sciences (DPS). The journal contains articles discussing the results of new research on astronomy, geology, meteorology, physics, chemistry, biology, and other scientific aspects of the Solar System or extrasolar systems."

#31 Second Law of Thermodynamics

[1]] Asimov, Isaac, "In the Game of Energy and Thermodynamics You Can't Even Break Even," Smithsonian Institute Journal, June 1970, p. 6

[2] Christian Answers, "Second Law of Thermodynamics—Does this basic law of nature prevent Evolution? Evolution versus a basic law of nature." http://www.christiananswers.net/q-eden/edn-thermodynamics.html. Accessed June 11, 2016.

[3] Wallace, T., True.Origin Archive, "Five Major Evolutionist Misconceptions about Evolution," 2016, https://www.trueorigin.org/isakrbtl.php. Accessed June 11, 2016.

[4] Sewell, Granville, "A second look at the second law," Mathematics Department, University of Texas, El Paso, Elsevier, Applied Mathematics Letters, January, 2011, http://www.math.utep.edu/Faculty/sewell/AML_3497.pdf. Accessed June 11, 2016.

#32 Irreducible Complexity

[1] Behe, Michael, Darwin's Black Box: The Biochemical Challenge to Evolution. Free Press; 2nd edition (March 13, 2006).

[2] Charles Darwin, On the Origin of Species, chapter 6 (p. 189), 1859, Murray: London

[3] Denton, Michael, Evolution: A Theory in Crisis. Adler & Adler; 3rd edition (April 15, 1986)

[4] Behe, Michael, Darwin's Black Box: The Biochemical Challenge to Evolution. Free Press; 2nd edition (March 13, 2006).

[5] Animated video of growth of bacterial flagellum. "Bacterial Flagellum - Evolution's Nightmare & Demise," https://www.youtube.com/watch?v=0N09BIEzDlI. Accessed June 12, 2016.

[6] Staff, Discovery Institute, About Irreducible Complexity: Responding to Darwinists Claiming to Have Explained Away the Challenge of Irreducible Complexity, September 2, 2010, http://www.discovery.org/a/3408, Accessed June 11, 2016.

Further Reference: Intelligent Design and Evolution Awareness Center, "Irreducible Complexity: The Challenge to the Darwinian Evolutionary Explanations of many Biochemical Structures," http://www.ideacenter.org/stuff/contentmgr/files/9147e04fc268407ac48a8915b73ef8e2/miscdocs/irreduciblecomplexity.pdf. Accessed June 11, 2016.

#34 The Giraffe

[1] The Big Zoo website, "Reticulated Giraffe " (November, 2004) http://www.thebigzoo.com/Animals/Reticulated_Giraffe.asp. Accessed June 11, 2016.

[2] Buzzle.Com, "Giraffe Facts," http://www.buzzle.com/articles/giraffe-facts.html, Accessed June 11, 2016.

[3] Wikipedia, "Giraffe," https://en.wikipedia.org/wiki/Giraffe, Accessed June 11, 2016.

"However, scientists disagree about just how much time giraffes spend feeding at levels beyond the reach of other browsers, and a 2010 study found that adult giraffes with longer necks actually suffered higher mortality rates under drought conditions than their shorter-necked counterparts. This study suggests that maintaining a longer neck requires more nutrients, which puts longer-necked giraffes at risk during a food shortage."

[5] Smerup, Morten, Funder, Jonas, et. al, "How can a normal-sized heart generate high blood pressure in the Giraffe?". The Official Journal of the Federation of American Societies for Experimental Biology (FASEB Journal), http://www.fasebj.org/content/25/1_Supplement/1045.8.short. Accessed June 11, 2016.

[6] Buzzle.Com, "Giraffe Facts," http://www.buzzle.com/articles/giraffe-facts.html, Accessed June 11, 2016.

They have the highest recorded blood pressure. 280/180mm Hg on average.

[7] Brøndum E., Hasenkam J.M., et. al., "Jugular venous pooling during lowering of the head affects blood pressure of the anesthetized giraffe." US. National Library of Medicine, National Institutes of Health, Oct. 2009, http://www.ncbi.nlm.nih.gov/pubmed/19657096. Accessed June 11, 2016.

Further Reference: Giraffe Conservation Foundation, Frequently Asked Questions About Giraffe, https://giraffeconservation.org/faqs/?v=7516fd43adaa. Accessed June 11, 2016.

[8] Lord Kelvin, Sir William Thomson, "Quotations," http://zapatopi.net/kelvin/quotes/http://zapatopi.net/kelvin/quotes/. Accessed June 11, 2016.

#35 Natural Selection

[1] Gould, Stephen J., famous evolutionist, "The Return of Hopeful Monsters," Natural History, vol. 86, June/July 1977, p 28

"The essence of Darwinism lies in a single phrase: Natural selection is the creative force of evolutionary change. No one denies that selection will play a negative role in eliminating the unfit. Darwinian theories require that it create the fit as well."

[2] Pesely, Gregory Alan, "The Epistemological Status of Natural Selection," Laval Theologique et Philosophique, vol 38, Feb 1982, p 74.

> "What is most unsettling is that some evolutionary biologists have no qualms about proposing tautologies as explanations. One would immediately reject any lexicographer who tried to define a word by the same word, or a thinker who merely restated his proposition, or any other instance of gross redundancy; yet no one seems scandalized that men of science should be satisfied with a major principle which is no more than a tautology."

[3] Stephens, Jim, 101 Proofs for God, Chapter 27 The Truth About Mutation, BookBaby Publishing, 2016.

#36 The Zoo

[1] Zimmer, Carl, "How Many Species? A Study Says 8.7 Million, but It's Tricky," New York Times, Aug. 23, 2011. http://www.nytimes.com/2011/08/30/science/30species.html?_r=0. Accessed June 11, 2016

[2] Klappenbach, Laura, Animals & Wildlife Expert, About.Com, "How Many Animal Species Inhabit Our Planet? Estimating the Number of Species in Each Animal Group," http://animals.about.com/od/zoologybasics/a/howmanyspecies.htm. Accessed June 11, 2016.

[3] Thompson, Andrea, LiveScience.com, "Greatest Mysteries: How Many Species Exist on Earth?" August 3, 2007, http://www.livescience.com/4593-greatest-mysteries-species-exist-earth.html#sthash.YMzxvQTQ.dpuf. Accessed June 11, 2016

#37 Information

[1] Dawkins, Richard, The Blind Watchmaker, page. 115. W. W. Norton & Company; (August 29, 1996)

[2] Sarfati, Jonathan, Refuting Evolution. p. 121 (Green Forest, AR, Master Books, 1999). Original information from W. Gitt, "Dazzling Design in Miniature," Creation Ex Nihilo, 20(1): 6, December 1997-February 1998.

[3] Spetner, L., Not by Chance, The Judaica Press, Inc., page. 131-143.

[4]] Sarfati, Jonathan, Refuting Evolution, Green Forest, AR, Master Books, 1999. page. 123 Original information from W. Wells, "Taking Life To Bits," New Scientist, 155 (2095): 30-33, 1997.

[5] Denton, M., Evolution: A Theory in Crisis, Adler and Adler Publishers, Inc. 1986, page. 328.

#38 Practice Makes Perfect

[1] Moskowitz, Clara, "Einstein's 'Biggest Blunder' Turns Out to Be Right," SPACE.com, November 24, 2010, http://www.space.com/9593-einstein-biggest-blunder-turns.html. Accessed June 12, 2016.

> "In 1917, Albert Einstein inserted a term called the cosmological constant into his theory of general relativity to force the equations to predict a stationary universe in keeping with physicists' thinking at the time. When it became clear that the

universe wasn't actually static, but was expanding instead, Einstein abandoned the constant, calling it the "'biggest blunder" of his life."

[2] Texas A&M University, ScienceDaily.com, "Einstein's Biggest Blunder? Dark Energy May Be Consistent With Cosmological Constant," November 28, 2007, https://www.sciencedaily.com/releases/2007/11/071127142128.htm. Accessed June 12, 2016.

Then, 12 years later, Edwin Hubble discovered that the universe is not static -- it is actually expanding. So Einstein scrapped his idea of a cosmological constant and dismissed it as his biggest blunder.

[3] Siemon-Netto, Uwe, "Analysis: Atheism worldwide in decline," UPI Religious Affairs, March. 1, 2005, http://www.upi.com/Business_News/Security-Industry/2005/03/01/Analysis-Atheism-worldwide-in-decline/UPI-20691109700930/. Accessed June 12, 2016.

[4] Siemon-Netto, Uwe, "Analysis: Atheism worldwide in decline," UPI Religious Affairs, March. 1, 2005, http://www.upi.com/Business_News/Security-Industry/2005/03/01/Analysis-Atheism-worldwide-in-decline/UPI-20691109700930/. Accessed June 12, 2016.

[5] Gray, Mark M., Center for Applied Research in the Apostolate, Georgetown University, "The Reverts: Catholics who left and came back.," June 19, 2012. http://nineteensixty-four.blogspot.com/2012/06/reverts-catholics-who-left-and-came.html. Accessed June 12, 2016.

See chart of retention rates among all faiths at this website.

#40 Chirality: Chemical Handedness

[1] McCombs, Charles, "Evolution Hopes You Don't Know Chemistry: The Problem With Chirality". Impact: Vital Articles on Science/Creation, Issue 371, May 2004. Page 2, paragraph 2. http://www.icr.org/i/pdf/imp/imp-371.pdf. Accessed June 12, 2016.

[2] McCombs, Charles, "Evolution Hopes You Don't Know Chemistry: The Problem With Chirality". Impact: Vital Articles on Science/Creation, Issue 371, May 2004. Page 2, paragraph 3. http://www.icr.org/i/pdf/imp/imp-371.pdf. Accessed June 12, 2016.

[3] McCombs, Charles, "Evolution Hopes You Don't Know Chemistry: The Problem With Chirality". Impact: Vital Articles on Science/Creation, Issue 371, May 2004. Page 3, paragraph 1. http://www.icr.org/i/pdf/imp/imp-371.pdf. Accessed June 12, 2016.

[5] Le Guennec, Patrick, Chirality.Org, "Describing Chirality: Chirality in life," December, 2002, http://www.chirality.org/homepage.htm. Accessed June 12, 2016.

[6] Refer to Wells, Jonathan, Icons of Evolution, Science of Myth? Why much of what we teach about evolution is wrong, Chapter 2, Regnery Press, Washington, DC, 2000

#41 The First Living Cell

[1] Bergman, Jerry, "Why the Miller–Urey Research Argues Against Abiogenesis," Institute for Creation Research, August 1, 2004, https://answersingenesis.org/origin-of-life/why-the-miller-urey-research-argues-against-abiogenesis/. Accessed June 12, 2016.
"The eukaryote protozoa, believed in Darwin's day to be as simple as a bowl of gelatin, are actually enormously complex. A living eukaryotic cell contains many hundreds of thousands of different complex parts, including various motor proteins.

Footnotes and Comments

These parts must be assembled correctly to produce a living cell, the most complex 'machine' in the universe—far more complex than a Cray supercomputer."

[2] Harter, Richard, "An analogy for the genome," February 9, 2002, http://richardhartersworld.com/cri/2002/analogy.html. Accessed June 12, 2016.

"Imagine a small walled town. Within it there is a diversified population of people performing different tasks. There is a butcher and a baker and an undertaker, guards at the gate and a refuse collector. The people in the town are good at their tasks but they are quite stupid so anything novel is a real problem for them. Fortunately there is a library in the town, a library which contains instructions for dealing with unusual situations."

[3] Brain, Marshall, "How Evolution Works: Question 3: Where Did the First Living Cell Come From?" HowStuffWorks.com, http://science.howstuffworks.com/life/evolution/evolution11.htm. Accessed June 12, 2016.

[4] Brain, Marshall, "How Evolution Works: Question 3: Where Did the First Living Cell Come From?" HowStuffWorks.com, http://science.howstuffworks.com/life/evolution/evolution11.htm. Accessed June 12, 2016.

[5] Brain, Marshall, "How Evolution Works: Question 3: Where Did the First Living Cell Come From?" HowStuffWorks.com, http://science.howstuffworks.com/life/evolution/evolution11.htm. Accessed June 12, 2016.

[6] Brain, Marshall, "How Evolution Works: Question 3: Where Did the First Living Cell Come From?" HowStuffWorks.com, http://science.howstuffworks.com/life/evolution/evolution11.htm. Accessed June 12, 2016.

[7] Wikipedia.org, "DNA repair," https://en.wikipedia.org/wiki/DNA_repair. Accessed June 12, 2016.

"DNA repair is a collection of processes by which a cell identifies and corrects damage to the DNA molecules that encode its genome."

[8] Koning, Ross E. 1994. Biology is the Study of Life!. Plant Physiology Information Website. http://plantphys.info/organismal/lechtml/biology.shtml. Accessed June 12, 2016.

[9] Biotopics.co.uk, "The Respiration Process," http://www.biotopics.co.uk/humans/respro.html. Accessed June 12, 2016.

"one of the 7 characteristic processes shared by all living organisms."

[10] Wikibooks.Org, "Structural Biochemistry/Properties of Living Organisms," http://en.wikibooks.org/wiki/Structural_Biochemistry/Properties_of_Living_Organisms. Accessed June 12, 2016.

[11] Bergman, Jerry, "Why the Miller–Urey Research Argues Against Abiogenesis," Institute for Creation Research, August 1, 2004, https://answersingenesis.org/origin-of-life/why-the-miller-urey-research-argues-against-abiogenesis/. Accessed June 12, 2016.

[12] Biello, David, Scientific American, "Man-Made Genetic Instructions Yield Living Cells for the First Time. Scientists create the first microbe to live under the instruction of

DNA synthesized in the lab.," May, 20, 2010,
http://www.scientificamerican.com/article.cfm?id=synthetic-genome-cell. Accessed June
12, 2016.

[13] Thomas, Brian, 2010. "Have Scientists Created a Living Cell?" Acts & Facts. 39 (7):
17. http://www.icr.org/article/5485/. Accessed June 12, 2016.

[14] Thomas, Brian, May 5, 2010. "Complicated Cells Leave No Room for Evolution.,"
Institute for Creation Research. http://www.icr.org/article/5353/. Accessed June 12,
2016.

[15] Anitei, Stefan, "The Smallest Genome: What's the Minimum DNA Amount for
Life? Even just 182 genes!" Dec. 13, 2007, http://news.softpedia.com/news/The-
Smallest-Genome-What-039-s-The-Minimum-DNA-Amount-for-Life-73763.shtml.
Accessed June 12, 2016.

[16] For further research, visit www.YouTube.com. Search for "animation of cell
membrane".

Suggested examples: "A Tour of the Cell,"
http://www.youtube.com/watch?v=1Z9pqST72is. This animation shows tens of
parts in a cell.

"Unlocking the Mystery of Life (Chapter 10 of 12)" shows the working of DNA,
RNA, proteins, and ribosomes. http://www.youtube.com/watch?v=gdBJt6sdDfI.
Accessed June 12, 2016.

#44 Murphy's Law

[1] Wikipedia.Org., "Murphy's law," https://en.wikipedia.org/wiki/Murphy%27s_law.
Accessed June 12, 2016.

[2] ScienceDaily.Com., "How many species on Earth? About 8.7 million, new estimate
says.," August 24, 2011.
https://www.sciencedaily.com/releases/2011/08/110823180459.htm Accessed June 12,
2016.

[3] Stephens, Jim, 101 Proofs for God, Chapter #41 The First Living Cell, 2016.

#45 The EYE

[1] ChemistryLand.com, "Electromagnetic Spectrum," Nov. 9, 2008,
http://www.chemistryland.com/CHM107Lab/Exp7/Spectroscope/Spectroscope.html.
Accessed June 12, 2016.

[2] Wikipedia.org, "Photoreceptor Cell,"
https://en.wikipedia.org/wiki/Photoreceptor_cell. Accessed June 12, 2016.

[3] Wikipedia.org, "Color vision," https://en.wikipedia.org/wiki/Color_vision. Accessed
June 12, 2016.

[4] Catchpoole, David, "An eye for detail: Why your eyes 'jitter',"
http://creation.com/an-eye-for-detail, Accessed June 12, 2016.

[5] Tom Wagner, "Darwin Vs. the Eye," Sept. 1, 1994,
https://answersingenesis.org/charles-darwin/darwin-vs-the-eye/, Accessed June 12, 2016.

Footnotes and Comments

[6]. Wikipedia.org, "Optic nerve," https://en.wikipedia.org/wiki/Optic_nerve, Accessed June 12, 2016.

[7] Award-winning science writer Carl Zimmer explains the "creation" of the organ so complex that it baffled even Darwin. The New York Academy of Sciences Magazine. October 9, 2009.

[8] Award-winning science writer Carl Zimmer explains the "creation" of the organ so complex that it baffled even Darwin. The New York Academy of Sciences Magazine. October 9, 2009.

[9] Wikipedia.org, "Eye," https://en.wikipedia.org/wiki/Eye, Accessed June 12, 2016.

[10] Bergman, Jerry, "Did eyes evolve by Darwinian mechanisms?" Creation Ministries International, http://creation.com/did-eyes-evolve-by-darwinian-mechanisms. Accessed June 13, 2016

[11] Duke-Elder, S.S., System of Ophthalmology, Volume 1: The Eye in Evolution. p. 237.

#46 Ants

[1] Wikipedia.org, "Ant". https://en.wikipedia.org/wiki/Ant. Accessed June 13, 2016

[2] Gross, M. 2012. How ants find their way. Current Biology. 22 (16): R618.

[3] Prabhakar, B., K. N. Dektar, and D. M. Gordon. 2012. The Regulation of Ant Colony Foraging Activity without Spatial Information. PLoS Computational Biology. 8 (8): e1002670.

[4] Avolio, Carla, "Chris Reid shows that Argentine ants can solve Towers of Hanoi," The University of Sydney, School of Biological Sciences, December 9, 2010, http://sydney.edu.au/news/sobs/1699.html?newsstoryid=6164. Accessed June 13, 2016

> "The result was exactly as predicted: the ants quickly established pheromone trails along the shortest path. But then we blocked the shortest paths, thus forcing the ants to find an alternative solution. As explained above, conventional wisdom dictates that the ants would not be able to adapt and would continue following their original trail that now leads nowhere."

> "Contrary to predictions, Argentine ants rapidly found the alternative shortest path, showing that they have the ability to adapt to sudden changes in their environment. But the speed with which they adapt depends on whether or not they had prior experience with the maze: colonies that had explored the maze hours before food was introduced, found the alternative solution quicker than colonies without such pre-exposure. This is a puzzling result, as the time between exploring the maze and the need to find an alternative solution when the original path is blocked, was at least 1 hour."

[5] Reid, C. R., D. J. T. Sumpter and M. Beekman. 2011. Optimisation in a natural system: Argentine ants solve the Towers of Hanoi. Journal of Experimental Biology. 214 (1): 50-58.

[6] Sherwin, Frank and Thomas, Brian, "Insect Arithmetic--Pure Genius!" Institute for Creation Research, http://www.icr.org/article/7536/. Accessed June 13, 2016

[7] Encyclopædia Britannica, Kids, "Ant Colony," http://kids.britannica.com/comptons/art-144467/An-ant-colony-has-several-entrances-leading-to-a-variety. Accessed June 13, 2016

[8] Wikipedia.org, "Ant". https://en.wikipedia.org/wiki/Ant. Accessed June 13, 2016

[9] Wikipedia.org, "Ant". https://en.wikipedia.org/wiki/Ant. Accessed June 13, 2016

[10] Wikipedia.org, "Ant". https://en.wikipedia.org/wiki/Ant. Accessed June 13, 2016

[11] Poppick, Laura, "Bizarre fire ants lock together and form big rafts to survive floods," NBCNEWS, Nov. 26, 2013, http://www.nbcnews.com/science/bizarre-fire-ants-lock-together-form-big-rafts-survive-floods-2D11660482. Accessed June 13, 2016

#47 Gratitude

[1] HeartMath Institute, The Mysteries of the Heart, animated video. . http://www.heartmath.org/templates/ihm/articles/infographic/2013/mysteries-of-the-heart/index.php. Accessed June 13, 2016.

[2] Fosar, Grazyna, and Bludorf, Franz, Wakeup-World.com, "Scientists Prove DNA Can Be Reprogrammed by Words and Frequencies," http://wakeup-world.com/2011/07/12/scientist-prove-dna-can-be-reprogrammed-by-words-frequencies/. Accessed June 14, 2016.

[3] Petre, Jonathan, "'Believers are happier than atheists'," The Telegraph, March 18, 2008, http://www.telegraph.co.uk/news/uknews/1581994/Believers-are-happier-than-atheists.html. Accessed June 13, 2016

#48 The Nitrogen Cycle

[1] Nitrogen Cycle. Learning diagrams from PBS Learning http://www.pbslearningmedia.org/asset/lsps07_int_nitrogen/?utm_source=teachersdomain_redirect/asset/lsps07_int_nitrogen/utm_medium=teachersdomain/asset/lsps07_int_nitrogen/utm_campaign=td_redirects. Accessed June 14, 2016.

#49 The Moon

[1] DeYoung, Donald B., "The Moon: A Faithful Witness in the Sky," http://www.icr.org/article/moon-faithful-witness-sky. Accessed June 14, 2016.

[2] Faulkner, Danny R., "A Perfect Partner, Special Feature: There's No Place Like Home," January 1, 2014. https://answersingenesis.org/astronomy/moon/a-perfect-partner/. Accessed June 14, 2016.

[3] Thomas, Brian, "Water in Rocks May Support Moon's Bible Origins," http://www.icr.org/article/7712/. Accessed June 14, 2016.

[4] DeYoung, Donald B., "The Moon: A Faithful Witness in the Sky," http://www.icr.org/article/moon-faithful-witness-sky. Accessed June 14, 2016.

[5] Institute for Creation Research. "Earth Was Created in a Wonderful Location: Our Sun Is Perfectly Located Within Our Galaxy." http://www.icr.org/earths-location/. Accessed June 14, 2016.

[6] DeYoung, Donald B., "The Moon: A Faithful Witness in the Sky," http://www.icr.org/article/moon-faithful-witness-sky. Accessed June 14, 2016.

Footnotes and Comments

[7] Hughes, David W., "The Open Question in Selenology," Nature, Vol. 327, 28 May 1987, p. 291.

"In astronomical terms, therefore, the Moon must be classed as a well-known object, but astronomers still have to admit shamefacedly that they have little idea as to where it came from. This is particularly embarrassing, because the solution of the mystery was billed as one of the main goals of the US lunar exploration program."

[8] Wikipedia, "Moon Rock," During the six Apollo surface excursions, 2,415 samples weighing 382 kg (842 lb) were collected, the majority by Apollo 15, 16, and 17. http://en.wikipedia.org/wiki/Moon_rock. Accessed June 14, 2016.

[9] Center for Scientific Creation, "48. The Origin of the Moon". http://www.creationscience.com/onlinebook/AstroPhysicalSciences9.html. Accessed June 14, 2016.

"Evolutionary theories for the origin of the Moon are highly speculative and completely inadequate.a The Moon could not have spun off Earth, because its orbital plane is too highly inclined. The Moon's nearly circular orbit shows that it was never torn from nor captured by Earth.b If the Moon formed from particles orbiting Earth, other particles should be easily visible inside the Moon's orbit; none are."

"The once popular theory that the Moon formed from debris splashed from Earth by a Mars-size impactor is now largely rejected, because the rocks that astronauts brought back from the moon are too similar to those of Earth. The impactor's material should have been quite different. (In Part II of this book, you will see why the loose rocks the astronauts brought back from the moon are so similar to Earth's rocks. Those rocks came from Earth.) Had a Mars-size impact occurred, many small moons should have formed.e Also, the impactor's glancing blow would have either be too slight to form our large Moon, or so violent that Earth would end up spinning too fast.f Besides, part of Earth's surface and mantle would have melted, but none of the indicators of that melting have been found.g Small particles splashed from Earth would have completely melted, allowing any water inside them to escape into the vacuum of space. However, Apollo astronauts found on the Moon tiny glass beads that had erupted as molten material from inside the Moon but had dissolved water inside! The total amount of water that was once inside the Moon probably equaled that in the Caribbean Sea.h Finally, a Mar-size impactor would heat up and evaporate much, if not all, of Earth's surface water. Earth would likely have experienced a runaway greenhouse effect, making earth permanently uninhabitable."

[10] Evolution News & Views, "How the Moon Supports the Privileged Planet Hypothesis," December 5, 2013, http://www.evolutionnews.org/2013/12/our_moon_still079861.html. Accessed June 14, 2016.

[11] DeYoung, Donald B., "The Moon: A Faithful Witness in the Sky," http://www.icr.org/article/moon-faithful-witness-sky. Accessed June 14, 2016.

[12] Lissauer, Jack J., "It's Not Easy to Make the Moon," Nature, Vol. 389, 25 September 1997, pp. 327–328.

#50 Scientists Are Wrong A Lot of the Time

[1] Newman, Judith, Discover Magazine, October 1, 2000, "20 of the Greatest Blunders in Science in the Last 20 Years, What were they thinking?" http://discovermagazine.com/2000/oct/featblunders. Accessed June 15, 2016.

[2] Shaw, Steven, Askmen.com, "Top 10: False Scientific Theories," http://www.askmen.com/top_10/entertainment/top-10-disproven-theories.html. Accessed June 15, 2016.

[3] Ioannidis, John P. A., PLOS Medicine, "Why Most Published Research Findings Are False," August 30, 2005. http://journals.plos.org/plosmedicine/article?id=10.1371/journal.pmed.0020124. Accessed June 15, 2016.

"Simulations show that for most study designs and settings, it is more likely for a research claim to be false than true. Moreover, for many current scientific fields, claimed research findings may often be simply accurate measures of the prevailing bias."

[4] Ethan, ScienceBlogs, "Most Scientific Theories Are Wrong," May 31, 2013, http://scienceblogs.com/startswithabang/2013/05/31/most-scientific-theories-are-wrong/. Accessed June 15, 2016.

"Scientific theories are only meant to have a certain range of validity! We know that the Big Bang doesn't explain what came prior to the Big Bang; we know that evolution doesn't explain the origin of life; we know that Airy's theory of isostatic compensation doesn't explain the motion of the Earth's crust over geologic timescales; we know that General Relativity doesn't explain the existence of antimatter."

[5] Simanek, Donald, "It'll Never Work," http://www.lhup.edu/~dsimanek/neverwrk.htm. Accessed June 15, 2016.

[6] WikiQuote, "Incorrect Predictions," https://en.wikiquote.org/wiki/Incorrect_predictions. Accessed June 15, 2016.

[7] English Teachers Network, "Predictions-Quotes," http://www.etni.org.il/quotes/predictions.htm. Accessed June 15, 2016.

"I think there is a world market for maybe five computers." -- Thomas Watson (1874-1956), Chairman of IBM, 1943

"Who the hell wants to hear actors talk?" -- H. M. Warner (1881-1958), founder of Warner Brothers, in 1927

"Heavier-than-air flying machines are impossible." -- Lord Kelvin, President, Royal Society, 1895

"Everything that can be invented has been invented." -- Charles H. Duell, Commissioner, U.S. Office of Patents, 1899

[8] Discover Magazine, September 1, 2008, "Einstein's 23 Biggest Mistakes: A new book explores the mistakes of the legendary genius." http://discovermagazine.com/2008/sep/01-einsteins-23-biggest-mistakes#.UvGzZfldXy0. Accessed June 15, 2016.

[9] Schilling, David Russell, "Knowledge Doubling Every 12 Months, Soon to be Every 12 Hours," Industry Tap into News, April 19, 2013. http://www.industrytap.com/knowledge-doubling-every-12-months-soon-to-be-every-12-hours/3950. Accessed June 15, 2016.

Footnotes and Comments

[10] Wikipedia.org, "Thomas S. Kuhn," http://en.wikipedia.org/wiki/Thomas_Kuhn. Accessed June 15, 2016.

> "Kuhn made several notable claims concerning the progress of scientific knowledge: that scientific fields undergo periodic "paradigm shifts" rather than solely progressing in a linear and continuous way, and that these paradigm shifts open up new approaches to understanding what scientists would never have considered valid before; and that the notion of scientific truth, at any given moment, cannot be established solely by objective criteria but is defined by a consensus of a scientific community. Competing paradigms are frequently incommensurable; that is, they are competing and irreconcilable accounts of reality. ... all objective conclusions are ultimately founded upon the subjective conditioning/worldview of its researchers and participants."

[11] Stanford Encyclopedia of Philosophy, "Thomas Kuhn," article revised Aug. 11, 2011. http://plato.stanford.edu/entries/thomas-kuhn/. Accessed June 15, 2016.

[12] Wells, Jonathan, Icons of Evolution: Science or Myth? Why much of what we teach about evolution is wrong. Introduction, Section: What is Evolution?" Regnery Publishing, 2000. http://www.iconsofevolution.com/intro/. Accessed June 15, 2016.

[13] Wells, Jonathan, Icons of Evolution: Science or Myth? Why much of what we teach about evolution is wrong. Introduction, Section: Science of Myth?" Regnery Publishing, 2000. http://www.iconsofevolution.com/intro/. Accessed June 15, 2016.

[14] Ben Stein, movie: Expelled: No Intelligence Allowed, http://topdocumentaryfilms.com/expelled-no-intelligence-allowed/. Accessed June 15, 2016.

[15] The Trivedi Foundation website: http://www.trivedifoundation.org/. Accessed June 15, 2016.

#51 Pollination

[1] Wikipedia.org, "Pollination": http://en.wikipedia.org/wiki/Pollination. Accessed June 15, 2016.

> "At least 100,000 species of animal, and possibly as many as 200,000, act as pollinators of the estimated 250,000 species of flowering plants in the world.[6] The majority of these pollinators are insects, but about 1,500 species of birds and mammals have been reported to visit flowers and may transfer pollen between them."

[2] Shroud University, "The Shroud Report." http://shroud2000.com/ArticlesPapers/Article-PollenEvidence.html. Accessed June 15, 2016.

[3] Fischer, J. Michael, adapted from the original article by John C. Iannone, "The Shroud of Turin - Evidence it is authentic.," "The Shroud as an ancient textile." http://www.newgeology.us/presentation24.html. Accessed June 15, 2016.

[4] TutorVista.com, "Plant Fertilization," http://biology.tutorvista.com/plant-kingdom/plant-fertilization.html. Accessed June 15, 2016.

[5] Choi, Charles Q., "Ancient Roots: Flowers May Have Existed When First Dinosaur Was Born," LiveScience, October 1, 2013. http://www.livescience.com/40088-flowers-existed-with-dinosaurs.html. Accessed June 15, 2016.

[6] Diffen.com, Botany section: "Cross Pollination vs. Self Pollination," http://www.diffen.com/difference/Cross_Pollination_vs_Self_Pollination. Accessed June 15, 2016.

#52 Garbage In, Garbage Out (GIGO)

[1] Wikipedia.org., "Garbage in, garbage out," https://en.wikipedia.org/wiki/Garbage_in,_garbage_out. Accessed June 15, 2016.

#54 Trophic Cascades and Wolves

[1] Sustainable Human, "How Wolves Change Rivers," February 17, 2014. http://sustainablehuman.com/how-wolves-change-rivers/. Accessed June 15, 2016.

[2] "Mission: Wolf, Education vs. Extinction. A Wolf's Role in the Ecosystem - The Trophic Cascade." http://www.missionwolf.org/page/trophic-cascade/. Accessed June 15, 2016.

[3] Smith, Douglas W., Peterson, Rolf O., and Houston, Douglas Bl, "Yellowstone after Wolves," Oxford Journals, BioScience, Volume 53, Issue 5, Pp. 330-340. http://bioscience.oxfordjournals.org/content/53/4/330.full. Accessed June 15, 2016. mals.

[4] Wikipedia.Org., "Trophic Cascade".http://en.wikipedia.org/wiki/Trophic_cascade. Accessed June 15, 2016.

Examples of this phenomenon include:
A 2-3 fold increase in deciduous woody vegetation cover, mostly of willow, in the Soda Butte Creek area between 1995 and 1999. Heights of the tallest willows in the Gallatin River valley increasing from 75 cm to 200 cm between 1998 and 2002. Heights of the tallest willows in the Blacktail Creek area increased from less than 50 cm to more than 250 cm between 1997 and 2003. Additionally, canopy cover over streams increased significantly, from only 5% to a range of 14-73%. In the northern range, tall deciduous woody vegetation cover increased by 170% between 1991 and 2006.

Importantly, the number of beaver (Castor canadensis) colonies in the Park has increased from one in 1996 to twelve in 2009. The recovery is likely due to the increase in willow availability, as they have been feeding almost exclusively on it. As keystone species, the resurgence of beaver is a critical event for the region. The presence of beavers has been shown to positively impact streambank erosion, sediment retention, water tables, nutrient cycling, and both the diversity and abundance of plant and animal life among riparian communities.

[5] Wikipedia.Org., "Trophic Cascade".http://en.wikipedia.org/wiki/Trophic_cascade. Accessed June 15, 2016.

Another example of the cascade effect caused by the loss of a top predator has to do with sea otters.

#56 Snowflakes

[1] Wikipedia.Org, "Snowflake," https://en.wikipedia.org/wiki/Snowflake. Accessed June 15, 2016.

[2] Wikipedia.Org, "Snowflake," https://en.wikipedia.org/wiki/Snowflake. Accessed June 15, 2016.

Footnotes and Comments

[3] Kljatove, Alexey (ChaoticMind75), flickr.com, Photostream, https://www.flickr.com/photos/chaoticmind75/page1. Accessed June 15, 2016.

[4] Libbrecht, Kenneth G., Snow Crystals.com, http://snowcrystals.com/. Accessed June 15, 2016.

[5] Post By Abraham. "Microscopic timelapse photography reveals the formation of snowflakes," http://twentytwowords.com/microscopic-timelapse-photography-reveals-the-formation-of-snowflakes/. Accessed June 15, 2016.

[6] Wikipedia.Org, "Snowflake," https://en.wikipedia.org/wiki/Snowflake. Accessed June 15, 2016.

[7] Website of Dr. Masaru Emoto. http://www.masaru-emoto.net/english/water-crystal.html. Accessed June 15, 2016.

[8] Website of movie: What The Bleep Do We Know? http://www.whatthebleep.com/. Accessed June 15, 2016.

#57 17-Year Cicadas

[1] Wikipedia.Org., "Cicada" https://en.wikipedia.org/wiki/Cicada. Accessed June 15, 2016.

[2] Wikipedia.Org., "Cicada" https://en.wikipedia.org/wiki/Cicada. Accessed June 15, 2016.

#58 The Cambrian Explosion

[1] Time Magazine. "Evolution's Big Bang," December 4, 1995 issue. See online: http://content.time.com/time/covers/0,16641,19951204,00.html. Accessed June 16, 2016.

[2] Jones, Steve, University College, London, Almost Like A Whale: The Origin Of Species Updated, p. 252, 1999

[3] Bohlin, Ray, "Another Big Bang?" May 27, 1996. https://www.probe.org/evolutions-big-bang/. Accessed June 16, 2016.

#60 Water

[1] U. S. Geological Survey, "How much water is there on, in, and above the Earth?" http://water.usgs.gov/edu/earthhowmuch.html. Accessed June 16, 2016.

[2] National Oceanic and Atmospheric Administration, U. S. Dept. of Commerce. "Are there oceans on other planets?" http://oceanservice.noaa.gov/facts/et-oceans.html. Accessed June 16, 2016.

   "Earth is the only known planet to have bodies of liquid water on its surface."

[3] Hall, Jack, "The Most Important Organism?" Ecology, September 12, 2011. http://www.ecology.com/2011/09/12/important-organism/. Accessed June 16, 2016.

[4] Laing, Robert L., "Section 14. Water: Twenty Three Unique Properties of Water." 2008, 20013. http://www.intelligentdesigntheory.info/unique_properties_of_water.htm. Accessed June 16, 2016.

[5] Water On The Web, "Student Reading - The Unique Properties of Water." (The ensuing discussion is adapted from Campbell, N.A. 1996. Biology (4th edition))

http://www.waterontheweb.org/curricula/bs/student/water/unique.html. Accessed June 16, 2016.

[6] Water On The Web, "Student Reading - The Unique Properties of Water." (The ensuing discussion is adapted from Campbell, N.A. 1996. Biology (4th edition)) http://www.waterontheweb.org/curricula/bs/student/water/unique.html. Accessed June 16, 2016.

[7] U. S. Geological Survey. Water Properties and Measurements: Section: The Water Around Us, http://ga.water.usgs.gov/edu/waterproperties.html. Accessed June 16, 2016.

[8] Laing, Robert L., "Section 14. Water: Twenty Three Unique Properties of Water." 2008, 20013. http://www.intelligentdesigntheory.info/unique_properties_of_water.htm. Accessed June 16, 2016.

[9] U. S. Geological Survey. Water Properties and Measurements: Section: The Water Around Us, http://ga.water.usgs.gov/edu/waterproperties.html. Accessed June 16, 2016.

[10] Water On The Web, "Student Reading - The Unique Properties of Water." (The ensuing discussion is adapted from Campbell, N.A. 1996. Biology (4th edition)) http://www.waterontheweb.org/curricula/bs/student/water/unique.html. Accessed June 16, 2016.

[11] Laing, Robert L., "Section 14. Water: Twenty Three Unique Properties of Water." 2008, 20013. http://www.intelligentdesigntheory.info/unique_properties_of_water.htm. Accessed June 16, 2016.

#61 Muscles

[1] Ludwig-Maximilians-Universität München, "Evolution of muscles: Fit as a sponge," June 28, 2012, http://www.en.uni-muenchen.de/news/newsarchiv/2012/2012_woerheide.html. Accessed June 17, 2016.

[2] University of Vienna, ScienceDaily.Com, "Searching for the origin of muscles," June 28, 2012. http://www.sciencedaily.com/releases/2012/06/120628145626.htm. Accessed June 17, 2016.

[3] Wikipedia.Org, "Muscular evolution in humans," http://en.wikipedia.org/wiki/Muscular_evolution_in_humans. Accessed June 17, 2016.

[4] Freudenrich, Craig, "How Muscles Work," HowStuffWorks.Com, http://health.howstuffworks.com/human-body/systems/musculoskeletal/muscle.htm. Accessed June 17, 2016.

[5] Wikipedia.Org, "List of muscles of the human body," http://en.wikipedia.org/wiki/List_of_muscles_of_the_human_body. Accessed June 17, 2016.

[6 Wikipedia.Org, "List of muscles of the human body," http://en.wikipedia.org/wiki/List_of_muscles_of_the_human_body. Accessed June 17, 2016.

#62 Common Sense

[1] Wikipedia.Org, "Common Sense".http://en.wikipedia.org/wiki/Common_sense. Accessed June 17, 2016.

Footnotes and Comments

[2] Wikipedia.Org, "Big Bang nucleosynthesis," http://en.wikipedia.org/wiki/Big_Bang_nucleosynthesis. Accessed June 17, 2016.

[3] White, Martin, Professor of Physics and Astronomy, UC Berkeley, "Big Bang nucleosynthesis," http://astro.berkeley.edu/~mwhite/darkmatter/bbn.html. Accessed June 17, 2016.

[4] Wikipedia.Org, "Spontaneous Generation," http://en.wikipedia.org/wiki/Spontaneous_generation. Accessed June 17, 2016.

"Disproof of the traditional ideas of spontaneous generation is no longer controversial among professional biologists."

[5] Encyclopaedia Britannica, "Spontaneous generation, Biological theory ," http://www.britannica.com/EBchecked/topic/560859/spontaneous-generation. Accessed June 17, 2016.

"By the 18th century it had become obvious that higher organisms could not be produced by nonliving material. The origin of microorganisms such as bacteria, however, was not fully determined until Louis Pasteur proved in the 19th century that microorganisms reproduce."

#63 Skin

[1] Wikipedia.Org, "Human Skin," http://en.wikipedia.org/wiki/Human_skin. Accessed June 18, 2016.

[2] Menton, David, "The Integumentary System (Skin)," Body of Evidence DVD Series. https://answersingenesis.org/store/product/body-evidence-3-integumentary-system-skin/?sku=30-9-335. Accessed June 18, 2016.

[3] Wikipedia.Org, "Sebaceous Glands," http://en.wikipedia.org/wiki/Sebaceous_glands. Accessed June 18, 2016.

[4] Wikipedia.Org, "Tactile Corpuscle," http://en.wikipedia.org/wiki/Tactile_corpuscle. Accessed June 18, 2016.

[5] Wikipedia.Org, "Nociception," http://en.wikipedia.org/wiki/Pain_receptors. Accessed June 18, 2016.

#64 Missing Links

[1] List of Transitional Fossils, Wikipedia, http://en.wikipedia.org/wiki/List_of_transitional_fossils. Accessed June 18, 2016.

[2] Sherwin, Frank, "Paleontology's Pelvic Puzzle," http://www.icr.org/article/7399/. Accessed June 18, 2016.

[3] Pelvic Anatomy, "Upright Posture and Health," http://www.upright-health.com/pelvic-anatomy.html. Accessed June 18, 2016.

[4] World Net Daily, "Anthropologist Resigns in 'Dating Disaster', Panel says professor of human origins made up data, plagiarized works.," Published: 02/19/2005, http://www.wnd.com/2005/02/29004/. Accessed June 18, 2016.

[5] Wikipedia.Org., "Piltdown Man," https://en.wikipedia.org/wiki/Piltdown_Man. Accessed June 18, 2016.

[6] Creation-Evolution Headlines, "Good-bye Heidelberg Man: You Never Existed," http://crev.info/2014/07/heidelberg-man-never-existed/. Posted July 11, 2014. Accessed June 18, 2016.

[7] Unesco, "The Peking Man World Heritage Site at Zhoukoudian," http://www.unesco.org/ext/field/beijing/whc/pkm-site.htm. Accessed June 18, 2016.

#65 Mitochondrial Eve, Y-Chromosome Adam

[1] Wikipedia.com. "Mitochondrion," http://en.wikipedia.org/wiki/Mitochondrion. Accessed June 18, 2016.

[2] Clark, Josh, "Are we all descended from a common female ancestor?" http://science.howstuffworks.com/life/evolution/female-ancestor.htm. Accessed June 18, 2016.

[3] Wikipedia.Com, "Y-Chromosome," http://en.wikipedia.org/wiki/Y_chromosome. Accessed June 18, 2016.

[4] Wikipedia.Com, "Y-Chromosome Adam," http://en.wikipedia.org/wiki/Y-chromosome_Adam. Accessed June 18, 2016.

[5] LiveScience Staff, "When Humans and Chimps Split," Dec. 19, 2005, http://www.livescience.com/3996-humans-chimps-split.html. Accessed June 18, 2016.

#68 Symmetry

[1] Dictionary.Com, "Symmetry," http://www.dictionary.com/browse/symmetry. Accessed June 18, 2016.

[2] Thesaurus.Com. Antonyms for "random," http://www.thesaurus.com/browse/random. Accessed June 18, 2016.

#69 The Archerfish

[1] Passary, Sumit, "No crosshair, no laser but archerfish always hits bull's eye. Guess why?" Tech Times, September 6, 2014. http://www.techtimes.com/articles/15027/20140906/no-crosshair-no-laser-but-archerfish-always-hits-the-bulls-eye-heres-how.htm. Accessed June 18, 2016.

[2] Gerullis, Peggy and Schuster, Stefan, "Archerfish Actively Control the Hydrodynamics of Their Jets," Volume 24, Issue 18, p2156–2160, 22 September 2014, http://www.cell.com/current-biology/abstract/S0960-9822(14)00922-1. Accessed June 18, 2016.

[3] Weird Nature – BBC, "Archer Fish Water Pistol," (3min 27sec), https://www.youtube.com/watch?v=S4G_MeUUZII. Accessed June 18, 2016.

NatGeoWild, "World's Deadliest - Fish 'Shoots' Prey with Water," (1 min 52 sec), https://www.youtube.com/watch?v=BcLLB5vijfk. Accessed June 18, 2016.

Wildvisuals. Our Wild World, "Archer Fish - Amazing Fish Shoots Water Bullets at Insects," (1 min 30 sec), https://www.youtube.com/watch?v=GhMi9Hw_wZ0. Accessed June 18, 2016.

[4] Wikipedia.Org., "Refraction," http://en.wikipedia.org/wiki/Refraction. Accessed June 18, 2016.

Footnotes and Comments

[5] O'Leary, Mary Beth, "Archerfish target shoot with 'skillfully thrown' water," EurekaAlert, The Global Source for Science News, September 4, 2014, http://www.eurekalert.org/pub_releases/2014-09/cp-ats082814.php. Accessed June 18, 2016.

#70 Healing

[1] Gabriel, Allen and Molnar, Joseph, "Wound Healing and Growth Factors," Medscape, October 5, 2015. http://emedicine.medscape.com/article/1298196-overview. Accessed June 18, 2016.

[2] Oswald, Rachel, "How Your Skin Works: How Skin Heals," HowStuffWorks: Health, http://health.howstuffworks.com/skin-care/information/anatomy/skin4.htm. Accessed June 18, 2016.

[3] Go Ask Alice, Columbia University, "How do wounds, cuts, scrapes, lacerations heal?" http://goaskalice.columbia.edu/how-do-wounds-cuts-scrapes-lacerations-heal. Accessed June 18, 2016.

[4] Wikipedia.Org, "Platelets" Section on Dynamics. http://en.wikipedia.org/wiki/Platelet. Accessed June 18, 2016.

[5] Wikipedia.Org. "Wound Healing". http://en.wikipedia.org/wiki/Wound_healing. Accessed June 18, 2016.

[6] Gabriel, Allen and Molnar, Joseph, "Wound Healing and Growth Factors," Medscape, October 5, 2015. http://emedicine.medscape.com/article/1298196-overview. Accessed June 18, 2016.

#71 Fruits

[1] Very, Christine, "Top 20 Fruits You Probably Don't Know," July 8, 2011, http://listverse.com/2011/07/08/top-20-fruits-you-probably-dont-know/. Accessed June 18, 2016.

[2] Very, Christine, "20 More Fruits You Probably Don't Know," July 23, 2011, http://listverse.com/2011/07/08/top-20-fruits-you-probably-dont-know/. Accessed June 18, 2016.

[3] Reference.Com, "How many types of fruits are there in the world," https://www.reference.com/food/many-types-fruits-world-ef78fe775fd75a9b. Accessed June 18, 2016.

[4] Stark Bros., "How Many Years Until Your Tree Bears Fruit?" http://www.starkbros.com/blog/how-many-years/. Accessed June 18, 2016.

[5] Reference.Com, "How many types of fruits are there in the world," https://www.reference.com/food/many-types-fruits-world-ef78fe775fd75a9b. Accessed June 18, 2016.

[6] Food Matters, "25 Powerful Reasons to Eat Bananas," August 14, 2012, http://foodmatters.tv/articles-1/25-powerful-reasons-to-eat-bananas. Accessed June 18, 2016.

[7] Szalay, Jessie, Live Science Contributor, "Bananas: Health Benefits, Risks & Nutrition Facts," September 29, 2014. http://www.livescience.com/45005-banana-nutrition-facts.html. Accessed June 18, 2016.

[8] Hagy, Chad, "14 Banana Health Benefits You Might Not Know About: A Banana a Day Might Keep the Doctor Away," Lifescript, December 21, 2015, http://www.lifescript.com/food/articles/0/14_banana_health_benefits_you_might_not_kn ow_about.aspx. Accessed June 18, 2016.

[9] Kayser, Matthew, "5 Health Benefits of Apples," Lifescript, May 23, 2007, http://www.lifescript.com/food/articles/0/5_health_benefits_of_apples.aspx. Accessed June 18, 2016.

[10] Best Health Magazine, "15 Health Benefits of Eating Apples," http://www.besthealthmag.ca/eat-well/nutrition/15-health-benefits-of-eating-apples. Accessed June 18, 2016.

[11] Alexander, Rose, "8 Reasons To Eat Pineapple, Tap Into The Health Benefits of This Tropical Fruit," LifeScript, August 10, 2015, http://www.lifescript.com/food/articles/0/10_reasons_to_eat_pineapple.aspx. Accessed June 19, 2016.

[12] Herrington, Diana, "13 Health Benefits of Oranges," Green Living, http://www.care2.com/greenliving/13-health-benefits-of-oranges.html. Accessed June 19, 2016.

#72 The Superb Lyrebird

[1] Davies, Gareth Huw, "Bird Songs," PBS, http://www.pbs.org/lifeofbirds/songs/. Accessed June 19, 2016.

"The musical detail would have impressed the great composers. The nightingale, for example, holds up to 300 different love songs in his repertoire. The canary may take 30 mini-breaths a second to replenish its air supply. The cowbird uses 40 different notes, some so high we can't hear them. The chaffinch may sing his song half a million times in a season."

"Indeed, British musician David Hindley slowed bird song down and discovered parallels between the skylark's blizzard of notes and Beethoven's Fifth Symphony; between the woodlark's mind-numbingly complex song and J.S. Bach's 48 Preludes and Fugues. It changes its tune according to the rules of classical sonata form."

"In most species, a male bird owning a territory is essential for attracting a female and breeding successfully. Males claim a territory by singing in it. They generally use shorter, simpler songs for territorial defense. They are addressing their songs to rival males. These territorial songs carry over long distances and convey detailed information about the location and identity of the singer. Gaps in the song enable the singer to listen for replies, and determine where their rival is and how far off."

"Birds can distinguish neighbors from strangers by individual differences in their songs. Males use this information to concentrate their defense efforts. They will not react aggressively against a neighbor as long as he stays on his own territory. But a singing stranger could mean a threat to the territory; a strong response is required to see this potential invader off."

"When they are trying to attract females onto their territory, males become operatic. They sing longer and more complex songs."

Footnotes and Comments

[2] Davies, Gareth Huw, "Bird Songs," PBS, http://www.pbs.org/lifeofbirds/songs/. Accessed June 19, 2016.

[3] Wikipedia.Org., "Lyrebird, Vocalizations and mimicry," http://en.wikipedia.org/wiki/Lyrebird. Accessed June 19, 2016.

[4] Adelaide Zoo, "Superb Lyrebird imitating construction work," https://www.youtube.com/watch?v=WeQjkQpeJwY#t. Accessed June 19, 2016.

Attenborough, David, "Amazing! Bird sounds from the lyre bird" - BBC wildlife, https://www.youtube.com/watch?v=VjE0Kdfos4Y#t. Accessed June 19, 2016.

National Geographic, "World's Weirdest - Bird Mimics Chainsaw, Car Alarm and More," https://www.youtube.com/watch?v=XjAcyTXRunY. Accessed June 19, 2016.

Amesreiter, Bernd, "Begging for Love, Lyrebird mimics car alarm, human speech and courtship act." https://www.youtube.com/watch?v=_2UcKFtwS5o. Accessed June 19, 2016.

Heidenreich, Barbara, "Awesome bird, the Lyre Bird mimicking like crazy!" https://www.youtube.com/watch?v=bCKxbJA3KpM. Accessed June 19, 2016.

Additional YouTube videos

Australian National University, "Humans aren't alone in grooving to the music" http://www.youtube.com/watch?v=5Js9DTOoYEM. Accessed June 19, 2016.

Adelaide Zoo "Adelaide Zoo Lyrebird 'Chook'," https://www.youtube.com/watch?v=E2f_7tdOgiQ. Accessed June 19, 2016.

Is It Possible: The Lyrebird," http://www.youtube.com/watch?v=xr-o7Cw9zA0, Accessed June 19, 2016.

Lee, Wen Hao, "Lyrebird: The Best Songbird Ever," https://www.youtube.com/watch?v=WA0tP-p7m40. Accessed June 19, 2016.

Sinhala News, "This Bird can TALK in 20 different voices!" https://www.youtube.com/watch?v=ocCPvl6mUmo. Accessed June 19, 2016.

[5] Simon, Matt, Wired.Com, "Absurd Creature of the Week: The Bird That Does Unbelievable Impressions of Chainsaws, Car Alarms," Wired: Science, February 7, 2014, http://www.wired.com/2014/02/absurd-creature-week-lyrebird/. Accessed June 19, 2016.

[6] Thomas, Abbie, "Winter call of the lyrebirds," ABC Science, http://www.abc.net.au/science/articles/2011/08/04/3284076.htm. Accessed June 19, 2016.

[7] Bristol, Marc, "How to Carve a Homemade Bamboo Flute," November 1982, http://www.motherearthnews.com/diy/how-to-carve-a-homemade-bamboo-flute-zmaz82ndzgoe.aspx#axzz3JAI6aOBd. Accessed June 19, 2016.

[8] Wikipedia.Org., "Absolute Pitch or Perfect Pitch," https://en.wikipedia.org/wiki/Absolute_pitch. Accessed June 19, 2016.

"Absolute pitch (AP), widely referred to as perfect pitch, is a rare auditory phenomenon characterized by the ability of a person to identify or re-create a given musical note without the benefit of a reference tone."

350

#73 Punctuated Equilibrium

[1] Adler, Jerry, and Carey, John, "Is Man A Subtle Accident?" Newsweek Magazine, November 3, 1980, page 95

[2] Jerry Adler and John Carey, "Is Man A Subtle Accident?" Newsweek Magazine, November 3, 1980, page 95

[3] Mayr, Ernst (1954). "Change of genetic environment and evolution" In J. Huxley, A. C. Hardy and E. B. Ford. Evolution as a Process. London: Allen and Unwin, pp. 157-180.

[4] Wikipedia.Org, "Punctuated Equilibrium, Theoretical mechanisms," http://en.wikipedia.org/wiki/Punctuated_equilibrium. Accessed June 19, 2016.

[5] Wikipedia.Org, "Punctuated Equilibrium," http://en.wikipedia.org/wiki/Punctuated_equilibrium. Accessed June 19, 2016.

[6] Wikipedia.Org, "Punctuated Equilibrium, Section on Stasis," http://en.wikipedia.org/wiki/Punctuated_equilibrium. Accessed June 19, 2016.

[7] Jerry Adler and John Carey, "Is Man A Subtle Accident?" Newsweek Magazine, November 3, 1980, page 95

[8] Eldredge, Niles, "Evolutionary Housekeeping," Natural History Magazine, February, 1982, page 79

[9] Eldredge, Niles, "Evolutionary Housekeeping," Natural History Magazine, February, 1982, page 79

#74 Proteins

[1] Innovateus, "How many Proteins exist in human body?" http://www.innovateus.net/health/how-many-proteins-exist-human-body. Accessed June 19, 2016.

[2] National Institutes of Health, "What are proteins and what do they do?" http://ghr.nlm.nih.gov/handbook/howgeneswork/protein. Accessed June 19, 2016.

[3] Lloyd, Emma, edited by Zaykoski, Leigh A., "An Introduction to Protein Molecules: The Building Blocks of Life," http://www.brighthub.com/science/medical/articles/6050.aspx. Accessed June 19, 2016.

[4] Parker, Gary, "The Origin of Life: DNA and Protein: Evidence of Creation?, February 6, 2016, https://answersingenesis.org/origin-of-life/dna-and-protein/. Accessed June 19, 2016.

[5] Dill, Ken A. and MacCallum, Justin L. "The Protein-Folding Problem, 50 Years On," Science, November 23, 2012, http://www.sciencemag.org/content/338/6110/1042.short. Accessed June 19, 2016.

[6] Parker, Gary, "The Origin of Life: DNA and Protein: Evidence of Creation?, February 6, 2016, https://answersingenesis.org/origin-of-life/dna-and-protein/. Accessed June 19, 2016.

#75 Hospice Workers

Footnotes and Comments

[1] Brotman, Barbara, Chicago Tribune, "Striking similarity of dying words, Longtime hospice nurse believes patients are glimpsing the afterlife," June 19, 2013, http://articles.chicagotribune.com/2013-06-19/news/ct-x-dying-words-0619-20130619_1_hospice-nurse-maggie-callanan-death-awareness. Accessed June 19, 2016.

[2] Harris, Trudy, Glimpses of Heaven, True Stories of Hope & Peace at the End of Life's Journey, Revell, 2008

[3] Feinberg,Jody, The Patriot Ledger, "Hospice nurse comforts the dying and bereaved through her work and new book," August 10, 2010, http://www.patriotledger.com/article/20100810/News/308109676. Accessed June 19, 2016.

[4] Harris, Trudy,"Guideposts, "Evidence of Life After Death, Is there proof of life after death? This hospice nurse has faith that her patients move on to heaven.," no date, https://www.guideposts.org/inspiration/life-after-death/proof-of-life-after-death-hospice-nurse?nopaging=1. Accessed June 19, 2016.

#76 200 Parameters for Life

[1] Ross, Hugh, "Fine-Tuning For Life On Earth (Updated June 2004)," http://www.reasons.org/articles/fine-tuning-for-life-on-earth-june-2004. Accessed June 19, 2016.

[2] Boyle, Tim, "Does Life Exist On Any Other Planet In The Universe? Another Look At SETI," (Adapted from chapter 15 of the book "The Creator and the Cosmos," by Hugh Ross) http://www.konkyo.org/English/DoesLifeExistOnAnyOtherPlanetInTheUniverseAnother LookAtSETI. Accessed June 19, 2016.

[3] Metaxas, Eric, "Science Increasingly Makes the Case for God. The odds of life existing on another planet grow ever longer. Intelligent design, anyone?" Wall Street Journal, December 25, 2014, http://www.wsj.com/articles/eric-metaxas-science-increasingly-makes-the-case-for-god-1419544568. Accessed June 19, 2016.

#77 God of the Gaps

[1] Wright, Ned, UCLA, Division of Astronomy & Astrophysics, "Fine tuned density of Universe at time of Big Bang. Flatness-Oldness Problem," http://www.astro.ucla.edu/~wright/cosmo_03.htm#FO. Accessed June 19, 2016.

[1] Wright, Ned, UCLA, Division of Astronomy & Astrophysics, "Fine tuned density of Universe at time of Big Bang. Flatness-Oldness Problem," http://www.astro.ucla.edu/~wright/cosmo_03.htm#FO. Accessed June 19, 2016.

[3] Science Daily, "Scientists Find Smallest Number Of Genes Needed For Organism's Survival," University of North Carolina, December 13, 1999. http://www.sciencedaily.com/releases/1999/12/991213052506.htm. Accessed June 19, 2016.

[4] Williams, Peter S., "The Big Bad Wolf, Theism and the Foundations of Intelligent Design," http://www.epsociety.org/library/articles.asp?pid=53&mode=detail. Accessed June 19, 2016.

[5] Boyle, Tim, "Does Life Exist On Any Other Planet In The Universe? Another Look At SETI," (Adapted from chapter 15 of the book "The Creator and the Cosmos," by Hugh Ross)

http://www.konkyo.org/English/DoesLifeExistOnAnyOtherPlanetInTheUniverseAnother
LookAtSETI. Accessed June 19, 2016.

[6] Villanueva, John Carl, "How Many Atoms Are There in the Universe?"July 30, 2009,
http://www.universetoday.com/36302/atoms-in-the-universe/. Accessed June 19, 2016.

[7] Swinburne, Richard, "The Argument from Design,"
http://www.orthodoxytoday.org/articles2/SwinburnDesign.php. Accessed June 19, 2016.

#78 Icons of Evolution

[1] Wells, Jonathan, Icons of Evolution: Science or Myth? Why Much of What We
Teach About Evolution Is Wrong, 2002, Regnery Publishing. Articles by Jonathan Wells,
http://www.iconsofevolution.com/articles.php3. Accessed June 19, 2016.

[2] Wells, Jonathan, "Survival of the Fakest," Discovery Institute, The American
Spectator, January 1, 2001. http://www.discovery.org/a/1209. Accessed June 19, 2016

[3] Wells, Jonathan, "Survival of the Fakest," Discovery Institute, The American
Spectator, January 1, 2001. http://www.discovery.org/a/1209. Accessed June 19, 2016

[6] Wells, Jonathan, "Critics Rave Over Icons of Evolution: A Response to Published
Reviews," Discovery Institute, June 12, 2002, http://www.discovery.org/a/1180.
Accessed June 19, 2016.

#79 The Heart

[1] McCraty, Rollin, Ph.D., The Energetic Heart: Bioelectromagnetic Interactions Within
and Between People, 2003, Institute of HeartMath, http://www.heartmath.org. Accessed
June 19, 2016.

#80 Four Fundamental Forces

[1] Carnegie Mellon University, "Science Notes: Fundamental Forces of Nature,"
http://environ.andrew.cmu.edu/m3/s3/06forces.shtml. Accessed on June 19, 2016.

[2] Georgia State University, "Hyperphysics," http://hyperphysics.phy-
astr.gsu.edu/hbase/forces/funfor.html. Accessed June 19, 2016.

[3] Schroeder, Gerald, "Science Has Finally Proven that Scientifically, There is a God,"
video from February 24, 2016, http://www.israelvideonetwork.com/science-has-finally-
proven-that-scientifically-there-is-a-god/. Accessed June 19, 2016.

> "Gerald Schroeder holds a doctorate in physics from MIT and has been on staff at
> the Weizmann Institute of Science, the Volcani Research Institute, the Hebrew
> University. In this video he gives an incredible explanation on the existence of G-d
> based on the laws of physics and nature. It all makes sense. You just need to follow
> his train of thought."

#81 The Definition of Impossible

[1] Brown, Walt, In the Beginning: Compelling Evidence for Creation and the Flood (8th
Edition), Center for Scientific Creation, December, 2008.

[2] Wikipedia.Org, "Amino Acid," http://en.wikipedia.org/wiki/Amino_acid. Accessed
June 20, 2016.

Footnotes and Comments

[3] Wikipedia.Org, "Protein," http://en.wikipedia.org/wiki/Protein. Accessed June 20, 2016.

[4] Kimball, J., "Proteins," http://users.rcn.com/jkimball.ma.ultranet/BiologyPages/P/Proteins.html. Accessed June 20, 2016.

[5] WiseGeek, "How Many Proteins Exist?" This source said the longest chain of amino acids is 26,926. http://www.wisegeek.org/how-many-proteins-exist.htm. Accessed June 20, 2016.

[6] Georgia State University, Hyperphysics, "Proteins," http://hyperphysics.phy-astr.gsu.edu/hbase/organic/protein.html. Accessed June 20, 2016.

[7] WiseGeek, "How Many Proteins Exist?" This source said the longest chain of amino acids is 26,926. http://www.wisegeek.org/how-many-proteins-exist.htm. Accessed June 20, 2016.

[8] Ell, Douglas, Counting To God, AttitudeMedia, 2014, page 106.

#83 RAS (Reticular Activating System)

[1] Phatak, Omkar, Activating System, March 3, 2014, http://www.buzzle.com/articles/reticular-activating-system.html. Accessed June 20, 2016.

[2] Blanton, Smiley, Living on Purpose, "The Reticular Activating System (RAS)," https://www.crgleader.com/ezine/livingonpurpose/LOP151.html. Accessed June 20, 2016.

[3] The Human Memory, "Neurons & Synapses," http://www.human-memory.net/brain_neurons.html. Accessed June 20, 2016.

Additional Reference: WiseGeek, "What Is the Reticular Activating System?" http://www.wisegeek.org/what-is-the-reticular-activating-system.htm. Accessed June 20, 2016.

#84 Homing Pigeons

[1] OneKind.Org, "Facts about pigeons," http://www.onekind.org/be_inspired/animals_a_z/pigeon/. Accessed June 20, 2016.

"Only 6 species can pass the mirror test, all mammals except for the pigeon."

[2] Urban Wildlife Society, "Answers to the Urban Wildlife Society's Gee Whiz Animal Quiz," http://www.urbanwildlifesociety.org/UWS/GeeWhizQuizAnswers.htm. Accessed June 20, 2016.

[3] SoftSchools.Com, "Pigeon Facts," http://www.softschools.com/facts/animals/pigeon_facts/589/. Accessed June 20, 2016.

[4] Pigeon Control Resource Centre. "21 Amazing Facts About Pigeons. Fact 4. The pigeon as a war hero," http://www.pigeoncontrolresourcecentre.org/html/amazing-pigeon-facts.html. Accessed June 20, 2016.

[5] Urban Wildlife Society, "Answers to the Urban Wildlife Society's Gee Whiz Animal Quiz," http://www.urbanwildlifesociety.org/UWS/GeeWhizQuizAnswers.htm. Accessed June 20, 2016.

[6] FirstBirdsInPigeons.com, "Pigeon Facts,"
http://www.fbipigeons.com/PIGEON%20FACTS.htm. Accessed June 20, 2016.

[7] Mora, Davison, Wild, & Walker, Nature.Com, "Letters to Nature: Magnetoreception
and its trigeminal mediation in the homing pigeon,"
http://www.nature.com/nature/journal/v432/n7016/abs/nature03077.html. Accessed June
20, 2016.

[8] Reardon, Sara, Science Magazine, "ScienceShot: Homing Pigeons Follow Their
Noses," Jan. 27, 2011, http://www.sciencemag.org/news/2011/01/scienceshot-homing-
pigeons-follow-their-noses. Accessed June 20, 2016.

[9] [6] FirstBirdsInPigeons.com, "Pigeon Facts,"
http://www.fbipigeons.com/PIGEON%20FACTS.htm. Accessed June 20, 2016.

[10] Evolution New & Views, "For Everything a Reason: Why Ants Walk Crooked and
Pigeons Circle Around," December 13, 2013.
http://www.evolutionnews.org/2013/12/for_everything080121.html. Accessed June 20,
2016.

[11] WikiHow, "How to Train a Homing Pigeon," http://www.wikihow.com/Train-a-
Homing-Pigeon. Accessed June 20, 2016.

#85 Spontaneous Generation

[1] Wikipedia.Org, "Spontaneous generation,"
http://en.wikipedia.org/wiki/Spontaneous_generation. Accessed June 20, 2016.

[2] Levine, Russell, and Evers, Chris, "The Slow Death of Spontaneous Generation
(1668-1859)," The National Health Museum: About Biotech,"
http://webprojects.oit.ncsu.edu/project/bio183de/Black/cellintro/cellintro_reading/Sponta
neous_Generation.html. Accessed June 20, 2016.

[3] Encyclopaedia Britannica, "Spontaneous Generation,"
http://www.britannica.com/EBchecked/topic/560859/spontaneous-generation. Accessed
June 20, 2016.

[4] [1] Wikipedia.Org, "Spontaneous generation,"
http://en.wikipedia.org/wiki/Spontaneous_generation. Accessed June 20, 2016.

[5] Wikipedia.Org, "Biogenesis," http://en.wikipedia.org/wiki/Biogenesis. Accessed June
20, 2016.

[6] All About Science, "What is Spontaneous Generation?"
http://www.allaboutscience.org/what-is-spontaneous-generation-faq.htm. Accessed June
20, 2016.

[7] InfoPlease, "Origin of Life: Spontaneous Generation,"
http://www.infoplease.com/cig/biology/spontaneous-generation.html. Accessed June 20,
2016.

[8] Wilkins, John S., "Spontaneous Generation and the Origin of Life," TalkOrigins,
April 26, 2004, http://www.talkorigins.org/faqs/abioprob/spontaneous-generation.html.
Accessed June 20, 2016.

Footnotes and Comments

[9] Wilkins, John S., "Spontaneous Generation and the Origin of Life," TalkOrigins, April 26, 2004, http://www.talkorigins.org/faqs/abioprob/spontaneous-generation.html. Accessed June 20, 2016.

#86 The Tongue

[1] Science Kids, "Human Body Facts: Fun Tongue Facts for Kids," http://www.sciencekids.co.nz/sciencefacts/humanbody/tongue.html. Accessed June 21, 2016.

[2] Wikipedia.Org, "Tongue," http://en.wikipedia.org/wiki/Tongue. Accessed June 21, 2016.

[3] Harmon Courage, Katherine, "Octopus Arms, Human Tongues Intertwine for Science," Scientific American, January 10, 2014, http://blogs.scientificamerican.com/octopus-chronicles/octopus-arms-human-tongues-intertwine-for-science/. Accessed June 21, 2016.

[4] Kids' Health, "Your terrifc tongue: Your Friendly Tongue," http://www.cyh.com/HealthTopics/HealthTopicDetailsKids.aspx?p=335&np=152&id=1832. Accessed June 21, 2016.

[5] Baidya, Sankalan, "20 Interesting Human Tongue Facts," http://factslegend.org/20-interesting-human-tongue-facts/. Accessed June 20, 2016.

[6] Arnold, Paul, "Mouth Bacteria. It's a Jungle in There," July 22, 2010, http://www.brighthub.com/science/genetics/articles/45935.aspx. Accessed June 21, 2016.

[7] KidsHealth, "Your Tongue," October, 2013, http://kidshealth.org/en/kids/tongue.html#. Accessed June 21, 2016.

[8] Klein, Sarah, Healthy Living, "8 Things You Probably Didn't Know About Your Tongue," October 13, 2014, http://www.huffingtonpost.com/2014/10/11/tongue-facts-health-info_n_5952850.html. Accessed June 21, 2016.

#87 PAIN

[1] Wikipedia.Org, "Congenital insensitivity to pain," https://en.wikipedia.org/wiki/Congenital_insensitivity_to_pain. Accessed June 21, 2016.

[2] The Oprah Winfrey Show, "The Little Girl Who Doesn't Feel Pain," November 8, 2005, https://www.youtube.com/watch?v=AqRcngt0-h0. Accessed June 21, 2016.

[3] Heckertnov, Justin, "The Hazards of Growing Up Painlessly," The New York Times Magazine, November 15, 2012. http://www.nytimes.com/2012/11/18/magazine/ashlyn-blocker-feels-no-pain.html?_r=0. Accessed June 21, 2016.

[4] Mohney, Gillian, Good Morning America, "Meet the Child Who Feels No Pain," Oct. 25, 2013, http://abcnews.go.com/Health/meet-toddler-feels-pain/story?id=20658484. Accessed June 21, 2016.

[5] Mohney, Gillian, Good Morning America, "Meet the Child Who Feels No Pain," Oct. 25, 2013, http://abcnews.go.com/Health/meet-toddler-feels-pain/story?id=20658484. Accessed June 21, 2016.

[6] BBC: Science: Human Body & Mind, "Nervous system – Touch: Pain and temperature,"

http://www.bbc.co.uk/science/humanbody/body/factfiles/touch/touch.shtml. Accessed June 21, 2016.

[7] The Free Dictionary, "Pain," http://medical-dictionary.thefreedictionary.com/Pain+receptors. Accessed June 21, 2016.

[8] Dafny, Nachum, Department of Neurobiology and Anatomy, The UT Medical School at Houston. "Neuroscience. Chapter 6: Pain Principles," http://neuroscience.uth.tmc.edu/s2/chapter06.html. Accessed June 21, 2016.

[9] Jrank.Org, "Touch," http://psychology.jrank.org/pages/634/Touch.html. Accessed June 21, 2016.

[10] Dafny, Nachum, Department of Neurobiology and Anatomy, The UT Medical School at Houston. "Neuroscience. Chapter 6: Pain Principles," http://neuroscience.uth.tmc.edu/s2/chapter06.html. Accessed June 21, 2016.

[11] The Free Dictionary, "Pain," http://medical-dictionary.thefreedictionary.com/Pain+receptors. Accessed June 21, 2016.

#88 The Waggle Dance of Honeybees

[1] National Geographic video, "World's Weirdest: Honeybee Dance Moves," http://video.nationalgeographic.com/video/weirdest-bees-dance. Accessed June 21, 2016.

[2] Wikipedia.Org, "Waggle Dance," https://en.wikipedia.org/wiki/Waggle_dance. Accessed June 21, 2016.

[3] N.C. State University, "The Honey Bee Dance Language," http://www.cals.ncsu.edu/entomology/apiculture/pdfs/1.11%20copy.pdf. Accessed June 21, 2016.

[4] Quitmeyer, Andrew, and Baich, Tucker, "The Waggle Dance of the Honeybee," Georgia Tech College of Computing, February 2, 2011. https://www.youtube.com/watch?v=bFDGPgXtK-U. Accessed June 21, 2016.

[5] Wikipedia.Org, "Waggle Dance," https://en.wikipedia.org/wiki/Waggle_dance. Accessed June 21, 2016

[6] wgbhstocksales Video: "Bee Waggle Dance," https://www.youtube.com/watch?v=Jc-mtUs-eis. Accessed June 21, 2016.

[7] N.C. State University, "The Honey Bee Dance Language," http://www.cals.ncsu.edu/entomology/apiculture/pdfs/1.11%20copy.pdf. Accessed June 21, 2016.

#89 Earthworms

[1] Wikipedia.Org, "Earthworm," https://en.wikipedia.org/wiki/Earthworm. Accessed June 21, 2016.

[2] University of Pennsylvania, "Earthworms: Earthworms Help the Environment," http://www.sas.upenn.edu/~rlenet/Earthworms.html. Accessed June 21, 2016.

[3] University of Michigan, BioKids, "Oligochaeta," http://www.biokids.umich.edu/critters/Oligochaeta/. Accessed June 21, 2016.

Footnotes and Comments

[4] University of Michigan, BioKids, "Oligochaeta," http://www.biokids.umich.edu/critters/Oligochaeta/. Accessed June 21, 2016.

[5] Wikipedia.Org, "Earthworm," https://en.wikipedia.org/wiki/Earthworm. Accessed June 21, 2016.

[6] Wikipedia.Org, "Earthworm," https://en.wikipedia.org/wiki/Earthworm. Accessed June 21, 2016.

[7] ScienceDaily, Imperial College London, "Mystery behind earthworm digestion solved," August 4, 2015, https://www.sciencedaily.com/releases/2015/08/150804142947.htm. Accessed June 21, 2016.

[8] Wikipedia.Org, "Earthworm," https://en.wikipedia.org/wiki/Earthworm. Accessed June 21, 2016.

[9] Biology Junction, "We Love Worms," http://www.biologyjunction.com/earthworm%20facts.htm#hatch. Accessed June 21, 2016

[10] University of Pennsylvania, "Earthworms: Earthworms Help the Environment," http://www.sas.upenn.edu/~rlenet/Earthworms.html. Accessed June 21, 2016.

[11] University of Pennsylvania, "Earthworms: Earthworms Help the Environment," http://www.sas.upenn.edu/~rlenet/Earthworms.html. Accessed June 21, 2016.

[12] Wikipedia.Org, "Earthworm," https://en.wikipedia.org/wiki/Earthworm. Accessed June 21, 2016.

[13] Wikipedia.Org, "Earthworm," https://en.wikipedia.org/wiki/Earthworm. Accessed June 21, 2016.

[14] University of Pennsylvania, "Earthworms: Earthworms Help the Environment," http://www.sas.upenn.edu/~rlenet/Earthworms.html. Accessed June 21, 2016.

#90 Copying Degradation

[1] Durston, Kirk, "An Essential Prediction of Darwinian Theory Is Falsified by Information Degradation," July 9, 2015. http://www.evolutionnews.org/2015/07/an_essential_pr097521.html. Accessed June 22, 2016.

[2] Mira, Alex, Ochmanemail, Howard, and Moran, Nancy A., Dept of Ecology and Evolutionary Biology, University of Arizona, "Deletional bias and the evolution of bacterial genomes," Trends in Genetics, October 1, 2001, ww.cell.com/trends/genetics/abstract/S0168-9525(01)02447-7?_returnURL=http%3A%2F%2Flinkinghub.elsevier.com%2Fretrieve%2Fpii%2FS0168952501024477%3Fshowall%3Dtrue. Accessed June 22, 2016.

[3] Petrov, Dmitri A., and Hartl, Daniel L., Department of Organismic and Evolutionary Biology, Harvard University, "High Rate of DNA Loss in the Drosophila melanogaster and Drosophila virilis Species Groups," http://petrov.stanford.edu/pdfs/11.pdf. Accessed June 22, 2016.

[4] Lynch, Michael, Department of Biology, Indiana University, "Rate, molecular spectrum, and consequences of human

mutation,"http://www.pnas.org/content/107/3/961.full.pdf+html. Accessed June 22, 2016.

[5] Durston, Kirk, "An Essential Prediction of Darwinian Theory Is Falsified by Information Degradation," July 9, 2015. http://www.evolutionnews.org/2015/07/an_essential_pr097521.html. Accessed June 22, 2016.

[6] Montelone, Beth A., Division of Biology, Kansas State University, "Mutation, Mutagens, and DNA Repair. Section V. DNA repair systems," Copyright 1998Montelone, Beth A., Division of Biology, Kansas State University, http://www-personal.k-state.edu/~bethmont/mutdes.html. Accessed June 22, 2016.

[7] Sunderland, Cooper, The Cell: A Molecular Approach. 2nd edition., DNA Repair, 2000.

Additional Reference: Nair, A.J., Principles of Biochemistry and Genetic Engineering, University Science Press, New Delhi, 2010

#91 Spider Webs

[1] Wikepedia.Org, "Spider Webs: Silk production," https://en.wikipedia.org/wiki/Spider_web. Accessed June 22, 2016.

[2] Wikepedia.Org, "Spider Webs: Silk production," https://en.wikipedia.org/wiki/Spider_web. Accessed June 22, 2016.

[3] Wikepedia.Org, "Spider Webs: Silk production," https://en.wikipedia.org/wiki/Spider_web. Accessed June 22, 2016.

[4] Wikepedia.Org, "Spider Webs: Silk production," https://en.wikipedia.org/wiki/Spider_web. Accessed June 22, 2016.

[5] HowStuffWorks.Com, "How Spiders Work: A Typical Spider Web," http://animals.howstuffworks.com/arachnids/spider5.htm. Accessed June 22, 2016.

#92 Emperor Penguins

[1] Wikipedia.org, "Emperor penguin," https://en.wikipedia.org/wiki/Emperor_penguin. Accessed June 22, 2016.

[2] Cool Antarctica, "Emperor Penguin (Aptenodytes Forsteri)," http://antarcticconnection.com/information/emperor-penguin-aptenodytes-forsteri/. Accessed June 22, 2016.

[3] Wikipedia.org, "Emperor penguin," https://en.wikipedia.org/wiki/Emperor_penguin. Accessed June 22, 2016.

[4] Cool Antarctica, "Emperor Penguin (Aptenodytes Forsteri)," http://antarcticconnection.com/information/emperor-penguin-aptenodytes-forsteri/. Accessed June 22, 2016.

[5] Wikipedia.org, "Emperor penguin," https://en.wikipedia.org/wiki/Emperor_penguin. Accessed June 22, 2016.

[6] Wikipedia.org, "Emperor penguin," https://en.wikipedia.org/wiki/Emperor_penguin. Accessed June 22, 2016.

Footnotes and Comments

[7] "Emperor Penguins Facts"
http://www.coolantarctica.com/Antarctica%20fact%20file/wildlife/Emperor-penguins.php. Accessed June 22, 2016.

[8] "Emperor Penguins Facts"
http://www.coolantarctica.com/Antarctica%20fact%20file/wildlife/Emperor-penguins.php. Accessed June 22, 2016.

#93 Camels

[1] San Diego Zoo, "Animals: Mammals: Camel: Ships of the desert,"
http://animals.sandiegozoo.org/animals/camel. Accessed June 22, 2016.

[2] KidsKonnect, "Camel Facts," https://kidskonnect.com/animals/camel/. Accessed June 22, 2016.

[3] British Llama Society, "All about Camels,"
www.britishllamasociety.org/camelids/camels/camels.html. Accessed June 22, 2016.

[4] Bradford, Alina, "Camels: Facts, Types & Pictures," June 3, 2014, LiveScience,
http://www.livescience.com/27503-camels.html. Accessed June 22, 2016

[5] Wikipedia.Org., "Camel: Ecological and behavioral adaptations,"
https://en.wikipedia.org/wiki/Camel. Accessed June 22, 2016.

#94 Whales

[1] Biowebpagevdl Wiki, "Whales Evolution,"
http://biowebpagevdl.wikia.com/wiki/Whales_evolution. Accessed June 28, 2016.

[2] Switek, Brian, Smithsonian.com, "How Did Whales Evolve?" December 1, 2010,
http://www.smithsonianmag.com/science-nature/how-did-whales-evolve-73276956/?no-ist. Accessed June 28, 2016.

[3] Parry, Wynne, LiveScience.com, "How Whales' Ancestors Left Land Behind"
http://www.livescience.com/28075-how-whales-ancestors-left-land.html. Accessed June 28, 2016.

[4] Sarfati, Jonathan, "Refuting Evolution—Chapter 5, Whale Evolution,"
http://creation.com/refuting-evolution-chapter-5-whale-evolution. Accessed June 28, 2016.

[5] American Museum of Natural History, "Whale Evolution,"
http://www.amnh.org/exhibitions/past-exhibitions/whales-giants-of-the-deep/whale-evolution. Accessed June 28, 2016.

[6] Wikipedia.Org, "Whale," https://en.wikipedia.org/wiki/Whale. Accessed June 29, 2016.

[7] Wikipedia.Org, "Whale," https://en.wikipedia.org/wiki/Whale. Accessed June 29, 2016.

[8] Wikipedia.Org, "Whale," https://en.wikipedia.org/wiki/Whale. Accessed June 29, 2016.

[9] Wikipedia.Org, "Whale," https://en.wikipedia.org/wiki/Whale. Accessed June 29, 2016.

#95 Archaea

[1] Wikipedia.org, "Archaea," https://en.wikipedia.org/wiki/Archaea. Accessed June 29, 2016.

[2] Frazer, Jennifer, Scientific American, "Archaea Are More Wonderful Than You Know," January 12, 2013, http://blogs.scientificamerican.com/artful-amoeba/archaea-are-more-wonderful-than-you-know/. Accessed June 29, 2016.

[3] WiseGeek, "What Are the Differences between Archaea and Bacteria?" http://www.wisegeek.org/what-are-the-differences-between-archaea-and-bacteria.htm#didyouknowout. Accessed June 29, 2016.

[4] Wikipedia.org, "Archaea," https://en.wikipedia.org/wiki/Archaea. Accessed June 29, 2016.

[5] Wikipedia.org, "Archaea," https://en.wikipedia.org/wiki/Archaea. Accessed June 29, 2016.

[6] Frazer, Jennifer, Scientific American, "Archaea Are More Wonderful Than You Know," January 12, 2013, http://blogs.scientificamerican.com/artful-amoeba/archaea-are-more-wonderful-than-you-know/. Accessed June 29, 2016.

[7] Deem, Rich, "The Incredible Design of the Earth and Our Solar System," http://www.godandscience.org/apologetics/designss.html. Accessed June 29, 2016.

[8] Wikipedia.org, "Archaea," https://en.wikipedia.org/wiki/Archaea. Accessed June 29, 2016.

[9] New Mexico Museum of Natural History and Science, "Archaea," http://treeoflife.nmnaturalhistory.org/archaea.html. Accessed June 29, 2016.

[10] Wikipedia.org, "Archaea," https://en.wikipedia.org/wiki/Archaea. Accessed June 29, 2016.

#96 Blood

[1] Smithsonian.com, "There are 37.2 Trillion Cells in Your Body," October 24, 2013, http://www.smithsonianmag.com/smart-news/there-are-372-trillion-cells-in-your-body-4941473/?no-ist. Accessed June 30, 2016.

[2] Guliuzza, Randy J., "Life-Giving Blood," http://www.icr.org/article/4823. Accessed June 30, 2016.

[3] American Society of Hematology, "Blood Basics," http://www.hematology.org/Patients/Basics/
(Excellent 52 sec video: https://youtu.be/R-sKZWqsUpw) Accessed June 30, 2016.

[4] WebMD article, "Heart Health Center," http://www.webmd.com/heart/anatomy-picture-of-blood. Accessed June 30, 2016.

[5] Bianco, Carl, "How Blood Works," http://health.howstuffworks.com/human-body/systems/circulatory/blood.htm/printable. Accessed June 30, 2016.

[6] [2] Guliuzza, Randy J., "Life-Giving Blood," http://www.icr.org/article/4823. Accessed June 30, 2016.

Footnotes and Comments

[7] U. S. National Library of Medicine, "Red blood cell production," https://www.nlm.nih.gov/medlineplus/ency/anatomyvideos/000104.htm. Accessed June 30, 2016.

[8] Bianco, Carl, "How Blood Works," http://health.howstuffworks.com/human-body/systems/circulatory/blood.htm/printable. Accessed June 30, 2016.

[9] Bianco, Carl, "How Blood Works," http://health.howstuffworks.com/human-body/systems/circulatory/blood.htm/printable. Accessed June 30, 2016.

[10] American Society of Hematology, "Blood Basics," http://www.hematology.org/Patients/Basics/. Accessed June 30, 2016.

#97 The Retina

[1] Stevens, John K., Associate Professor of physiology and biomedical engineering, Originally appeared in "Reverse Engineering the Brain," Byte, April 1985, p. 287. Quoted from: http://www.creationscience.com/onlinebook/ReferencesandNotes9.html. Accessed June 30, 2016.

[2] Sanders, Robert, Media Relations, UC Berkeley, March 28, 2001, "Eye strips images of all but bare essentials before sending visual information to brain," http://www.berkeley.edu/news/media/releases/2001/03/28_wers1.html. Accessed June 30, 2016.

[3] Calkins, Joseph, "Design in the Human Eye," http://www.creationmoments.com/content/design-human-eye. Accessed June 30, 2016.

[4] Wikipedia.org, "Choroid," https://en.wikipedia.org/wiki/Choroid. Accessed June 30, 2016.

[5] Bergman, Jerry and Calkins, Joseph, Creation Research Society Quarterly, "Why the Inverted Human Retina Is a Superior Design," https://www.creationresearch.org/crsq/articles/45/45_3/CRSQ%20Winter%2009%20Retina.pdf. Accessed June 30, 2016.

[6] Bergman, Jerry and Calkins, Joseph, Creation Research Society Quarterly, "Why the Inverted Human Retina Is a Superior Design," https://www.creationresearch.org/crsq/articles/45/45_3/CRSQ%20Winter%2009%20Retina.pdf. Accessed June 30, 2016.

[7] Bergman, Jerry and Calkins, Joseph, Creation Research Society Quarterly, "Why the Inverted Human Retina Is a Superior Design," https://www.creationresearch.org/crsq/articles/45/45_3/CRSQ%20Winter%2009%20Retina.pdf. Accessed June 30, 2016.

#98 Acacia Trees and Ants

[1] Quatr.us, formerly History for Kids, "History of Farming: Ancient and Medieval Farming – History of Farming," http://quatr.us/economy/farming/. Accessed July 1, 2016.

[2] Piper, Ross. Extraordinary Animals: An Encyclopedia of Curious and Unusual Animals. Westport, CT: Greenwood Press, 2007. 1-3. Print.

[3] Themes of Parasitology Blog, "Relationship Advice: Acacia Trees and Ants," March 23, 2012, http://bio390parasitology.blogspot.com/2012/03/relationship-advice-acacia-trees-and.html. Accessed July 2, 2016.

[4] Bartz, Paul, "Ants who garden,"
http://www.creationmoments.com/radio/transcripts/ants-who-garden. Accessed July 2,
2016.

[5] Themes of Parasitology Blog, "Relationship Advice: Acacia Trees and Ants," March
23, 2012, http://bio390parasitology.blogspot.com/2012/03/relationship-advice-acacia-
trees-and.html. Accessed July 2, 2016.

[6] Marietta College, "Acacia Ants"
http://w3.marietta.edu/~biol/costa_rica/animals/acacia_ants.htm. Accessed July 2, 2016.

[7] Wikipedia, "Vachellia cornigera," (Bullhorn Acacia),
https://en.wikipedia.org/wiki/Vachellia_cornigera. Accessed July 2, 2016.

[8] Max Planck Institute for Chemical Ecology, "Ants Protect Acacia Plants Against
Pathogens," January 15, 2014, http://www.ice.mpg.de/ext/index.php?id=1057. Accessed
July 2, 2016.

[9] McDaniel College, "Ant-acacia mutualism,"
http://www2.mcdaniel.edu/Biology/eco/mut/mutualism.html. Accessed July 2, 2016.

#99 Complexity, Equilibrium, and Energy Costs

[1] The American Heritage® New Dictionary of Cultural Literacy, Third Edition,
Copyright © 2005 by Houghton Mifflin Company.

[2] Snoke, David W.; Cox, Jeffrey; and Petcher, Donald, "Suboptimality and complexity
in evolution," Complexity Journal, Volume 21, Issue 1,
http://onlinelibrary.wiley.com/doi/10.1002/cplx.21566/abstract. Accessed July 2, 2016.

[3] Luskin, Casey, "Peer-Reviewed Paper Reveals Darwin's Unavoidable Catch-22
Problem," December 27, 2015,
http://www.evolutionnews.org/2015/12/6_of_our_top_st101881.html. Accessed July 2,
2016.

[4] Luskin, Casey, "Peer-Reviewed Paper Reveals Darwin's Unavoidable Catch-22
Problem," December 27, 2015,
http://www.evolutionnews.org/2015/12/6_of_our_top_st101881.html. Accessed July 2,
2016.

[5] Luskin, Casey, "Peer-Reviewed Paper Reveals Darwin's Unavoidable Catch-22
Problem," December 27, 2015,
http://www.evolutionnews.org/2015/12/6_of_our_top_st101881.html. Accessed July 2,
2016.

[6] Gauger, Ann, "Waiting for Mutations: Why Darwinism Won't Work," Sept. 23, 2015,
http://www.evolutionnews.org/2015/09/waiting_for_mut099631.html. Accessed July 2,
2016.

[7] Luskin, Casey, "Peer-Reviewed Paper Reveals Darwin's Unavoidable Catch-22
Problem," December 27, 2015,
http://www.evolutionnews.org/2015/12/6_of_our_top_st101881.html. Accessed July 2,
2016.

#100 Quality Control and Error Correction

Footnotes and Comments

[1] The Royal Swedish Academy of Sciences, Press Release, October 7, 2015, http://www.nobelprize.org/nobel_prizes/chemistry/laureates/2015/press.html. Accessed July 2, 2016.

Additional references for DNA replication and repair mechanisms

Illustration - DNA Structure and cell division process (pdf 650 kB) by Jarnestad, Johan, The Royal Swedish Academy of Sciences, http://www.nobelprize.org/nobel_prizes/chemistry/laureates/2015/fig_ke_en_15_dn astructure.pdf. Accessed July 2, 2016.

Illustration – DNA Base excision repair mechanism (pdf 495 kB) by Jarnestad, Johan, The Royal Swedish Academy of Sciences, http://www.nobelprize.org/nobel_prizes/chemistry/laureates/2015/fig_ke_en_15_ba seexcisionrepair.pdf. Accessed July 2, 2016.

Illustration - Mismatch repair mechanism. (pdf 1,5 Mb) by Jarnestad, Johan, The Royal Swedish Academy of Sciences, http://www.nobelprize.org/nobel_prizes/chemistry/laureates/2015/fig_ke_en_15_mi smatchrepair.pdf. Accessed July 2, 2016.

Illustration - Nucleotide excision repair (pdf 537 kB) by Jarnestad, Johan, The Royal Swedish Academy of Sciences, http://www.nobelprize.org/nobel_prizes/chemistry/laureates/2015/fig_ke_en_15_nu cleotideexcisionrepair.pdf. Accessed July 2, 2016.

[2] Mirsky, Steve, Scientific American.Com, "2015 Nobel Prize in Chemistry," October 7, 2015, http://www.scientificamerican.com/podcast/episode/2015-nobel-prize-in-chemistry/. Accessed July 2, 2016.

[3] Yan, Holly, and Melvin, Don, CNN.Com, "Nobel Prize for chemistry awarded to 3 scientists for DNA repair studies," October 7, 2015, http://www.cnn.com/2015/10/07/world/europe/nobel-prize-chemistry/. Accessed July 2, 2016.

[4] Mirsky, Steve, Scientific American.Com, "2015 Nobel Prize in Chemistry," October 7, 2015, http://www.scientificamerican.com/podcast/episode/2015-nobel-prize-in-chemistry/. Accessed July 2, 2016.

[5] Sample, Ian, and Randerson, James, The Guardian.Com, "Nobel prize for chemistry: Lindahl, Modrich and Sancar win for DNA research," October 7, 2015 https://www.theguardian.com/science/2015/oct/07/lindahl-modrich-and-sancar-win-nobel-chemistry-prize-for-dna-research. Accessed July 2, 2016.

[6] Sample, Ian, and Randerson, James, The Guardian.Com, "Nobel prize for chemistry: Lindahl, Modrich and Sancar win for DNA research," October 7, 2015 https://www.theguardian.com/science/2015/oct/07/lindahl-modrich-and-sancar-win-nobel-chemistry-prize-for-dna-research. Accessed July 2, 2016.

[8] Dictionary.com. "Quality Control," http://dictionary.reference.com/browse/quality-control. Accessed July 2, 2016.

#101 The Messiah

[1] Wikipedia.org. "List of best-selling single-volume books," https://en.wikipedia.org/wiki/List_of_best-selling_books. Accessed July 2, 2016.

[2] ChristianAnswers.net, "About the Bible," http://www.christiananswers.net/bible/about.html. Accessed July 2, 2016.

[3] Wikipedia.org, "Francis of Assisi," https://en.wikipedia.org/wiki/Francis_of_Assisi. Accessed July 2, 2016.

[4]. Wikipedia.org, "Stigmata," https://en.wikipedia.org/wiki/Stigmata. Accessed July 2, 2016.

[5]. Wikipedia.org, "Stigmata," https://en.wikipedia.org/wiki/Stigmata. Accessed July 2, 2016.

[6] Know What You believe.Com, "Is The New Testament Reliable As A Historical Record?" http://knowwhatyoubelieve.com/believe/evidence/bible_reliability.htm. Accessed July 2, 2016.

[7] Know What You believe.Com, "Is The New Testament Reliable As A Historical Record?" http://knowwhatyoubelieve.com/believe/evidence/bible_reliability.htm. Accessed July 2, 2016.

[8] Wikipedia.Org, "Plato: Textual sources and history," https://en.wikipedia.org/wiki/Plato. Accessed July 2, 2016.

[9] Freedom Poet, Dakota Voice.com, "Did Plato Really Exist?" March 22, 2008. http://www.dakotavoice.com/2008/03/did-plato-really-exist/. Accessed July 2, 2016.

[10] FaithFacts.org, "Manuscript Evidence for the Bible: An Outline: Reliability of the New Testament as Historical Documents," http://www.faithfacts.org/search-for-truth/maps/manuscript-evidence. Accessed July 2, 2016.

Images – Copyright Information

Image 1. Artist's concept of human evolution, but incomplete.

© 2016. Nari M. Hanna. Used by permission.

Image 2. Artist's concept of male and female evolution.

© 2016. Nari M. Hanna. Used by permission.

Image 3. Sticks.

Public Domain. Altered by Jim Stephens: cropped, flipped, rotated, and changed to greyscale. https://pixabay.com/en/branch-stick-wooden-tree-plant-34379/

Image 4. Primate feet.

Licensed under a Creative Commons Attribution Share-Alike 3.0.
http://www.bigfootencounters.com/images/primatefeet.htm

Image 5. Chemical reactions and neurotransmitters.

Public Domain. "Drawing illustrating the process of synaptic transmission in neurons".
Date: 2009-12-30, first publication of original unknown.
Source: http://www.nia.nih.gov/alzheimers/publication/alzheimers-disease-unraveling-mystery/preface
Author: Looie496, US National Institutes of Health, National Institute on Aging.
Altered by Jim Stephens: cropped and changed to greyscale.

Image 6. Darwin vs. Actual Fossils.

© 2016 Created by Jim Stephens.

Image 7. DNA Replication.

Public Domain. This work has been released into the public domain by its author,
LadyofHats. https://commons.wikimedia.org/wiki/File:DNA_replication_en.svg
Altered by Jim Stephens: changed to greyscale.

Image 8. Mousetrap.

© 2016. Created by Jim Stephens from a personal photo.

Image 9. Dog breeding.

CC0 Public Domain. Free for commercial use. No attribution required. Use of three images altered by Jim Stephens: rotated, cropped, and changed to greyscale.
https://pixabay.com/en/hound-dog-scent-animal-biology-153773/
https://pixabay.com/en/dog-english-pet-animal-mammal-fur-48321/
https://pixabay.com/en/hound-animal-biology-dog-mammal-153051/

Image 10. Single cell bacteria.

CC0 Public Domain. Free for commercial use. No attribution required.
https://pixabay.com/en/school-education-science-diagram-40847/
Altered by Jim Stephens: changed to greyscale.

Image 11. Tree of Life vs. Orchard.

© 1999. Jonathan Sarfati. Used by permission. From: <u>Refuting Evolution</u>, pgs 38, 39

Image 12. Types of Skin.

Licensed under the Creative Commons Attribution-Share Alike 3.0 Unported license.
"Layers of the skin," Date: October, 2012. Authors: Madhero88 and M.Komorniczak
Source: https://en.wikipedia.org/wiki/File:Skin_layers.png.
Altered by Jim Stephens: changed to greyscale.

Image 13. Changes from Chimpanzee to Human Feet.

CC0 Public Domain. Free for commercial use. No attribution required.
Altered by Jim Stephens: Cropped, repositioned, changed to greyscale.
https://pixabay.com/en/monkey-chimpanzee-sweet-425140/
https://pixabay.com/en/chimpanzee-monkey-apes-sitting-88993/
https://pixabay.com/en/feet-foot-sole-ten-1291554/

Image 14. All Links are Missing.

© 2016. Nari M. Hanna. Used by permission.

Image 15. Honeybee Waggle Dance.

Licensed under the Creative Commons Attribution 2.5 Generic license.
"Figure-Eight-Shaped Waggle Dance of the Honeybee (Apis mellifera). A waggle run
oriented 45° to the right of 'up' on the vertical comb (A) indicates a food source 45° to
the right of the direction of the sun outside the hive (B). The abdomen of the dancer
appears blurred because of the rapid motion from side to side."
Date: July, 2004. Source: Chittka L: Dances as Windows into Insect Perception.
Author: (Figure design: J. Tautz and M. Kleinhenz, Beegroup Würzburg.)
https://commons.wikimedia.org/wiki/File:Waggle_dance.png
Altered by Jim Stephens: changed to greyscale.

Image 16. Spider Web Building Steps.

Licensed under the Creative Commons Attribution-Share Alike 4.0 International license.
Altered by Jim Stephens: Text reformatted, color changed to greyscale.
https://commons.wikimedia.org/wiki/File:Orb_web_building_steps-01.svg

Image 17. Missing Whale Ancestors, all of them.

All of the following images were altered by Jim Stephens: repositioned, changed to greyscale.

"Hippopotamus." CC0 Public Domain. Free for commercial use. No attribution required.
https://pixabay.com/en/hippopotamus-animal-hippo-big-40150/
"Question Mark." CC0 Public Domain. Free for commercial use. No attribution required.
https://pixabay.com/en/question-mark-confirmation-question-838656/
"Blue Whale." Public Domain from Clipart Panda, 2014
http://www.clipartpanda.com/clipart_images/humpback-whale-drone-video-35175251

The following images are licensed under GNU Free Documentation License, Version 1.2 or
any later version and under the Creative Commons Attribution 3.0 Unported license.

"Indohyus." Date: 23 December 2007. Author: Nobu Tamura
https://commons.wikimedia.org/wiki/File:Indohyus_BW.jpg

Images – Copyright Information

Front Cover: Image Copyrights and References to Chapters on that subject.

1. Giraffe: Chapter 34, https://pixabay.com/en/giraffe-africa-national-park-kenya-756444/

2. Brain: Chapter 16, https://pixabay.com/en/brain-anatomy-human-science-health-512758/

3. Moon: Chapter 49, https://pixabay.com/en/moon-satellite-space-crater-sky-1370052/

4. Camel: Chapter 93, http://www.freeimages.com/photo/camel-1507449

5. Flowers: Chapter 2, https://pixabay.com/en/flowers-farmers-market-market-stall-1323632/

6. Ant: Chapters 46 and 98, https://pixabay.com/en/hymenoptera-ant-head-rossa-macro-1037434/

7. DNA: Chapters 21 and 30, "Animation of a rotating DNA structure." Author: brian0918™

Licensing: Public domain. This work has been released into the public domain by its author, brian0918. This applies worldwide. https://commons.wikimedia.org/wiki/File:ADN_animation.gif

8. Eye: Chapters 45 and 97, https://pixabay.com/en/eye-green-girl-close-up-face-skin-1227700/

9. Chimpanzee: Chapters 12 and 13, https://pixabay.com/en/solar-system-sun-planet-11596/

10. Lottery: Chapter 28, https://pixabay.com/en/lotto-balls-gambling-lottery-864035/

11. Heart: Chapter 79, http://www.freeimages.com/photo/heart-1414885

12. Planets: Chapters 14 and 76, https://pixabay.com/en/solar-system-sun-mercury-venus-439046/

13. Fruit: Chapter 71, https://pixabay.com/en/fruit-basket-grapes-apples-pears-1114060/

14. Wolf: Chapter 54, https://pixabay.com/en/wolf-face-fur-close-wild-animal-1336224/

Front Cover: Image Copyrights and References to Chapters on that subject.

15. Chirality: Chapter 74,
https://commons.wikimedia.org/wiki/File:Chirality_with_hands.svg

> Licensing: Public domain. This file is in the public domain in the United States because it was solely created by NASA. NASA copyright policy states that "NASA material is not protected by copyright unless noted".

16. Empire State Bldg: Chapter 67, https://pixabay.com/en/empire-state-building-usa-1081929/

17. Mathematics: Chapters 29, 37, and 81, https://pixabay.com/en/mathematics-pay-count-school-936697/

Back Cover: Image Copyrights and References to Chapters on that subject.

1. Anatomy: **Chapters 1 and 61,** http://www.freeimages.com/photo/anatomy-1428238

2. Missing Links: **Chapter 64,** Copyright 2016. Nari M. Hanna, used by permission

3. Whale: **Chapter 94,** https://pixabay.com/en/humpback-whale-natural-spectacle-436120/

4. Archer Fish: **Chapter 69,** https://pixabay.com/en/brain-anatomy-human-science-health-512758/

5. Healing Wound: **Chapter 70,** https://pixabay.com/en/arm-wound-pain-injury-patient-1214997/

6. Light Spectrum: **Chapters 59 and 97,** https://pixabay.com/en/lines-rainbow-colors-spectrum-color-520430/

7. Fetus: **Chapter 43,** http://www.freeimages.com/photo/feto-evolution-2-1426787

8. Worm: **Chapter 89,** https://pixabay.com/en/worm-vermiculture-humus-earth-soil-1140767/

9. Bat: **Chapter 42,** https://pixabay.com/en/bat-dracula-animal-mammal-biology-147038/

10. Cicada: **Chapter 57,** https://pixabay.com/en/cicada-insects-nature-115913/

11. Tongue: **Chapter 86,** https://pixabay.com/en/tongue-mouth-mammal-human-anatomy-181725/

12. Kittens: **Chapter 5,** https://pixabay.com/en/kittens-cat-cat-puppy-rush-555822/

13. Butterfly: **Chapters 19 and 20,** https://pixabay.com/en/butterfly-linen-red-black-cloth-1358845/

14. Suckling Pigs: **Chapter 43,** https://pixabay.com/en/pig-piglets-farm-agriculture-1089118/

15. Trees: **Chapter 39,** https://pixabay.com/en/woods-forest-nature-landscape-tree-1072819/

16. Fossil Fish: **Chapters 18 and 58,** http://www.freeimages.com/photo/fish-761-1342970

17. Pollen: **Chapter 51,** https://pixabay.com/en/pollen-varieties-magnified-1056342/

18. Emperor Penguin: **Chapter 92,** https://pixabay.com/en/penguins-emperor-antarctic-life-429134/

19. Spider Web: **Chapter 91,** http://www.freeimages.com/photo/spiders-net-1529149

20. Books: **Chapter 37,** http://www.freeimages.com/photo/books-1562581

21. Red Blood Cells: **Chapter 96,** https://pixabay.com/en/blood-blood-plasma-red-blood-cells-75302/

22. Homing Pigeon: **Chapter 84,** https://pixabay.com/en/pigeon-homing-bird-close-up-372496/

About the Author

Jim Stephens grew up in Illinois and Wisconsin and has since lived on both the East and West Coasts. He graduated in 1972 from Northwestern University at the top of his class in Industrial Engineering and Management Sciences.

Looking for the purpose of life and true happiness, he hitchhiked to California. There he encountered the scientific and understandable God of principles and universal laws that he could believe in. This grew into many profound experiences in his spiritual life.

He developed a passion to share inspirational experiences and research into God's nature, God's creation, and God's plan for human beings.

He has had the good fortune to travel throughout the United States, around the world two times, and over forty times to Japan and Korea as a program organizer and lecturer.

His wife is native-born Japanese and they have five grown children, all married and building families.

He and his wife led a marriage ministry for five years and have helped countless relationships.

This book is the result of a profound experience with God after Jim prayed to offer the rest of his life to help bring God's literal kingdom on earth.

Write to him at 101ProofsForGod@gmail.com.